GLOBAL RESPONSES TO MARITIME VIOLENCE

GLOBAL RESPONSES TO MARITIME VIOLENCE

Cooperation and Collective Action

Edited by Paul Shemella

Stanford Security Studies
An Imprint of Stanford University Press
Stanford, California

Stanford University Press
Stanford, California

Printed in the United States of America on acid-free, archival-quality paper

Library of Congress Cataloging-in-Publication Data

Global responses to maritime violence : cooperation and collective action / edited by Paul Shemella.
    pages cm
  Includes bibliographical references and index.
    ISBN 978-0-8047-9203-5 (cloth : alk. paper) — ISBN 978-0-8047-9841-9 (pbk : alk. paper)
    1. Sea-power.   2. Sea-power—International cooperation.   3. Security, International.   4. Piracy—Prevention.   5. Maritime terrorism—Prevention. I. Shemella, Paul, editor.
    VA10.G55 2016
    364.16′4—dc23

2015034999

    ISBN 978-0-8047-9863-1 (electronic)

Typeset by Newgen in 10/14 Minion

This book is dedicated to the professionals with whom we have been privileged to teach, as well as the thousands of international colleagues who have taught us. Special thanks must go to those in peril on the sea.

Contents

Preface   ix

Contributors   xi

1   Introduction   1
    Paul Shemella

    PART I: Examining Maritime Violence

2   Maritime Terrorism: An Evolving Threat   11
    Peter Chalk

3   Terrorist Targeting   30
    Paul Shemella

4   Armed Maritime Crime   49
    Peter Chalk

    PART II: Riding the Storm

5   Integrated Strategies Against Maritime Violence   71
    Paul Shemella

6   Assessing Maritime Governance   88
    Paul Shemella

7   Global Port Security   104
     Charles J. Reinhardt

8   Maritime Domain Awareness   124
     Timothy J. Doorey

9   The Role of Institutional Leadership   142
     Robert Schoultz

10   The Maritime Legal Framework   162
     Aubrey Bogle

11   Managing Maritime Incidents   179
     James Petroni

     PART III: Case Studies

12   Defeating the Sea Tigers of LTTE   203
     Rohan Gunaratna

13   Suppressing Piracy in the Strait of Malacca   224
     Lawrence E. Cline

14   Maritime Violence in the Sulu Sea   243
     Thomas R. Mockaitis

15   Maritime Crime in the Gulf of Guinea   265
     Peter Chalk

16   Yemen: The Case for a Coast Guard   282
     Aubrey Bogle

17   Conclusion   298
     Paul Shemella

     Index   305

Preface

Plugging the Gaps

THIS BOOK IS ALL ABOUT GAPS. THE TRANSITION BETWEEN land and sea reveals governance and capacity deficits that challenge even the most well resourced countries. And those disconnects, which include legal and institutional ambiguities, grow larger with distance from the beach. No government can confront the political and operational issues found in the maritime domain without substantial assistance from its neighbors. A storm at sea is a compelling image that haunts maritime security officials everywhere. Calm water is frequently difficult to find. The book you are about to read attempts to help them locate it.

The Center for Civil-Military Relations (CCMR) at the Naval Postgraduate School published a book in 2011 on the threat from terrorism and government responses to it (*Fighting Back: What Governments Can Do About Terrorism*, Stanford University Press). Since that time, we have come to believe that a second volume focused on the maritime aspects of terrorism and other maritime threats—a sequel, if you will—could add value to our efforts to help international colleagues build vital maritime security capacity. CCMR has been teaching seminars and workshops on fighting terrorism for civilian and military officials from more than 145 countries since 2002. We now use *Fighting Back* as a standard reference work for all those courses; it is our intent to use this book in the same way—to help other governments develop a broad and deep understanding of what we call "Maritime Violence."

Many US government organizations and institutions are involved in help-ing friendly governments build tactical maritime security capacity, but pro-grams targeting the strategic level of decision-making are in short supply. Operational assistance to our maritime colleagues is definitely a good thing, but most governments need even more help at the national and regional levels. Virtually every maritime security threat is transnational, and some of them reside on the high seas. Lasting maritime security requires the cooperation of national institutions, regional partners, and maritime nations from all over the world. Leaving the treatment of interstate *conflict* to other authors, we fo-cus on an array of challenges to maritime security requiring international *co-operation:* maritime terrorism, piracy, sea robbery, maritime smuggling, and port security. Our title comes from the rubric we have been using to link these activities together; each of them features, or benefits from, maritime violence.

Three factors complicate a government's efforts to maintain security in the maritime domain. The first is imposed by international law, the second by in-stitutional roles, and the third by limited resources. Governance in maritime areas brings all these considerations together, not always smoothly, adding complexity to an already difficult problem. International law has shaped each nation's maritime space, opening the door to both institutional and interna-tional conflicts. National and international institutions clash along the seams that delineate maritime zones, cooperating where they can, but competing for resources where they must. No government has enough resources to protect everything, especially in the global maritime domain through which most of the world's trade must pass. Territorial seas and exclusive economic zones are difficult; the high seas are much harder. Where does one even start?

We started with teaching, and now we are ready to write the book. This is more than an edited volume; it reflects the complex cross-cutting classroom discussions we have engaged in collectively with our international colleagues. Despite the ambiguities, a few things *are* clear. States need to govern their maritime spaces better and invest more in developing maritime security ca-pacity. National institutions must work as a team, and governments around the world will have to find ways to cooperate for the common good. In this book, we hope to advance a number of practical ideas that governments can use to protect their societies against maritime threats, meet the difficulties that arise, and peacefully exploit the *opportunities* that lie alongside those challenges.

Contributors

Editor

Paul Shemella retired from the Navy at the rank of Captain in 1996 after a career in Special Operations. During his military service, he planned and executed operations in Latin America, Europe, and other regions. He earned a Master's Degree in National Security Affairs at the Naval Postgraduate School and attended the Kennedy School of Government at Harvard University as a Senior Fellow in National Security. Captain Shemella has been with the Center for Civil-Military Relations (CCMR) since 1998. He is currently the CCMR Africa Program Manager, having developed and managed programs for Combating Terrorism and Maritime Violence. Captain Shemella is assisted in these efforts by a network of civilian and retired military faculty members drawn from the Naval Postgraduate School, civilian universities, government organizations, and the private sector. Captain Shemella is the principal author and editor of *Fighting Back: What Governments Can Do About Terrorism*, published by Stanford University Press in 2011.

Contributors

Aubrey Bogle served as a line officer in the US Navy from 1967–1983 and Coast Guard (1983–2001). His postgraduate degrees include a Master of Arts degree in Economics (1971) and a Juris Doctorate degree (1980), both from Vanderbilt

University. He has been active in CCMR programs since 2003. His military service includes five afloat tours and Coast Guard staff legal assignments. He also has extensive operational service in the Middle East on the 5th Fleet/US Navy Central Command Staff (1992 and 1997–1999). Mr. Bogle served on the faculty of the Naval War College as Deputy Director of the International Law Division, lecturing on a wide range of international law topics at the college and in South America. In 2001, Mr. Bogle retired from active military service, and accepted a position at the Defense Institute of International Legal Studies (DIILS) He retired in 2011, having served as Regional Program Director for DIILS programs in the United States Central Command and the US Pacific Command.

Peter Chalk is a Senior Policy Analyst with the RAND Corporation, Santa Monica, California. He has worked on a range of projects, including studies examining low-intensity conflict threats in the Philippines, Thailand, Indonesia, India (Kashmir), Pakistan, and Sri Lanka. Prior to joining RAND, Dr. Chalk was an Assistant Professor of Politics at the University of Queensland, Brisbane, and a Postdoctoral Fellow in the Strategic and Defense Studies Centre of the Australian National University, Canberra. He is a specialist correspondent for *Jane's Intelligence Review* and Associate Editor of *Studies in Conflict Terrorism*—one of the foremost journals in the international security field. Dr. Chalk has regularly testified before the US Senate on issues pertaining to national and international terrorism and is the author of numerous books, book chapters, monographs, and journal articles dealing with various aspects of low-intensity conflict in the contemporary world. Dr. Chalk has taught regularly for CCMR since 2005.

Lawrence E. Cline completed a career as an intelligence officer and Middle East Foreign Area Officer in the US Army. His military service featured tours of duty in Egypt, Lebanon, El Salvador, and Somalia, as well as Joint Staff and Special Forces assignments. He holds an MA in International Relations from Boston University. Dr. Cline earned a PhD in Political Science from the State University of New York at Buffalo, writing a dissertation on Islamic insurgent movements. He has published a number of articles on international security and internal security affairs in various academic journals and has given numerous conference paper presentations and lectures on aspects of low-intensity conflicts. He has been a regular faculty member for the CCMR academic program "Civil-Military Responses to Terrorism" since 2002. In

2006, Dr. Cline volunteered for recall to active duty and served as an intelligence advisor in Iraq.

Timothy J. Doorey is a Lecturer and Maritime Security Program Manager for the Center for Civil-Military Relations (CCMR). Prior to joining CCMR in 2009, he served twenty-eight years as a naval intelligence officer. Captain Doorey's last assignment on active duty was as the Senior Intelligence Officer at the Naval Postgraduate School, where he developed and taught graduate-level intelligence courses and mentored US and allied officers. During his career, Captain Doorey provided direct tactical, operational, and strategic-level intelligence support for US and coalition operations around the world. Captain Doorey has master's degrees from the Naval War College in Newport, RI (National Security and Strategic Studies) and the Naval Postgraduate School (National Security Affairs), and he was the Navy's Federal Executive Fellow at Harvard University's John M. Olin Institute for Strategic Studies. Captain Doorey now develops and leads in-residence and mobile education teams for CCMR in all regions of the world.

Rohan Gunaratna is a specialist of the global threat environment, with expertise in Asia, the Middle East, and Africa threat groups. He is head of Singapore's International Centre for Political Violence and Terrorism Research (ICPVTR), one of the largest specialist counterterrorism research and training centers in the world. He is also Professor of Security Studies at the S. Rajaratnam School of International Studies, Nanyang Technological University, Singapore. Gunaratna serves on the advisory board of the International Centre for Counter-Terrorism in The Hague. He is a member of the International Advisory Board of the International Institute for Counter-Terrorism in Israel, member of the Steering Committee of George Washington University's Homeland Security Policy Institute, and Member of the Board of Homeland Security Services Pte Ltd. Gunaratna was a Senior Fellow both at Fletcher School for Law and Diplomacy and at the US Military Academy's Combating Terrorism Center at West Point.

Thomas R. Mockaitis is Professor of History at DePaul University. He earned his BA in European History from Allegheny College in Meadville, PA, and his MA and PhD in Modern British and Irish History from the University of Wisconsin–Madison. Professor Mockaitis is the author of numerous books on terrorism and insurgency, the most recent of which bears the title, *Osama* *bin Laden: A Biography.* He co-edits the journal *Small Wars and Insurgencies* and frequently provides commentary regarding terrorism issues on a variety of radio and television networks. Professor Mockaitis is a renowned expert on government responses to irregular security threats. He has lectured at military educational institutions all over the world, including the Royal Military Academy Sandhurst (UK). In 2004, Dr. Mockaitis held the Eisenhower Chair at the Royal Military Academy of the Netherlands. He has been a regular faculty member of CCMR since 2003.

James Petroni retired in 2002 from a long career in public safety. He is currently an active consultant in the field of international and homeland security, addressing the threat potentials of both human and natural catastrophes. Beginning in the fire service, Mr. Petroni acquired experience in a wide variety of emergency management disciplines, often serving in significant roles during California's major emergencies. A longtime faculty member at the California Specialized Training Institute, Mr. Petroni pioneered emergency management procedures that have been adopted around the world. He has served as a consultant and lecturer to various federal agencies, including the Department of Defense, the Federal Emergency Management Agency, the Federal Bureau of Investigation, the Central Intelligence Agency, the Department of State, and the United States Congress. Mr. Petroni has worked closely with a number of foreign governments on disaster and terrorism training programs. He has been a regular CCMR faculty member since 2006.

Charles J. Reinhardt is a career-long transportation industry professional with thirty-five years of experience serving the aviation, rail, motor-carrier, and waterborne modes and supporting multimodal transportation infrastructure development projects on behalf of governments and private investors. In this capacity he has participated in a broad range of engagements for clients in more than thirty countries worldwide. Since 2004 he has lectured at CCMR on topics related to port security, maritime piracy, critical infrastructure protection, and international law. Mr. Reinhardt is a former ship's officer with service in both the Naval Reserve and Merchant Marine. He holds a professional license as a marine engineer and is certified by the Federal Aviation Administration as a multiengine-rated commercial pilot and flight instructor. Mr. Reinhardt received a BS degree in Marine Engineering from the US Merchant Marine Academy and an MBA in Finance and Accounting from Columbia University.

Robert Schoultz entered the US Navy after graduating from Stanford University with a BA in Philosophy. During a thirty-year career in special operations, Captain Schoultz served in operational and staff assignments in Germany, the United Kingdom, and Panama. He held command positions at both the 0–5 and 0–6 levels. He earned a master's degree in National Security and Strategic Studies from the Naval War College. Captain Schoultz was a fellow at the US Naval Academy's Center for Military Ethics and subsequently served as the Director of Officer Development at the Naval Academy. After leaving the Navy, he directed the Master of Science in Global Leadership program at the University of San Diego for six years. He currently manages "Fifth Factor Leadership" in San Diego, California, which offers consulting, corporate education, and keynote speaking. Captain Schoultz has been associated with the Center for Civil-Military Relations since 2003.

GLOBAL RESPONSES TO
MARITIME VIOLENCE

1 Introduction

Paul Shemella

WITH THIS BOOK WE OFFER CONTEXT-BASED ANALYSIS OF maritime security imperatives, as well as practical approaches to facing some of the world's most challenging threats. The authors use the collective noun *maritime violence*, reviving the title of a *Jane's Special Report* on the subject published almost twenty years ago.[1] That rubric did not "stick" in the literature but, having explored combinations of violence in the maritime domain for years, we think it should have.[2] We understand maritime violence to be a set of threats short of war, occurring in or at the edge of the maritime domain, that includes terrorism, insurgency, piracy, armed robbery at sea, and maritime smuggling, along with other crimes such as oil bunkering and illegal fishing.[3] Given that all these threats are closely related, scholars need an umbrella term that links them together. We offer a typology in Figure 1.1 that describes what we think of as an ecosystem of related threats. As in biological ecosystems, the activities listed—as well as the remedies—are interconnected. The sea itself has always been a violent place, and man's activities on the sea have taken a similar turn. If political and business leaders, acting together, wish to create a climate of security within which all citizens can thrive, they will have to tame the "outlaw sea" that laps at their shores.[4]

There is no shortage of evidence regarding the rise of global maritime violence. At the terrorism end of the spectrum, it was reported during the writing of this book that al-Qaeda in the Islamic Maghreb (AQIM) is preparing a maritime suicide unit to carry out attacks against shipping in and around

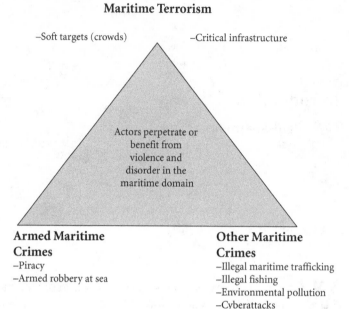

Maritime Terrorism

–Soft targets (crowds)   –Critical infrastructure

Actors perpetrate or benefit from violence and disorder in the maritime domain

Armed Maritime Crimes
–Piracy
–Armed robbery at sea

Other Maritime Crimes
–Illegal maritime trafficking
–Illegal fishing
–Environmental pollution
–Cyberattacks
–Fuel bunkering

FIGURE 1.1 The maritime violence ecosystem
NOTE: Industrial accidents and natural disasters require many of the same institutional responses as maritime terrorism.

the Mediterranean Sea.[5] At the opposite end of our continuum, the navy of the Ivory Coast seized two Chinese fishing vessels, operating illegally in the country's waters during November 2014. The ships were impounded until the Chinese government paid a fine of US $200K.[6] While Ivory Coast managed to send a message to governments that would steal from its rich fisheries (and collect revenue in the process), Sierra Leone's lack of port security has allowed the Ebola virus to return from offshore to rekindle that nation's deadly outbreak.[7] We will show how governments—even those with limited resources—can impose positive changes that can spread through the maritime violence ecosystem. They do this by creating the broadest possible climate of security in the maritime domain.

Maritime security begins behind the beach. Governments are challenged to provide security on the land areas they control (or, too often, do not really control). Ashore is where governments develop maritime laws and build maritime security institutions. Ashore is where criminal activity originates, and from where criminals extend their networks. The maritime domain is significantly more challenging for governments to control; it is a transition zone fraught with ambiguity. Institutional jurisdictions overlap inside territorial seas, but in exclusive economic zones (EEZs) it is governments that overlap. On the high seas, the lines disappear altogether. Securing the broadest maritime domain requires a large number of governments and an enormous amount of resources. Maritime spaces—internal, coastal, regional, and global—too often remain without formal governance, leaving room for terrorists, pirates, and other criminals to operate with near impunity. Maritime security requires governments to leave familiar, perhaps comfortable surroundings and seek out those who perpetrate, or benefit from, maritime violence.

To begin Part I, Peter Chalk explains in Chapter 2 that maritime terrorism, though rare to date, appears to be evolving into a greater threat (especially with Mumbai-style events now falling under the maritime rubric). Even though strategic and formal linkages with pirates and other criminals are unproven, the general lawlessness of the maritime domain creates opportunities for terrorism. Paul Shemella discusses in Chapter 3 how maritime terrorists might decide which targets to attack. Using a variation of the US Special Forces target-analysis model, applied to a fictitious maritime country, he provides a useful methodology for "thinking like a terrorist," whereby planners can anticipate which targets are most likely to be attacked. In Chapter 4, Peter Chalk examines piracy and sea robbery, introducing the umbrella term *armed maritime crime* (as opposed to other maritime crimes, more ubiquitous but less spectacular). He concludes by evaluating the advantages and disadvantages of using private armed security guards for preventing acts of piracy. Other maritime crimes, as well as industrial accidents and natural disasters, did not warrant separate chapters, but all these activities are discussed in the relevant chapters of Part II. A detailed example of illegal maritime trafficking activities can be found in the Yemen case study in Part III.

Part II begins with maritime strategy, the art of creating the best possible outcomes with a perennially scarce resource base. In Chapter 5, Paul Shemella examines the process of creating holistic maritime strategies that incorporate all sectors of government. Integrated strategies can lead to the integrated actions leaders must be prepared to execute. The suggested methodology organizes strategic thought at two levels: political and operational. Shemella characterizes strategy as a forcing function that fuses together a wide range of resources, explaining how the maritime sector of government fits into a broader institutional mix. In Chapter 6, he focuses on how governments can assess their own maritime governance, a wide-ranging set of activities that creates preconditions for effective maritime security. While describing the functions and subfunctions of maritime governance, Shemella avers that, given the political will (not always a given), there are two sides to the maritime security coin: governance and capacity. Strategy is the act of governing; the assessment of governance is a measure of capacity.

In one manifestation of capacity, maritime security is a key component of border security. If borders are the skin of a nation, ports are cuts that can become infected. Charles Reinhardt examines in Chapter 7 what we call *global port security*, an image meant to evoke the interconnectivity of the world's ports. His command of the commercial details comes from a career inside the maritime industry. Reinhardt discusses the balance between commerce and security, covering everything from international treaties to the potential for cyberattacks. Comprehensive port security is much more than maintaining healthy national skin; it requires close and persistent cooperation among institutions and nations. In Chapter 8, Timothy Doorey discusses maritime intelligence as both a product and a source of what the United States calls *maritime domain awareness*. No government can succeed in the maritime domain while suffering from what we sometimes call "sea blindness." Whether it is illegal fishing vessels, Ebola-infected citizens, pirates, or terrorists, national sovereignty rests on a government's ability to know what is going on out there.

In Chapter 9, Robert Schoultz writes in more personal terms about leadership. He argues that institutions are more important than individuals, and that individuals must work hard to improve institutions while they have the chance. Imposing change on institutions is a difficult process, especially in the maritime sector, but the chapter examines how good leaders can do it. Good leadership is so basic it is often assumed; Schoultz takes us all back to school on how to lead institutions generally—and maritime security institutions in particular. In Chapter 10, Aubrey Bogle, an operator as well as a lawyer, discusses the legal regime that underpins all government activities in the global maritime domain. Going further, Bogle imagines what a legal framework might actually look like for a typical maritime government. This chapter underscores the complexity of legal issues that dominate the maritime domain and reminds all of us that managing maritime law requires maritime lawyers.

James Petroni, a former firefighter and emergency manager, introduces a system for managing maritime catastrophes in Chapter 11. His maritime adaptation of the US Incident Command System (ICS) provides a practical example of Schoultz's reminder that leaders must figure out how to delegate management functions so they can concentrate on leading. Conceptually as well as operationally, ICS connects maritime threats from human actors to random industrial accidents and natural disasters. Institutions with the capacity to respond to maritime terrorism can also serve governments and populations inevitably affected by circumstance.

In Part III, we introduce a series of case studies, selected to illustrate some of the major themes of the book. In Chapter 12, Rohan Gunaratna examines Sri Lanka's campaign against the Sea Tigers of the LTTE insurgency. Finally developing a strategy right out of Clausewitz, the Sri Lankan Navy identified and targeted the enemy's center of gravity—the maritime logistics network that supported the ground force. The inclusion of this case illustrates the diversity of maritime threats, demonstrating how governments and their maritime security institutions must adapt to changing circumstances. The campaign against the Sea Tigers also illustrates the value of international cooperation, and especially intelligence sharing. This case, almost more than any other, reminds maritime governments just how bad things can get. In Chapter 13, Lawrence Cline discusses regional measures to suppress piracy in the Strait of Malacca. This case study is instructive for its successes, but also for its failures. The Strait of Malacca is geostrategically fated to suffer from some degree of armed maritime crime, and it must be overseen by governments, cooperating wherever they can. Thomas Mockaitis examines the under-studied maritime insurgencies (with an admixture of terrorism) in the Sulu Sea region in Chapter 14, highlighting the difficulty of getting regions and national governments to rise above history and religion. Mockaitis makes the observation that violence on the coastal fringes of the maritime domain, exposed to the open ocean, can sometimes be more serious than on the sea itself. The Sulu Sea, with its national and international dimensions, has much to teach students of maritime violence.

Peter Chalk analyzes the Gulf of Guinea's variations on maritime crime in Chapter 15. This region has claimed the title of highest piracy threat in the world, but Chalk explains that the largest share of the problem is actually sea robbery and fuel theft (armed and unarmed forms of maritime crime). Given the disparity between challenges and resources (added to the fact that regional and national maritime security strategies have been developed), the Gulf of Guinea may be emerging as the "poster child" for international maritime security cooperation. Without it, these nations will not be able to exploit their own marine resources to generate the national wealth they so desperately need. In Chapter 16, Aubrey Bogle explains the rationale for (and roles of) Yemen's Coast Guard that he helped to develop. The chapter provides a comprehensive account of multiple maritime threats facing an under-resourced maritime security institution. This case illustrates the need for governments to be amenable to creating new maritime security institutions—even at the expense of old ones—while at the same time providing a steady stream of resources. Whether or not Yemen remains a unitary state, the need for a coast guard (or two) will endure.

Chapter 17 aims to integrate the foregoing ideas into a holistic approach to the problem of managing maritime violence, prescribing a set of precepts we think will lead most governments to the outcomes they seek. Throughout this book we evoke the image of a government riding out a storm at sea. But this is a storm that never recedes completely. Maritime violence can only be managed by governments doing the best they can with what they have, and then acting together. The following chapters give the reader a glimpse of how governments can do just that.

Notes

1. Samuel Pyeatt Menefee, "Trends in Maritime Violence," *Jane's Intelligence Review Special Report*, 1996.

2. This term fits very well with David Kilcullen's argument that the world's population has become—and will continue to be—more urban, more connected, and more coastal. See David Kilcullen, *Out of the Mountains: The Coming Age of the Urban Guerrilla* (New York: Oxford University Press, 2013).

3. Terrorism and insurgency are not the same thing. Insurgents use terror from time to time, but terror is not the defining characteristic of an insurgency. If insurgents are not successful, they often devolve into terrorist organizations, dependent on the use of terror to accomplish any of their goals.

4. William Langewiesche coined the term *outlaw sea* in his thought-provoking 2004 book by the same name. See William Langewiesche, *The Outlaw Sea: A World of Freedom, Chaos, and Crime* (New York: North Point Press, 2004).

5. "Al Qaeda Planning Kamikaze Attacks on Ships in Mediterranean, Cables Claim," *The Guardian*, February 25, 2015, http://www.theguardian.com/2015/feb/25/.

6. "Ivory Coast Seizes Two Chinese Trawlers in Fishing Dispute," *Africa Markets Today*, November 28, 2014 (Reuters).

7. "Nearly Halted in Sierra Leone, Ebola Makes a Comeback by Sea," *New York Times*, February 28, 2015.

I EXAMINING MARITIME VIOLENCE

2 Maritime Terrorism

An Evolving Threat

Peter Chalk

THE MARITIME REALM REMAINS PARTICULARLY CONDUCIVE TO the type of irregular or unconventional threat contingencies that have come to characterize transnational security in the contemporary era. A vast area covering 139,768,200 square miles,[1] most of this environment takes the form of high seas that lie beyond the strict control of any single state—meaning they are, by definition, devoid of any form of sovereign jurisdiction. These over-the-horizon oceans are fringed and linked by a complex lattice of territorial waters, estuaries, and riverine systems that, due to a lack of resources or will (and in some cases both), frequently lack an effective regime of coastal surveillance. Compounding matters is the largely unregulated nature of the international trading system—a trait that is designed to minimize cost and maximize turnover but that also inevitably exposes maritime commerce to nefarious criminal designs.[2] Combined, these attributes and practices have served to infuse the planet's aquatic expanse with the same type of unpredictable and lawless qualities that Thomas Hobbes once famously wrote ensured life as "nasty, brutish, and short."

One particular threat that academics, intelligence analysts, law enforcement officials, and politicians have begun to take increasingly serious note of is the exploitation of the maritime realm to facilitate terrorist logistical and operational designs. Indeed, commentators in various countries now appear to believe that the next major strike against Western interests is as likely to emanate from a maritime theater as from a land-based one. Exacerbating concerns is the fear that militant extremists will be able to significantly enhance their operational capacity to impede shipping in key strategic sea-lanes of communication (SLOCs) by establishing mutually beneficial alliances with pirates.

This chapter examines the scope and dimensions of maritime terrorism[3] in the modern age. It discusses the reasons why militant extremists have traditionally shunned non-land-based theaters and the factors that appear to have caused a shift in this operational calculus. Specific terrorist scenarios are examined, including the use of the maritime environment to execute mass casualty attacks, cause economic disruption, and facilitate the movement of weapons and personnel. Finally, the chapter considers the potential nexus between maritime terrorism and piracy in the Gulf of Aden (GoA)—one of the world's most important trading routes and the region where the fear of such a convergence has been greatest.

Track Record of Maritime Terrorism

Historically, the world's oceans have not been a major locus of terrorist activity. Indeed, according to RAND's Chronology of International Terrorism, less than 2 percent of all global attacks conducted since 1968 have taken place at sea or been directed at maritime platforms. To be sure, part of the reason for this empirical paucity stems from the fact that many organizations have neither been located near coastal regions nor had the necessary means to extend their physical reach beyond purely local theaters. Additionally, several fundamental requirements for conducting effective maritime strikes have not traditionally been available to terrorist groups due to limited resources. Notably, these include possession of mariner skills, access to appropriate assault and transport vehicles, and expertise in certain specialist capabilities (e.g., surface and underwater demolition techniques).[4]

The inherently conservative nature of terrorists in terms of their chosen attack modalities is a further factor accounting for the lack of sea-borne strikes. Precisely because groups are constrained by ceilings in operational finance and skill sets, most have deliberately adhered to tried-and-tested methods that are known to work, which offer a reasonably high chance of success and whose consequences can be relatively easily predicted.[5] More specifically, in a world of finite human and material assets, the costs and unpredictability associated with expanding to the maritime realm have typically trumped any potential benefits that might be garnered from initiating such a change in operational direction.

One final consideration that has relevance to the relative lack of terrorist incidents at sea is the nature of potential maritime targets themselves. Because these platforms for the most part remain out of sight, they are generally not at the forefront of public interest, something that is particularly true of commercial vessels. Hence, attacking a ship is unlikely to attract widespread attention, as—unlike land-based venues—they do not often abut major centers of population and are not immediately media accessible. This opaqueness is important, since terrorism, at its root, is a tactic that can only be effective if it is able to demonstrate and communicate its relevance through *visible* acts of violence.[6]

A Change in the Terrorist Operational Calculus?

In spite of these considerations, a modest yet highly discernible spike has taken place in high-profile terrorist incidents at sea over the past fourteen years. Equally, a number of significant maritime terrorist plots have been aborted or prevented prior to execution. The more notable of these incidents are set out in Table 2.1. This heightened level of activity has galvanized fears in the West that terrorists, especially militants motivated by transnational jihadist designs, are developing the capability and intent to conduct highly damaging attacks at sea. If this is in fact the case, why might terrorists be seeking to expand their operational agenda to the maritime environment?

Three possible rationales would seem to have relevance. First, attacks at sea constitute a viable means for inflicting mass coercive punishment on enemy audiences. Second, maritime strikes offer terrorists an additional means for causing economic destabilization. Third, in several respects the expansive global container complex provides extremists and militants a useful logistical channel for facilitating the covert movement of weapons and personnel. Each of these potential motivational drivers is discussed in more detail below.

Maritime Terrorism as a Means of Causing Mass Casualties

Ever since the attacks of 9/11, the presumed wisdom that terrorists wanted "a lot of people watching rather than a lot of people dead" has been turned on its head.[7] The 2001 suicide strikes on the Pentagon and World Trade Center,

TABLE 2.1 Selected high-profile maritime attacks and plots, 2000–2010

Year	Group	Incident
2000	al-Qaeda	Suicide bombing of USS *Cole* at the Port of Aden
2001	al-Qaeda, Jemaah Islamiah (JI)	Plot to bomb the USS *The Sullivans* and Sembawang wharves in Singapore
2002	al-Qaeda	Suicide bombing of MV *Limburg* off the coast of Yemen
2002	al-Qaeda	Planned bombings of Western commercial carriers transiting the Strait of Hormuz
2003	Gerakan Aceh Merdeka (GAM)	Hijacking of MV *Penrider* as it was en route from Singapore to Penang
2003	al-Qaeda	Plots to bomb Western shipping interests in the Mediterranean and Strait of Gibraltar
2004	Jamaat al-Tawhid wa'a-Jihad	Attacks against the Khor al-Amaya and al-Basra oil terminals in Iraq
2004	Abu Sayyaf Group (ASG), JI	Bombing of *Super Ferry 14* in the Philippines
2004	Hamas, al-Aqsa Martyrs Brigade	Suicide attack against the Port of Ashdod in Israel
2005	al-Qaeda in Iraq	Mortar attacks against two US naval ships docked at the Port of Aqaba
2005	al-Qaeda	Plots to bomb Israeli cruise liners sailing to Turkey
2005	Unidentified Islamist militants	Attacks against the *Seaborne Spirit* off the coast of Somalia
2003–present	Movement for the Emancipation of the Niger Delta (MEND), Niger People's Volunteer Force (NDPVF), Niger Delta Vigilante (NDV)	Attacks against offshore oil platforms and drilling platforms in the Niger delta
2009	al-Qaeda and affiliates	Various plots to attack gas lines between Israel and Egypt and Israeli ships passing through the Suez Canal
2009	al-Qaeda	Plot to attack a US battleship in Tobruk, Morocco
2010	Abdullah Azzam Brigades	Suicide bombing of the US warship MV *Star* in the Strait of Hormuz
2010	al-Qaeda	Plot to hijack and detonate oil tankers and other offshore energy platforms/infrastructure in non-Muslim seas

which collectively killed nearly 3,000 people, were clearly aimed at maximizing collateral civilian damage. Militant strikes around the world during the subsequent fourteen years have been similarly motivated and, while not as destructive, have certainly been animated by the same apparent desire to inflict as much damage and misery as possible. The specter of mass casualty terrorism has accordingly emerged with increased alacrity and although most security concerns in this regard have focused on land-based targets (notably surface transportation, sports stadiums, shopping malls, and airports), certain maritime assets could also be vulnerable to such contingencies. This is particularly true of passenger ships.

Cruise liners are often singled out as ideal venues for orchestrating attacks intended to maximize civilian casualties. These vessels typically transport thousands of people, with some of the larger carriers having passenger manifests upwards of 4,000.[8] Moreover, because companies such as Royal Caribbean, Carnival, and Holland America largely cater to affluent American and European tourists, they provide a high-prestige target that would likely resonate with the type of absolute extremist Islamist intent that currently lies at the forefront of international terrorism concerns. That said, actually destroying a cruise liner would be an extremely difficult undertaking, as these vessels are constructed with safety as the foremost priority. Hulls are double lined and, in most cases, interiors are compartmentalized with largely (though not fully)[9] watertight systems in place. Overcoming these safeguards would require, at a minimum, several highly powerful bombs as well as a sophisticated understanding of the structural integrity of the intended target—particularly in terms of being able to identify locations where simultaneous explosions could be expected to cause the most damage. As a result, most commentators agree that attempting to sink a cruise ship would be an extremely difficult proposition and is probably well beyond the existing capabilities of known terrorist groups.[10]

Passenger ferries constitute a different threat altogether. Although not as symbolic as cruise liners, these vessels represent a highly "soft" target in terms of potential mass-casualty terrorism. Many of the commercial ships currently in operation move tens of hundreds, if not thousands, of people in a single crossing. This is especially true in the developing world, where ferries notoriously sail at or well over designated capacity limits. As such, they exhibit the same body-rich environment that cruise ships do. What sets ferries apart from their tourist cousins, however, is that they are far more susceptible to cataclysmic attack. Several factors account for this inherent vulnerability.

First, extant security measures at passenger terminals vary greatly and, even in developed littoral states such as the Netherlands, Canada, the United Kingdom, and the United States, are not nearly as extensive as those employed for cruise liners (much less aircraft). The very need to accommodate high volumes of embarking traffic in as efficient a manner as possible necessarily precludes the latitude for carrying out concerted checks on baggage, cars, trucks, and people.[11] Indeed, instituting even minimal precautionary measures can have the effect of generating huge delays and backlogs. The Port of Dover on the English south coast provides a case in point. In the immediate aftermath of the July 2005 London underground bombings, all motorists leaving the terminal for Calais in northern France were subjected to a slightly more rigorous regime of predeparture scrutiny and examination. Although individual inspections and questions generally took no more than a few minutes per vehicle, combined they served to create traffic jams that extended over four miles.[12]

Second, the vetting of those working aboard ferries is ad hoc and partial, reflecting the seasonal and highly transient nature of these personnel. Background checks, to the extent that they occur, are generally aimed at verifying past employers and rarely embrace wider criminal investigations. Throughout much of Asia and Africa, it is unlikely that any consistent form of examination takes place, largely because owner-operators lack the means (and frequently the willingness) to do so, something that is particularly true for foreign nationals. Maritime experts generally concur that the absence of effective staff/crew scrutiny represents a significant point of vulnerability for commercial ferry companies, providing extremists with an ideal opening to covertly place insiders on board targeted vessels for strike and/or logistical purposes.[13]

Third, and in common with cruise liners, ferries sail along predefined routes according to set departure and arrival times. By definition, these schedules have to be made widely available to the paying public and, as a result, are easily accessed through a broad array of mediums and conduits, ranging from travel guides and port terminals to the Internet.[14] Itineraries are, in short, both fixed and highly transparent, availing terrorists with a reasonably accurate cartographic picture that can be used to gauge the point at which vessels are most susceptible to attack and interception. The Abu Sayyaf Group (ASG) in the southern Philippines provides a good example of an organization that has conspicuously planned many of its maritime assaults around information of this sort.[15]

Finally, certain features in the specific construction of ferries serve to weaken their wider structural integrity and safety. This is especially true of vessels that transport vehicles. Colloquially known as *ro-ros* (roll on, roll off), these ships are deliberately built with large, open car decks to avail the efficient embarkation and disembarkation of cars, trucks, vans, and motorbikes. Unfortunately, this particular design format makes them acutely sensitive to subtle shifts in their centers of gravity, largely because they necessarily lack stabilizing bulkheads in their lower sections. Abrupt movements of automobiles that have been improperly secured or sudden accumulations of even small amounts of water[16] could, under such conditions, realistically cause a ferry to list or even fully capsize.[17]

The ASG bombing of Philippine *Super Ferry 14* in 2004 is a good example of the extensive human damage that can result from an attack against a passenger ferry. In this instance, 116 people were killed in an operation that involved a total planning cycle of only a couple of months and which was executed using a highly crude improvised explosive device—sixteen sticks of dynamite hidden in a hollowed out television set.[18] Other good indicators of the potential loss of life can be derived from ferry accidents such as the 1994 sinking of the MS *Estonia* in the Baltic Sea (852 deaths),[19] the 1987 MS *Herald of Free Enterprise* tragedy in Belgium (193 fatalities), and the 2014 MV *Sewel* disaster in South Korea (300 drowned, mostly schoolchildren).[20]

Apart from passenger ships, concern exists that terrorists could seize a liquefied natural gas (LNG) tanker and detonate it as a floating bomb near an area of human habitation in what would amount to a maritime equivalent of 9/11. Channels feeding the LNG terminals at Everett, Massachusetts, and Elba Island, Georgia, in the United States are often highlighted as particularly vulnerable in this regard, as they respectively lie proximate to the major population centers of Boston and Savannah.[21] However, as Martin Murphy notes, while LNG has the potential to cause a massive explosion, the mechanics of actually carrying out an operation of this sort are problematic at best:

If LNG is to be used as a weapon a series of steps need to take place, each one of which has to be successful even though each one has a significant chance of failure. The tank containing the LNG has to be breached. Sufficient liquid has to be released to form a pool. This must not be ignited immediately. Instead it needs time to warm and form a cloud that must rise and drift over an area where it could cause damage. Once this cloud hits a suitable ignition source it must be within the flammability range and that range must be maintained consistently through the cloud such that the flame can burn back to the pool, which is the fuel source, where it will form a "pool fire."[22]

Maritime Terrorism as a Means of Causing Economic Destabilization

Besides mass casualties, it has been suggested that the maritime realm offers terrorists a viable theater in which to execute attacks that are designed to trigger mass economic destabilization. This is seen to have particular relevance to the global al-Qaeda network, which has repeatedly affirmed that carrying out attacks that can deliver a crippling blow to the Western financial, commercial, and trading systems is the most effective way of waging jihad against the United States and its partner nations. This tactical bent was given concrete expression in 2004 when Bin Laden announced a "bleed-to-bankruptcy" strategy that was explicitly aimed at destroying the financial and commercial lifeline that underpins the current global capitalist system.[23]

One of the most commonly postulated scenarios for causing economic destabilization is an attack designed to shut down a port or block a SLOC in order to disrupt the mechanics of the "just in time, just enough" international trading system.[24] Because very little redundancy is built into the modern global economy (for reasons of cost efficiency), even small delays in delivery could potentially have large-scale ramifications, particularly for strategic and perishable commodities. As Michael Richardson, a senior fellow at the Institute of Southeast Asian Studies (ISEAS) in Singapore, observes:

> The global economy is built on integrated supply chains that feed components and other materials to users just before they are required and just in the right amounts. That way inventory costs are kept low. However, because these supply chains have no excess capacity, if they are disrupted, it will have repercussions around the world, profoundly affecting business confidence.[25]

Certainly the closure of a major waterway such as the Suez Canal, the Panama Canal, the Strait of Gibraltar, the Strait of Hormuz, or the Straits of Malacca and Singapore (75 percent of world trade moves through one of these choke points) would have a serious effect on global commerce. In the case of the Suez Canal, for instance, rerouting Asian cargoes bound for Europe would result in a mammoth increase in fuel costs, compelling ocean carriers to add a special bunker surcharge of anywhere between US $200 and $500 per TEU.[26] For a cargo loaded off the Arabian Peninsula, the most viable alternative passage would be around the Cape of Good Hope. This would lengthen a vessel's journey by around 4,700 nm, adding an estimated US $4 million to an average shipment in extra fuel costs.[27]

That said, decisively disrupting the operation of the contemporary international shipping system through a campaign of terrorism would be difficult. With the exception of the Suez and Panama Canals, very few SLOCs are truly noninterchangeable and would require, at most, only 1–2 days extra steaming time in the event of closure.[28] Actually blocking a choke point would pose problems on several levels and even in the case of highly narrow straits would require several vessels to be scuttled at once—a formidable task.[29] Major ports such as Rotterdam, Vancouver, Singapore, New York, and Los Angeles are also largely immune to wholesale closure, both on account of their size and because of the rigorous security standards they enact. Even if a full suspension of all loading/off-loading functions did occur, ships could be fairly easily diverted (albeit at a cost) to alternative terminals, thus ensuring the continued integrity of the intermodal transportation network.[30]

While long-term or widespread disruption to the global economy is unlikely, it is certainly possible that an act of maritime terrorism could cause temporary financial damage. The suicide strike on the MV *Limburg* in 2002 is a good example. Although the incident only resulted in three deaths (including the two bombers), it directly contributed to a short-term collapse of international shipping in the GoA; led to a 48-cent per-barrel rise in the price of Brent crude oil; and due to the tripling of war risks, premiums levied on ships transiting the gulf resulted in a 93 percent drop in container terminal throughput at the Port of Aden that cost the Yemeni economy an estimated US $3.8 million a month in lost anchorage revenues.[31]

Terrorists could also sabotage maritime critical infrastructure, such as offshore refining and drilling platforms.[32] As noted in Table 2.1. Jama'at al-Tawhid wa'a-Jihad carried out such an operation in 2004, attacking the Khor al-Amaya and al-Basra oil terminals in Iraq, while strikes against rigs and pipelines in the Niger delta have been a consistent tactic of the Movement for the Emancipation in the Niger Delta (MEND), Niger Delta Vigilante (NDV), and Niger Delta People's Volunteer Force (NDPVF). Again, however, these assaults have largely failed to cause long-term harm, either internationally or in terms of local production.

In sum, although maritime attacks have the potential to deliver a strategic blow to the global economy, the likelihood of this occurring is not high. At most, the effects would be localized and short term, as indeed they were in the case of the MV *Limburg* as well as the assaults on the Khor al-Amaya and al-Basra oil terminals two years later.[33] Moreover, it is arguable whether purely economically oriented attacks truly animate the minds of terrorists, their public rhetoric notwithstanding. In the absence of human fatalities, these strikes have little ability to satisfy the desire for immediate, visible effects—not to mention the bloodlust—that has become so intrinsic to militant extremist action in the post-9/11 era.

Terrorist Movement of Weapons and Personnel

Approximately 112,000 merchant vessels, 6,500 ports and harbor facilities, and 45,000 shipping bureaus constitute the contemporary international maritime transport system, linking roughly 225 coastal nations, dependent territories, and island states.[34] This expansive network, which caters for around 80 percent of commercial freight, has been the focus of considerable attention by maritime security analysts and intelligence officials, largely because it is widely seen to represent a viable logistical conduit for availing the covert movement of terrorist weapons and personnel. At least four factors underscore this perceived vulnerability.

First, the sheer volume of commercial goods and commodities that is moved by container ships effectively eliminates the possibility of comprehensive checks once cargo reaches its port of destination. Indeed, experts universally acknowledge that trying to inspect all incoming freight—or even a significant random sample—without unduly interrupting the contemporary dynamic of oceanic exchange is neither possible nor economically tenable given the number of boxed crates involved.[35] Even in terminals with advanced X-ray and gamma-ray scanning technologies, inspection rates remain minimal. In the United States, for instance, a mere 10 percent of the roughly 6 million containers that arrive in the country every year can be expected to have undergone some sort of scrutiny.[36]

Second, the highly complex nature of the maritime conveyance supply chain creates a plethora of opportunities for terrorist infiltration. Unlike other freight vessels that typically handle payloads for a single customer loaded at port, container ships deal with cargoes from hundreds of companies and individuals, which in most cases are received and transported from inland warehouses characterized by various forms of on-site security. For even a standard shipment, numerous agents and parties would be involved, including the exporter, the importer, the freight forwarder, a customs broker, excise inspectors, commercial trucking and/or railroad firms, and dockworkers, as well as harbor feeder craft and the ocean carrier itself. Each point of transfer along this spectrum of movement represents a potential source of vulnerability for the overall security and integrity of the consignment, providing terrorists with numerous openings to "stuff" or otherwise tamper with its contents.[37]

Third, and directly related to the above, is the rudimentary nature of the locks that are used to seal containers. Existing devices offer little if any protection, and often consist of nothing more than a plastic tie or bolt that can be quickly cut and then reattached using a combination of superglue and heat.[38] Most commercial shipping companies have been reluctant to develop more resistant mechanisms, given the costs involved.[39] Moves to develop so-called smart boxes equipped with GPS transponders and radio frequency identification devices (RFIDs) that emit signals if they are interfered with, have run into similar problems and have not, at the time of writing, been embraced with any real degree of enthusiasm by the international maritime industry.[40]

Fourth, the effectiveness of point-of-origin inspections for containerized freight is highly questionable. Many resource-constrained states in Asia and Africa fail to routinely vet dockworkers, do not require that truck drivers present valid identification before entering an off-loading facility, and frequently overlook the need to ensure that all cargo be accompanied by an accurate manifest. Even richer nations in Western Europe and North America are not devoid of these types of deficiencies. Privacy regulations in the Netherlands, for instance, preclude the option of comprehensive security vetting for port employees without first gaining their permission. In the words of one Dutch expert, "I would be amazed if harbor employees at Rotterdam, Antwerp, or Amsterdam were required to undergo any form of mandatory background criminal check." In the United States, some 11,000 truck drivers enter and leave the Long Beach terminal in Los Angeles with only a standard driver's license, while Singapore, which has arguably one of the world's most sophisticated commercial maritime terminals, does not require shipping companies to declare goods on their vessels if they are only transiting through the country's port.[41]

Several high-profile cases have involved terrorists (and their backers) deliberately exploiting maritime conveyance. Historically, this was the favored means by which Irish republican Catholic sympathizers in the United States and sponsoring regimes such as Libya armed the Provisional IRA.[42] For much of its struggle against the Sri Lankan state, the Liberation Tigers of Tamil Eelam (LTTE) depended on a global munitions procurement network that centered around eleven oceangoing freighters colloquially known as the Sea Pigeons.[43] Al-Qaeda is thought to have transported the explosives it used for the 1998 East Africa embassy bombings by sea and later reportedly ran its own dedicated fleet of commercial vessels to smuggle weapons.[44] The two individuals who carried out the attack against the Port of Ashdod were smuggled into Israeli territory in a specially modified cargo container that been trucked in from the Gaza Strip. The crate was designed with a hidden compartment that was used to store the terrorists, their weapons, food, water, and sleeping accommodations. Notably, the attackers managed to evade security measures that were far stricter than those required under the International Ship and Port Facility Security (ISPS) Code.[45] And in 2014, Israel intercepted a Panamanian-flagged vessel that was allegedly being used to send advanced Iranian M-302 surface-to-surface missiles to Hamas militants in the Gaza Strip.[46]

While most concern is directed at freighters in terms of furthering terrorist logistical designs, it is important to note that maritime assets can be employed in other ways to facilitate land-based assaults. A case in point are the Mumbai strikes of 2008, which consisted of coordinated shootings and bombings that left 164 people dead and more than 300 wounded.[47] The ten Lashkar-e-Taiba (LeT) members who conducted the mission sailed from Karachi on a Pakistani cargo ship. En route, they hijacked an Indian fishing trawler and, after murdering the crew, forced the captain to take them into the waters off the coast of Mumbai (after which he was beheaded), where they moored for three days. The attack team eventually came ashore in a pair of inflatable dinghies that they landed at two different sites in the southern part of the city.[48] Infiltrating in this manner availed the LeT squad with two key advantages: First, it allowed the terrorists to bypass stringent security checkpoints at the frontier or at airports. Second, it enabled them to avoid arousing the suspicion of the Indian coast guard.[49] Further, the incident graphically underscored Delhi's inability to effectively monitor its coastline—something that undoubtedly informed and factored into LeT operational planning.[50]

A Convergence Between Maritime Terrorism and Piracy?

For several years fears have arisen that an "unholy alliance" could occur between pirates and terrorists, a nexus similar to the one that characterized the political militarization of the drug trade in Latin America during the 1990s and, more recently, Afghanistan following the rise of the Taliban. These concerns have been especially marked with respect to potential threat contingencies in the GoA, a key trading corridor that has not only witnessed a major surge in armed maritime crime since 2008 (see Chapter 3) but which also abuts two major zones of terrorist activity: al-Shabaab in Somalia and al-Qaeda in the Arabian Peninsula (AQAP) in Yemen.

Various claims have been put forward attesting to a presumed piracy-terrorism convergence in this region. In 2011 the head of the United Nations counterpiracy unit, Colonel John Steed, asserted that an informal arrangement had been concluded between al-Shabaab and maritime bandits operating out of the port city of Harardhere (then under rebel Islamist control), whereby the former had agreed to provide base security and weapons in exchange for a cut of the latter's profits.[51] There have also been allegations that AQAP and al-Shabaab have jointly sought to further the goal of economically crippling the West by working in tandem with pirates to shut down the strategically important Strait of Bab el-Mandeb at the bottom of the Red Sea.[52] Finally, periodic assertions have arisen that Somali pirates have trained Islamist militants in offensive boarding techniques and opened transit havens in Yemen (for a fee) to allow al-Shabaab to consolidate an offshore presence near AQAP.[53]

Despite these various claims, the purported tie between piracy and terrorism in the wider vicinity of the GoA remains problematic for at least three reasons. First and arguably most significantly, speculation of a concerted convergence between the two threats remains just that—speculation. Certainly any substantive evidence has yet to emerge supporting the thesis that either al-Shabaab or AQAP has sought to establish concrete ties with Somali pirates, much less moved to translate such links into actual operations. Second, a fundamental disconnect exists between the objectives of terrorists and pirates in this part of the world. The former seek to undermine maritime trade as part of a concerted "bleed-to-bankruptcy" strategy aimed at exploiting the assumed "Achilles' heel" of the West—the economy. This agenda is diametrically opposed to the interests of the latter, whose business depends on a thriving system of commercial shipping. Third, the very notion of piracy is anathema to the jihadi moral code, which views the criminal practice as directly counter to the values of "social justice" for which it purportedly stands. It is noteworthy that to this day the most effective counterpiracy drives to have ever occurred in Somalia took place in 2006, a period when al-Shabaab—in the guise of the Islamic Courts Union (ICU)—was briefly in power.

While there is reason to be skeptical of an operational nexus emerging between armed maritime crime and terrorism, the possibility of militants seeking to mimic the activities of criminal syndicates should not be ruled out. It is highly unlikely that the enormous windfall of profits that have been made through hijackings—which now average in the range of US $4–5 million (see Chapter 4)—have not been lost on AQAP or al-Shabaab, who could well seek to supplement their respective war chests through similar endeavors. Certainly a precedent exists for this type of militant fund-raising, as the examples of the Movement for the Emancipation in the Niger Delta, or MEND (see Chapter 15), and the ASG in the Southern Philippines attest.

Conclusion

In many respects the maritime environment constitutes a viable terrorist theater given its expanse, lack of regulation, esoteric character, and general importance for global trade. That said, it is essential that the overall level threat be put in context. While numerous attack scenarios are possible, only a relative few are likely to fall within the purview or capacity limits of known groups. Spectacular events such as detonating a cruise ship, shutting down major ports, or simultaneously scuttling vessels to block critical SLOCs would seem to be more in the realm of fantasy than fact. However, scenarios involving the exploitation of the supply chain for logistical purposes or the critical breach of a passenger ferry to cause mass casualties do represent realistic dangers. Security analysts necessarily need to focus on these contingencies in terms of overall threat mitigation and consequence management efforts.

Notes

1. This equates to some 2.42 times the planet's terrestrial surface area.

2. Rupert Herbert-Burns, "Terrorism in the Early 21st Century Maritime Domain," in Joshua Ho and Catherine Zara Raymond, eds., *The Best of Times, the Worst of Times: Maritime Security in the Asia-Pacific* (Singapore: World Scientific Publishing, 2005), 157.

3. For the purposes of this chapter, maritime terrorism will be defined as the undertaking of politically motivated criminal violence—or associated activities in furtherance of such acts—within the maritime realm using or directed against vessels or fixed platforms at sea and/or members of their passengers or crew and coastal facilities and settlements, including tourist resorts, port areas, and port towns and cities.

4. Interviews, Institute of Defense and Strategic Studies (IDSS), Singapore, September 2005. See also Paul Wilkinson, "Terrorism and the Maritime Environment" and Brian Jenkins, Bonnie Cordes, Karen Gardela, and Geraldine Petty, "A Chronology of Terrorist Attacks and Other Criminal Actions Against Maritime Targets," both in Eric Ellen, ed., *Violence at Sea* (Paris: International Chamber of Commerce, 1986).

5. This point is directly taken up by Bruce Hoffman in his "The Modern Terrorist Mindset: Tactics, Targets and Technologies (University of Colorado, The Beyond Intractability Project, Conflict Information Consortium, October 1997).

6. For a discussion on this aspect of the terrorist phenomenon, see Peter Chalk, *West European Terrorism and Counter-Terrorism: The Evolving Dynamic* (London: Macmillan, 1996), Chapter 1.

7. This phrase was first attributed to Brian Jenkins, who rejected the argument that terrorists were not willing to draw the line at mass casualty attacks. See Brian Jenkins, *The Likelihood of Nuclear Terrorism* (Santa Monica, CA: RAND, 1985), 6; and Bruce Hoffman, *Inside Terrorism* (London: Victor Gollancz, 1998), 198.

8. The world's two largest cruise ships, the Royal Caribbean's *Oasis of the Seas* and *Allure of the Seas*, are each able to hold up to 6,296 passengers.

9. It would be impossible to construct a cruise liner that has a fully compartmentalized watertight system in place, as the recreational and luxury-oriented nature of these vessels necessarily requires an on-board configuration that is open and accessible (within the constraints of allowable safety limits).

10. Interviews, maritime security analysts, London and Kuala Lumpur, September 2005.

11. In Britain, for instance, cars and coaches are inspected on a random, selective basis. Freight vehicles are rarely, if ever, checked. As one former defense intelligence official opined: "Ferries are their own worst enemies: [the industry is] designed to transport a high volume of people as conveniently, cheaply, and quickly as possible. Most operators simply do not have the infrastructure—or willingness—to carry out a comprehensive regimen of security checks." Author interview, former UK defense intelligence official, London, September 2005.

12. Interviews, UK Customs and Excise officials, London, September 2005.

13. Author interviews, maritime analysts and intelligence officials, Singapore, London, Amsterdam, and Washington, DC, August and September 2005.

14. In the UK, for instance, the schedules and itineraries of all ferry companies operating out of the country can be accessed on the web via www.ferries.co.uk.

15. Interviews, Ministries of Home Affairs and Foreign Affairs, Singapore, September 2005.

16. According to one US-based maritime security analyst, as little as a foot of water accumulated in a single location could upset a ship's center of gravity through the so-called free-surface effect. Interview, Washington, DC, August 2005.

17. It should be noted that certain countries have moved to address this specific structural vulnerability. In the UK, for instance, ferries are now constructed with drains in their car decks to prevent the free-surface effect. Many also have additional buoyancy devices, such as air-filled tanks strapped to either side of the vessel.

18. Peter Chalk, *The Maritime Dimension of International Security* (Santa Monica, CA: RAND, 2008), 26.

19. For more on this disaster, see William Langewiesche's chapter on the Estonia sinking, pages 127–95.

20. Michael Greenberg, Peter Chalk, Henry Willis, Ivan Khilko, and David Ortiz, *Maritime Terrorism: Risk and Liability* (Santa Monica, CA: RAND, 2006), 99–100; Rory Knight and Deborah Pretty, *The Impact of Catastrophes on Shareholder Value* (Oxford: Templeton College, 1997); Catherine Lawson and Roberta Weisbrod, "Ferry Transport: The Realm of Responsibility for Ferry Disasters in Developing Nations," *Journal of Public Transportation* 8/4 (2005), 17–31; "Insurance Claims to Exceed $110 M," *Lloyd's List*, September 29, 2004; "South Korea Ferry Disaster," *The Guardian*, available online at http://www.theguardian.com/world/south-korea-ferry -disaster, as of August 26, 2014.

21. See, for instance, Eben Kaplan, "Liquefied Natural Gas: A Potential Terrorist Target?" *Council on Foreign Relations Backgrounder*, February 27, 2006, available online at http://www.cfr.org/natural-gas/liquefied-natural-gas-potential-terrorist -target/p9810, as of August 26, 2014; and Cindy Hurst, "The Terrorist Threat to Liquefied Natural Gas: Fact or Fiction," *Analysis of Global Security*, February 2008, available online at http://www.iags.org/hurstlng0208.pdf, as of August 26, 2014.

22. Martin Murphy, *Small Boats, Weak States, Dirty Money* (New York: Columbia University Press, 2009), 221.

23. See Matthew Hunt, "Bleed to Bankruptcy," *Jane's Intelligence Review* (January 2007), 14–17; "Bin Laden: Goal Is to Bankrupt the US," *CNN.com*, November 1, 2004, available online at http://www.cnn.com/2004/WORLD/meast/11/01/binladen .tape/, as of December 19, 2009; and Douglas Jehl and David Johnston, "In Video Message, bin Laden Issues Warning to US," *New York Times*, October 30, 2004.

24. Author interviews, Control Risks Group and Lloyd's, London and Amsterdam, September 2005. See also Catherine Zara Raymond, "Maritime Terrorism, a Risk Assessment: The Australian Example," in Joshua Ho and Catherine Zara Raymond,

eds., *The Best of Times, the Worst of Times* (Singapore: World Scientific Publishing, 2005), 179; and Martin Murphy, *Maritime Terrorism: The Threat in Context* (London: International Institute of Strategic Affairs Adelphi Paper 388, 2007), 20.

25. Michael Richardson, *A Time Bomb for Global Trade* (Singapore: Institute of Southeast Asian Studies, 2004), 7.

26. Twenty-foot equivalent unit.

27. "Avoiding Piracy by Sailing Around the Cape of Good Hope Is a Costly Business," Baltic International Maritime Council (BIMCO), November 23, 2009, available online at https://www.bimco.org/Reports/Market_Analysis/2009/1123_Avoiding _piracy.aspx, as of August 26, 2014.

28. By contrast, rerouting around the Cape of Good Hope as opposed to transiting through the Suez Canal would lengthen a vessel's journey by around three weeks, adding an estimated US $1.5 to $2 million to an average shipment in terms of extra fuel, time, and labor.

29. Sinking any sizable vessel with a high waterline would require the perpetrating group to have access to a large quantity of explosives, the time and means to transport this material, and the expertise to know where to place bombs to cause a critical breach. These logistical and knowledge barriers would pose formidable barriers for a single attack, much less an assault to target two or three ships.

30. Peter Chalk, *The Maritime Dimension of International Security* (Santa Monica, CA: RAND, 2008), 23.

31. Ben Sheppard, "Maritime Security Measures," *Jane's Intelligence Review* (March 2003), 55; Richardson, *A Time Bomb for Global Trade*, 70; Rupert Herbert-Burns, "Terrorism in the Early 21st Century Maritime Domain," in Ho and Raymond, eds., *The Best of Times, the Worst of Times: Maritime Security in the Asia-Pacific*, 165.

32. Paul Shemella develops a methodology for evaluating the relative attractiveness of maritime critical infrastructure to terrorist attack in Chapter 3.

33. In the Khor al-Amaya and al-Basra attacks, two suicide boats were driven toward the terminals but exploded before they made contact. Following the incident, the price of oil rose but quickly fell back as it did after the *Limburg* incident. See Murphy, *Small Boats, Weak States, and Dirty Money*, 207; and "Oil Prices Rise on Fears of Attacks on Iraqi Resources," *Taipei Times*, April 27, 2005.

34. Interviews, Lloyd's of London, London, September 2005. See also Herbert-Burns, "Terrorism in the Early 21st Century Maritime Domain," 158–59; and OECD, *Security in Maritime Transport: Risk Factors and Economic Impact* (Paris: OECD, July 2003).

35. Interviews, maritime experts and intelligence officials, Singapore, London, and Rotterdam, September 2005. See also John Fritelli et al., *Port and Maritime Security: Background and Issues for Congress* (Washington, DC: Congressional Research Service, RL31733, December 30, 2004), 4; Catherine Zara Raymond, "Maritime Terrorism, a Risk Assessment," in Ho and Raymond, eds., *The Best of Times, the Worst of Times*, 187; and N. Brew, "Ripples from 9/11: The US Container Security Initiative and Its Implications for Australia," *Current Issues Brief 28* (2003), 5.

36. Robert Block, "Security Gaps Already Plague Ports," *Wall Street Journal*, February 23, 2006.

37. Fritelli, *Port and Maritime Security: Background and Issues for Congress*, 9; James Hoge and Gideon Rose, eds., *How Did This Happen* (New York: Public Affairs, 2001), 188.

38. See, for instance, J. Saunders, "Marine Vulnerability and the Terrorist Threat," *International Maritime Bureau* (London: International Chamber of Commerce, 2003), 4.

39. A standard seal can be purchased for a few cents if ordered in bulk, whereas more robust versions might run to several hundreds of dollars.

40. Interviews, Department of Homeland Security Liaison officials, US Embassy, Singapore, and London, September 2005. In bulk order form, these types of technologies would cost at least US $500 per container. Shipping companies have also been reluctant to make such investments, given that even more advanced boxes cannot offer anything approaching 100 percent infallibility.

41. This is largely due to a fear that if declarations on all cargoes were made mandatory irrespective of whether or not Singapore was the final port of call, the resulting red tape would deflect trade north to Malaysia.

42. Murphy, *Small Boats, Dirty Money, Weak States*, 345; "Arming the IRA: The Libya Connection," *Economist*, March 31, 1990.

43. For more on the LTTE's international procurement network, see Peter Chalk, "The Liberation Tigers of Tamil Eelam's (LTTE) International Organization and Operations: A Preliminary Analysis," *CSIS Commentary* No. 77 (March 2000).

44. Richardson, *A Time Bomb for Global Trade*, 14–15; Murphy, *Small Boats, Dirty Money, Weak States*, 345–46.

45. See Bill Watson, "In Search of the Trojan Horse," *Fairplay*, April 8, 2004; "Palestinians and al-Qaeda Bond Through Ship Container," *DEBKAfile*, March 17, 2004; and Akvia Lorenz, "The Threat of Maritime Terrorism to Israel," *Maritime Terrorism Research Center*, September 19, 2007, available online at http://www.maritime terrorism.com/2007/09/19/the-threat-of-maritime-terrorism-to-israel/, as of August 26, 2014.

46. "Israel Halts Weapons Shipment from Iran," *BBC News*, March 5, 2014, available online at http://www.bbc.com/news/world-middle-east-26451421, as of August 27, 2014.

47. The attack venues included the Chhatrapati Shivaji Terminus (CRT, the city's main train station), the Cama and Albless Hospital, the Trident-Oberoi and Taj Mahal Palace hotels, and Nariman House (a commercial-run complex run by the Jewish Chabad Lubavich movement).

48. "Mumbai Terror Attacks," *CNN*, September 18, 2013, available online at http://www.cnn.com/2013/09/18/world/asia/mumbai-terror-attacks/, as of August 27, 2014.

49. See Angel Rabasa, Robert D. Blackwill, Peter Chalk, Kim Cragin, C. Christine Fair, Brian A. Jackson, Brian Michael Jenkins, Seth G. Jones, Nathaniel Shestak, and Ashley J. Tellis, *The Lessons of Mumbai* (Santa Monica, CA: RAND, 2009), 4.

50. See, for instance, Sunita Parikh, "Mumbai Attacks Highlight Shortcomings in Indian Terror Response," *Beacon*, December 5, 2008; and Padma Rao Sundarji, "How India Fumbled Response to Mumbai Attack," *McClatchy Newspapers*, December 3, 2008.

51. Jonathan Saul and Camila Reed, "Shabaab-Somali Pirate Links Growing: UN Advisor," *Reuters*, October 20, 2011. See also, "Pirates Reached an Agreement with al-Shabaab," *SeaNews Turkey*, February 28, 2011; Valter Vikko, "Al-Shabbab: From External Support to Internal Extraction—A Minor Field Study on the Financial Support from the Somali Diaspora to al-Shabaab," Working Paper, Department of Peace and Conflict Research, Uppsala University, March 2011, 23; and Shima Keene, *Maritime Piracy, Somalia*, Security Economics Programme, Institute for Statecraft, 2011. According to Colonel Steed, al-Shabaab initiated the deal largely because it had become increasingly desperate for funding to counter Kenyan-led offensives against its main operational and logistical bases.

52. See, for instance, Bruce Riedel, "When Terrorists and Pirates Merge," *Daily Beast*, February 13, 2010.

53. Bruno Schiemsky, "Piracy's Rising Tide: Somali Piracy Develops and Diversifies," *Jane's Intelligence Review*, January 20, 2009.

3   Terrorist Targeting
Paul Shemella

N O GOVERNMENT HAS ENOUGH RESOURCES TO PROTECT all its citizens and property against terrorism all the time. It is often said that terrorists have to be successful only once, but that governments must be successful every time. Imagine how difficult it must be for a government to claim it has enacted the right policies and executed brilliant strategies against terrorism, only to suffer a terrorist attack the very next day. Well-resourced and wise governments are successful—until they are not. Their citizens will give them credit for protecting them—until they do not. Under-resourced leaders face much longer odds, as well as the credibility risk that comes with failure. The most realistic goal for government, then, is not to prevent *all* attacks, but to prevent those attacks that do the greatest harm to the most people for the longest time. In other words, governments must find a way to prioritize their defensive efforts, distributing more resources for defending against the most devastating attacks and fewer resources for other, less devastating, attacks. This is certainly a sensible approach, but how might a government actually do it?

The process of protecting against major terrorist attacks begins with a comprehensive assessment of the risks associated with *all* threats to a society. Let us assume that a country has undertaken such an assessment, and that terrorism is near the top of its list of prioritized risks.[1] If terrorism is enough of a threat to draw precious national resources away from more productive uses, the government must ensure that the money is spent as effectively and efficiently as possible. There are essentially two types of terrorist targets: soft and hard. Soft targets, it is generally agreed, are individuals and groups of people. People move from place to place, making individuals somewhat more challenging for terrorists to attack, but crowds are abundant and vulnerable. Attacks on individuals are always serious, but unless the victim is a key leader or beloved national figure, the damage to society is limited. Attacks on crowds are valued by terrorists because of the fear they create in the society as a whole, and because they make governments look helpless.[2]

Hard targets are "hard" because they are structures, but they are also harder to attack. Within the context of terrorism, the most attractive hard targets can be classified under the rubric *critical infrastructure*. The US Department of Homeland Security's definition of critical infrastructure is simple enough to serve as a useful construct for this global examination:

> Critical infrastructure are the assets, systems, and networks, whether physical or virtual, so vital to the United States that their incapacitation or destruction would have a debilitating effect on security, national economic security, national public health or safety, or any combination thereof.[3]

Critical infrastructure is difficult to attack in the sense that private companies and governments normally provide some security.[4] Facilities, however, are also easier for terrorists to plan against because they are stationary.[5] Airplanes, trains, and other vehicles follow routine, often predictable, movements. Critical infrastructure, whether owned by the private sector or by the government, is attractive to terrorists because it sustains the standards of civilization most human beings have come to expect. The *systems* that define critical infrastructure now constitute an *obligation* of governments worldwide; indeed, the reliability of such systems has become a measure of a government's legitimacy. Such systems provide—at a minimum—electricity, water, heating, food, communications, and transportation. Many of the same systems are also critical to the success of private-sector business and vital to the economy.[6] Finally, certain key resources are sometimes considered alongside critical infrastructure because of their iconic status or emotional value to the nation.[7] The comprehensive list of generic critical infrastructure is long, so it is often broken into bite-sized pieces or "sectors." The US list looks something like this:

Agriculture and Food	Banking and Finance
Chemical Commercial Facilities	Communication
Critical Manufacturing	Dams and Locks
Defense-Industrial Base	Emergency Services
Energy	Government Facilities
Healthcare and Public Health	Information Technology
National Monuments and Icons	Nuclear Reactors
Materials and Waste	Postal and Shipping
Transportation Systems	Water Supply Systems

Much of the critical infrastructure at risk lies in the maritime domain. Of the world's 193 countries, 153 have at least a small coastline.[8] Those that do not have coasts often contain large lakes, a chain of lakes, or a system of navigable rivers.[9] This chapter will describe the analytical method for critical infrastructure assessment taught by the authors to security officials world-wide. The focus here will be on maritime critical infrastructure, an analysis that serves as a bridge to evaluating the attractiveness of all critical infrastructure to terrorists. A generic list of maritime critical infrastructure might look like this:

Container Terminals	Bridges
Tunnels	Offshore Oil/Gas Platforms
Offshore Gas Platforms	Coastal Pipelines
Container Ships	Ferry Vessels
Dams and Locks	LNG/LPG Tankers
Shoreside Storage Tanks	Shoreside Power Plants
Desalination Plants	Offshore Storage Facilities
Cruise Ships	Pier Facilities

So, if you happen to be a terrorist wishing to strike maritime critical infrastructure for maximum impact, how do you choose a target? We are not terrorists, but we can attempt to think as they do. Unless government officials are willing to do that, security resources will be wasted, terrorists will be more able to conduct effective sabotage, and the very fabric of advanced societies will be threatened.

Thinking Like a Terrorist

In order to answer the question "Which pieces of maritime critical infrastructure are most attractive to terrorists?" we can assume that terrorists evaluate attractiveness in a systematic way. Even terrorists try to avoid wasting resources, but their overriding concern is failure. A failed terrorist attack makes the government appear strong and the attackers seem weak. Citizens are more likely to support a strong government, and they do not fear what they perceive as weak. When terrorists decide to attack something, they must try to maximize the probability the attack will succeed. As Edward Luttwak reminds us, the horizontal dimension of strategy places governments on the same level as their opponents at all levels, each side looking for advantage over the other in a dynamic contention of wills.[10] What, then, might the target-analysis process for a terrorist organization look like?

One way to imagine this would be to study how the government side analyzes targets. Legitimate military forces everywhere have developed target-analysis processes to help them choose the right targets and to plan the most effective attacks on their opponents. In the US, special operations forces have used a process known as *CARVER*, now woven into their tactical DNA.[11] The acronym breaks down into a series of judgments based on assessment criteria, and the assignment of raw scores (numbers between 0 and 10) to each criterion. Those assessment criteria are:

- *Criticality*. How important is the target to the overall operation of a system of critical infrastructure? The clearest example is an electricity grid. Here, the target could be a single component of the grid that forms a critical node upon which the whole system depends.
- *Accessibility*. How easily could one or more attackers reach the target with enough equipment to destroy it? This assessment criterion only determines whether the saboteurs can get to the target, not whether they can actually destroy it (that will come later when we examine vulnerability).
- *Recuperability*. How difficult would it be for the enemy to replace, repair, or bypass the damaged portion of a facility to be attacked? This is measured in terms of days, weeks, months, or even years. Such a judgment takes quite a bit of research, but the Internet has made much of the required information available—to everyone.

- *Vulnerability.* How easy would it be to destroy the target once it is accessed? All of the assessment criteria work together to provide the attacker with a comprehensive analysis of the target. Vulnerability, for instance, is not very important if the attacker cannot get close enough to launch an attack.
- *Effect.* What would be the military, political, economic, psychological, and sociological impacts of the attack—at the scene and beyond? For American forces engaged in sabotage, the effect on the population would hopefully be minimized. Effects are the *reason* for an attack but, without the other criteria, they cannot be assessed.
- *Recognizability.* Is the target clearly recognizable? Can the attacker(s) actually see it under the conditions likely to prevail during the attack?

On the terrorist side, the same methodology would seem to offer an effective guide, but some modifications might make it work better.[12] Having done some informed speculation, we offer a terrorist version of the process, called *CARVES.*

- *Criticality.* From a terrorist perspective, the criticality of a target to the infrastructure system that serves the people is moderately important. Conventional forces would target the system to deny the enemy some military advantage, but the target of terrorists would be society itself. Among many examples, the October 2014 opening of Lithuania's LNG terminal provided maritime critical infrastructure for terrorists (and Russians) to plan against.[13]
- *Accessibility.* With their limited resources, terrorists must consider accessibility more than conventional armies do. If a government wants to seal off a piece of critical infrastructure—or a stadium full of sports fans—it might be able to render a target so difficult to approach that terrorists decide to strike somewhere else (and there are always plenty of other targets).
- *Resilience.* This is a better word to use here than recuperability (which is not a word at all). In the context of modern terrorism, *resilience* has come to mean more than just the time it takes to get a system back on line. Governments have started to use the term because it carries psychological meaning; a resilient society is less vulnerable to the fear terrorists attempt to generate.

- *Vulnerability.* Assuming terrorists can gain access to the target, vulnerability measures the ease with which the critical node in the system can be taken out. Often a target will be vulnerable but inaccessible, or it can be accessible but largely invulnerable to destruction. The higher the vulnerability of a target, the more resources a government (or the private sector) must dedicate to making it inaccessible.
- *Effects.* Terrorist attacks are the ultimate "effects-based operations."[14] Terrorism, after all, is a form of theater designed to create fear in a wide audience. Those killed in a bombing are not the real victims; the victims are *everywhere* in the target society. The assessment criterion *effects* should be one of the most important elements in the terrorist target-analysis process (the plural form is used here to highlight the common terrorist desire to generate cascading and holistic effects).
- *Symbolism.* The target-analysis process used by terrorists would have to include an evaluation of the target's symbolic value. The inclusion of monuments and other iconic structures as "key resources" recognizes that they are prime targets for terrorism. Symbolism is important, but how important is it relative to the other assessment criteria?[15]

Weighting Factors

Some assessment criteria in the CARVES model are more important than others. But how would we account for that? The easiest way would be to assign weighting factors to each criterion. These numbers would remain fixed during the assessment process, ensuring that the final result takes the differences into account. If all the assessment criteria were of equal importance to terrorists, then the analysis process could be a simple matter of assigning raw scores to each criterion for the target being assessed. That evaluation would yield something useful, but not something useful enough.[16]

Terrorists have their own, sometimes unique, strategic objectives, and not all targets offer the best way to achieve them. We can say that, in a general sense, terrorists wish to create as much havoc as possible. Although the long-term absence of a critical service, say electricity, would be a nice-to-have result for terrorists, the short-term removal of these services from the population would be enough to make the government look weak and the people to feel fear. This suggests that criticality and resilience are less important than accessibility or vulnerability.[17] Moreover, if society is to be disrupted, then the effect of the attack should be among the most important assessment criteria (especially if economic damage is a strategic objective). Finally, the terrorist love of symbolism would merit a high weighting factor for that criterion.

The following are suggested weighting factors for each assessment criterion in the putative CARVES methodology. These numbers are intended for the general case—that is, terrorist organizations that behave as we normally expect. They are, however, subject to change on the basis of idiosyncratic terrorist objectives and usage over time by counterterrorism analysts and industry experts.[18]

- *Criticality:* 3
- *Accessibility:* 5
- *Resilience:* 2
- *Vulnerability:* 5
- *Effects:* 8
- *Symbolism:* 7

In this notional target-analysis process, the weighting factors are multiplied by raw scores for each criterion—as applied to a particular potential target. A total score is then calculated for each target, using a matrix format. The result would be a rank-ordered target list from which terrorists could choose the target most likely to help them achieve their strategic objectives.[19]

Public Security

Crowds are attractive targets for most terrorist organizations, but people are not listed as critical infrastructure. Consequently, one would have to ask whether the suggested model could be used to analyze the attractiveness of large groups. If governments wish to preserve their legitimacy, they must find a way to manage the risk to groups of citizens standing closely together in outdoor markets, indoor malls, and stadiums (some crowds are embedded in critical infrastructure, such as cruise ships and ferries, enhancing the attractiveness of those potential targets). Two assumptions will help: First, crowds are always attractive to terrorists; they are both critical and symbolic by definition. Second, terrorists do not care about how fast governments can clean up after them; mass casualties alone achieve the objective. That leaves public security planners with the assessment criteria of accessibility, vulnerability, and effects. Governments can protect people at major events staged in sports stadiums and convention halls, but protecting them in the open is a real challenge.

Part of that challenge is to impose, on the public at large, security requirements that reduce the freedom of each individual. Closed-circuit television, frequent searches, traffic stops, and other measures are more acceptable in some publics than in others. Governments must convince their citizens that public security cannot be achieved without some sacrifice. Citizens of the United States, for instance, are extremely sensitive to any curtailment of personal freedom. People in Britain, Singapore, and many other countries are less concerned. A place on this continuum is often the result of recent experience, but also of culture and tradition. It is important to recognize that most individuals will gladly give up some of their freedoms in the aftermath of a terrorist attack, but also that they will want those freedoms back after a reasonable period without terrorist activity. This dynamic can be factored into terrorist target analysis and be exploited.

For complete public security, then, governments must imagine how terrorists can hurt their citizens directly, through attacks on crowds, or indirectly, through attacks on critical infrastructure that expose large numbers of people. Some maritime targets offer both hard and soft targets in the same package. In Chapter 2, for example, Peter Chalk argued that passenger ferries are more attractive targets than cruise ships. The CARVES method validates this conclusion. But there are other places where crowds gather at sea or near the water's edge.[20] Governments should be thinking like the terrorists looking for those places.

Tactics and Tradecraft

How might terrorists carry out successful attacks in the maritime environment? As explained in the previous chapter, the requirement for specialized skills partly explains the paucity of maritime terrorist attacks to date. But what if terrorists could acquire the requisite skills from pirates and smugglers, or simply outsource tactical operations to them? Martin Murphy asks why, with all the challenges of the maritime environment, terrorists are still interested in operating at sea. The answer, he says, is that they must move people, weapons, materiel, and money over long distances and in large quantities to support land campaigns.[21] With the increasing scrutiny governments place on security ashore, the relatively lawless maritime environment offers a more attractive alternative.

Once terrorists become more comfortable with maritime challenges—whether they develop organic capabilities or contract their operations—myriad opportunities emerge. The most frightening involve hijacking large ships in or near port facilities. One can think of four roles that captured ships can perform in the terrorist playbook: iconic targets (cruise ships), economic targets (oil tankers), mass casualty targets (ferries), and weapons (gas tankers).[22] While ships present the most significant maritime targets, they are not the only ones a terrorist organization might deem attractive. Bridges, offshore energy platforms, power plants, dams, and piers provide lucrative options for publicity and carnage. Even in such a target-rich environment, however, terrorists (and perhaps their criminal partners) would find a series of obstacles before them.

The maritime environment is vast and remote, but the coastal areas needed for training and staging are not devoid of people. It is difficult to hide full-mission-profile rehearsal activities from the fishermen and smugglers who ply the same waters and use the same beaches. Foreign fighters must hide themselves in rural areas; in cities they require "tradecraft" skills similar to those of intelligence operatives.[23] Logistics, especially those of bringing in large amounts of explosives, cannot go completely unnoticed. As many of the case studies in this volume attest, such training and preparation are difficult, and the low numbers of maritime attacks reflect that.[24] The lack of clear evidence (at least so far) that terrorists have partnered with criminals reminds us that each has different motives; criminals want to make money, whereas terrorists want publicity. For smugglers and pirates, violence is bad for business.[25]

The terrorist planning cycle also complicates successful outcomes. Would-be attackers must progress from broad-target selection, through a surveillance phase, to specific-target selection, attack planning, and attack rehearsals. Stopping an attack becomes a matter of decreasing the odds that each stage in the cycle will be successful. Say, for instance, that the probability of maritime terrorists finding a class of target they have the capability to attack is 90 percent, and the chances of them finding a suitable point target without being detected by security forces hover around 50 percent. Multiplying these probabilities would tell us there is a 45 percent chance of terrorists being successful to that point (and if the remaining stages of the planning cycle can be estimated at less than 100 percent, the odds for a successful attack decrease even more). The target-analysis tool suggested here provides counterterrorist planners with a method of putting themselves inside the minds of terrorists engaged in this cycle. That, it seems to us, is the only way to develop the insight needed for generating effective defensive strategies.

Protecting "Maritima"

The terrorist target-analysis model can be applied to a long list of maritime targets, allowing counterterrorism experts to produce a prioritized list. Working in small but diverse groups, experts can use the suggested model to provide decision makers with enough collective judgment to help them allocate scarce resources for protecting the most attractive targets from terrorist attack. Let us imagine a maritime country with a typical array of critical infrastructure, both at sea and ashore. Map 3.1 provides a map of "Maritima," a fictional developing country with an extensive maritime domain and an economy dependent on the sea, estuaries, and lakes. Maritima's citizens live in peace, but let us imagine that a terrorist organization threatens to attack in unspecified ways, in retaliation for the government's foreign policy decisions. These terrorists have demonstrated elsewhere in the region that they possess the capability to attack maritime targets, signaling that the government must craft a defensive strategy for protecting them. The Maritima situation presents an opportunity to use the target-analysis model to demonstrate how governments can redistribute defensive resources on the basis of target attractiveness.

The government, using a series of expert working groups, has identified six maritime targets of potential interest to the terrorist group. The group has shown, through previous attacks in neighboring countries, a targeting philosophy that places high value on short-term disruption and symbolism. Their objectives do not seem to include mass casualties but rather sensational attacks with maximum physical damage. Academic and government studies suggest that this terrorist group might wish to demand changes to government policies, but apparently does not aim to reconstruct Maritima society at large. The terrorists are thought to have sanctuaries in the mountains that lie near the eastern border, but no training camps have been located. Maritima authorities, in coordination with regional partners, are searching for terrorist

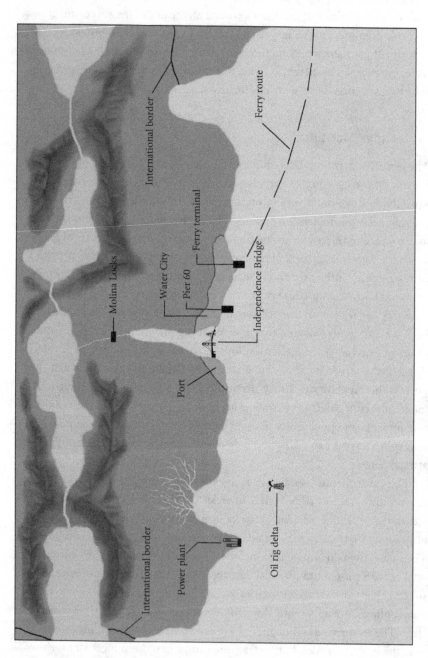

MAP 3.1 The fictional maritime nation of Maritima

planning cells in coastal cities, linked together by passenger ferries and airports. The government is analyzing the following maritime targets:

1. *Offshore Oil Platform "Delta."* This platform is located within sight of Maritima's coastline. "Delta" is one of four such platforms that pump crude oil from beneath the ocean bottom and transfer it by pipeline to a refinery in the country's major port. Delta is larger than the other platforms, which are separated from one another by a distance of 10 miles. The facilities lie 25 miles offshore of the country's most attractive beaches, where tourists visit year-round. None of these platforms has ever been attacked. Small, lightly armed patrol boats, which belong to the government, patrol the area. A small private security force guards the platforms themselves.

2. *Power Plant #1.* This conventionally fired electricity-generating facility is located at the shoreline, 30 miles from the nearest town, and takes its cooling water directly from the ocean. Plant #1 is the only power plant in the country situated on the coast; there are five others, all inland, and they draw their cooling water from the country's large freshwater lakes (the other five plants are not pictured on Map 3.1). All six power plants are connected in a nation-wide network. Although plans are in place for hydroelectric projects, Maritima has no alternative sources of power. There has never been an attack on one of these power plants, which are guarded only by private security forces. Government security personnel have not developed close contacts with these guards, and no emergency drills have been conducted.

3. *Molina Locks.* A canal that allows small cargo vessels to transport goods throughout the mountainous country connects Maritima's numerous large lakes to each other (interior roads, mostly made of gravel, are washed out regularly). The system of lakes also links Maritima's productive central valley and growing region with markets in two neighboring countries. The lakes are connected to the country's central estuary through a multistep locking system that raises and lowers cargo ships transiting in both directions. The locks are named for Yasiel Molina, the country's first president. Because the government realizes the critical role these structures play in the economy, the Maritima armed forces provide security.

4. *Independence Bridge.* A new suspension bridge spans the entrance to a large estuary that extends inland for thirty miles in the center of the country. On one side is the country's largest port facility. On the other side is the national capital, Water City, with a population of over one million. This newly

constructed bridge has been named "Independence" to commemorate the establishment of Maritima as an independent country in the middle of the twentieth century. Because of its location, the bridge carries a large number of trucks that bring goods between the city and the port facility for import and export.

5. *Water City Shopping Arcade.* One of Water City's major destinations for wealthy residents and tourists is a former commercial fishing wharf that has been transformed into a large public space. The wharf extends 200 yards into the ocean on pilings, and it supports shops and restaurants, as well as a small amusement park. Many people use the pier for fishing, while surfers ride waves all around the structure. Private guards, hired by the mall's businesses and the pier's owner, provide security that focuses on preventing theft. There is no visible government presence.

6. *Oceangoing Ferry.* Because of its mountainous borders with two neighboring countries, Maritima has developed a system of oceangoing ferries that carry passengers and vehicles between Water City and regional capitals. The system uses three ships of 325 feet in length, with a capacity for up to 100 cars and trucks. The trip from Water City to each foreign destination is about eight hours over seas that can become rough at certain times of the year. The first ferry to be launched was named *Maritima* and remains a source of pride for the country's citizens.

Armed with the information above (and certainly much more), experts would convene a series of working sessions to rank the six potential targets in order of attractiveness to the threatening terrorist organization. These experts, drawn from Maritima's intelligence agencies, the private sector, academia, law enforcement, and perhaps the military, would sit down with the target-analysis tool and begin to consider all assessment criteria for each target. Starting with a blank template, the group would decide, through extensive debate, which targets should draw the greatest share of security resources and which would need the least. The end product might look something like Table 3.1.

Interpreting the Table

The Maritima analysts have calculated, using the CARVES tool, that the Molina Locks would be the most attractive of the six maritime targets to

TABLE 3.1 Target analysis table for Maritima

Intended target	Criticality (×3)	Accessibility (×5)	Resilience (×2)	Vulnerability (×5)	Effects (×8)	Symbolism (×7)	Total
Oil platform	$2 \times 3 = 6$	$5 \times 5 = 25$	$2 \times 2 = 4$	$7 \times 5 = 35$	$7 \times 8 = 56$	$1 \times 7 = 7$	**133**
Power plant	$3 \times 3 = 9$	$8 \times 5 = 40$	$4 \times 2 = 8$	$6 \times 5 = 30$	$3 \times 8 = 24$	$1 \times 7 = 7$	**118**
Molina Locks	$9 \times 3 = 27$	$3 \times 5 = 15$	$8 \times 2 = 16$	$8 \times 5 = 40$	$8 \times 8 = 64$	$6 \times 7 = 42$	**204**
Bridge	$7 \times 3 = 21$	$9 \times 5 = 45$	$5 \times 2 = 10$	$2 \times 5 = 10$	$4 \times 8 = 32$	$8 \times 7 = 56$	**174**
Shopping arcade	$1 \times 3 = 3$	$9 \times 5 = 45$	$3 \times 2 = 6$	$9 \times 5 = 45$	$8 \times 8 = 64$	$2 \times 7 = 14$	**177**
Ferry	$4 \times 3 = 12$	$6 \times 5 = 30$	$6 \times 2 = 12$	$7 \times 5 = 35$	$4 \times 8 = 32$	$6 \times 7 = 42$	**163**

NOTE: Rank order of attractiveness:

1. Molina Locks
2. Shopping arcade
3. Bridge
4. Ferry
5. Oil platform
6. Power plant

terrorist planners. We can see from the numbers that the analysts worried about the absence of an alternative method for moving commerce between the coast and the interior. They seem to think that the locks are easy to approach (especially by terrorists in the guise of seamen) but that strong military security would complicate accessibility to the locks themselves. Were saboteurs able to actually place explosive charges on the locks, the analysts seem to have concluded that much damage could be wrought to the system. If that were to happen, the numbers tell us that the analysts also worried about the time it would take to get the locking system back in operation. The effects of a successful attack on the locks would be economically significant, and the symbolic name of the target might add to its attractiveness.

The analysts have also concluded that the power plant is the least attractive terrorist target. The plant is only one of six networked facilities in a small country, and its temporary loss would not result in anything but a temporary local power failure. The plant is fairly accessible and distinctly vulnerable, but those assessment criteria do not make up for the low effects, resilience, and symbolism ratings. The government cannot ignore security for this piece of critical infrastructure, but it would probably not invest additional security resources. Assuming terrorists analyze the power plant target the same way, these assessment criteria would work together to dampen the target's attractiveness to them.

It is in the middle group of potential targets that the government must consider some agonizing tradeoffs. In this case, the bridge, the shopping arcade, and the ferry system are all worthy of extra security (the main risk from the oil platform appears to be environmental, and incident management personnel—like those detailed in Chapter 11—would have to maintain a high level of readiness). The bridge is critical and accessible, but it is a large structure that would be difficult for terrorists to damage catastrophically. They could perhaps hijack a vessel or an airplane and crash it into the bridge, but such a complex operation would be very difficult to execute. Standing government security forces at the port and airport could probably increase vigilance to the point at which terrorists would decide not to attempt it.[26]

Both the shopping arcade and the passenger ferry would be attractive targets for the mass casualties that could be generated. The arcade is extremely accessible and quite vulnerable to a bloody attack that could be filmed by the media, almost as it happens (as in Mumbai). The ferry could also be attacked catastrophically, but its greatest window of vulnerability is at sea, where the most sensational effects are out of public view. Optimized for carrying vehicles, oceangoing ferries are prone to accidents and easy to sink with explosives, but security at embarkation could be enhanced without many additional resources.[27]

Maritima's government might well decide that increased vigilance by existing security forces would suffice for the power plant and the ferry. Perhaps it would also conclude that national police forces should be positioned in the arcade and near the bridge. Increasing police presence on the pier would have to be discrete enough not to discourage public enjoyment of the facilities there. Additional security around the bridge might be less obtrusive, but it would certainly be more expensive. Military forces guarding the lock system could increase their readiness for an attack, perhaps with additional forces and an extended perimeter. The government could also increase the number of patrol boats securing the oil platforms, but all of this costs money. Tradeoffs would have to be made, depending on available intelligence regarding specific terrorist capabilities and intent.

Conclusion

All governments must develop defensive strategies against terrorism in a way that guarantees reliable operation of the critical systems that sustain the normal functioning of a society. At the same time, they must conserve enough resources to provide the governance their populations expect. The balancing of security with individual and commercial freedom is a daily struggle for political leaders. In a country dependent on the sea, the prevention of maritime terrorism illustrates this dilemma quite well.

The value of the target-analysis tool lies not in the numbers themselves but in the *debate* over the numbers. When a member of the expert working group wrestling with a target's assessment criteria must defend the numbers he offers to others, he is forced to think about a target as the attacker would. If he is not able to convince his peers, someone else's numbers will find their way into the table. The assessment tool allows governments to turn the judgment of experts into numbers that political leaders can understand. Those leaders will then have the raw material for making decisions about utilization of the people's resources so that they may defend them efficiently as well as effectively.

And where does a government go from there? It cannot simply allocate sufficient resources and move on to other business. The terrorist planning cycle is dynamic, and so must be the counterterrorist planning cycle. As the threat changes, so must the readiness to respond. Part of that process should require specially selected operational personnel to play the role of terrorists attempting to penetrate the security forces arrayed against them. So-called red-teaming is a time-tested method for determining whether terrorists can access and damage the actual targets. Results from such exercises can inform the experts who debate CARVES numbers in the government's terrorist target-analysis process.

Critical infrastructure, key resources, and crowds cannot be protected solely with government security forces. This is especially true with regard to maritime assets and systems. The size and complexity of much maritime infrastructure require extensive private investment. Virtually all the potential targets in Maritima would require some private ownership, along with the security forces that go with it. How the government structures public-private security partnerships can be just as important as the ways it distributes its own security resources. Private-sector representatives should be included in the expert working groups that debate the assessment criteria we have suggested.[28]

Governments must also invest resources in communicating—with terrorists, and with their own citizens. Policies on readiness for, and responses to, terrorism and maritime criminality should be articulated publicly at the highest levels. Terrorists need to know that governments have the will and the resources to protect their societies. Citizens must know that governments have the capacity to protect them personally, as well as the systems that sustain them. Public affairs officials should be empowered to reveal the existence of analytical processes through which governments determine how to protect the assets terrorists wish to attack. Such announcements should be deliberately vague, but the processes themselves need to be well defined and practiced.

Notes

1. See Paul Shemella, *Fighting Back: What Governments Can Do About Terrorism* (Stanford, CA: Stanford University Press, 2011), 117–30.

2. Transportation systems, particularly air and rail, reside in the overlap between soft and hard targets. Attacking these systems provides a terrorist the opportunity to kill randomly (one aim), while simultaneously disrupting essential transportation for large numbers of people (a second aim).

3. US Department of Homeland Security website (December 2013), http://www.dhs.gov.

4. Governments do not always provide enough security to deter terrorists from attacking critical infrastructure. See "Q&A: Hostage Crisis in Algeria," *BBC News*, January 21, 2013, http://www.bbc.com/news/world-africa-21056884.

5. Critical infrastructure may also be "hard" in the sense that it takes more explosive power to damage it, but that is not always the case. For example, a bullet fired into the cracking tower can disable an oil refinery more effectively than high explosives placed on a less critical node. Devastating cyberattacks require no explosives at all.

6. This list would include roads, railroads, and air and maritime transportation networks, as well as systems for transferring money.

7. In the United States, the list of key resources would include the Statue of Liberty, the Washington Monument, and many other structures.

8. *The CIA World Fact Book*, 2013, https://www.cia.gov/library/publications/the-world-factbook.

9. For example, the Caspian Sea, the African Great Lakes region, or landlocked Paraguay.

10. Edward Luttwak, *Strategy: The Logic of War and Peace* (Harvard College, 1987), vii.

11. US Army Field Manual (FM) 34–36, *Special Forces Intelligence and Electronic Warfare Operations* (1991), Appendix D. *Recuperability* and *recognizability* are nonwords that convey the precise meaning sought.

12. Terrorists certainly have access to FM 34–36. They can just as certainly adapt the methodology to their specific needs.

13. This facility has the potential to supply all of Lithuania's requirements for natural gas, and perhaps supply those of Latvia and Estonia as well. See, "Russia's Hold on the Baltics Loosens," *Stratfor*, October 24, 2014.

14. Now a NATO term of art.

15. I have omitted the assessment criterion *recognizability* on the terrorist side of the ledger. As a former special operations officer, I have always believed that *recognizability* is a subset of *accessibility*. If an attacker cannot see the target—or if he has not studied it enough during preparation to be able to identify it—then the target is not vulnerable to attack. This suggests that governments and private-sector owners should consider hiding or disguising certain pieces of critical infrastructure.

16. Interestingly, the Special Forces target-analysis model does not include weighting factors.

17. Most governments place more importance on resilience, figuring that people will blame them even more for a long-term loss of services. Terrorists, however, might not care as much about the long term, as long as they are able to demonstrate the capability to deny those services for a few hours (and take credit for it).

18. Some terrorist groups actually shun publicity; others adopt a "bleed-to-bankruptcy" strategy that places more importance on resilience. This suggests that analysts must first adapt the target-analysis model for the group of highest concern.

19. The US Coast Guard uses a vulnerability-analysis process that might also provide a model. The process is similar to CARVER, but it focuses on domestic vulnerabilities through the lens of the government itself. "Maritime Domain Awareness Requirements Validation" (US Coast Guard, 2003), PowerPoint presentation.

20. For a thorough account of the Mumbai attacks, see David Kilcullen, *Out of the Mountains* (New York: Oxford University Press, 2013), 52–66.

21. Martin N. Murphy, *Small Boats, Weak States, Dirty Money: The Challenges of Piracy* (New York: Columbia University Press, 2009), 374.

22. Ibid., 199.

23. For an extended discussion of the terrorist tradecraft challenge, see Scott Stewart, "Examining the Elements of Terrorist Tradecraft," *Stratfor*, August 14, 2014.

24. Even in cases like Mumbai, where most evidence indicates that Pakistan had a major supporting role, maritime attacks require extensive training. For a summary of the alleged Pakistani role, see Azmat Khan, "New Evidence of Pakistan's Role in Mumbai Attacks?" *PBS/Frontline*, June 28, 2012, available online at http://www.pbs .org/wgbh/pages/frontline/afghanistan-pakistan/david-headley/new-evidence-of -pakistans-role-in-the-mumbai-attacks/.

25. The assumption that terrorists, pirates, and smugglers are cooperating systematically derives partly from the fact that all these criminal activities have the same set of root causes, from poverty to poor maritime governance.

26. In an effort to avoid failure, terrorists adhere to a lengthy planning cycle that exposes them to observation. Detection by security authorities, or the general public, is an ever-present danger.

27. The *Super Ferry* 14 attack in the Philippines in 2004 destroyed the ship and caused 116 deaths. These effects were produced by a small amount of dynamite, hidden inside a television set.

28. Seminars on maritime energy security, conducted by the US Africa Command in Maputo, Mozambique, and Accra, Ghana in 2014, included the participation of industry representatives. The value of the resulting dialogue was obvious to all.

4   Armed Maritime Crime

Peter Chalk

A S OBSERVED IN CHAPTER 2, THE VAST AND LARGELY
unregulated nature of the oceanic realm makes it especially vulnerable to irregular and/or unconventional threats. Besides terrorism, another prominent challenge that has emerged with increased prominence in
recent times is *armed maritime crime* (AMC), a term that includes maritime
piracy. Once considered a scourge consigned to the annals of history, this
particular issue has taken on heightened relevance in a growing number of
regions around the world, with incidents now having become a common occurrence off the Horn of Africa (HoA), the Gulf of Guinea (GoG), and the
territorial waters of several countries in Southeast and South Asia.

This chapter focuses on the evolving dynamic of AMC in the modern
era. It discusses the scope and dimensions of this particular manifestation
of maritime disorder, the main dangers associated with attacks, and the key
contributing factors that account for its recent growth. The chapter then goes
on to consider the potential role of private security companies (PSCs) in combating AMC, paying specific attention to the implications these entities have
for wider norms of order at sea.

For the purposes of the analysis, AMC is defined as "an act of boarding
or attempting to board any ship with the apparent intent to commit theft or
any other crime and with the apparent intent or capability to use force in furtherance of the act." This is the definition of piracy used by the International
Maritime Bureau (IMB).[1] It is broader than the conceptualization adopted

under the 1982 United Nations Convention on the Law of the Sea (UNCLOS), which restricts its focus to attacks that only take place on the high seas.[2] The UNCLOS delineation is problematic, as the majority of criminal maritime incidents occur either in territorial or coastal waters. The IMB definition also abolishes the traditional two-ship requirement for classifying an incident, meaning that attacks from a raft or the dockside would also be counted as an act of AMC.

Modern-Day AMC: Scope and Dimensions

Armed maritime crime has emerged as an increasingly visible threat to national and international security in recent years. Between 2009 and March 2013, a total of 1,904 actual and attempted attacks were recorded around the world, which equates to an average of around thirty acts per month.[3] Although 2013's total of 264 incidents represents a significant decline from the high point of 445 recorded in 2010—largely due to a sharp decline in hijackings and robberies off the HoA—AMC continues to have a marked presence in several parts of the world, particularly in the waters off Indonesia and Nigeria (see Figure 4.1). Moreover, while numbers are down, it is still too early to conclude that AMC in the wider Somali Basin has been effectively neutralized, as the fundamental land-based drivers of maritime crime in this part of the world (governance voids, lack of economic opportunity, poverty, and corruption) have yet to be addressed, much less comprehensively mitigated.

Official statistics of AMC likely underplay the true extent of the problem in the modern age, possibly by as much as 50 percent. The reason for this is that many ship owners have a vested interest in *not* reporting attacks for fear that doing so will merely serve to increase their maritime insurance rates. In addition, there appears to be a generic concern over vessels being laid up (and, hence, not making money) for weeks, if not months, while postattack investigations are completed. In short, unless a robbery results in significant loss, owner-operators generally calculate that it makes more (economic) sense to simply accept the attack as the inevitable risk of doing business in the maritime realm.[4]

Three main types of AMC have historically occurred in global waters. At the low end of the spectrum are anchorage thefts of ships at harbor. Maritime muggers normally carry out these attacks, taking advantage of relatively lax

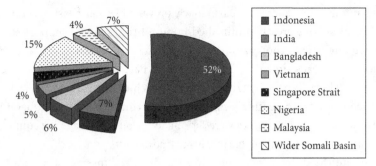

FIGURE 4.1 Main regional distribution of AMC attacks, 2013

security procedures at many ports around the world. Perpetrators are usually armed with knives and pistols and typically target a vessel's stocks, cash, and portable high-value goods with an average theft of between US $5,000 and $10,000.[5]

More serious is the ransacking of vessels in territorial waters or on the high seas. Well-armed gangs conduct these assaults, typically boarding a freighter with the intent to steal its cargo. In many cases, crews are killed or thrown overboard during or after the attack—a pattern that has been especially common in Southeast Asia. Not only does this have immediate implications for human life, it could also seriously threaten the safety of maritime navigation, especially if a vessel is left to drift in a congested sea-lane of communication (SLOC).[6]

At the high end of the spectrum are assaults that involve the outright hijacking of ships. Traditionally, much of this activity was directed at seizing and reconverting vessels for the purpose of illegal trading. Often referred to as the *phantom ship phenomenon*, this form of piracy has followed a common pattern.[7] First, a carrier would be seized and its cargo off-loaded onto a lighter (a type of flat bottomed barge) that had been moored alongside. It would then be renamed and re-registered under a flag of convenience (FoC), usually using bureaus in Panama, Belize, Malta, Cyprus, Honduras, the Bahamas, or Liberia.[8] With its assumed identity in place, the ship would take on a fresh payload (normally after offering extremely competitive terms for its transfer) that would be diverted and sold in an alternate port—often with the complicity of local officials. The vessel would then adopt yet another name and flag, and the whole cycle of fraud would commence once again.[9]

Phantom ship frauds were particularly prevalent in Southeast Asia during the 1990s but have greatly diminished in recent times due to more effective regional intelligence cooperation. In addition, a number of states have moved to decisively crack down on the corruption that facilitated many of these swindles. This is especially true of China, which by the turn of the millennium had become increasingly concerned that criminal syndicates operating from and through its territory were serving to seriously damage the country's reputation as a safe and reliable maritime trading hub.[10]

Despite the drop in phantom ship frauds, hijackings remain a serious concern. These attacks are now generally undertaken for the more straightforward purpose of extorting money, and it is this style of AMC that has characterized much of the illicit activity reported off the HoA/Somali Basin since 2008. According to a report from the World Bank, gangs operating in this wider vicinity earned an estimated US $400 million in ransoms between 2005 and 2012.[11] While the tempo of hijackings in these waters has declined—reflecting more concerted moves to "harden" vessels transiting the area, better adherence to shipping advisories put out by the IMB, and the deterrent effect of international naval patrols in the GoA[12]—attacks have surged in Nigeria, where syndicates have exhibited a capacity to operate more than 170 nautical miles from shore.[13]

Dangers Associated with Armed Maritime Crime

There are at least four reasons why the international community should care about AMC. First, attacks represent a direct threat to the lives and welfare of the citizens of a variety of flag states. Between 2009 and the end of 2013, nearly 4,000 crew were taken hostage and held against their will. Fatalities and injuries have also been apparent, especially in the Gulf of Guinea and around the Indonesian archipelago. Overall, thirty-three people have lost their lives to AMC since 2009, with a further 299 having been subjected to some sort of physical injury or abuse.[14]

Second, armed maritime crime has a direct economic cost in terms of insurance premiums, ransom payments, stolen cargoes, delayed trips, naval deployments, mitigation measures, and prosecutions. According to an estimate from "Oceans Beyond Piracy," a project of the Denver-based One Earth Future Foundation, the combined financial impact of piracy off the Somali coast alone, between 2010 and 2012, ran from a low of US $19.3 billion to a potential high of $25 billion.[15]

Third, AMC attacks have the potential to cause a major environmental disaster. The "nightmare scenario" is a mid-sea collision between an unmanned vessel and an oil tanker. The resultant discharge of petroleum would not only cause possibly irreparable damage to offshore resources and marine life, it could seriously harm extended stretches of fertile coastline.[16] Such effects would have particular significance to any littoral state that relies on the seas as a primary source of protein for indigenous consumption and regional export.[17] Moreover, if governments are viewed as ineffective in containing the environmental fallout, such circumstances could act as a trigger for political condemnation or even censure. The lessons from the *Deepwater Horizon* oil spill in the Gulf of Mexico are instructive in this regard. Although responsibility for the disaster lay strictly with British Petroleum (BP), the Obama administration's handling of the crisis generated widespread criticism from Republicans and Democrats alike.[18]

Finally, armed maritime crime can erode political stability and legitimacy by encouraging corruption. This has been evident in a number of states, including China, the Philippines, Indonesia, Brazil, Peru, India, and Bangladesh. The range of official complicity has included everything from providing intelligence on shipping movements and manifests, to facilitating the rapid discharge of stolen cargoes. In regions of endemic corruption, practices have also extended to actually constraining coastal patrols whenever they appear to be making substantial progress in denying attacks. Nigeria represents a case in point. Here, members of the navy have vigorously decried government decisions to cut their funding—claiming that such moves reflect the dissatisfaction of central members of the administration who have actively colluded with maritime gangs operating in the Niger delta.[19]

Factors Associated with the Rise of AMC in the Contemporary Era

Global AMC has traditionally been fed by three underlying drivers: the enormous volume of freight that moves by sea (which provides numerous targets of opportunity);[20] the increased dependence of ships on passing through narrow choke points (which has made these vessels vulnerable to mid-sea interception from fast-attack craft launched from shore);[21] and the inherently opaque nature of the maritime environment (which has constrained options for effective policing over both high seas and coastal/territorial waters). The contemporary manifestation of AMC reflects the continued salience of these drivers in addition to six further contributing factors.

First, there has been an increased trend toward skeleton crews, reflecting both attempts to reduce overhead costs and contemporary advances in maritime navigation technology. Even some of the largest oceangoing vessels today operate with crews of only between a dozen and twenty. This "bare-bones" complement has negated the option of carrying out concerted antipiracy watches and greatly facilitated the technical ease by which boarding parties can take control of a ship they seize.[22]

Second, there have been competing demands for scare security resources in the post-9/11 era. Since al-Qaeda's attacks in New York and Washington, many states have moved to erect expensive systems of homeland security (either voluntarily or under pressure) focused on tightening land and air borders and safeguarding components of critical infrastructure. Where this has occurred in countries already struggling to monitor their shorelines, it has further reduced already stretched budgets for coastal surveillance and, in so doing, increased their exposure to criminal penetration.[23]

Third, grinding poverty and chronic governance voids in Somalia have contributed to AMC off the Horn of Africa. The incidence of maritime crime in this part of the world is a direct manifestation of the general lawlessness, chaos, and lack of licit economic opportunities[24] that has been such an endemic feature of the country since the fall of the Siad Barre dictatorship in 1991.[25] As noted above, international naval patrols in the GoA, together with the more risk-sensitive attitude of ships transiting these waters, has helped to ameliorate the problem, at least in the short term. However, such measures are largely premised on the faulty assumption that AMC can be best contained at its endpoint—on the sea. Until more concerted attention is given to addressing the territorial "push" factors that lie at the root of maritime crime in this part of the world, a resurgence of incidents cannot be ruled out.

Fourth, owner-operators are increasingly more willing to pay ever-larger ransoms. Whereas in the early 2000s negotiated settlements averaged around US $150,000, today they range from $4–$5 million.[26] Table 4.1 details some of the more prominent sums that have been made to Somali-based syndicates since 2008. Although attempts have been made to outlaw the payment of ran-

TABLE 4.1 Prominent ransom payments to Somali-based syndicates since 2008

Ship name	Date of hijack	Flag state/owner	Amount of ransom (US$)
SV *Le Ponant*	April 2008	France	$2 million
MV *Stella Maris*	July 2008	Japan	$2 million
MV *Bunga Melati Dua*	August 2008	Malaysia	$2 million
MV *Bunga Melati Lima*	August 2008	Malaysia	$2 million
MV *Iran Deyanat*	August 2008	Iran	$2 million
MT *Irene*	August 2008	Japan	$1.6 million
MV *Stolt Valor*	September 2008	Hong Kong	$2.5 million
MV *Fiana*	September 2008	Ukraine	$3.2 million
MV *Sirius Star*	November 2008	Saudi Arabia	$3 million
MT *Ariana*	May 2009	Greece	$2.6 million
MV *Horizon*	July 2009	Turkey	$2.75 million
MV *Alakrana*	October 2009	Spain	(Allegedly) $3.3 million
MV *De Xin Hai*	October 2009	China	$4 million
CEC *Future*	November 2009	Denmark	(Allegedly) $1–2 million
VLCC *Maran Centarus*	November 2009	Greece	$7 million
MV *Samaho Dream*	April 2010	South Korea	$9.5 million
Jih Chun Tsai No 68	March 2010	Taiwan	$8 million
Rak Afrikana	April 2010	St. Vincent and Grenadines	$1.2 million
Motivator	July 2010	Marshall Islands	$4.97 million
Suez	August 2010	Panama	$2.1 million
Asphalt Venture	September 2010	Greece	$3.6 million
MV *Olib G*	September 2010	Malta	$3 million
MT *Fairchem Bogey*	September 2010	Marshall Islands	$8 million
York	October 2010	Singapore	$4.5 million
Izumi	October 2010	Panama	$4.5 million
Polar	October 2010	Barbados	$7.7 million
Panama	October 2010	Liberia	$7 million
Yuan Xiang	November 2010	China	$3.6 million
Albedo	November 2010	Malaysia	$1.2 million

(*continued*)

TABLE 4.1 *(continued)*

Ship name	Date of hijack	Flag state/owner	Amount of ransom (US$)
Haniball II	November 2010	Panama	$2 million
Ems River	December 2010	Germany	$3 million
Jahan Moni	December 2010	Bangladesh	$4 million
Vega 5	December 2010	Liberia	$5 million
Thor Nexus	December 2010	Thailand	$5 million
Renaur	December 2010	Panama	$6 million
Khaled Muhieddine	January 2011	Togo	$2.5 million
Hoang San Sun	January 2011	Mongolia	$4.5 million
Blida	January 2011	Algeria	$3.5 million
Beluga Nomination	January 2011	Germany	$5 million
Eagle	January 2011	Norway	$4 million
Irene SL	February 2011	Greece	(Allegedly) $13.5 million
Sinin	February 2011	Malta	$4 million
Savina Caylyn	February 2011	Italy	$11 million
SV ING	February 2011	Denmark	$3 million
Dover	February 2011	Panama	$3.5 million
Zirku	March 2011	United Arab Emirates	$12 million
Sinar Kudus	March 2011	Indonesia	$4.5 million
Susan K	April 2011	Antigua	$5.7 million
Rosalia D'Amato	April 2011	Italy	$6 million
Gemini	April 2011	Singapore	$4.05 million
MT Liquid Velvet	October 2011	Greece	$4 million
MT Enrico Levoli	December 2011	Italy	$9 million
Leila	February 2012	Panama	$2 million
Free Goddess	February 2012	Greece	$5.7 million

soms (by linking them to material support for terrorism), these efforts have so far been unsuccessful. Indeed, in February 2011 a UK court of appeal ruled that monies extorted from shipping companies were actually recoverable as a "sue and labor" expense.[27] The shipping industry, for its part, appears to have an unwritten rule to settle as quickly as possible, calculating that even million-dollar payouts are preferable to losing entire vessels and manifests. In addition, owner-operators are generally keen to fast-track transactions, realizing that the longer negotiations last, the longer their vessels are out of operation and not making money.[28]

A final contributing factor has been the global proliferation of arms. The range of weapons currently available on the international black market is truly enormous, including everything from pistols and assault rifles to heavy-caliber machine guns and rocket-propelled grenades (RPGs).[29] Many of these munitions can be procured relatively cheaply (which opens up a large buyer's market), providing maritime criminals with the means to operate on a higher and significantly more lethal and sophisticated level. As Noel Choong, the current director of the IMB's Piracy Reporting Centre in Kuala Lumpur, remarks: "Five to six years ago, when pirates attacked, they used machetes, knives and pistols. Today they come equipped with AK-47s, M-16s, rifle grenades and RPGs."[30]

A common denominator in most, if not all, of these factors is money. Ship owners have inadvertently made their vessels vulnerable to attack due to cost considerations. At the same time, they have provided a very strong incentive (through ransoms) for impoverished communities to engage in maritime crime. Littoral states have been unwilling or unable to secure their coastlines due to a lack of resources. Concurrently, the competitive nature of the global arms market has availed even poorly resourced gangs the necessary hardware to contemplate ever more audacious and complex operations.

Role of Private Security Companies in Countering Armed Maritime Crime

Growing international concern over AMC has prompted various PSCs to make their services available to help protect commercial vessels and offshore platforms. This has been especially evident in the wider Somali Basin, which until 2012 existed as the world's most prominent zone of armed criminality at sea. According to David Johnson, the chief executive officer of the UK-based Eos Risk Management, business opportunities for protecting ships off the HoA more than tripled with the regional onset of AMC post-2008.[31] At least twenty-two major companies have operated in this vicinity (see Table 4.2), arguing that they constitute a vital force multiplier to existing naval patrols in the GoA by providing professional protection that is uniquely tailored to the specific requirements of their customers. Most are headquartered out of the

TABLE 4.2 Main PSCs that are or have been active off the HoA

Company	Corporate headquarters
Drum-Cussac	UK
Dryad Maritime Intelligence Service	UK
Maritime Risk Solutions	UK
EoS Risk Management	UK
Maritime and Underwater Consultants (MUSC)	UK
Protection Vessels International (PVI)	UK
Geo and Shield Consulting	UK
Lotus	Yemen
Hollowpoint Protection	US
HP Terra-Marine International	US
Marque Star	US
Maritime Asset Security and Training (MAST)	UK
ISSG Holdings	Seychelles
REDfour MSS	UK
Olive Group	UK
Neptune Maritime Security	UK/Australia
Secopex	France
Saracen International	South Africa/US
Xe Services (formerly Blackwater)	South Africa/US
Templar Totan	US
Espada Logistics and Security	US
Muse Professional Group	Ukraine

SOURCES: "Private Security Companies Called in to Combat Somali Piracy," *The Strategist,* September 10, 2009; Jerry Mazza, "Why Is Blackwater/Xe in Somalia?" *Online Journal,* available online at https://butnerblogspot.wordpress.com/2010/01/18/ as of October 30, 2015; Katherine Houreld, "Companies Hire 'Shipriders' Against Somali Pirates," *Associated Press,* June 5, 2009; Sandra Jontz, "Hired Guns Secure Ships, Stir Controversy," *Stars and Stripes,* February 15, 2010.

UK (although many also operate sub-branches in other parts of the world) and have a strong military or law enforcement background. They typically consist of a few permanent staff and a small office, relying on electronic media to advertise their services. Additional personnel and equipment are only procured on a case-by-case basis—usually after a contract with a client has been signed—which allows these firms to run their businesses with limited capital outlays.[32]

The range of services offered by PSCs has spanned the spectrum from advice and training to active defense assistance (lethal and nonlethal), with the recovery of hijacked vessels and, in a few cases, the provision of escort and patrol boats.[33] Certain companies have also been tangentially involved in both land-based and multilateral operations. In 2010, for instance, several Middle Eastern countries directly affected by the spread of organized crime off the HoA (known as the "donor" states) called for private expressions of interest to help develop a land-based maritime force for the semiautonomous province of Puntland in Somalia. Saracen International responded to and won the tender, although in 2011 the effort was suspended on the grounds that training such a unit contravened the standing United Nations arms embargo against Somalia.[34]

Several parties have welcomed the growing presence of PSCs protecting ships off the HoA. The United States has been largely favorably inclined, with the former assistant secretary in the State Department's Bureau of Political-Military Affairs, Andrew Shapiro, observing in 2012 that to date: "not a single ship with privately contracted armed security personnel aboard has been pirated."[35] Despite some early reservations, the IMB has similarly exhibited growing support for PSCs, crediting at least some of the drop in AMC incidents off the HoA to the increased use of these companies.[36] Maritime insurance companies have also supported the employment of contractors, with some slashing premiums by as much as 40 percent for vessels hiring their own security.[37]

The endorsement of PSCs reflects some important advantages these companies have over purely state-led counterpiracy initiatives. First of all, they are able to provide one-on-one protection, which is obviously beyond the capacity of multinational naval deployments (as resources necessarily have to be spread out among numerous vessels).[38] They also have a definite deterrent value—reflected by Shapiro's observation that no ship with armed guards on board has yet been successfully hijacked. Finally, they play an important role in burden-sharing because they shift the onus of mitigating piracy and AMC back to the shipping industry—which, until recently, effectively "free-rode" off the back of costly coalition task forces patrolling the GoA.

Increased acceptance of PSCs off the Horn of Africa, as well as growing acknowledgment of some of their benefits, has generated calls to expand their use to other parts of the world affected by AMC. However, while private security contractors do have certain advantages, their employment on a wider scale should proceed cautiously, not least because they have some significant limitations that have yet to be addressed.

One major drawback is that clear rules of engagement (ROEs) on the use of force at sea have yet to be fleshed out, much less institutionalized. There is a particular need for greater cognizance of the consequences of opening fire against suspected pirates and insurgents who are subsequently found to be innocent. To attain this level of awareness, it is critical that a solid international legal framework regulating the use of PSCs and their ROEs be developed. Just as importantly, an internal culture that encourages these companies to seek sound legal guidance on the potential consequences of their activities needs to be fostered. Accidental death or injury, for instance, could expose contractors—and conceivably those that employ them—to exorbitant liability claims and, worse, criminal charges.[39] Indicative of the potential problems that can arise is the case of the two Italian Marines—Massimiliano Lattore and Salvatore Girone—who in February 2012 wrongfully killed a pair of Indian fishermen they mistook for pirates off the coast of Kerala. As of this writing, the servicemen were awaiting trial in Delhi on charges of involuntary manslaughter, facing potential prison terms of ten years.[40]

A related difficulty is the absence of a public registry that can be used to audit and verify the bona fides of the various firms providing armed guards to commercial vessels. In many cases, shipping companies will be forced to rely on the sales pitch of a PSC, which is hardly an objective basis for making an informed decision on whether to hire the firm. The winding down of military operations in Iraq and Afghanistan has exacerbated these problems, as it has increased the number of companies entering the maritime security market as part of the next private security "gold rush." In the absence of any formal vetting procedure, it will be extremely difficult to ascertain whether these contractors have an established and reliable track record in the provision of maritime (as opposed to land-based) security and protection.[41]

PSCs are also expensive. Providing a robust external escort costs between US $10,000 and $100,000, depending on the length of the accompanied trip, while an on-board three-man security detail typically runs between $21,000 and $50,000 per transit.[42] Although larger owner-operators are able to contemplate such outlays, they are well beyond the means of small- and medium-sized shipping companies. Unfortunately, it is these so-called "mom-and-pop" operators that constitute the bulk of attacks off the Horn of Africa, presently accounting for around two-thirds of all hijackings in the region.[43]

A further problem stems from agreements that have been made between PSCs and local government agencies to rent coastal boats and surveillance craft for escort duties. Practices such as these can have the effect of stirring controversy, as they necessarily redirect (frequently scarce) resources away from the provision of public security services to the protection of vessels belonging to PSC clients.[44]

On a practical level, stationing armed guards on a ship creates additional bureaucratic complexities for any commercial voyage involving numerous ports of call. In most cases, entry is only granted after all weapons are lodged with competent port authorities and, in certain instances, upon payment of a fee that is directly charged against the presence of munitions. These requirements obviously extend moorage transit times, costing shipping companies both in terms of extra port levies and delayed onward movements of cargo.[45] If vessels attempt to bypass these stipulations by not declaring the presence of weapons/armed personnel, they are effectively in breach of the right of innocent passage and subject to the legal penalties of the state concerned.[46]

Another consideration has to do with the fact that traditional flag states normally do not register ships that carry weapons. The employment of security contractors equipped with assault rifles, machine guns, pistols, and other munitions could therefore encourage a shift to FoCs that are characterized by laxer standards and legal requirements. This would further exacerbate the existing opaque and unregulated nature of the maritime industry—something that could, ironically, work to the direct advantage of criminals (and terrorists). Signs of such a trend are already becoming apparent. A 2010 article written for *Lloyd's List*, for instance, revealed that German ship owners operating routes near or adjacent to the HoA were looking to flag their vessels in FoC states such as the Bahamas, Belize, Bermuda, Honduras, Liberia, and Panama, specifically to avoid stringent national regulations that prohibit the use of armed guards.[47]

Additionally, it should be remembered that the growing acceptance of PSCs off the HoA reflects the unique nature of attacks in this part of the world (major hijackings on the high seas). In many respects, this is an anomaly, as armed maritime crime in other regions tends to take the form of offshore cargo thefts, the mitigation of which in most cases is invariably viewed as more appropriately falling to coast guards and marine police. This is true of even violence-prone waters such as the Gulf of Guinea (see Chapter 16), where, despite kidnappings and killings, there has yet to be a general call for the widespread use of privatized security.

Finally, the employment of PSCs proceeds from the assumption that AMC can best be addressed at sea. This is at odds with the basic reality that some of the most important drivers for AMC—corruption, the absence of governance, poverty, and lack of economic opportunity—stem from land. Until these underlying factors are dealt with, the resort to armed guards will remain, at best, no more than a stopgap measure.

Conclusion

Long considered a thing of the past, armed maritime crime remains an enduring threat to maritime shipping, trade, and commerce. Well-armed gangs continue to rove several parts of the world, exhibiting a proven ability to operate far from shore and take control of large oceangoing vessels. The existence of these groups reflects a maritime environment that is at once rich in targets and poor in regulation, where the actions of shipping companies have unwittingly served to alter favorably the risk-benefit calculus of engaging in maritime crime. While attacks have to be seen in the context of the overall magnitude of the international maritime industry (which in 2009 generated revenues in excess of US $8 trillion), it is clear that they carry important implications for human, economic, political and, potentially, environmental security.

To be sure, PSCs have been able to blunt some of the armed criminal activity that has occurred off the Horn of Africa. However, significant questions remain over the wisdom of extending these services to other parts of the world. Mitigation measures need to account for these concerns and reflect that, in the final analysis, the duty to provide safe passage is fundamentally an obligation of sovereign states—a responsibility that is enshrined as a key pillar of the UNCLOS regime.

Notes

1. See International Maritime Bureau (hereafter referred to as IMB), *Piracy and Armed Robbery Against Ships: Report for the Period 01 January–31 December 2009* (London: IMB, January 2010), 3.

2. Article 101 of UNCLOS defines piracy as "any illegal acts of violence or detention, or any act of depredation, committed for private ends by the crew or passengers of a private ship or private aircraft, and directed: (i) on the high seas, against another ship or aircraft, or against persons or property on board such ship or aircraft; (ii) against a ship, aircraft, persons or property in a place outside the jurisdiction of any State." See UNCLOS, "Part VII: High Seas," available online at http://www.un.org/depts/los/convention_agreements/texts/unclos/part7.htm, as of May 27, 2014.

3. IMB, *Piracy and Armed Robbery Against Ships: Report for the Period 01 January–31 December 2013* (London: IMB, January 2014), 5–6; IMB, *Piracy and Armed Robbery Against Ships: Report for the Period 01 January–31 March 2014* (London: IMB, April 2014), 5–6.

4. As Noel Choong, director of the IMB's Southeast Asian office in Kuala Lumpur, Malaysia observes: "A lot of ships, when nothing [major] is stolen, they do not want to report because [there is] a lot of paperwork, a lot of hassle. Sometimes, the shipmasters want a clean record. The bad thing is if they do not report another ship is going to get robbed." Cited in "Safer Waters: Global Piracy on the Wane. But Reported Attacks on Singaporean Ships and in Southeast Asian Waters Remain High," *Today*, March 26, 2014.

5. Peter Chalk, "The Evolving Dynamic of Piracy and Armed Robbery in the Modern Era," *Maritime Affairs* 5/1 (Summer 2009), 3.

6. See, for instance, Mark Valencia, "Piracy and Terrorism in Southeast Asia," in Derek Johnson and Mark Valencia, eds., *Piracy in Southeast Asia* (Singapore: ISEAS, 2005), 80–81.

7. In a number of instances, ship owners were also thought to have arranged the hijacking of their vessels in order to defraud hull insurers.

8. For an excellent overview of FoCs and how they have been exploited for criminal and terrorist purposes, see Catherine Meldrum, "Murky Waters: Financing Maritime Terrorism and Crime," *Jane's Intelligence Review* (May 2007).

9. Peter Chalk, "The Evolving Dynamic of Piracy and Armed Robbery in the Modern Era: Scope, Dimensions, Dangers and Policy Responses," *Maritime Affairs* 5/1 (2009), 3–4. For a good overview of the mechanics of the phantom ship phenomenon, see Jayant Abyankar, "Phantom Ships," in Eric Ellen, ed., *Shipping at Risk* (London: International Chamber of Commerce, 1997), 58–75.

10. In the mid-1990s, for instance, many shipping companies threatened to boycott ports in southern China as a direct result of the high incidence of phantom ship attacks that were taking place in the so-called Hainon-Luzon-Hong Kong (HLH) terror triangle. See Robert Beckman, Carl Grundy-Warr, and Vivian Forbes, "Acts of Piracy in the Malacca Straits," *Maritime Briefing* 1 (1994); Kazuo Takita and Bob Couttie, "ASEAN Pressured to Act Against Pirates," *Lloyd's List* 29 (May 1992); and Michael Pugh, "Piracy and Armed Robbery at Sea: Problems and Remedies," *Low Intensity Conflict and Law Enforcement* 2/1 (1993), 11.

11. "Horn of Africa Piracy 'Netted $400m' from 2005–12," *BBC News*, November 2, 2013, available online at http://www.bbc.co.uk/news/world-africa-24783828, as of May 27, 2014.

12. Naval flotillas in the GoA include Combined Taskforce 151 (CTF-151), the European Union's Operation Atalanta, and NATO's Operation Ocean Shield. For more details on these deployments, see Peter Chalk, "Piracy off the Horn of Africa: Scope, Dimensions, Causes and Responses," *Brown Journal of World Affairs* (Spring/Summer 2010), 97–100.

13. IMB, *Piracy and Armed Robbery Against Ships: Report for the Period 01 January–31 December 2013*, 21. See also Joe Brock and Jonathan Saul, "Nigerian Offshore Attacks Surge as Pirates Advance, Violence Increases," *Reuters*, February 21, 2013.

14. IMB, *Piracy and Armed Robbery Against Ships: Report for the Period 01 January–31 December 2013*, 11.

15. Jonathan Bellish, *Economic Cost of Somali Piracy* (Denver, CO: One Earth Future Foundation, 2012), 7. The World Bank arrived at an even higher figure of $18 billion—tallied just for the year 2012. See Teo Kermellotis, "Somali Pirates Cost Global Economy '$18 Billion a Year,'" *CNN*, April 12, 2013, available online at http://edition.cnn.com/2013/04/12/business/piracy-economy-world-bank/, as of May 27, 2013.

16. See, for instance, Greg Chaikin, "Piracy in Asia: International Cooperation and Japan's Role," in John and Valencia, eds., *Piracy in Southeast Asia*, 127; Jayant Abyankar, "Piracy and Ship Robbery: A Growing Menace," in Hamzah Ahmad and Akira Ogawa, eds., *Combating Piracy and Ship Robbery* (Tokyo: Okazaki Institute, 2001); and Valencia, *Piracy and Politics in Southeast Asia*, 114.

17. Any state that suddenly finds itself in a position in which it is unable to provide staples such as fish confronts the danger of mass protests and violence. Although not marine related, the 2008 Asian rice crisis is indicative of the sorts of problems that could arise.

18. See, for instance, "Obama Draws Bipartisan Criticism for Using Oil Spill to Push Energy Policy," *Fox News*, June 16, 2010, available online at http://www.foxnews.com/politics/2010/06/15/obamas-pitch-energy-speech-gulf-crisis-infuriates-republicans/, as of February 18, 2011; and Neela Banerjee, "Report Critical of Government Response to Gulf Oil Spill," *Los Angeles Times*, October 6, 2010.

19. Author interviews, Nigerian Navy officials, Abuja, September 2008. See also Stephanie Hanson, "Combating Maritime Piracy," Council on Foreign Relations, January 27, 2009, available online at http://www.cfr.org/publication/18376/combating_maritime_piracy.html? as of February 10, 2009.

20. Approximately 80 percent of the world's trade moves by sea, representing around 93,000 merchant vessels, 1.25 million seafarers, and almost 6 billion tons of cargo. Since the end of World War II, seaborne trade has doubled every decade. See David Rosenberg, "The Political Economy of Piracy in the South China Sea," in Bruce Elleman, Andrew Forbes, and David Rosenberg, eds., *Piracy and Maritime Crime* (Newport, RI: Naval War College Press, 2010); and Bellish, *The Economic Costs of Piracy*, 6.

21. Major choke points include the Panama Canal, the Suez Canal, the Strait of Hormuz, the Strait of Bab el-Mandeb, the Malacca Strait, the Bosphorus Strait, the Gibraltar Strait, and the Gulf of Aden. The high volume of shipping that passes through these bottlenecks necessarily forces vessels to significantly reduce speed in order to ensure safe passage (in the Bosphorus Strait, for instance, at least six accidents occur every one million transit miles), which dramatically increases their exposure to attack. See, for instance, Ali Köknar, "Maritime Terrorism: A New Challenge for NATO," *Energy Security*, January 24, 2005.

22. Interviews, maritime security analysts, Amsterdam and London, September 2005. See also "Stormy Waters: Q&A Counter-Piracy," *Jane's Homeland Security Review* (October/November 2009), 19.

23. Peter Chalk, *The Maritime Dimension of International Security: Terrorism, Piracy, and Challenges for the United States* (Santa Monica, CA: RAND, 2008), 12.

24. An average Somali fisherman earns around US $650 a year from legal trawling, whereas the potential payoff from a single hijacking could be as much as $10,000. See, for instance, Lesley Anne Warner, "From Sea to Shore," *Journal of International Peace Operations* 5/4 (January–February 2010), 13.

25. Chalk, "Piracy off the Horn of Africa," 94.

26. "Ransoms to Pirates Remain a Spiraling Illegal Tax on the 90% of World's Goods That Move by Sea," *Maritime Executive Newsletter* 11/97 (May 16, 2013); Manoj Nair, "Marine Piracy Losses Hit a Record $7b Last Year," *Gulf News*, February 7, 2011; John Payne, "Piracy Today: Fighting Villainy on the High Seas," *Wall Street Journal*, April 8, 2010.

27. Eoin O'Cinneide, "Ransoms Get Green Light," *TradeWinds*, January 28, 2011, available online at http://www.tradewinds.no/andalso/article574970.ece, as of January 28, 2011.

28. Peter Chalk, Laurence Smallman, and Nicholas Burger, *Countering Piracy in the Modern Era: Notes from a RAND Workshop to Discuss the Best Approaches for Dealing with Piracy in the 21st Century* (Santa Monica, CA: RAND, 2009), 6.

29. For a concise overview of the dynamics of the global proliferation of light weapons and their impact on substate violence and criminality, see Gideon Burrows, *Kalashnikov AK47* (Oxford: New Internationalist, 2006).

30. Interview, IMB, Kuala Lumpur, August 2006.

31. "Splashing, and Clashing, in Murky Waters," *Economist*, August 20, 2009, available online at http://www.globalsecurity.org/org/news/2009/090820-piracy.htm, as of January 31, 2010.

32. See, for instance, Carolin Liss, "Anti-Piracy Escorts in the Malacca Straits," in Claude Berube and Patrick Cullen, eds., *Maritime Private Security* (New York: Routledge, 2012), 55; Carolin Liss, "Private Military and Security Companies in the Fight Against Piracy," in Graham Gerard Ong-Webb, ed., *Piracy, Maritime Terrorism and Securing the Malacca Straits* (Queensland: Griffith University Press, 2006); "Blackwater Sets Sights on Somali Pirates," *Virginian-Pilot*, October 18, 2008; Abayomi Azikiwe, "Where Do Calls to Intervene in Somalia Come From?" *Workers World*, June

19, 2008, available at http://www.workers.org/2008/world/somalia_0626, as of February 2, 2010; and "Private Security Firms Join Battle Against Somali Pirates," *Fox News.com*, October 26, 2008, available at http://www.foxnews.com/printer_friendly _story/0,3566,444103,00.html, as of February 1, 2010.

33. One example was Xe (formerly Blackwater), which in 2008 offered a dedicated vessel, the *McArthur*, for escort duties. The ship was equipped with a helicopter pad and a storage shed capable of holding two small MD-530 aircraft. Due to a lack of interest, however, the *McArthur* was pulled from service in January 2010 and listed for sale at a purchase price of US $3.7 million (in 2008, the vessel was valued at $15 million). See Louis Hansen, "Blackwater Sets Sights on Somali Pirates," *Virginian-Pilot*, October 18, 2008; and Bill Sizemore, "Xe Pulls Plug on Its Counter-Piracy Venture; Ship up for Sale," *Virginian-Pilot*, January 5, 2010.

34. Peter Chalk, "Private Practice," *Jane's Intelligence Review* (January 2012), 10. For an overview of the proposed force, see "Puntland Maritime Police Force: A Vital Component of the Piracy Solution," Garow, Puntland State of Somalia, December 1, 2012.

35. Andrew Shapiro, "Expanding Private Sector Partnerships Against Piracy," remarks to the US Chamber of Commerce, March 13, 2012.

36. See, for instance, IMB, *Piracy and Armed Robbery Against Ships: Report for the Period 01 January–31 December 2013*, 24. The drop in AMC attacks off the HoA surprised a number of maritime security specialists who actually thought the resort to PSCs would worsen the problem by triggering an "arms race" with pirate syndicates.

37. In 2008, the UK-based Hart Group launched the first joint venture with an insurance firm. Under the terms of the arrangement, all ships using the firm's guards would benefit from significantly lower rates when sailing past Somalia. See "Private Security Firms Join Battle Against Somali Pirates," *Strategist*, September 10, 2009; "Potential Hikes in Shipping Rates Involving Gulf of Aden Transits," Gerson Lehrman Group, September 29, 2008.

38. Christopher Spearin, "A Private Security Solution to Somali Piracy?" *Naval War College Review* (Autumn 2010), 61–62; "'Ships Need Armed Guards,' Says Security Firm Chief," *Maritime Global Net*, October 20, 2008, available online at http://www .mgn.com/ as of October 2010.

39. See Katherine Houreld, "Companies Hire 'Shipriders' Against Somali Pirates" *Associated Press*, June 05, 2009; and Sandra Jontz, "Hired Guns Secure Ships, Stir Controversy." *Stars and Stripes*, February 15, 2009.

40. "UNGA President to Raise Italian Marines Issue with India," *Times of India*, March 19, 2014, available online at http://timesofindia.indiatimes.com/india/UNGA -president-to-raise-Italian-marines-issue-with-India/articleshow/32287415.cms, as of May 28, 2014; "Italy Says Arrest of Marines Sets 'Very Dangerous Precedent,'" *Associated Press*, April 5, 2012.

41. Steven Jones, "Implications and Effects of Maritime Security on the Operation and Management of Vessels," in Rupert Herbert-Burns, Sam Bateman, and Peter Lehr, *Lloyd's Handbook of Maritime Security* (London: CRC Press, 2009), 107; Houreld,

"Companies Hire 'Shipriders' Against Somali Pirates"; Britta Rinehard, "Armed Guards on Merchant Vessels," *Civil Military Fusion Centre* (November 2011); Spearin, "A Private Security Solution to Somali Piracy?" 63–64.

42. Author interviews, London and Hong Kong, February 2010. See also *The Economic Cost of Somali Piracy, 2011*, 17; and Tim Fish, "Private Security Firms Step up Anti-Piracy Ops in Gulf of Aden," *Jane's Intelligence Review*, May 15, 2007.

43. Peter Chalk, Laurence Smallman, and Nicholas Burger, *Countering Piracy in the Modern Era: Notes from a RAND Workshop to Discuss the Best Approaches for Dealing with Piracy in the 21st Century* (Santa Monica, CA: RAND, 2009), 3.

44. Carolin Liss, "Losing Control? The Privatisation of Anti-Piracy Services in Southeast Asia," *Australian Journal of International Affairs* 63/6 (2009), 390–403.

45. See, for instance, Nick Blackmore, "New Tricks: Examining Anti-Piracy Tactics," *Jane's Intelligence Review* (December 21, 2009).

46. In October 2013, for instance, the Indian Coast Guard impounded the *Seaman Guard Ohio*, a US-owned merchant vessel, and arrested thirty-three personnel on board for failing to produce papers authorizing it to carry weapons while sailing off the southern coast of Tamil Nadu. See "Following Arrests, India Charges 33 Aboard Armed US Ship," *Maritime Executive Newsletter* 11/210 (October 23, 2013); and "MV Seaman Guard Ohio: India Police Arrest Crew of US Ship," *BBC News*, October 18, 2013, available online at http://www.bbc.com/news/world-asia-india-24577190, as of May 28, 2014.

47. Chalk, "Private Practice," 12.

II RIDING THE STORM

5   Integrated Strategies Against Maritime Violence

Paul Shemella

T HE SUCCESSFUL MANAGEMENT OF MARITIME VIOLENCE CALLS
for a comprehensive set of civil-military strategies, executed continuously over time. There is no "victory" at the end of this campaign, only the stability that comes with sound maritime governance. In this volume, we have been using the term *maritime violence* to describe a category of activities characterized by violence or the threat of violence in the maritime domain.[1] This category does not include state-on-state conflict at sea, conducted by powerful nations with global reach. It does include situations in which warships are used against pirates, drug traffickers, and other non-state actors. But most maritime violence is managed by maritime law enforcement agencies, working within multiple domestic jurisdictions and complex international legal frameworks. Such a diverse grouping of government responses must have a common thread beyond the fact that they take place in the maritime domain. That common thread is strategy.

The word *strategy* means different things to different people, and that limits its usefulness. Simply stated, strategy does four things: First, it provides a clear vision of success and how to achieve it. Second, strategy shows a government how to employ its scarce resources in the most effective and efficient manner. Third, it forms a necessary bridge between policy and operations. Fourth, strategy connects the ends needed, the means available, and the ways to use those means toward the achievement of the government's political objectives. Strategy is not a legal framework or a financial plan—although both are essential elements of a maritime campaign. It is a logical sequence of actions that connects decision-makers with the citizens they represent. Strategy needs to be written, but it is not fixed. Indeed, the key to making strategy effective is building in a process of measurement and adjustment. Strategy is a continuous cycle of improving a government's position relative to the threats it faces.[2]

Strategies for managing maritime violence have two basic levels: political and operational.[3] The political level focuses on a spectrum of government institutions, matching roles and objectives to particular ministries and agencies. Each ministry or agency then develops an operational strategy to support its assigned role and reach the broad objectives listed. Managing maritime violence is a process of organizing a government's institutions around specific maritime security roles and then making sure those institutions can fulfill them. Institutions fulfill their roles by anticipating the missions that will be required, and securing the resources needed to successfully complete those missions. They must then develop the *capacity* to generate capable forces whenever the need arises. Strategy is also a "forcing function" that makes it necessary for all maritime security institutions—and other government institutions—to work collectively for a common set of political objectives. It is the sheet music that brings an institutional symphony into harmony.

Government Toolkit

Every government has a "toolkit" into which it can reach for the basic building blocks of strategy. For strategies against maritime violence, the range of instruments available normally includes the following:

- *Diplomacy.* The complex legal framework, as well as the international nature of maritime issues, requires a strong diplomatic component for maritime strategies.
- *Information.* Governments are obliged to send messages to a variety of audiences, both friend and foe. This is particularly important for maritime issues, which do not command the continuous attention of the public.
- *Maritime Law.* Both domestic and international maritime laws involve multiple parties and a dynamic technological landscape. The legal code must be kept one step ahead of terrorists, pirates, and other

criminals. Maritime law is a specialty within the legal profession for a reason.

- *Maritime Law Enforcement.* This is the main instrument for establishing and maintaining security in a country's maritime domain. The responsible institutions are normally called coast guards or maritime law enforcement agencies.

- *Military Forces.* Most governments have naval forces. Some have a marine corps or maritime component of the army. In many countries, these institutions have the responsibility, but limited capability, to patrol the extensive maritime space their governments wish to monitor. In more than a few countries, military forces are not permitted to enforce the law within territorial seas and internal waters.

- *Economic Means.* A significant aspect of maritime governance is providing the resources needed to increase security in the maritime domain. This includes the protection of maritime critical infrastructure at sea and ashore. Economic policies also include employment programs that can help alleviate the root causes of maritime violence.[4]

- *Financial Means.* Many governments use sanctions and seizures to deny financial assets to terrorists, pirates, and other criminals operating in the maritime domain. Financial "task forces" can also use the flow of money through a terrorist or criminal network to identify key individuals. A key part of using the financial tool is to reduce the vulnerability of government officials to corruption.[5]

- *Maritime Intelligence.* The branches of civilian or military intelligence that gather, analyze, and disseminate intelligence information regarding the maritime domain. This intelligence is largely civilian and very much international. Maritime domain awareness and maritime intelligence work in tandem to produce the raw materials for strategy.

- *Commercial Activities.* The commercial sector of a government's economy includes maritime transportation and the exploitation of marine resources. These industries rely on public-private partnerships aimed at achieving the proper balance between commerce and security.

- *Emergency Management.* Often working with commercial partners, governments must develop the capacity to manage the consequences of a terrorist attack, industrial accident, or environmental disaster in the maritime domain. Maintaining a robust capacity to manage maritime incidents helps to prevent or deter them. Emergency management prowess is also a fundamental element of government legitimacy.

- *Population.* Civil society and individual citizens can be the most powerful tools a government possesses with which to fight maritime violence. In the extensive maritime space, labor and trade organizations can provide important information on what is happening at sea, in lakes and rivers, and along the coast. At the individual level, fishermen are especially good sources of information.

These tools are the building blocks for strategy development, to be mixed together in various combinations for maintaining or reestablishing security in the maritime domain.[6]

Net Assessment

The first requirement of strategic development is to identify what (or who) threatens the state and its population. An "all-hazards" approach to this task reveals all possible maritime events for which the government must maintain the ability to respond. Starting with a long list of threats illuminates the range of maritime responses that may become necessary. Since all responses compete for the same government resource base, a process of risk assessment must ensue.[7] Only after the most significant risks are identified can a government mobilize its maritime resources in the most effective and efficient manner.[8]

As a family, *maritime violence* brings terrorists, armed maritime criminals, smugglers, and even greedy corporations into the threat picture.[9] The next step in the strategy process is to identify the specific groups capable of harming people or destroying property, and to assess them relative to government assets. This is normally done through a process of *net assessment*, a listing of relative strengths and weaknesses. The resulting four-way matrix shows where the government must invest in shoring up its own vulnerabilities, where it can exploit adversary weaknesses, and where it can find opportunities for strategic advantage. This process can help governments identify what their adversaries need, as well as suggest how those needs can be denied or taken away. The identification of these areas of vulnerability can be understood as strategic "centers of gravity."[10]

The centers of gravity suggested by a net assessment will reflect both the common and the unique characteristics of individual threats; they will also remind governments how their maritime adversaries might be assessing *them*. Situational lists point to separate strategies for different threats. Wise governments will develop strategies that have both wide and narrow applications. However, even if separate strategies have a lot in common, they must also account for the unique characteristics of each threat.

Table 5.1 lists the strengths and weaknesses for a typical government and its adversaries. Any government with a similar list would have a place to start

TABLE 5.1 Net assessment

Threats		Governments	
Strengths	*Weaknesses/ vulnerabilities*	*Strengths*	*Weaknesses/ vulnerabilities*
Extensive maritime domain (AMC, smuggling)	Leadership (terrorism)	Legitimacy	Lack of capacity
Number of maritime targets (terrorism, AMC)	Ideology (terrorism)	Potential resources	Weak maritime governance
Networks (terrorism, smuggling)	Cost (terrorism)	International organizations	Government corruption
Financing (terrorism, AMC, smuggling)	Training (terrorism, AMC)	Popular support	Poverty
	Lack of trust (terrorism, AMC, smuggling)	Moral values	Unemployment
	Operational difficulties (terrorism, AMC)	Maritime law	Illiteracy
	Unit cohesion (terrorism)		Isolated populations
	Distance (smuggling)		
	Visibility (smuggling)		
	Money transfers/ storage (terrorism, AMC, smuggling)		

building its various strategies against maritime violence. Looking at the columns, we can see immediately that there are both common and unique items. By focusing strategies against common centers of gravity, governments can ensure that their resources are distributed as widely and intelligently as possible. This increases the value of their investments and can lead to better operational performance. If, for instance, pirates and maritime drug traffickers rely on the same logistics network, the disruption of that network will have a dual impact. Vulnerabilities unique to each threat can also be accommodated in a focused strategic calculation.

Ends, Ways, Means, and Measures

The strategic calculation begins with identifying both political- and operational-level ends. These objectives should correspond as closely as possible to the centers of gravity previously identified.[11] The accumulation of political-level ends can lead the government to the end state it wishes to achieve (e.g., complete confidence in the ferry system). End states are based on a set of outcomes derived from measures of effectiveness comprising inputs (effort) and outputs (results). At the operational level, efforts are the most common form of measurement; at the political level, results become easier to tabulate. But it is *outcomes* that permit governments to adjust strategy until they get it right. End states allow them to declare victory and channel their precious resources into some other public good.

The critical path to desired outcomes runs through the ends achieved with the tools available. Those building strategy must first work from the general to the specific, then from the specific back to the general. The "bridge" for linking the general to the specific, called *ways*, is where creativity comes into the equation. For example, the instrument of information can be used in various ways to bring about the desired end. If that end is a reduction in ship hijackings, the government can use "information" to announce a policy of zero tolerance, to broadcast a counternarrative to pirate claims that they are taking back what is rightfully theirs, and to reassure shipping companies that their assets will be protected as long as they conform to certain operating procedures while traveling in pirate-infested waters.

Means take the form of tools and instruments available at all levels. At the political level, the means are almost exclusively government institutions. At the operational level, the means are capabilities developed by civilian and military operating units within each ministry or agency. If a government wishes, for instance, to reduce the number of pirate attacks on its merchant ships, it will have to empower the appropriate institution, perhaps a maritime law enforcement agency, to develop an operational strategy. Other agencies can be called on to assist, but the lead institution remains responsible for execution. In this case, the means might include ships, planes, and small units trained to board pirate craft at sea. Such means, of course, go beyond capabilities into the realm of capacity. Capability is being able to do something once. Capacity, on the other hand, enables the operational unit to utilize particular capabilities day after day, until the operational and political outcomes have been achieved. Against maritime violence, for which all strategies are long-term, capacity is what counts.[12]

Ends, ways, means, and measures thus form the "bones" of strategy, a speech pattern for the development of strategic narrative. Measures provide the feedback loop that indicates when a strategy needs to be adjusted. Perhaps the best example of maritime strategic adjustment is the incorporation of private armed security guards for merchant ships sailing around the Horn of Africa (discussed in Chapter 4). For effective responses to maritime violence, we suggest governments pursue political and operational ends, through ways and means, for three interlocking substrategies. These three components require different mixes of government tools, yielding a family of mutually supporting strategies.[13] The three substrategies are characterized as follows:

- *Core Strategy.* Continuous, comprehensive, and long-term efforts to dry up the root causes of maritime violence. Core strategies guide the good governance that makes all individuals part of a just society, one in which economic gain and political expression are sought by law-abiding citizens cooperating with each other.
- *Offensive Strategy.* Immediate and midterm actions taken to interdict, arrest, capture, or kill individuals and groups that use the maritime domain for criminal activity, or threaten citizens and their property. These strategies are the primary responsibility of the security sector but necessarily involve other institutions.
- *Defensive Strategy.* Protects critical maritime infrastructure, key resources, and citizens in the maritime domain from terrorism and criminal attack. If such attacks cannot be prevented, the defensive strategy guides a government's efforts to manage the consequences

of those attacks (discussed in Chapter 11). These strategies normally require the participation of the private sector.

The family of strategies against maritime violence has now grown considerably. Deconstructing the family into its component parts—and then reconstructing it—can ensure that nothing is overlooked and that the final set of strategies coheres. Deconstruction also helps to keep the operational strategies firmly in support of their political counterparts. The hierarchy of substrategies potentially breaks out into eighteen separate components (2 levels of strategy, times 3 kinds of strategy, times 3 different threats—terrorism, AMC, and smuggling). The list appears long and complicated, but it is not. For one thing, each of the substrategies focuses on a specific type of maritime violence, and at a specific level. The deconstruction allows strategists to apply the ends-ways-means-measures formula to each narrow set of activities for maximum impact. After all the substrategies are formulated and coordinated, a comprehensive strategic document can be put back together as the sum of its parts.

Defensive Strategy for Maritima

Chapter 3 introduced a method of analyzing the vulnerability of maritime infrastructure, applying it to the fictional country of Maritima. We will again turn our attention to Maritima to illustrate the process for constructing a set of strategies against maritime violence. Maritima faces a clear terrorist threat, but as a coastal developing nation, it must also deal with armed maritime crime. The AMC threat manifests as what we called *armed robbery at sea* in Chapter 4. There have been no incidents of high-seas piracy in Maritima or the wider region, but a thriving network of illegal maritime traffickers is transporting cocaine over the beach and into the dense urban waterfront of Water City.

Selecting maritime terrorism as a sample threat—and with some imagination—the foregoing summary is enough to begin roughing out a defensive strategy for Maritima.[14]

Political Level
Political End #1: The citizens of Maritima understand that the government is taking all possible measures to protect them from terrorist attack.

Ways for Political End #1

1.1 Make public announcements explaining what the government has done.

1.2 Strengthen the climate of security nationwide.

1.3 Make it clear that those who might wish to attack citizens and their property will be arrested and prosecuted to the fullest extent of the law.

Means for Political End #1 (institutions listed by function)

1.1 Information (primary) with support from Tourism and Transportation.

1.2 Interior (primary) with support from Defense.

1.3 Justice (primary) with support from the legislature, Information, and Interior.

Measures of Effectiveness for Political End #1
(track these over time)

- Polling data, featuring questions on how secure ordinary citizens feel.

- Number of threats by extremist groups toward maritime infrastructure.

- Number of attacks by extremist groups within the country and its maritime domain.

Operational Level
Operational End #1: Make public announcements explaining what the government has done.[15] (Ministry of Information lead)

Ways for Operational End #1

1.1 Use traditional media to send messages to target audiences.

1.2 Exploit opportunities afforded by the Internet and social media.

1.3 Use television in creative ways to inform the public.

Means for Operational End #1

1.1 Government-controlled newspapers and radio.

1.2 Government websites and Facebook/Twitter accounts.

1.3 Government television stations, international television broadcasts.

Measures of Effectiveness for Operational End #1 (track these over time)[16]

- Number of public announcements by the government.
- Number of newspaper articles favorable to government efforts.
- Number of Facebook "Likes" on government explanations.
- Number of favorable Twitter comments.
- Number of television infomercials.[17]

Operational End #2: Strengthen the climate of security nationwide. (Ministry of the Interior lead)

Ways for Operational End #2

2.1 Increase security posture at Molina Locks.

2.2 Increase security checks at ferry terminal.

2.3 Increase security patrols in Water City harbor.

Means for Operational End #2

2.1 National police coordinate with army to increase number of soldiers guarding the Molina Locks. Expand the effective security perimeter with law enforcement personnel.

2.2 Replace the private security company at the ferry terminal with national police personnel.

2.3 Direct coast guard to double the number of patrols in Water City harbor.

Operational End #3: Make it clear that those who might wish to attack citizens and their property will be punished to the fullest extent of the law. (Ministry of Justice lead)

Ways for Operational End #3

3.1 Strengthen antiterrorism laws.

3.2 Publicize trials of terrorism suspects.

3.3 Warn extremists (and would-be extremists) that violence as political expression will not be tolerated.

Means for Operational End #3 (Ministry of Justice lead)

3.1 Work with the legislature to review and update the legal framework for terrorism offenses and punishments.

3.2 Work with the Ministry of Information to increase media coverage of terrorism trials.

3.3 Work with the president and the rest of his cabinet to schedule speeches explaining/justifying Maritima's law enforcement approach to terrorism.

Examining the defensive strategy hierarchy, we can see how the pieces come together. Political-level ways become operational-level ends. Measures of effectiveness are applied to each political-level end as a method of determining whether the strategy is producing the outcome sought the by the government of Maritima. If the government gets the political-level objectives right, the hierarchy can be constructed as a strategic outline for the daunting task of actually writing a set of documents. The accumulation of political measures will then lead to the broader outcome desired.[18] Strategy is a complicated undertaking that can be organized through persistent logic and simplified through clear writing.[19] No strategy can be effective if it is incomplete, inconsistent, or unreadable.

Broken Windows

One theory of policing, made popular in the 1990s by Rudolph Giuliani, the mayor of New York City, suggests that reducing petty crime (fixing broken windows) will result in fewer acts of major crime. This approach appeared to work in New York, and many police chiefs in the United States subscribe to it.[20] In the maritime context, a government that is able to suppress low-level smuggling, sea robbery, illegal fishing, toxic waste dumping, fuel bunkering, and anything else that inhibits its ability to exercise routine governance can perhaps expect to experience a lower incidence of terrorism, piracy, and large-scale illegal maritime trafficking. As discussed in Chapter 6, *maritime governance* is a comprehensive set of activities, undertaken through maritime security and other institutions, aimed at reducing the level of lawlessness that naturally pervades these undergoverned spaces. Can the broken-windows approach be effective in the maritime domain?[21]

Terrorists, insurgents, pirates, and big-time traffickers operate more successfully within a climate of general lawlessness—whether or not they work together, or are even aware of each other. Illegal maritime activity provides the backdrop for the sharing of smuggling routes, boats, sanctuaries, and fraud, as well as specialized individuals comfortable in and around the water (the Sea Tigers of LTTE rode with smugglers before they had their own boats). If you're a terrorist wishing to hijack a vessel to use as a weapon, you might want to outsource the job to pirates rather than train and equip your own team. If you're a pirate in need of small arms and am-munition, you might buy them from a smuggler. If you're a drug trafficker, perhaps you can find a secure beach on which to land a boat in the middle of the night, courtesy of maritime insurgents. Tactical marriages of conve-nience happen all the time—if the government is not there to prevent them. Petty criminality is the "universal solvent" for more significant maritime mayhem.

Tom Mockaitis explains in Chapter 14 how the Lahad Datu insurgents blended into normal seaborne traffic to escape detection from the authori-ties of two countries, not necessarily cooperating with anyone. Even without criminality, the maritime environment provides cover and concealment to insurgents and terrorists. Larry Cline describes in Chapter 13 how the govern-ments of Indonesia, Singapore, and Malaysia cooperate to police the Malacca Strait. Such regional efforts enable governments to find out what is going on "out there." An important part of the broken-windows approach is to foster trust between the police and the local community. So it is with drying up petty maritime crime: maritime law enforcement institutions must talk to fishermen, seafarers, dockworkers, and private security personnel every day in an effort to get to know "the neighborhood."

Prerequisites for Good Strategy

The first ingredient needed for making successful strategy is a thorough as-sessment of the risks associated with specific maritime threats.[22] Starting with an all-hazards framework, threats in the maritime domain must be evalu-ated in terms of the potential for public harm. Scarce government resources can then be apportioned according to risk rather than political or personal considerations. A series of increasingly focused assessments will lead strate-gists to the conclusions needed for laying a set of maritime violence strategies in place. If, for instance, terrorism does not rank high on the list of priori-tized maritime risks, the government can direct more thought and resources to something that does. Many countries are plagued with illegal maritime trafficking (primarily arms, drugs, and people). Others are afflicted with sea robbery (from petty cash, to petroleum, to the ships themselves). Still others worry about high-seas piracy. Each of these risks requires a different set of strategies.

Secondly, government institutions need clear guidance, and that guidance must come from the top. This guidance would include an end-state vision (e.g., a country free of maritime violence in all its forms), statements of policy (e.g., "we will never pay ransom to pirates"), and a political-level strategy. Without such guidance, thoroughly debated and then written down, institutions will vie with one another for roles and the associated resources. The political-level strategy organizes the whole government so that a whole-of-government approach can guide the development and execution of operational-level strategies for each institution. Just as importantly, the assignment of roles and resources from the highest level can encourage government institutions to coordinate their actions. This is especially true if the political strategy distributes roles and resources in ways that increase interdependency. In the maritime arena, with its many overlapping jurisdictions and capabilities, that interdependency is critical.

The third prerequisite is an interagency process. The roles clarification that comes with a political strategy provides the sheet music. But creating harmony is more than just having clear institutional roles. There must be a mechanism for interagency coordination—indeed, for interagency decision-making. The process is difficult, however, because institutions do not easily develop the kind of trust upon which individual relationships depend. The best measure of institutional trust is whether or not one of them is willing to share credit for a successful action. Sound institutional relationships rest on two pillars: complementarity and reciprocity. Each must have something the other does not have, and each must be willing to do something *for* the other. Individual trust is relatively easy to cultivate; institutional trust can be developed, but it takes time and leadership.[23] Without trust, even sharing information is difficult; with it, institutions can move beyond information sharing to collaboration. When they collaborate, using complementary skill sets, institutions can create something that did not exist before. Good strategy is the best example of institutional collaboration, especially in the maritime domain.[24]

The final major prerequisite is capacity. Before government institutions can coordinate (and, perhaps, collaborate) they must be able to fulfill their own assigned roles. High-capacity institutions are built on visionary leadership, but several other characteristics are important. Every organization has an optimum size, and most institutions are far too large.[25] Leaner institutions are faster and more efficient, especially if individuals within them trust each other. Smaller and faster, they can focus on fewer core roles, especially if they can count on other institutions to focus on complementary roles. They can also benefit from a decentralized organizational structure and a philosophy of empowering individuals all the way down the organizational ladder.[26]

Conclusion

The development and execution of strategies against maritime violence does not conform to a single rigid formula. However, the approach described in this chapter can go a long way toward providing maritime planners with a blueprint for operations that satisfy the political objectives of their elected leaders. The context for good strategy in the maritime domain includes governance and capacity. One without the other is not sufficient to confront and defeat maritime violence. Strategy guides both maritime governance at the national level and the application of operational capacity at the institutional level. Good strategy can bind a government and its people together in the pursuit of lasting security in the maritime domain.

We have tried to demonstrate that strategy can be formulated through a logical process that connects political objectives to available resources. If the process can be made to involve a wide spectrum of government institutions, resulting strategies will lead to measurable results on three fronts: root causes, threats, and vulnerabilities. In the case of maritime violence, the most important root cause is the environment itself. To the extent that resources allow, the vastness of the environment can be mitigated by increased maritime domain awareness (MDA), discussed in Chapter 8. The improvement of MDA leads, simultaneously, to better governance and an increased capacity to confront waterborne threats. The intelligence derived from better MDA also enhances a government's ability to defend its citizens and protect the infrastructure that powers their societies.

Having developed good strategies, government officials must be able to explain them to average citizens (a strategy in itself). Strategies against maritime violence are more difficult to explain because the maritime domain is less familiar to the public to begin with. Even though every family depends on them, seas, harbors, and river systems are largely out of sight—until terrorists and other criminals bring them into focus. Maritime security institutions, linked by ends, ways, and means, must garner enough resources to maintain a high level of readiness. Governments must make the effort to continually educate the public regarding what those forces are ready to do and why.

Even with good strategies, single governments cannot defeat—or even manage—maritime violence in isolation. As with all transnational threats, real solutions in the maritime domain are regional, sometimes global. Fortunately, many of the world's regions most affected by maritime violence are banding together in both planning and execution. The governments that control the Strait of Malacca have undertaken a host of regional approaches to mitigating piracy, as discussed in Chapter 13 of this volume. Similarly, the four nations that border the Gulf of Thailand have been integrating the actions of their maritime security institutions through a series of joint education and training events.[27] The African Union (AU) has gone still further, declaring in a Maritime Strategy document the goal of creating a "Common EEZ."[28] Regional efforts in the Gulf of Guinea are discussed in Chapter 15. Like interagency responses within a single government, regional responses to maritime violence can be a forcing function that can foster the critical cooperation that has eluded most countries for a long time.

Notes

1. The term *maritime domain* in this chapter includes a government's internal waters, territorial sea, contiguous zone, exclusive economic zone, and—where that government has capable forces to contribute to global maritime security—the high seas.

2. Successful strategy is sometimes called a *virtuous cycle*, while the unsuccessful kind is often referred to as a *vicious cycle*.

3. See Edward Luttwak, *Strategy: The Logic of War and Peace* (Harvard College, 1987), 82–90. See also "Missiles as Strategy for Israel and Gaza," *International Herald Tribune*, July 10, 2014.

4. For a prime example of the potential for economic instruments to reduce maritime violence, see "Pirates v Economists," *Economist*, July 12, 2014, http://www .economist.com/news/middle-east-and-africa/21606882-new-weapon-against-somali -bandits-free-trade-pirates-v-economists.

5. The economic tool can (and should) be used to pay maritime security officials a high enough wage so they are not tempted by bribery.

6. This list is a modification of the traditional DIMEFIL list that forms the basis of the US government's strategic approach to national security.

7. For instance, if the threat from tropical cyclones poses the most risk of harm, the government will have to allocate a substantial portion of its maritime resources to dealing with the consequences (and perhaps some to predicting the weather). Those resources will not be available for fighting terrorists or pirates.

8. A thorough discussion of risk assessment, written by James Petroni, can be found in Paul Shemella, *Fighting Back: What Governments Can Do About Terrorism* (Stanford, CA: Stanford University Press, 2011), 117–30.

9. If the list of threats includes environmental pollution or resistance to defensive measures for commercial infrastructure, corporations can sometimes be seen as having an adversarial relationship with the government.

10. Clausewitz's term is borrowed here, with respect. If it is not completely consistent with his analysis of war, the point is the same.

11. This is simply the basis for an asymmetric approach to strategy.

12. Compounding the challenge for governments is that terrorists can succeed with only the capability to do something once (see Mumbai). Capacity is needed on the government side for denying them the opportunity to use that capability. Pirates, on the other hand, require the capacity to mount a campaign in order to be considered a menace to society. Either way, government capacity is required for the long-term resolution of these problems.

13. This insight borrows from Ian O. Lesser, *Countering the New Terrorism* (Santa Monica, CA: RAND, 1999), 126–40.

14. There is not enough space (and not enough country detail) here to include a notional ends-ways-means-measures breakdown for other maritime threats, but the process would be the same. The statements themselves are abbreviated for simplicity.

15. The operational-level *end* should match one of the political-level *ways*.

16. This strategic hierarchy would not be complete without listing MOE for Operational Ends #2 and #3, but that exercise is left to the reader. A second hierarchy would begin with a second political end and its supporting structures.

17. Note that all these operational MOE are measures of effort, but that the political measures they support indicate results.

18. To illustrate the concept of *outcome*, we could use the example of the United States' War on Terror. The outcome (unintended as it was) has been *more* terrorism, illustrated most clearly by the emergence of the self-styled "Islamic State" (IS). The only conclusion we can draw from this is that America's strategy thus far has been ineffective.

19. The pattern-generated outline also helps strategists avoid the chaos that often results from unstructured brainstorming by groups of very smart people.

20. This theory was first articulated in 1982. See George L. Kelling and James Q. Wilson, "Broken Windows," *Atlantic Monthly*, March 1982. The theory is controversial in some quarters, but it has demonstrated the value of bringing ordinary citizens closer to the police and making them feel safer.

21. The other side of this argument would be that spreading out scarce maritime resources to police nonviolent crime prevents governments from concentrating their assets to deal with violent crime. The best strategy might be to hedge assets and be reasonably ready to do both.

22. Threats and risks are not the same thing. A process to analyze threats might reveal that a government has done so much to reduce the threat of a particular form of maritime violence that it no longer poses a significant risk.

23. See Stephen M. R. Covey, *The Speed of Trust: The One Thing that Changes Everything* (New York, NY: Free Press, 2006). This is primarily a business book, but Covey's principles of trust building can be applied directly to interagency cooperation. Governments, most of which do have a bottom line, could learn a lot from business.

24. For more on leadership and institutional cooperation, see Chapter 9 of this volume.

25. For an interesting discussion of optimum group size, see Malcolm Gladwell, *The Tipping Point* (New York: Little Brown, 2003), 179.

26. For an illuminating discussion of how the flow of information through an organization can yield better decision-making, see Alex Pentland, *Social Physics* (New York: Penguin Press, 2014), 32–42.

27. The Gulf of Thailand Initiative (GOTI) has featured courses on three levels: command, staff, and tactical. Instruction has been provided by CCMR and the US Coast Guard since 2011.

28. See "2050 Africa's Integrated Maritime Strategy" (AIM Strategy), African Union, Version 1.0, 2012. The document combines many of the principles described in this chapter.

6 Assessing Maritime Governance

Paul Shemella

GOOD GOVERNANCE AT SEA BEGINS ASHORE. LEADERS WHO cannot govern their cities, towns, and villages effectively perform still worse in the maritime territory for which they are responsible. Almost all countries have remote areas sometimes referred to as *ungoverned spaces* within which formal governments do not matter much.[1] But no space is truly ungoverned; where there is human activity, someone is always in charge. Extending formal governance into the maritime domain is difficult for even the most capable governments; it is indeed an environment of freedom, chaos, and crime.[2] This chapter reviews the functions expected of governments in their maritime spaces and suggests ways to assess the performance of the activities associated with those functions.

The business of government is about doing collectively what individuals cannot do for themselves. Citizens in maritime regions are often isolated from central authority, either by circumstances of birth or livelihood, or because they want to avoid the scrutiny of government officials.[3] Whether they play by the rules or not, citizens who live by the sea are different from other citizens. These are subcultures at work, brought together by geography, hardship, and the increased freedom to act as they wish. Leaders and administrators must find ways to give them a feeling of inclusion in a fulfilling social enterprise—the nation-state. Governments that do not make this effort set the stage for maritime violence of all kinds. Disorder in the maritime domain is normal, but in describing the high seas—and certain very large port cities—Martin Murphy goes on to characterize them as "anarchic."[4] Better maritime governance is long overdue.

Maritime governance is a set of functions shaped by long-term programs and the resources needed to finance them. Although some of the functions deal with dangerous threats to the nation's security, others do not. Some functions are routine. Good governance is, in fact, the practice of making *everything* routine. But even the routine requires robust maritime institutions that translate good intentions into successful programs. When dangerous maritime threats are deterred, their potential consequences are avoided. Consequently—albeit gradually—people decide to trust the government to protect them and their interests. Over time, maritime governance can become largely a matter of knowing what is happening in the maritime domain, maintaining readiness to deal with threats, providing essential services, and generating wealth.

Governing the Maritime Domain

Individuals matter a great deal in government, especially those in leadership positions, but governments must act through institutions. Creating the right institutions, as well as the processes that allow them to act together, is the foundation of maritime governance. In order to do that, we must know the functions around which government must build those institutions, whether those institutions are actually performing their assigned functions, and how well they are doing it. We must also understand the connections among particular functions—that is, the ecosystem. Maritime governance produces best when institutions work as a team. There are two levels of analysis in this chapter: a simplified listing of maritime governance functions, and a more comprehensive layout of functions, subfunctions, and capabilities. For each level, we will suggest methodologies for assessing performance.[5]

Level I Examination

Maritime Domain Awareness

The subfunctions in this category include maritime patrol, surveillance, and intelligence. *Maritime domain awareness* (MDA) is a US term that describes a universal function. It is the effective understanding of anything associated with the global maritime domain that could impact the security, safety, economy, or environment of the United States and any other country with maritime spaces.[6] Jeff Kline argues that there are three requirements for effective responses to maritime threats: knowledge, platforms, and law.[7] MDA (or whatever else it is called) provides the knowledge piece.

Surface and air platforms must be capable of covering a vast area in all weather conditions, establishing and maintaining a persistent presence. A visible presence deters lawless behavior, and even the *threat* of seeing government surveillance platforms tends to moderate criminal activity. Many maritime nations do not have vessels capable of operating throughout the exclusive economic zone (EEZ), or if they have vessels, they lack a sufficient number of them. Still more do not have capable aircraft. Virtually all of them lack the operational funding to establish a persistent presence where it is needed.

Aircraft can be an effective surveillance tool, flying to the EEZ boundary, often in less than one hour, and patrolling thousands of square miles of sea more quickly than ships. Such coverage, however, comes at great cost. For example, a Lockheed C-130 transport plane can cost in excess of US $100M, and costs more than $10K per hour to operate.[8] Smaller, less expensive aircraft have shorter ranges and reduced loiter times. Moreover, aircraft cannot duplicate the personal contact with fishermen and other mariners that is afforded by surface platforms. Surveillance and intelligence gathering are best conducted by a combination of patrol boats, ships, and aircraft, suggesting regional approaches that maximize numbers and distribute costs.

To offset the high cost of operating ships and aircraft on the high seas, some governments may leverage technology. For example, the Automatic Identification System, referred to as AIS, is required by international law for ships over 300 gross tons, operating in the global maritime environment. AIS-equipped ships report key information via electronic transmission—information that provides positional and identification data to a central monitoring site. Many regional fisheries require AIS transmitters to monitor compliance with fisheries permits in national or regional waters. There are two limitations to the AIS system, one legal and one behavioral. Vessels weighing less than 300 gross tons are not required to broadcast, and vessels with AIS do not always turn it on (especially those engaged in criminal activity). Nonetheless, AIS is an essential tool.

Maritime intelligence is the product of monitoring and surveillance. The gathering, fusion, and dissemination of maritime intelligence facilitate all other aspects of maritime governance. From foreign naval threats, to maritime violence, to weather prediction, to the safety of individuals, maritime intelligence allows governments to remain tuned in to the pulse of life in the maritime domain. The integration of domestic intelligence structures and processes is an extremely complex task; the development of regional and international intelligence efforts is even more daunting. Shared intelligence forms a common operating picture (COP) that brings institutions closer together; compartmented intelligence creates gaps that can be exploited by the very criminals governments are trying to monitor. Maritime intelligence will be discussed in detail in Chapter 8.

Maritime Safety

The subfunctions of maritime safety include inspecting merchant vessels, maintaining the currency of maritime safety laws, enforcing safety regulations for boaters, and operating maritime safety education programs.

Maritime safety is a routine function, aimed at reducing the threat to human life, property, and the environment itself. It is anything *but* routine, however, once a major incident intervenes. Reducing the risks from disaster in the maritime domain requires a lot of resources. The return on that investment can be measured in terms of lives saved, vessels in service, or oil not discharged into the environment. The 1994 sinking of the *Estonia* ferry cost 852 lives. The 1989 *Exxon Valdez* oil spill cost more than US $2B. The wreck of the *Costa Concordia* cost 32 lives and economic losses in the billions. Chapter 11 of this volume examines how governments can best manage these kinds of incidents.

Shipping is the most international of all the world's great industries—and one of the most dangerous. It has long been recognized that the best way of improving safety at sea is by developing international regulations that are followed by all seafaring nations. Indeed, the first task of the International Maritime Organization (IMO) was to adopt a new 1960 version of the International Convention for the Safety of Life at Sea (SOLAS), the most important of all treaties dealing with maritime safety. Since that time, IMO has been involved at the human level of safety, developing the International Safety Management (ISM) Code, made mandatory under SOLAS.[9]

Individual governments develop appropriate maritime safety laws and regulations to ensure that owners understand the requirements to operate within their waters. These requirements apply to recreational boaters as well as fishermen and other commercial operators. Weather forecasting and dissemination are important adjuncts. Educational programs directed at the maritime community further reduce the likelihood of accidents and incidents, diminishing the need for disaster response as well as search and rescue operations.

Traditional Maritime Security

The term *traditional maritime security* refers to security at the state level (as opposed to *human security*, which operates at the individual level). Included in this category are the functions of maintaining military readiness and devising mechanisms to coordinate maritime operations with neighboring countries.

Some governments require robust naval forces, but others do not. As much of this book argues, contemporary maritime threats for most countries do not involve war on the high seas. The Sri Lankan Navy's war against the maritime wing of the Tamil Tigers insurgency, detailed in Chapter 12, is an exception that proves the rule. Most governments are concerned about irregular threats to citizens and property in their own waters. That often means maritime law enforcement is more useful than naval power. A process of maritime risk assessment should be undertaken to determine requirements. If naval forces are needed, they must at least be trained and organized to cooperate with law enforcement. In some cases, existing naval forces will have to be given law enforcement authority, or perhaps reduced in size to free up resources needed to create new maritime law enforcement institutions.

Enforcement of Customs and Maritime Law

This function requires the establishment of national laws and regulations, the acquisition and maintenance of specialized equipment, law enforcement training and education, and the development of interdiction capacity. Violations of customs and maritime laws degrade the national sovereignty, which rests on a government's ability to know what goods are coming in and leaving by sea, as well as who is moving them. Maritime nations must have institutions with the capacity to find out.

In order to develop the capacity for maintaining a clear picture of what is happening in the commercial sector, customs and other law enforcement institutions must have the specialized training and equipment needed to detect and interdict illegal shipments entering or leaving the country's maritime domain. Resource constraints may prevent governments from establishing and maintaining the law enforcement institutions they need, prompting creative solutions. No matter which institutions perform these functions, governments must develop a method of measuring the effectiveness of interdiction and seizure efforts.

Protection of Natural Resources

Conflict at sea is often related to the competition for natural resources. Military confrontation is less common, but the stakes for China and its neighbors over borders in the South China Sea bring the potential for such conflict. More commonly, illegal fishing, smuggling, and dumping of waste are major concerns for countries with weak governance and low capacity. Indeed, illegal fishing and dumping have been cited as justification for piracy.[10]

As discussed in Chapter 10, the maritime legal framework provides all governments with rules regarding where they are permitted to extract hydrocarbons and minerals from the seabed. A framework, however, is merely a framework; maritime boundaries are disputed and international courts are active. But the seabed is fixed, and although some arguments are more difficult than others, diplomacy can lead to agreement. Illegal, unlicensed, and unregulated (IUU) fishing and dumping of waste, on the other hand, require active maritime patrolling regimes. The migration of high-value fish resources brings with it a need for law enforcement at sea.[11] Policing the EEZ is a resource-intensive effort that many governments simply cannot afford; thus, they lose a valuable source of protein and lucrative commercial opportunities. Governments that have law enforcement institutions with adequate capacity not only protect their fisheries but also gain a source of revenue from imposing fines on violators.

Maritime Search and Rescue

At any given moment, numerous citizens from every maritime nation are located somewhere in the global maritime domain. Some of them will be placed in danger, or even killed, by weather, a collision at sea, an industrial accident, or a violent act of crime. The percentages might be low, but they are all worthy of rescue by the societies to which they belong. Maritime search and rescue (SAR) is a human security issue governments should be prepared to address with all the resources they can gather. Neglecting this function has the immediate effect of diminishing the credibility of a government in the eyes of its people.

The crowded nature of the maritime space necessitates the designation of one agency, perhaps a coast guard, as the lead for SAR operations. That institution must possess or control the assets and training required for operations in all weather conditions throughout the maritime domain. As with other aspects of maritime governance, domestic SAR constitutes a collective effort among multiple maritime security institutions. Operations on the high seas—or in waters not effectively controlled by a single national authority—warrant international cooperation. The 1979 United Nations Search and Rescue (SAR) Convention was aimed at developing an international SAR plan. Although the obligation of ships to go to the assistance of vessels in distress was enshrined both in tradition and in international treaties (e.g., SOLAS, 1974), until the adoption of the SAR convention, no international system covered search and rescue operations.[12]

Disaster Response

This critical function starts with the prevention of environmental disasters resulting from weather or industrial accidents. It requires intensive, specialized training and the pre-staging of enough equipment to mount a successful response. Not all disasters are natural; fortunately, the institutions a government needs in the event of a natural disaster can be used as the foundation for the capacity to manage the consequences of maritime terrorism.

Ineffective responses to disaster put national leaders as well as other citizens at risk. Any government that mismanages these events forfeits a legitimacy that can take years to recover. Leaders can also use successful disaster management to *bolster* legitimacy. When people need them the most, institutions capable of restoring the quality of life they have come to expect can strengthen the relationships that bind a society together. Investment in this functional area can have a high payoff, and lack of investment can doom a government.[13] The specific requirements for managing maritime disasters are elaborated in Chapter 11 of this volume.

Port Operations and Security

Port facilities, with all of their critical infrastructure and enormous economic value, lie at the edge of the maritime domain. And that is the point. Ports are where jurisdictions and responsible institutions come together. They offer a transition zone from land to sea and back. If borders are the skin of a nation-state, ports represent cuts into which infection can enter the body. Ports can be a source of great wealth. For example, the Port of Abidjan accounts for 91 percent of foreign trade and 85 percent of customs revenue for the government of Ivory Coast.[14] Ports are nodes in a worldwide network of maritime transportation that moves almost all of the world's commerce, but to fulfill this function they must be secure. Connectivity with the rest of the world gives maritime nations and their people an important advantage within a globalized family of nations; they *think* globally. Port security is discussed in this context in Chapter 7.

Level I Assessment

Now that we have listed and described the basic maritime governance functions, we must look for a way to evaluate how well a particular government is performing those functions. In the absence of a formal assessment process, individuals or whole institutions can measure effectiveness in these areas by means of a simple self-assessment. Table 6.1 lists the functions and subfunctions described above, organized as a table.[15] The table allows anyone with specialized maritime knowledge to assign a raw score between 1 and 10 to each function. This is a place to start. If we did not begin with something like this, a formal and complex assessment process would be difficult to comprehend.

The act of assigning numbers to functions is not trivial, especially as a group exercise. Numbers must be defended, and that gives them meaning. Small, diverse groups of experts on each function can make valuable inputs to institutional leaders facing critical restructuring decisions. This scenario sets up a useful workshop format—for classrooms, or for the staff structures of decision-makers. A simple Level I assessment can kick-start a series of strategy and planning efforts, to be refined further through a more detailed and comprehensive evaluation of how maritime governance can be improved.

Level II Examination

A follow-on process of description and assessment can now be conducted at what we will call Level II. This process borrows heavily from the *Maritime Security Sector Reform (MSSR) Guide* developed by the US Agency for International Development (USAID).[16] The guide was designed to assist partners of the United States in reforming their maritime security sectors. The framework can be adapted to small nations as well as large ones. The MSSR is a comprehensive guide that all governments can use to restructure maritime security institutions, preparing the way for better performance at the political and operational levels.

TABLE 6.1 Maritime governance assessment: Level One

Maritime area of focus	Score 1–10 (10) = high level of capacity
Maritime Domain Awareness: Patrols, monitoring, maritime intelligence gathering and fusion, interagency information sharing	
Maritime Safety: Inspection, maritime safety laws, boating safety regulations, maritime safety education	
Traditional Maritime Security: Military training and readiness, number/type/condition of tactical assets, interoperability with maritime partner agencies, coordination with neighboring countries/global maritime forums	
Enforcement of Customs and Maritime Law: National maritime laws and regulations, tactical equipment and assets, law enforcement training, interdiction capability and seizure rates	
Protection of Natural Resources (EEZ Enforcement): Fisheries-related training, drafting and enforcement of resource protection laws, fisheries law-enforcement assets and officers, international agreements, participation in international treaties and forums	
Maritime Search and Rescue: Search and rescue (SAR) capability, SAR assets, SAR training, SAR communications (C3), participation in international agreements and forums	
Disaster Response: Environmental disaster prevention, response training and exercises, pre-staging of response equipment, mitigation, interagency/ international coordination	
Port Operations and Security: Effectiveness of port authority agencies, maintenance/condition of facilities, security of facilities, participation in international agreements/treaties and forums	
Total	

SOURCE: Copyright 2015, Brad Sultzer, used by permission.

Level II places maritime governance functions and subfunctions (along with required capabilities) into the wider maritime sector. This approach recognizes that the maritime sector of government overlaps three others: civil justice, criminal justice, and the commercial sector.[17] Such a scheme broadens the analysis and catalyzes a more inclusive assessment process. Level II has the potential to inform leadership about the most efficient ways to improve maritime governance while strengthening maritime security and revitalizing the maritime sector of the economy. Level II analysis and assessment can lead to an integrated network of government institutions and private companies, working in cooperation with one another to protect and empower the people who live by the sea. One of the most difficult challenges of any government is to create and sustain a sense of national identity; maritime nations—especially archipelagos—are blessed from birth with a unifying theme.

On the broader Level II canvas, many of the functions listed in Level I are broken out separately from maritime governance. This typology reflects the requirement for a more detailed analysis. Typologies are merely devices for organizing the process; as long as every function and subfunction is included, results can be optimized. Level II functions can be categorized as maritime governance, maritime civil and criminal authority, maritime defense, maritime safety, maritime response and recovery, and maritime economy. The functions and subfunctions of Level II are listed in Table 6.2.

As with Level I, the functions cluster related activities without corresponding to particular actors or institutions. That is possible because roles and responsibilities for most of them vary with different national contexts. The subfunctions listed are not mutually exclusive; variations on the theme of maritime governance, for instance, cross multiple functional areas.[18] The eight subfunctions can be summarized as follows:

1. *Maritime mission.* Balancing safety and security measures; facilitating licit maritime commerce; maintaining freedom of navigation; protecting the marine environment; improving the lives of citizens in the maritime domain; and educating the public regarding the importance of the maritime economy fall under this rubric.

2. *Maritime agency organization.* Designating institutional roles and responsibilities within the maritime sector, while facilitating interagency and international coordination in support of national maritime strategies, characterize this subfunction.

3. *Maritime law and policy.* Developing, assessing, refining, and promulgating maritime law, policy, and regulations are included in this cluster. Without a legal and policy framework, maritime strategies cannot be implemented.

4. *Diplomatic and foreign affairs support.* This subfunction brings foreign affairs institutions into the mix, coordinating between civil and criminal law enforcement, as well as foreign counterparts, for the accomplishment of national goals.

TABLE 6.2 Level Two: Functions and subfunctions

Functions	Maritime governance	Maritime civil and criminal authority	Maritime defense	Maritime safety	Maritime response and recovery	Maritime economy
Subfunctions	• Maritime mission • Maritime agency organization • Maritime law and policy • Diplomatic and foreign affairs support • Maritime programs • Maritime professionals • Maritime agency outreach and stakeholder coordination • Accountability and oversight	• Enforcement of civil and criminal laws • Integrated border management • Judicial sector support • Port security • Vessel security • Supply-chain security • Maritime environmental enforcement	• Maritime defense administration • Maritime defense forces • Maritime situational awareness and maritime domain awareness	• Maritime safety administration • Flag state control • Fishing and small vessel safety and operations management • Maritime safety management • Mariner licensing administration • Aids to navigation infrastructure, equipment, and maintenance	• Emergency response administration • Incident management • Search and rescue • Fire • Environmental • Maritime defense assistance to civil authorities • Investigation and after-action analysis	• Economic activity regulation and management • Commercial ports • Transport • Market conditions

SOURCE: *Maritime Security Sector Reform Guide*, USAID, September 2010.

5. *Maritime programs.* Developing and enforcing regulations in support of national-level objectives is the subfunction that unites these activities.

6. *Maritime professionals.* Recruiting, training, educating, and retaining maritime professionals for all maritime safety and security programs are among the activities included in this cluster.

7. *Maritime agency outreach and stakeholder coordination.* This set of activities brings communications specialists into the vital role of encouraging input and coordination of policymaking from a wide spectrum of maritime security stakeholders, as well as providing information to all those affected by maritime security issues.

8. *Accountability and oversight.* This subfunction is all about making certain that policy development and implementation are conducted in a transparent, accountable, and ethical manner.

Level II Assessment

Assessing maritime governance at the next level obliges governments to list the critical capabilities a government might need to develop in order to fulfill the subfunctions listed in Table 6.2. This process allows them to connect the readiness to discharge maritime governance functions with cost-effective ways to use whatever means are available. In this regard, such an exercise mimics the ends-ways-means-measures strategy calculation introduced in Chapter 5 of this volume. Critical capabilities are roughly the same in all maritime nations (further suggesting multinational cooperation), but the specific tasks that generate them depend on national resources and country-specific strategies.[19] It is the capabilities that will be measured—initially to provide a more detailed snapshot, then over time to reveal trends.

The Level II assessment uses a two-phased set of measures: "approach measurement indicators" and "delivery measurement indicators," illustrated in Table 6.3. Approach indicators assess the extent to which plans, processes, programs, and other efforts have been identified to develop or support a specific capability; delivery indicators assess whether and to what extent those approaches are being implemented to achieve the desired objectives. The division into two sets of indicators produces richer discussions and better diagnostic insight. Even the best-conceived maritime security strategy is worth

TABLE 6.3 Level Two: Approach and delivery indicators and definitions

Qualitative indicator range	Quantitative indicator range	Approach indicator definition	Delivery indicator definition	Comments and remarks
Normal	0–2	Some activity may exist to evidence the capability being measured, but such activities are not part of formal plans, policies, processes, or programs.	The capability is infrequently employed (0–30% of the time) and its contribution to positive outcomes is minimal.	Recognizes the existence of some effort or activity, even though it may not stem from formalized plans, policies, or programs. Also recognizes scattered or disconnected efforts (often at the individual or local level).
Modest	3–5	Organized, if basic, approaches to the capability exist, and efforts are in place to address weaknesses.	The capability is not consistently employed (30–60% of the time) and outcomes are erratic or unpredictable.	Recognizes that there may not be consistency of effort but that various levels of organization exist.
Moderate	6–8	Organized activities supporting the capability are professional, formalized, and supported by adequate budget levels.	The capability is mostly employed (60–90% of the time) and produces adequate outcomes.	Shows sophistication and organization toward achieving a stated goal or objective. Even if capabilities are not consistently used or do not exist across the entirety of the maritime domain, outcomes are adequate.
Significant	9–10	Activities are formalized, planned, funded, assessed, and adjusted on a continual basis, evidencing a significant level of capability in this area.	The capability is consistently employed (90% of the time or higher) and produces effective and efficient outcomes. Capability reviews ensure the capability is upgraded if/when circumstances require.	More robust capacity exists and is being sustained. Efforts are made continually to improve capacities across the maritime domain.

SOURCE: *Maritime Security Sector Reform Guide*, USAID, September 2010.

nothing unless it is actually implemented.[20] In other words, approach indicators measure *governance*, while delivery indicators measure *capacity* (sustained capability over time).

Critical capabilities can be identified in a series of workshops populated by maritime professionals from all stakeholder institutions. It is a tedious process, but the end product will enable other groups of experts to assign approach and delivery indicators to each capability. The process also acts as a "forcing function" to drive cooperation among stakeholders, both public and private. A meaningful assessment of critical capabilities, subfunctions, and functions for maritime governance would then be consolidated with similar assessments for the other five functions (each with their subfunctions and critical capabilities). If the right institutions and individuals dedicate themselves to this long-term process, the outcome may well be a better set of strategies against maritime violence, as well as improved approaches to maritime governance generally.

Conclusion

Every maritime nation can use both Level I and Level II analysis and assessment. Each country, however, brings with it a unique set of political, geographic, social, and economic issues. Maritime governance initiatives—and maritime security sector reform more generally—fall into three general categories of context. The first could be called *preventive* in that measures must be undertaken to fill gaps in maritime governance. The second category could be called *responsive* in that direct actions must be taken immediately against perpetrators of maritime violence. The third category of context could be called *restorative* in that failures of maritime governance stem from conflict or war, requiring the assistance of the international community.[21] Each of the context categories, in separate ways, leads to the maritime governance analysis and assessment frameworks introduced here.

We have suggested that the evaluation of maritime governance should be a two-step procedure. Short educational programs lend themselves to Level I analysis and assessment, but much more time is needed for Level II. In short, Level I is an effective snapshot to introduce the concept; Level II is a long-term process for diverse groups of officials engaged in reforming the maritime sector of government. Better maritime governance, in the final analysis, is the same as good governance ashore—providing jobs, infrastructure, and security. Governance is a climate within which citizens can find options and opportunities to live law-abiding, productive lives.

Governance and capacity are two sides of the same coin; one does not work without the other. It is often said that there is no development without security, and no security without development.[22] But maritime violence is not just a threat to the developing world. The problem of maritime disorder without strong authority could (and sometimes does) extend well beyond the borders of weak states.[23] Better governance by individual nations, synchronizing their actions with neighboring states, can help diminish the level of maritime disorder and lead to outcomes that benefit everyone.

Notes

1. For a thorough analysis of this phenomenon, see Anne L. Clunan and Harold A. Trinkunas, *Ungoverned Spaces: Alternatives to State Authority in an Era of Softened Sovereignty* (Stanford, CA: Stanford University Press, 2010).

2. This theme is best expressed in William Langewiesche, *The Outlaw Sea: A World of Freedom, Chaos, and Crime* (New York: North Point Press, 2004).

3. Many coastal regions are growing rapidly to become power centers distant from central government. With that growth comes crime in a different form; individuals and organizations can hide in plain sight. For a detailed explanation of the coastal urbanization trend, with its implications for insurgency, see David Kilcullen, *Out of the Mountains: The Coming Age of the Urban Guerrilla* (New York: Oxford University Press, 2013).

4. Martin N. Murphy, *Contemporary Piracy and Maritime Terrorism: The Threat to International Security* (London: The International Institute for Strategic Studies, 2007), 73–74.

5. We will call them "Level I" and "Level II," a convention unique to this book.

6. "National Plan to Achieve Maritime Domain Awareness for the National Strategy for Maritime Security," Department of Homeland Security, Washington, DC, October 2005, available online at http://www.dhs.gov/national-plan-achieve-maritime-domain-awareness.

7. See Scott Jasper, *Securing Freedom in the Global Commons* (Stanford, CA: Stanford University Press, 2010), 73.

8. These figures were taken from lectures the Center for Civil-Military Relations (CCMR) by Brad Sultzer, Commander, US Coast Guard (Ret.).

9. For more information on the IMO's efforts regarding maritime safety, visit http://www.imo.org/en/OurWork/Safety/Pages/Default.aspx. The SOLAS treaty itself can be found online at https://treaties.un.org/doc/Publication/UNTS/Volume%201184/volume-1184-I-18961-English.pdf.

10. "Somali Pirates Tell Their Side of the Story: They Want Only Money," *International New York Times*, September 30, 2008, available at http://www.nytimes.com/2008/10/01/world/africa/01pirates.html.

11. During a 2011 CCMR seminar in Sri Lanka, participants identified IUU fishing as the most significant maritime threat. The fact that Sri Lanka, at that time, was still recovering from a decades-long maritime insurgency underscores the importance of illegal fishing.

12. The UN Treaty on Search and Rescue resulting from the Hamburg Conference can be found online at https://treaties.un.org/doc/Publication/UNTS/Volume%20 1405/volume-1405-I-23489-English.pdf.

13. See Paul Shemella, *Fighting Back: What Governments Can Do About Terrorism* (Stanford, CA: Stanford University Press, 2011), 205–21.

14. English translation of the draft Maritime Strategy for the Government of Ivory Coast, dated July 22, 2012.

15. This table was developed by Brad Sultzer, Commander US Coast Guard (Ret.).

16. United States Agency for International Development (USAID), *Maritime Security Sector Reform (MSSR) Guide*, September 2010.

17. Ibid., 4.

18. Ibid., 5.

19. Space available here does not permit us to include a listing of capabilities and tasks. That country-specific exercise is best left to a working group of experts from the focus government.

20. This assessment device is drawn from the Baldrige National Quality Program, National Institute of Standards and Technology, "Criteria for Performance Excellence," 2009–10, available online at www.baldrige.nist.gov/PDF_files/2009_2010_Business_Nonprofit_Criteria.pdf

21. This typology is borrowed from John F. Sandoz, "Maritime Security Sector Reform," *United States Institute of Peace Special Report*, May 2012, 7.

22. This quote is quite often attributed to Kofi Annan, but many others have said it.

23. Martin N. Murphy, *Small Boats, Weak States, Dirty Money* (New York: Columbia University Press, 2009), 411.

7   Global Port Security

Charles J. Reinhardt

ACCESS TO WORLD MARKETS VIA MARITIME TRADE IS essential to the health and well-being of virtually every economy in the world. It is difficult to think of any nation that does not possess a natural resource or produce a unique product that is in demand elsewhere. At the same time, almost every country lacks certain strategically important commodities, goods, or products. Lacking an adequate domestic supply, those items must be imported to sustain economic growth. And given the shipment volumes and physical characteristics of these cargoes, their intrinsic values, and the distances over which they must be moved, transportation via waterborne service is often the only practical way to accommodate this trade.

Ports, terminals, and related supporting infrastructure have vital roles in facilitating these transactions, enabling commerce to flow smoothly and efficiently. They represent critical nodes in broader maritime transportation networks and thus warrant protection. But in contrast to a country's national borders that restrict or limit movement, ports have a completely opposite role. Rather, they serve as international gateways, designed to support the fast and efficient movement of oceangoing vessels as well as their cargoes and passengers. This fundamental nature of ports makes them vulnerable to a multitude of potential threats and creates the possibility that they could be used as a means of access by those who wish to inflict harm.

This darker side of ports has not gone unnoticed. The need for port security to deal with a number of obvious threats has long been recognized, whether it be to deter the smuggling of contraband, narcotics, or other illegal substances; to prevent shippers and importers from evading customs duties and tariffs; or simply to stop everyday criminal activities such as pilferage and common theft. During times of war, port security might receive increased attention, but with the return of peace, vigilance is relaxed and complacency reigns.

However, the terrorist attacks in the United States on September 11, 2001 changed attitudes in many countries. This change stemmed from the realization that ports could be used as transit points for transporting terrorists and their tools of destruction across national borders. Under more dire scenarios, they could even serve as points of entry for weapons of mass destruction— with the potential to cause widespread damage, loss of life, and severe social and economic dislocations. Thus, in the aftermath of 9/11 many countries have come to view port security as a fundamental and integral element of their overall national defense strategies.

A new sense of urgency has emerged, one in which world governmental bodies, national regulatory agencies, private terminal and vessel operators, and industry and trade associations have joined together in an effort to develop an effective global response to potential threats emanating from ports and the broader maritime domain. This chapter highlights what those activities have been and how they have evolved over time. As background, and to underscore the scope of the port security challenge, information is presented on the current level of the global seaborne merchandise trade and the world fleet of commercial vessels used to transport those cargoes. The chapter also provides an overview of the typical port types and ownership structures found around the world, followed by a discussion of regulatory protocols that have emerged to enhance port security, and how that process has unfolded over time. The chapter concludes by providing insights into practical port security measures that have achieved a demonstrated record of effectiveness and success.

Global Foreign Trade

International foreign trade allows countries to participate in those global markets where their goods can compete on the basis of price, quality, and reliability of supply. Exports can yield important benefits by expanding domestic employment opportunities, enhancing relationships between trading countries, and serving as a means to earn foreign exchange to offset the currency drain caused by needed imports. Similarly, foreign trade also allows countries to access goods from distant markets that may be of strategic importance to their economies. In the event a country lacks a particular natural resource or the means of production to make certain goods, that deficiency can be made up through imports from foreign sources.

It should be noted that foreign commerce has the effect of creating a degree of interdependency between countries, and this can have positive consequences. The common benefits resulting from fair and balanced trade tend to enhance bilateral partnerships and promote peace and stability. In fact, knowing the identities of key trading partners and the types of commodities that comprise those trade flows represents valuable intelligence when formulating national foreign policies. This information can be found readily, using various publicly available documents from the International Monetary Fund[1] and the United Nations *Commodity Trade Statistics Database (Comtrade)*,[2] among other sources. Key policy- and decision-makers should be keenly aware of the role and importance international trade has in their national economies, as measured by the relative share imports and exports represent of total gross domestic product (GDP). This metric serves to highlight the exposure a country would have, should there be a disruption in foreign trade, and it can serve to justify making investments in defensive strategies to prevent such a disruption. Information on foreign trade and GDP can be obtained from national treasury ministries or intergovernmental agencies such as the International Monetary Fund. These data values can also be obtained from *The World Factbook*, an open-source document published online by the Central Intelligence Agency.[3]

The value of merchandise and goods moving globally in international foreign trade during 2012 totaled US $18.3 trillion[4] and represented 9.2 billion tons[5] of freight traffic. At the same time, the seaborne share of total trade accounted for 80 percent[6] of the movement of all goods transported globally in terms of tonnage volume and for a substantial share of the total value. Much of this seaborne traffic was between countries separated by oceans. Other segments encompassed traffic principally comprising relatively low-value bulk commodities and/or those being moved over long distances. In either case, shipment by sea was the only practical method of transportation given the inherent efficiency of the waterborne mode. In addition to being the low-cost alternative, marine transportation is also the least fuel-intensive on a per-ton-mile basis of freight moved. This affords the added benefit of giving it the smallest "carbon footprint" when it comes to contributing greenhouse gases to the environment.[7]

The cargoes moving in seaborne trade fall into four general categories that include commodities vital to the economies of almost every nation. Dry cargoes and the major bulks account for over half of all shipments and include cargoes ranging from coal, food grains, metallic ores, and fertilizer to finished steel, automobiles, and heavy equipment. The liquid bulks that include crude petroleum, petroleum products, and liquefied gases account for another 30 percent of the remaining total trade. Traffic moving in containerized liner service, which is normally used to transport higher value goods such as consumer products, accounts for most of the balance of seaborne trade, or about 16 percent of the total.[8] During the period of 2000–2012, total seaborne trade increased at the average compound annual growth rate of 3.5 percent, though the rates of growth did vary by segment. For instance, containerized trade increased the most rapidly, at an average rate of 7.8 percent annually, reflecting the migration of manufacturing from the established economies in Europe, North America, and North Asia to China, India, and the countries of Southeast Asia. Commodities moving in the dry- and liquid-bulk services grew at the average rate of 2.3 percent and 6.0 percent, respectively, over the same period.

Vessel Flag Registry

In addition to vessel types, the country of vessel registry, the *flag state*, is also an important characteristic of the world fleet of commercial vessels and one that can have important implications when it comes to port security. Under international law, ships engaged in foreign commerce must be registered to a flag state. Historically, much of the commerce occurring between countries was conducted mainly on a bilateral basis, often employing ships registered under the flags of both nations (with a smaller portion of the trade being handled by third-party flagged vessels known as cross-traders). Currently, however, every county, whether coastal or landlocked, has the right to have ships flying its flag operating on the high seas.[9]

Traditional national flag or "closed" registries typically define regulatory schemes or impose other restrictions that limit ownership to national interests (citizens and corporations), specify permitted crew nationalities, or impose taxes and fees as well as other conditions, each of which can impact the cost of vessel operations.

In contrast, open ship registries, sometimes called *flags of convenience*, allow foreign (non-national) ownership and may impose fewer regulations or lower taxes and fees. Thus, vessel operators who flag their ships in open registries may have lower operating costs when compared to vessels flagged under traditional national registries. As a result of these advantages, open registries now account for a dominant share of all ships flagged for international trade.[10] As shown in Table 7.1, data for the thirty-five largest fleets, as of January 2013, revealed that the following top eleven open registries accounted for more than half of the world's total shipping capacity when measured in deadweight tons.[11]

The fact that a dominant share of total world fleet is flagged in small countries that may lack the resources and commitment to ensure an effective regulatory environment raises serious concerns about matters related to both safety and security.[12]

TABLE 7.1 Flag registry worldwide

International registry	Fleet deadweight tons	Share of world fleet total (%)	Cumulative share (%)
Panama	350,506	21.5	21.5
Liberia	198,032	12.2	33.7
Marshall Islands	140,016	8.6	42.3
Bahamas	73,702	4.5	46.8
Malta	68,831	4.2	51.0
Isle of Man	22,629	1.4	52.4
Antigua and Barbuda	14,142	0.9	53.3
Bermuda	12,378	0.8	54.0
Tanzania	8,815	0.5	54.6
St. Vincent and the Grenadines	4,919	0.3	54.9
Cayman	4,310	0.3	55.2
Subtotal top international registries	898,280	55.2	
All other vessel registries	730,443	44.8	100.0
World fleet total	**1,628,723**	**100.0**	

SOURCE: Review of Maritime Transportation, 2013.

Characteristics of a Modern Port

There is a tendency by some to think of ports as being well-defined areas with discrete borders, all coming under the control of a single entity. Often, this is not the case; diffusion of authority, common to many ports, can complicate the task of achieving effective security. To illustrate this point, consider the port of Boston, Massachusetts, located in the northeast quadrant of the United States. Although the port of Boston has historical importance that dates back to colonial times, it is relatively small when compared with other ports around the United States and the rest of the world. In 2013 it ranked only twenty-eighth in terms of total cargo tonnage volume handled by all other US ports.[13] However, given its size and scale, Boston is representative of many ports and harbor areas found elsewhere, making it a valid reference for comparison.

The single largest port entity in Boston is the quasi-state agency of the Massachusetts Port Authority, known as MASSPORT, which owns approximately a dozen different waterfront properties. These parcels include marine terminals for handling containers, automobiles, passengers, and bulk cargoes. In addition, MASSPORT is also responsible for three area airports and other holdings that are within close proximity to the waterfront. In some cases, MASSPORT directly operates the facilities, and in others its role is strictly that of a landlord with little or no operating responsibilities. Rather, these facilities are operated by tenants who rent the property from MASSPORT for their own proprietary purposes or who use it to meet the needs of others on a common-use basis.

But the holdings owned and controlled by MASSPORT represent only a small fraction of the total number of facilities and waterfront-dependent activities within the broader harbor district. Information compiled by the US Army Corps of Engineers reveals the existence of scores of docks and other marine facilities operated by dozens of private-sector interests.[14] These include terminals for handling petroleum products, natural gas, sand, and gravel; waterfront parks and residential developments; electrical generating stations; and many other enterprises and entities whose daily operations require tidewater access. Complicating this situation further is the fact that the harbor area encompasses at least thirteen separate cities, towns, local municipalities, and jurisdictions, each with its own police, fire, and emergency services organizations. With no single harbor entity responsible for port security, users and stakeholders must collaborate to keep the port secure.

Similar conditions now exist in many ports around the world—even those traditionally operated by a single government entity. This is because development and renewal of port infrastructure is a highly capital-intensive endeavor that can include dredging to accommodate increasingly larger vessels; managing complex and costly facility designs and construction requirements; and outfitting marine terminals with very expensive cargo-handling equipment, including container cranes. Consequently, it has become increasingly common for governments to enter into private-public partnerships (PPPs).[15] Typically, these involve some form of lease, privatization, or concession arrangement with an investment group that assumes the up-front development responsibilities and day-to-day operating control in exchange for the payment of a lease, rent, or royalty fee. As a result, an independent private operator now manages many port facilities that were once closely held and controlled by a government entity. This change in structure can have profound implications with respect to the emphasis placed on port security unless regulatory controls and responsibilities are clearly defined and implemented as part of the privatization process.

Closing the Gaps

How do governments ensure that gaps related to jurisdiction, coordination, intelligence gathering, and information sharing do not result in port security being compromised? In the United States, the US Coast Guard, by combining its regulatory, enforcement, education, and coordination functions, fulfills the critical role of bringing together the many diverse members that comprise the broader port community. Typically, the Coast Guard conducts regular port-user group meetings; sponsors industry-wide security and safety symposia; and promotes Internet-based management tools, such as the Department of Homeland Security's *Homeport*.[16]

One outgrowth of these efforts has been the establishment of joint harbor operations centers (JHOCs) at selected US ports. The JHOCs foster collaboration, for instance, between the Coast Guard and the Navy, institutions with clearly defined, separate missions during peacetime. The JHOC concept recognizes that the information requirements needed to provide port security and infrastructure protection are vast, and that sharing that information requires strong interagency linkages. Consequently, JHOCs are organized with formal liaison positions and data-sharing protocols that serve effectively to merge regulatory, law enforcement, and antiterrorist-force protection information sources, capabilities, and procedures. Thus, the JHOC structure provides an effective model for fusing the intelligence and coordinating the multiagency operations to help secure the maritime domain.[17]

Another program that has been implemented to close gaps in the battle against criminal activity and potential acts of terrorism has been the creation of a national network of regional intelligence fusion centers. Located in states and major urban areas across the United States, fusion centers are designed to empower front-line law enforcement, public safety, fire service, emergency response, public health, critical-infrastructure protection, and private-sector security personnel to understand the local implications of national intelligence. Fusion centers provide interdisciplinary expertise and situational awareness to help inform better decision-making at all levels of government. They conduct analyses and facilitate information sharing while assisting law enforcement and homeland security partners in preventing, protecting against, and responding to crime and terrorism.[18] The Commonwealth Fusion Center in Massachusetts is one such operation, and it plays an important role in strengthening security at the port of Boston.[19]

Role of the IMO

The International Maritime Organization (IMO) is the United Nations agency with 170 member countries that is responsible for the safety and security of shipping and the prevention of marine pollution by ships.[20] The purpose of the organization is to provide the machinery for cooperation among governments, and to facilitate the adoption of the highest practicable standards.[21]

The IMO's first task was to adopt a new version of the International Convention for the Safety of Life at Sea (SOLAS). Achieved in 1960, SOLAS was the most important of all treaties dealing with maritime safety. The IMO then turned its attention to facilitating international maritime traffic and load lines, as well as the carriage of dangerous goods, while revising the system of measuring ship tonnage.

Over time, and in the aftermath of subsequent maritime casualties (e.g., the 1967 *Torrey Canyon* oil spill disaster), IMO member countries adopted additional measures, laws, and treaties. These included, *inter alia*, the prevention of tanker accidents; the enhancement of radio communications and messaging; mandated standards for the training, certification, and watchkeeping of seafarers; and the regulation of ship breaking, demolition, and recycling.[22] Also during this period, incidents of terrorism on the world stage made it necessary for the IMO to address issues related to maritime security.

The hijacking of *Achille Lauro* by Palestinian terrorists in 1985 led to the adoption of the Rome Convention for the Suppression of Unlawful Acts Against the Safety of Maritime Navigation.[23] Attacks by al-Qaeda twenty years later led to the adoption of the International Ship and Port Facility Security (ISPS) Code. ISPS is a comprehensive set of measures—designed to enhance the security of both ships and port facilities—developed in response to the perceived threats to critical elements of global transportation infrastructure, as well as to the adjacent centers of population and economic activity.[24] ISPS is now a mandatory part of the SOLAS Convention. It has been ratified by 162 states, representing 98.8 percent of the international merchant shipping community.[25]

Breaking Down ISPS

The key provisions of ISPS support a standardized and consistent framework for cooperation between governments, local administrations, and industry stakeholders for identifying and evaluating potential security-related risks for both ships and ports. The code also establishes the respective roles and responsibilities of these organizations for ensuring maritime security. This process is accomplished in two phases; first, conducting a security assessment, and second, creating a security plan to deal with possible contingencies.

The *port facility security assessment* is a precursor for developing and updating the *port facility security plan*. The assessment encompasses a series of steps designed to identify the critical infrastructure requiring protection; determine the possible threats to these assets and the likelihood of their occurrence; prioritize assets for security enhancements; and address those vulnerabilities and weaknesses that are most likely to be targets for exploitation.[26]

Upon completion of the assessment, a *port facility security plan* must be developed and maintained. At a minimum, the plan must address the following:

- Measures designed to prevent weapons or any other dangerous substances and devices intended for use against persons, ships, or ports, the carriage of which is not authorized, from being introduced into the port facility or on board a ship;

- Measures designed to prevent unauthorized access to the port facility, to ships moored at the facility, and to restricted areas of the facility;
- Procedures for responding to security threats or breaches of security, including provisions for maintaining critical operations of the port facility or ship/port interface;
- Procedures for responding to any security instructions that the contracting government in whose territory the port facility is located may give at security level 3;
- Procedures for evacuation in case of security threats or breaches of security;
- Duties of port facility personnel assigned security responsibilities and of other facility personnel on security aspects;
- Procedures for interfacing with ship security activities;
- Procedures for the periodic review and update of the plan;
- Procedures for reporting security incidents;
- Identification of the port facility security officer, including 24-hour contact details;
- Measures to ensure the security of the information contained in the plan;
- Measures designed to ensure effective security of cargo and the cargo-handling equipment at the port facility;
- Procedures for auditing the port facility security plan;
- Procedures for responding in case the ship security alert system of a ship at the port facility has been activated; and
- Procedures for facilitating shore leave for ship's personnel or personnel changes, as well as access of visitors to the ship, including representatives of seafarer welfare and labor organizations.
- Finally, the plan must designate security officers and define their responsibilities, as well as establish communication and notification protocols.

Because the ISPS Code is an amendment to the SOLAS Convention, all 162 member-state parties to that agreement are required to comply with its provisions for both port and vessel security. The IMO does not maintain a list of countries that are not in compliance with the code, nor could a comprehensive list of noncompliant countries be found using other public domain sources.[27] However, evidence exists that countries do maintain their own lists of ports and facilities not in compliance with ISPS so they can exercise more effective port state control with respect to vessels calling on their country from suspect areas. Recent industry and press reports cite Nigeria as an example of an area that has received heightened scrutiny from the United States Coast Guard.[28]

Beyond the ISPS Code

Container Security Initiative

Some countries have gone beyond simply implementing the requirements of ISPS, instituting additional security provisions designed specifically to address other security concerns, including those related to containerized cargoes. One such program, developed in the United States, is the Container Security Initiative (CSI), enacted as part of the Security and Accountability for Every Port Act (or SAFE Port Act) of 2006.[29] The mission of CSI is to identify, and then either examine or search, maritime containers that may pose a security threat *before* they are loaded aboard a vessel for shipment to the United States. To achieve this goal, the United States has stationed teams of Customs and Border Protection (CBP) officers in participating foreign countries and ports to work with host government counterparts. Their task is to identify and prescreen containers, and to develop investigative leads related to any cargo destined for the United States that may have been targeted for use in a terrorist threat.

As part of this process, CBP officers work with host customs administrations to establish security criteria for identifying high-risk containers. Nonintrusive inspection (NII) and radiation detection technologies are used to screen high-risk containers before they are loaded aboard a vessel to be shipped to the United States. CSI is reported to be operational at ports in North America, Europe, Asia, Africa, the Middle East, and Latin America. As of midyear 2014, CBP facilities were operational at 58 foreign ports and were able to prescreen over 80 percent of all maritime containerized cargo imported into the United States.[30] Further, CSI provides for bilateral information sharing with reciprocal provisions that enable customs officials from partner nations to operate from US ports so they can monitor exports being shipped to their countries.

Customs-Trade Partnership Against Terrorism

The SAFE Port Act also established the Customs-Trade Partnership Against Terrorism (C-TPAT) as a voluntary government–private sector partnership program to strengthen the overall security of the international supply chain as well as US border security. The partnership also aims to facilitate the movement of secure cargo through the supply chain by providing incentives to participants meeting or exceeding program requirements. It was designed with the goal of encouraging widespread participation from members of the broader transportation network, including importers; customs brokers; freight forwarders; air, sea, and land carriers; contract logistics providers; and other entities in the international supply chain and intermodal transportation system.

In exchange for implementing and maintaining security practices (based on prescribed criteria), participants may receive certain benefits that can include a reduction in the "high-risk" threshold used by the Automated Targeting System (ATS). ATS is the system used to assign terrorism-related risk for all cargoes entering the United States. Program participants would benefit from this by receiving fewer cargo inspections and expediting release of cargoes. They would also be among the first shippers allowed to move cargoes in the event supply chains should ever be compromised or otherwise face a serious security threat.

The SAFE Framework

Many of the goals and objectives defined under the US SAFE Port Act and embodied in CSI and C-TPAT have been adopted by other governments and entities, including the European Commission and the intergovernmental World Customs Organization (WCO), which represents 179 countries. The WCO's SAFE Framework of Standards to Secure and Facilitate Global Trade (SAFE Framework) was adopted in 2005 as a nonbinding instrument comprising customs standards aimed at securing international trade without impeding trade flow.[31] The SAFE Framework employs a two-pillar approach; the first resembles CSI, whereas the second has features similar to C-TPAT.

The first pillar of the SAFE Framework sets standards for customs-agency-to-customs-agency network arrangements to maximize both the security and the facilitation of the international trade supply chain as cargo shipments and transport conveyances move between nodes in the global trading system. It calls for customs administrations to work cooperatively with common and accepted methods to receive electronically information in advance on imports, exports, and in-transit cargoes and then analyze this information to determine if the shipment represents a risk to national scrutiny. Consignments determined to be potentially high risk may then be examined, preferably by using nonintrusive inspection techniques. This approach is claimed to both enhance security and facilitate trade flows because shipments deemed to be low risk need not be scanned or physically inspected.

The second pillar sets standards for customs administrations to establish partnerships with private-sector business operators to gain their participation and ensure the safety and security of international trade supply chains. The main focus of this pillar is on the creation of an international system for identifying private businesses, designated as authorized economic operators[32] or AEOs, that offer a high degree of security guarantees with respect to their roles in the global supply chain. In exchange for their voluntary cooperation, these AEO business partners receive tangible benefits in the form of expedited processing and other measures.

One fundamental difference does exist, however, between the security protocols rolled out by the United States and those rolled out by countries represented by the World Customs Organization. The SAFE Framework explicitly rejects the US congressional mandate calling for 100 percent scanning of all maritime containers entering the United States. WCO member states consider this approach unnecessary, too costly, and counter to the dual goals of optimizing cargo security and facilitating trade. The proponents of the SAFE Framework believe a multilayered risk-management approach, designed to target and inspect *suspect* cargo, is superior to the 100 percent scanning of all containers. Such an approach is thought to avoid a significant workload burden, serving to free up resources that can then be focused on those containers presenting a greater potential risk.

Global Workforce of Seagoing Personnel

On a particular day, almost any one of the roughly 50,000 large merchant vessels—each with at least twelve or more seafarers likely on board—could appear on the horizon and request entry to a port. To minimize security risk, port officials would have to vet the crews as well as the ships. The magnitude of this challenge is underscored by information gathered by the Baltic and International Maritime Council (BIMCO), a large industry trade group, which estimates the global supply of commercial shipboard personnel currently totals approximately 1.5 million seafarers.[33] To deal with this situation, national governments and international regulatory bodies have adopted upgraded requirements for tamper-resistant seafarer identity documents (SIDs). Indeed, the ISPS Code has mandated the creation of SIDs that use biometric information to provide proof positive of a seafarer's identity. While fingerprints may now be the most commonly used biometric identifier, others available include facial recognition, iris scan, retina scan, and DNA authentication.

In each case, the biometric identifier used is unique to a particular individual and can be used to provide proof positive of that person's identity. However, it assumes that a person's true identity is authenticated before that information is entered into a secure database. A fully functioning system also requires that the biometric information be stored on a tamper-proof ID card, and that an ID card reader be located at each access control point. Finally, each access control point must have the equipment necessary to remeasure the appropriate biometric identifier on the person being checked for comparison with the information shown on the card. Procedures developed collaboratively by the International Maritime Organization and the International Labor Organization call for governments to maintain secure databases on SIDs they have issued.

Cybersecurity Threats

Moving freight along international supply chains relies heavily on information. For each shipment, various commercial documents need to be exchanged between parties to the transaction, including the shipper, consignee, freight forwarder, ocean carrier, and any financial institutions that may be involved. Modern information technology makes it possible to handle the massive amounts of information involved in these transactions quickly and efficiency through the use of proprietary software products, industry standard applications, private computer networks, and the worldwide web. World commerce has become so dependent on the near-instantaneous flow of this information that, without the associated information technology (IT) systems and infrastructure, global trade would grind to a halt. The vital need for reliable and robust information systems makes these systems and networks critical infrastructure that warrants generous protection resources.

Beyond the disruption of international trade flows and severe economic dislocations, in a world increasingly operating with zero inventories and just-in-time strategies, cyberattacks could be used to manipulate information systems to create a serious breach in security. One such attack in Europe underscores the dire consequences that could result. In June 2013, Belgian and Dutch authorities reported that drug smugglers had employed professional hackers to aid in the illicit transport of more than two metric tons of heroin and cocaine through the port of Antwerp and on into the Netherlands. The hackers did this by emailing a "Trojan horse" virus to install keystroke-logging devices to capture passwords, allowing them to gain control of port computers and container-terminal operating systems. After executing this breach, the criminals were then able to monitor "their" container for special treatment—ultimately, to have it unloaded and delivered at a time and location of their choosing—all the while avoiding the scrutiny of port staff.[34] The same approach could just as easily have been used to bypass security to bring in any other type of contraband, including a weapon of mass destruction.

A July 2013 paper published by the Brookings Institution's Center for Twenty-First Century Security and Intelligence observed that US port facilities rely as much upon networked computer and control systems as they do upon port facilities and stevedores to ensure the flow of maritime commerce. However, unlike the critical infrastructure in other sectors of the economy, little attention has been paid to the networked information technology systems that serve as the backbone for port operations. Further, the report found no cybersecurity standards had been promulgated for US ports, nor had the US Coast Guard, the lead federal agency for maritime security, been granted authority to establish cybersecurity standards. This gap was cited as a serious threat to national security.[35] As governments become more reliant on information systems, they too will be ever more vulnerable to cyberattacks.

Role of Technology

The task of security checking inbound seaborne cargoes arriving at ports can be daunting, given the velocity and volume by which much of the freight handled in international trade is now being moved. Technology can aid by providing a helpful first line of defense against the smuggling of contraband, and by serving as a force multiplier for the agents and officials tasked with this responsibility. These devices include passive radiological sensors and monitors able detect ionizing radiation of the type that might be associated with a nuclear device or a "dirty" bomb. They are commonly deployed at fixed and mobile locations around ports to scan containers as soon as they are landed, when they are shifted between the dock and a storage yard, and when they enter or leave the port complex.

Various types of imaging devices are also in use to conduct nonintrusive inspections of cargo containers—devices that have evolved from industrial applications and the medical diagnostics field. Typically, these employ high-energy X-rays or gamma rays to create radiographic images, and they offer the potential to make closed cargo containers transparent to the trained eye of an inspector. However, these scanning devices only provide a preliminary assessment because the technology is still evolving. Yet, they can be useful as a first step in screening suspect containers and singling out those that warrant further inspection.

Thermal sensing is a scanning alternative that does not use ionizing radiation and is very effective at creating images based on temperature gradients. These devices are able to detect subtle temperature differences and can be used to reduce the threats to national security posed by uncontrolled cross-border movement and the smuggling of human cargoes. In addition, this technology may also make it possible to help bring to an end the tragic outcomes that can result when migrants and stowaways attempt to use shipping containers as a means to cross national borders.

While scanning can be an effective timesaving tool, the technology is expensive to deploy and, given the current state of the art of this equipment, it is far from foolproof. At the present time, physical inspection remains the most effective and reliable method for determining whether or not contraband is in a container. The down side of physical inspection is that it is very time consuming, and it can take several hours for a single, standard, 40-foot ocean container to be unloaded (stripped), inspected, and then reloaded (stuffed) again. Therefore, physical inspection has to be reserved for those containers believed to be of highest risk.

Conclusion

Creating effective port security may require a cultural shift in the way governments, organizations, and institutions think and set priorities. It may not be possible to enhance security without changing long-established patterns of behavior and making substantial commitments of time and resources. Therefore, it is important to be able to explain both the need and the urgency for taking action. One way to build support is by educating key policy- and decision-makers about the importance of ports and the possible consequences that could result from a security failure.

Best practices call for an integrated approach to information gathering and intelligence sharing, and this can also require a shift in long-standing patterns of past behavior. Accordingly, it is important to coordinate the collection and evaluation of all potentially relevant security-related data and facilitate the flow of information between the central government and local government agencies (and among the local agencies themselves). Governments must define missions and responsibilities for the relevant agencies, granting the authority and resources needed to fulfill those roles. They must then implement methods and procedures for rapidly disseminating security alerts and warnings, and establish liaison mechanisms for sharing information with neighboring countries, world bodies, and foreign trading partners.

The importance of maritime domain awareness has been stressed elsewhere in this book. MDA constitutes a critical first step when it comes to port security. Effective control must be exercised over all ports and territorial waters. Only a state has the right to determine which vessels should be allowed to enter its ports. The preferred goal should be to interdict dangerous cargoes before they enter the country, not to find them after they have arrived.

Notes

1. The International Monetary Fund (IMF) is an organization of 188 countries working to foster global monetary cooperation, secure financial stability, facilitate international trade, promote high employment and sustainable economic growth, and reduce poverty around the world. IMF publishes the *Directions of Trade Statistics Yearbook* annually, and it shows the value of foreign trade for each of its trading partners on a country-pair basis. This information can be sourced at http://www.imf.org/external/pubs/cat/longres.cfm?sk=20721.

2. The United Nations compiles data on commodity-level trade between countries and their trading partners and publishes it annually in the *International Trade Yearbook*. This information can be obtained online at http://comtrade.un.org/db/help/ServiceMessage.aspx?rowID=556.

3. The CIA's *World Factbook* provides detailed country-level information about national economies, demographics, transportation capabilities, and infrastructure,

and it can be accessed online at https://www.cia.gov/library/publications/the-world
-factbook/.

4. United Nations, *2012 International Trade Statistics Yearbook*, Vol. II, Table A, 3.
This information can be accessed at http://comtrade.un.org/pb/first.aspx.

5. United Nations, UNCTAD, *Review of Maritime Transport 2013*, 7. The United
Nations Conference on Trade and Development (UNCTAD) annually profiles trends
and developments in the ocean shipping sector of the global economy. Current and
past editions can be accessed online at http://unctad.org/en/publicationslibrary/
rmt2013_en.pdf.

6. *Review of Maritime Transport 2013*, xi. While the most recently available UN
data indicate 80 percent of world commerce moves by seaborne trade, other maritime
industry sources commonly report that volume to be in the range of 80 to 90 percent.
The 90 percent figure is commonly cited without reference, but the actual number
depends on how trade is measured.

7. Large, oceangoing vessels have traditionally used low-cost heavy residual oil
for bunker fuel. However, the high sulfur content of this type of fuel contributes to
air pollution. Regulations by IMO and individual countries are currently phasing in
mandates for the use of low-sulfur fuel alternatives. For additional information on the
environmental advantages of marine transportation versus other modes, please see
http://www.worldshipping.org/industry-issues/environment/air-emissions/carbon
-emissions.

8. Selena Yan, *Measuring the Importance of Seaborne Trade*, IMSF Annual Meeting 2013, Clarksons Research, 6. See http://www.imsf.info/media/1027/world-seaborne
-trade-commodity-trends.pdf.

9. The United Nations Convention on the Law of the Sea (UNCLOS) I establishes a legal framework that governs the use of the oceans. UNCLOS, Part VII, Article 90 enumerates the right of navigation and, specifically, prescribes that every
state, whether coastal or landlocked, has the right to sail ships flying its flag on the
high seas. For additional details, see http://www.un.org/depts/los/convention_agree
ments/texts/unclos/unclos_e.pdf.

10. Many countries have cabotage laws. These restrict domestic coastwise trades
involving the movement of passengers and cargoes to ships registered under that
state's own national flag.

11. *Review of Maritime Transport 2013*, 56. The top eleven pure open-registry fleets
accounted for 55 percent of the total world fleet. Additionally, 73 percent of the total
fleet capacity was "flagged out"—that is, registered in countries that were different
than the owner's nationalities.

12. Tina Shaugnessy and Ellen Tobi, "Flags of Inconvenience: Freedom and Insecurity on the High Seas," *Journal of International Law & Policy* (Philadelphia: University of Pennsylvania Press, 2007), 1–3.

13. Based on statistics published by the American Association of Port Authorities
(AAPA) for the year 2012. See http://www.aapa-ports.org/Industry/content.cfm?Item

Number=900&navItemNumber=551 and click on US Waterborne Foreign Trade 2013 Port Ranking by Cargo Volume.

14. http://www.navigationdatacenter.us/ports/ports.htm. Click on Port Facility Worksheet.

15. See http://ppp.worldbank.org/public-private-partnership/sector/transpor tation/ports.

16. For additional details see the DHS Homeport website at https://homeport .uscg.mil/mycg/portal/ep/home.do.

17. Robert Watts, "Maritime Critical Infrastructure Protection: Multi-Agency Command and Control in an Asymmetric Environment," *Homeland Security Affairs* (Naval Postgraduate School Center for Homeland Defense and Security, 2005). Complete article can be found online at http://www.hsaj.org/?fullarticle=1.2.3.

18. See the DHS website at http://www.dhs.gov/state-and-major-urban-area -fusion-centers.

19. For more background, see http://www.mass.gov/eopss/home-sec-emerg-resp/ fusion-center/fusion-center-overview.html.

20. See http://www.imo.org/About/Pages/Default.aspx.

21. Ibid.

22. IMO regulations are put into force through individual conventions that are adopted by member nations. Currently, an overwhelming majority of the member nations are signatories to the conventions involving safety and security. A list of each convention and the member countries that are party to it can be found at: http:// www.imo.org/blast/blastDataHelper.asp?data_id=18188&filename=HILIGHTSIMO5 0YRSARECORDOFSUCCESS.pdf.

23. *Singapore Journal of International & Comparative Law* 1998, 543.

24. See the IMO website at http://www.imo.org/About/Pages/Default.aspx.

25. Natasha Brown (NBrown@imo.org), Public Information Services, IMO, in an email to the author.

26. A detailed example of how the Ministry of Transportation and Communications of Taiwan reviews and evaluates port facility security assessments can be found on the MOTC website at http://www.motcmpb.gov.tw/MOTCMPBWeb/wSite /public/Data/f1375081197112.pdf.

27. This is one of the frequently asked questions (FAQ) addressed on the IMO website: http://www.imo.org/blast/mainframe.asp?topic_id=897#who.

28. As recently as December 2014 many Nigerian port facilities still failed to achieve compliance with ISPS. However, this does not mean ships from those facilities will be banned from entering the United States, rather, only that conditions of entry may be imposed, subjecting them to increased scrutiny. See http://www.marsec review.com/2014/12/nigeria-isps-compliance-hits-38/.

29. *Security and Accountability for Every Port Act of 2006*, Public Law 109-347, October 13, 2006. See http://www.gpo.gov/fdsys/pkg/PLAW-109publ347/pdf/PLAW -109publ347.pdf.

30. This information is available online at http://www.cbp.gov/border-security/ports-entry/cargo-security/csi/csi-brief.

31. This information is available online at http://www.wcoomd.org/en/topics/facilitation/instrument-and-tools/tools/safe_package.aspx.

32. An AEO may be any entity participating in the international supply chain, including manufacturers, importers, exporters, carriers, ports, airports, brokers, consolidators, warehouse service providers, terminal operators, etc.

33. BIMCO is an accredited NGO that provides a wide range of services to a global membership of stakeholders that has vested interests in the shipping industry, including ship owners, operators, managers, brokers. See http://www.maritimemanpower.com/wp-content/uploads/2014/11/Manpower-Study-highlights.pdf.

34. An account of this case is available online at http://onlinepubs.trb.org/online pubs/conferences/2014/MTS2014/Caldwell.pdf.

35. The report can be found online at http://www.brookings.edu/research/papers/2013/07/03-cyber-ports-security-kramek.

8 Maritime Domain Awareness

Timothy J. Doorey

THE PREREQUISITE FOR PROTECTING A COUNTRY'S MARITIME domain is a timely and comprehensive understanding of all maritime activity occurring within that nation's inland waterways, territorial seas, exclusive economic zone (EEZ), and adjacent high seas. With over 70 percent of the Earth's surface covered by water, this is a daunting task indeed for even the world's wealthiest and most technologically advanced maritime countries. The unprecedented—and unsuccessful—multinational search effort to locate any sign of wreckage from the missing Malaysian Airlines Flight 370 in the Andaman Sea and Indian Ocean in early 2014 demonstrates just how much of the world's maritime domain remains *mare incognitum*. This chapter is designed to assist countries and organizations in their efforts to enhance the understanding of maritime activity within—and adjacent to— their jurisdictions.

Efforts to detect, identify, track, and evaluate maritime activity within a specified geographic area are often referred to as achieving maritime domain awareness or MDA. However, this term is both overused and imprecise. MDA often means different things to different people from a range of organizations. Some believe MDA is primarily a technical problem, which can be solved by purely technical solutions, such as increased sensors, satellites, and computer systems to detect, track, and evaluate maritime activity. Others see it as an extension of law enforcement investigations and intelligence work ashore, since all illegal activity at sea is conceived, planned, and implemented by state and non-state actors on land, long before it reaches the water's edge.

Part of the problem with the maritime domain awareness concept is the term itself. While the *maritime domain* is rather straightforward in that it pertains to a specified maritime environment, what does *awareness* actually mean? Does MDA require up-to-the-minute knowledge of the location, course, speed, and identification of every ship or boat afloat, in a given area, no matter its size or displacement? Does MDA mean intricate knowledge of every vessel's ownership, including the thousands of vessels registered in countries such as Panama, Liberia, and the Marshall Islands? Does MDA mean that we know the contents of every shipping container transported by the thousands of massive cargo ships afloat? What about the crews? Does achieving MDA imply that we know the identities and motivations of the thousands of merchant officers and seamen sailing the seas, or leaving and entering commercial ports every day? Are we certain that these crews don't include individuals affiliated with either terrorist or criminal organizations?

According to the United Nations International Maritime Organization (IMO), *maritime domain awareness* (MDA) is defined as

> the effective understanding of anything associated with the maritime domain that could impact the security, safety, economy, or environment.[1]

The US Navy's Office of Maritime Domain Awareness, the Department of Defense's Executive Agent for MDA, uses a slightly expanded—but equally ambitious—definition for MDA:

> the effective understanding of anything associated with the global Maritime Domain that could impact the security, safety, economy, or environment of the United States. The Maritime Domain is "all areas and things of, on, under, relating to, adjacent to, or bordering on a sea, ocean, or other navigable waterway, including all maritime-related activities, infrastructure, people, cargo, vessels, and other conveyances.[2]

In practice, it is unrealistic to believe that any nation could achieve such an omniscient understanding of its maritime domain. Even the United States, with its vast federal, state, and local resources, including the Department of Defense (DOD), Department of Homeland Security (DHS), and various law enforcement agencies, routinely falls short of this goal, as evidenced by the vast quantities of illegally smuggled people, drugs, and other contraband that successfully enter the country every year by maritime conveyance.

Geography alone plays a major role in determining a nation's ability to meet its MDA challenge. Smaller nations—such as Slovenia, with its short coastline between Italy and Croatia in the Gulf of Trieste; Lebanon, with its proximity to Cyprus; Cameroon, with its proximity to Equatorial Guinea's capital, Malabo (on the island of Bioko); and Jordan, whose only seaport of Aqaba is surrounded by Israel, Egypt, and Saudi Arabia—have relatively small maritime domains to monitor and patrol. On the other hand, countries with vast maritime domains—such as the large-island and archipelagic nations like Australia, the Philippines, and Indonesia—must contend with maritime areas often many times larger than the nation's landmass. This enormous MDA task must be accomplished with limited surveillance and patrol assets.

History of Maritime Domain Awareness

Maritime domain awareness is a relatively new term for what has been traditionally referred to as *maritime intelligence*. Prior to 1994 and the establishment of 200-nautical-mile exclusive economic zones (EEZs) as part of the United Nations Convention on the Law of the Sea (UNCLOS) treaty, nations had relatively small maritime jurisdictions to monitor and police. Beyond territorial waters, on what was commonly referred to as the high seas, most nations were concerned primarily with universally recognized crimes such as piracy and slave trading, which were thankfully rare. Before the Cold War came to an end and UNCLOS came into effect, maritime intelligence was primarily the responsibility of national navies, which focused their efforts almost exclusively against the naval capabilities and location of enemy warships, submarines, and the troop and arms carriers of other nations. National and regional law enforcement agencies—such as coast guards and maritime police—conducted limited maritime intelligence gathering in support of law enforcement efforts. This was done in parallel with navy intelligence work (usually with limited resources) to detect domestic and transnational non-state maritime threats such as drug, arms, and human smuggling and trafficking; sea-based terrorism; piracy; dumping of toxic waste; and illegal, unreported and unregulated (IUU) fishing.[3]

Historically, maritime intelligence had been limited to visual observation at sea and from ashore, augmented by the work of paid informers, spies, and naval attachés snooping around ports, shipyards, and the naval and merchant shipping offices of potentially hostile nations. Prior to the widespread adoption of wireless telegraphy at sea and ashore in the early twentieth century, the range and effectiveness of maritime intelligence could only be marginally improved through enhanced optics and increased elevation. However, with radio, and the subsequent development and deployment of radar, reconnaissance satellites, and various acoustic sensors later in the twentieth century, navies were now able to dramatically extend their understanding of the maritime domain beyond visual range. Some navies developed advanced intelligence-collection capabilities to intercept, exploit, and geo-locate the radio and radar signals emanating from enemy ships and submarines at sea, thus giving them ever-greater knowledge of enemy naval activity.

Great Britain, with assistance from its wartime ally, Russia, led the way during World War I with a string of successes by the Admiralty's legendary Room 40, where British naval intelligence intercepted and decrypted many of the Imperial German Navy's operational communications.[4] Across the Atlantic, the US Navy's Office of Naval Intelligence (ONI) expanded from its modest beginnings in 1882 as a small branch of the Bureau of Navigation to become the premier maritime intelligence service by the mid-twentieth century. US Naval Intelligence, with invaluable contributions from its wartime allies, played a major role in winning World War II. During the Cold War, with critical support from its NATO allies, the United States monitored Soviet and Warsaw Pact naval operations successfully for decades.[5] Today, ONI and its many counterparts around the world continue tracking both state and non-state maritime activity and threats, including piracy off the coast of Somalia, the Gulf of Guinea, and Southeast Asia.[6]

Changing Maritime Threat Environment

Over the past few decades, national and international attention have begun to shift away from looking exclusively at traditional naval threats toward state and non-state transnational criminal actors in the maritime domain. This new emphasis has been the result of two major developments. First, with the signing of UNCLOS, maritime nations assumed the obligation to protect not only their traditional territorial seas, but also their new 200-nautical-mile EEZs.[7] At the same time, nations became increasingly concerned by myriad transnational maritime threats such as IUU fishing, maritime smuggling, sea-based terrorism, and environmental damage caused by the illegal dumping of toxic chemicals. Even the age-old scourge of piracy was making a strong comeback, with over 400 reported attacks on shipping recorded between 1980 and 1984 alone.[8]

The second development was the ending of the Cold War. When the threat posed by Soviet and Warsaw Pact navies started to recede, Western governments were able to focus their navies' surveillance and reconnaissance assets—and intelligence services—on non-state maritime threats, specifically drug trafficking. This transition from traditional to nontraditional maritime threats required naval intelligence to make many technical, legal, and cultural changes, but soon navies were making significant contributions to interagency and multinational law-enforcement interdiction efforts. Many governments were also becoming increasingly aware of the scope and lethality of transnational threats at sea, making them national security threats rather than low-level criminal activity. This forced many governments to reevaluate military and law enforcement organization roles and missions, and to reallocate dwindling defense resources against these threats in the maritime domain.

National security officials watched with alarm the rapid growth in transnational crime in the global maritime commons, including the proliferation of weapons of mass destruction. The events of September 11, 2001 highlighted the potential threat of maritime terrorism, and the vulnerability of the United States (and, by inference, all maritime nations) to terrorists using maritime conveyance to inflict mass casualties and economic damage. Maritime intelligence would have to play a major role in preventing terrorist attacks in the maritime domain, and reducing transnational criminal activity. RADM Jonathan W. White, USN, Director of the US Navy's Office of Maritime Domain Awareness, writes:

> Operational, intelligence, and law enforcement communities have long had responsibilities for different aspects of the Maritime Domain. After the attacks of September 11, 2001, the Federal government recognized the importance of aligning Federal government maritime security programs and initiatives to share information and promote a shared, effective understanding of the maritime environment.[9]

These new and growing transnational threats have placed increasing demands and requirements on maritime intelligence and MDA. For example, when the US Navy and its NATO allies' maritime intelligence services tracked

Soviet warships and submarines during the Cold War, it was a challenging but rather straightforward process. One could assume that a Soviet warship, merchant vessel, or submarine leaving a Soviet port and flying a Soviet flag would also have a Soviet crew, with Soviet cargo, receiving orders from Moscow. The same cannot be said about commercial shipping today. The flag flying from the stern of a merchant tanker, cargo ship, fishing trawler, or cruise ship is all but meaningless in determining if that vessel presents a potential threat or is engaged in illegal activity.

The extensive use of *flags of convenience* (or open registry) now accounts for a very large percentage of the world's merchant fleet. In 2010, just three countries—Panama (22.63%), Liberia (11.14%), and the Marshall Islands (6.10%)—accounted for over 40 percent of the world's top ship registries (flag states).[10] As for the crews of these and other ships, over 1.2 million merchant seafarers are involved in international trade by sea worldwide, which means that less than half of one percent of the population moves 90 percent of the world's freight over the seas that cover the Earth's surface.[11] While this indicates merchant shipping is highly efficient, properly vetting all seafarers is a complex endeavor, requiring extensive and continuous interagency and international cooperation.

Then there is the cargo itself. Nations have the responsibility to verify that the cargo entering their ports every day does not contain contraband, or worse, a weapon of mass destruction. But how can they be certain? In 2006, the *Xin Los Angeles*, the largest container ship afloat at the time, carried 9,600 twenty-foot equivalent units (TEU). As of 2013, the largest container ship being built could carry 18,000 TEU.[12] In late 2014, South Korea's Hyundai Heavy Industries delivered the second in a series of five 19,100-TEU cargo ships to China Shipping Container Lines.[13] It would take an army of trained container inspectors months to properly inspect even a fraction of the containers moving through the world's ports, and since time is money for these commercial shippers, it is not surprising that commercial shipping companies have resisted delaying cargoes for inspection by law enforcement officials trying to stop smuggling, human trafficking, and, in recent years, bombs.[14]

Complicating the detection challenge even further, resource-rich transnational criminal organizations (TCOs) now routinely use semi- and even fully submersible submarines to smuggle drugs and other contraband from South America into Central America and possibly even directly into the United States.[15] TCOs are also exploiting weaknesses in commercial and governmental information technologies. Today, cyberthreats to commercial shipping must also be taken into consideration, as more and more shipping information and activities migrate from the physical to the virtual world.[16] For example, in June 2013, Belgian authorities uncovered a two-year-long drug-smuggling operation, valued at about US $220 million, in which the perpetrators hacked into the port of Antwerp cargo-handling system to track their drug shipments (detailed in Chapter 7).[17] Could well-funded terrorist groups acquire similar skills and technologies?

Selected Institutional Solutions

Over the past two decades, a number of governmental and nongovernmental organizations have responded to the challenges posed by maritime transnational threats in a variety of ways. Much of their effort has focused on enhancing MDA, which, in turn, allows them to better allocate their limited patrol and interdiction assets. The following examples of national, multinational, and nongovernmental MDA institutions provide a rich body of knowledge and experience for nations to investigate as they work to enhance their own MDA capabilities.

Joint Interagency Task Force—South
In 1988, the US Congress pressured the Department of Defense (DOD) to divert some of its extensive intelligence, surveillance, and reconnaissance (ISR) resources against what had been viewed as a law enforcement problem: drug trafficking from South America to the southern United States. Following the terrorist attacks on September 11, 2001, these DOD efforts were expanded to cover other transnational maritime threats to national security and coordinated with the newly established Department of Homeland Security (DHS), whose functions included close-in MDA, customs, and border control.[18] In 1989, Joint Task Force Four (JTF-4) was established in Key West, Florida to better coordinate the various DOD and law enforcement counterdrug monitoring and surveillance efforts in the Eastern Pacific and Caribbean. This effort evolved into a truly joint, interagency, and multinational command. In 1999, it was renamed the Joint Interagency Task Force South (JIATF-South), serving as an interagency and multinational command with liaison officers from the four military services, nine separate federal agencies, and eleven partner nations.[19] Because of its unparalleled success, JIATF-South has often

been labeled the "gold standard" for interagency and multinational cooperation, successfully supporting US and allied maritime and air interdiction efforts in the Western Hemisphere.[20]

International Maritime Bureau's Piracy Reporting Centre

In 1992, the International Maritime Bureau (IMB) in London, responding to increasing piracy and armed robbery at sea, established the Piracy Reporting Centre (PRC) in Kuala Lumpur, Malaysia, making it the first nongovernmental organization to take on the MDA challenge, albeit for a specific transnational threat. From its modest beginnings, the IMB/PRC has evolved into a robust 24/7/365 watch, with a hotline to receive reporting from commercial ships of all types and merchant shipping organizations. When it receives credible reports of piracy or armed robbery at sea activity, it quickly notifies the local authorities in the region and also provides timely warnings to other commercial ships operating in the vicinity. The centre also produces and disseminates comprehensive reports on piracy trends by region, and posts updated maps of piracy and armed robbery at sea activity on its website.[21]

Australia's Border Protection Command

The Australian government's inadequate response to specific maritime incidents contributed to the creation of its interagency Border Protection Command and Maritime Intelligence Fusion Center. In April 2003, the Australian Federal Police discovered a Tuvalu-flagged, North Korean–owned, merchant cargo ship named the *Pong Su* delivering 150 kg (330 lb.) of heroin to Australia's southern coast. When the Australian authorities ordered the *Pong Su* into port, the ship attempted to flee into international waters. After a four-day chase—during which visual and radar contact were lost—the authorities were able to regain contact and direct Australian Special Air Service commandos to seize the vessel after fast-roping onto its deck by helicopter.[22] The ship was then commandeered into Sydney Port, where the crew was arrested. However successful, the incident highlighted many coordination problems among the numerous agencies responsible for Australia's vast maritime domain. In 2004, the government's Taskforce on Offshore Maritime Security reported to parliament that the separate agencies under Customs, Border Protection, and Defence all had significant offshore maritime patrol, response, and interdiction capabilities. These resources were merged to form the Joint Offshore Protection Command (JOPC). Other functions, including fisheries enforcement, were added to the mix, and in 2006 the JOPC was renamed the Border Protection Command or BPC.[23] The BPC's watch center, located in Canberra, is staffed by personnel from Defence, Customs, Fisheries Management Authority, and the Australian Quarantine Inspection Service, and is augmented by other agencies when required.[24]

The Philippines' National Coast Watch System (CWS)

In response to increases in regional terrorism by the Abu Sayyaf Group (ASG) and Jemaah Islamiah (JI), as well as to piracy and kidnapping by criminal organizations, the government of the Philippines—with assistance from Australia and the United States—established a national coast-watch system, or CWS. First conceptualized in 2006, CWS came into being on November 28, 2008. Originally called Coast Watch South (since it was focused on threats in the southern region of the 7,000-island archipelago), it was later renamed Coast Watch System and expanded to cover the entire nation.[25] In 2011, Philippines President Benigno Aquino signed Executive Order 57, which formally designated CWS a national system.[26] In 2013, the US defense firm Raytheon was awarded an $18-million contract to design and build a National Coast Watch Center.[27] The CWS concept is a superb model for nationwide coastal surveillance and integration. It remains to be seen, however, if the government of the Philippines can muster sufficient resources, effect the necessary interagency cooperation, and find the political will to operate and maintain the numerous radar stations, sensors, and watch centers. Moreover, the government will need to recruit, train, and retain the technicians and watch personnel needed to make the CWS a viable nationwide MDA capability.[28]

Singapore's Information Fusion Centre

Few nations are as dependent on the safe and efficient movement of commerce by sea as the city-state of Singapore.[29] To enhance regional maritime domain awareness and facilitate regional maritime information-sharing cooperation and collective analysis, Singapore established the multinational Information Fusion Centre (IFC) in 2009 at Changi Command and Control Centre. The IFC is linked to more than sixty-five agencies in thirty-five countries. In addition to its state-of-the-art information technologies, the IFC hosts twenty-four international liaison officers, or ILOs, to rapidly coordinate its efforts with partners in the region and beyond.[30] Singapore's Information Fusion Centre defines its area of interest (AOI) to extend westward to the Gulf of Oman (60 degrees east), north to Pakistan and Taiwan (23 degrees; 67 minutes), east to Banda Sea (130 degrees east) and south to above Australia

(12 degrees south). While the AOI is a very large area, heavily trafficked by national, regional, and international shipping, extensive technological investment in sensors and computer systems—along with its strong institutional partnerships—enables the IFC to achieve adequate granularity to provide timely support to interdiction forces if required.

South Africa's MDA Centres

In response to the expanding threat of Somalia-based piracy in East African waters, and increased piracy and armed robbery at sea in the Gulf of Guinea, the South African navy is establishing two maritime domain awareness (MDA) centres. One will be in Durban to cover the east coast, with a second at Silvermine in Cape Town to cover the west coast. The South African centres will be linked to other Southern African Development Community (SADC) MDA centres to exchange perishable maritime information more effectively. Numerous collection and sensor sources, such as mobile shore radars, automatic identification system (AIS) links, and fixed coastal radars are monitored at these centres, helping South Africa and other SADC maritime countries build a common operating picture of what is happening in their areas of interest. The MDA centres will be operated under the Chief of Defence Intelligence but in cooperation with the SADC, which will send liaison officers and watch standers to assist. Similar MDA centres are already in operation in Angola and Namibia.[31]

India's Coastal Security Measures

In the wake of the Mumbai attacks, the Indian government has become increasingly concerned about its vulnerability to seaborne infiltration. The investigation into the government's response to the attacks highlighted a lack of coordination by multiple government institutions, the failure to share intelligence, and a very slow response overall. The maritime dimension alone involved over fifteen agencies, ranging from navy, coast guard, customs, intelligence agencies, port authorities, the shipping ministries, state governments, and fisheries departments. Multiple investigations revealed that many of these agencies were working at cross-purposes.[32] The Modi administration is trying to establish a National Maritime Authority (NMA) to improve policy-making and the coordination of coastal security. Despite slow progress, India has implemented a number of coastal security measures since the Mumbai attacks, including a fledgling coastal radar network to link state marine police stations (only Phase I is operational). While many international security experts fear

India's port and coastal security remain vulnerable, senior Indian military and security officers believe "many gaps" have been plugged in their anti-terror infrastructure. They also claim to have achieved swifter dissemination of "actionable intelligence" to security forces to prevent impending attacks.[33]

The above are just a small sample of the numerous national and international governmental and nongovernmental efforts under way to improve regional MDA. Their experiences—added to many others—provide a rich body of knowledge any nation confronted with the MDA challenge can incorporate into its maritime security education and training programs.

Building Blocks for Successful MDA Efforts

All the national, international, and nongovernmental MDA organizations discussed above demonstrated the following common traits and principles.

Limited Scope for MDA Efforts

All the organizations profiled have carefully limited either their geographic or their functional areas of responsibility (AOR) which, if not limited by geography, are aimed against specific maritime threats such as piracy, drug trafficking, smuggling, IUU, etc. Such limitations were imposed to avoid diluting scarce collection, monitoring, and fusion center analytical and reporting resources. Usually, at a minimum, a nation's maritime domain extends to its EEZ boundaries under UNCLOS. Beyond the AOR is the area of interest, or AOI, from which maritime threats can also originate. While the AOR is mandated by UNCLOS EEZ claims, the AOI is determined by the organization. In the case of JIATF-South, the AOR and AOI are the same since it is the preferred interdiction zone. In the case of the IMB's Piracy Reporting Centre, the AOR and AOI are also the same (global), but functional responsibilities are limited to piracy and armed robbery at sea (what Peter Chalk calls *armed maritime crime* in Chapter 4).

Organizations such as Singapore's IFC and JIATF-South can expand their regional and functional limitations if they feel they have the technological capacity and international partnerships to cover a greater area. JIATF-South, for example, nearly doubled its area of responsibility in October 2003 in response to the post-9/11 terrorism threat. The task force now defines its joint operating area, or JOA, as all the sea and territory between 120 and 27 degrees west and below 30 degrees north—a 42-million-square-mile area.[34] JIATF-South was also able to expand its functional JOA because it had demonstrated the ability (with over two decades of experience) to monitor a smaller area against a single threat—drug trafficking. Nations without extensive technological capabilities and formal partnerships would be wise to limit the extent of their AOIs until they can demonstrate capacity and confidence.

Interagency and Multinational Approaches

Whenever possible, the MDA centers discussed here have developed an extensive interagency and multinational approach to their efforts. An interagency and multinational approach is usually essential for success. Many of the centers even reach out to nongovernmental organizations such as the private companies in the commercial shipping, fishing, and tourism sectors. These private-sector assets can provide detailed information that will greatly enhance national and international MDA efforts. Most shipping companies are willing to cooperate with governmental MDA efforts if by doing so they enhance their maritime clients' security, while also speeding up the cargo-handling process.[35]

Mix of High and Low Technology

In 2007, the US Navy embarked on a frenzied effort to improve its MDA capabilities. Much of the effort was focused around high-tech solutions to various MDA challenges. Unfortunately, many of the proposed solutions did not survive the dramatic budget reductions after the recession of 2008. However, the Navy's MDA enhancement efforts did produce excellent national and international dialogue on emerging MDA challenges. The undertaking also identified a number of new procedures and low-cost, commercial, off-the-shelf (COTS) MDA systems and technologies that could easily be purchased and integrated into its existing MDA efforts. Some of these key MDA tools and systems include the following.

Integrated Coastal Radar and Visual Observation Posts. Most nations have limited surface-radar coverage of their ports, harbors, and coasts. However, these systems are usually not integrated, and they provide only a fraction of the MDA picture to only a limited number of maritime security organizations. While not exactly high tech, coastal radar and observation posts, both fixed and mobile, can provide significant information to maritime security command centers. Mounting such systems at a higher elevation—on hills, towers, or even on aircraft—can greatly extend their effective ranges. Inclusion of electronic support measure (ESM) sensors can extend detection ranges even farther through a phenomenon called *ducting*. These systems can be augmented (or replaced) by human resources. Prior to and during World War II, for example, Australia established an extensive coast-watcher network, manned by 700 volunteers. The network extended from New Guinea in the west to Vanuatu in the east, over 1,200 nautical miles or 2,200 kilometers.[36] Such efforts, combined with a robust secure communication network, can assist governments tremendously in understanding maritime activity within their maritime domains.

Automatic Identification System (AIS). This device is an automatic tracking system used by ships, maritime patrol aircraft, and various vessel trafficking services (VTS) to identify and locate vessels at sea. Information provided by AIS equipment, such as the vessel's unique identification, position, course, and speed, is displayed on a screen to assist the vessel's officers and allow maritime authorities to track and monitor vessel movements.[37] The 2002 International Maritime Organization's International Convention for the Safety of Life at Sea (SOLAS) treaty included a mandate that required most vessels over 300 gross tons (GT) on international voyages to fit an AIS transceiver on board. This was the first mandate for the use of AIS equipment, and it affected approximately 100,000 vessels. Ships fitted with AIS transceivers and transponders can be tracked by AIS base stations located along coastlines or, when out of range of terrestrial networks, through a growing number of satellites that are fitted with special AIS receivers capable of resolving a large number of discrete signatures.

Integrated Weather Prediction Data. In order to minimize time and fuel costs, merchant shipping companies seek the most efficient route a carrier can take from point A to point B. While merchant ships will occasionally take a longer and more circuitous route to avoid areas of known pirate activity or maritime conflict, the most common reason a merchant ship diverts from the most efficient route is extreme-weather avoidance. Every MDA effort should have access to timely weather prediction information for its area of responsibility and area of interest. Fortunately, many of these maritime weather forecasts are available online at no cost. For example, the US Navy's Fleet Numerical Meteorology and Oceanography Center or FNMOC, in Monterey, California, and the Joint Typhoon Warning Center (JTWC) in Pearl Harbor, Hawaii, routinely post many of their predictive products.[38]

Common Reporting Standards for Contacts of Interest

Passing time-perishable information between agencies and nations requires common reporting standards to ensure that the information is easily
understood by the recipient and quickly forwarded to the operational forces
responsible for acting on that information. This challenge is more difficult
than it appears. Unlike the global aviation system, the maritime transportation system has evolved over centuries into an uneven patchwork of policies
supported by incompatible sensor and information systems.[39] Agencies, governments, and the commercial sector must work closely together to develop
common reporting standards that can be easily implemented. This will require commercial entities to change their historic "culture of secrecy."[40] It will
also require MDA professionals to work together to overcome the endemic
institutional barriers to timely communications and warning.

Training and Education

Developing and maintaining a current and useful common operational picture of one's maritime domain requires much more than sensors and platforms; it requires a highly educated and trained workforce able to make sense
out of the massive amount of data it will receive daily, turning it into actionable intelligence. These professionals must also have the skills needed to share
data with other law enforcement and regulatory agencies in a timely manner,
and in a digestible format. Failure to properly educate and train the MDA
workforce could lead decision-makers and operational force commanders to
act on erroneous or misleading "intelligence." This will quickly undermine
the MDA fusion center's credibility and utility. MDA training and education
efforts should be strategically designed, and driven by the current and future
needs of the organization, with an emphasis on joint, interagency, and multinational perspectives on information collection and analysis.

Training and education are not the same. Training focuses on doing things
right; education teaches us to do the right things. Operational forces are only
effective if decision-makers can develop the most effective strategies to employ them properly (see Chapter 5). All the organizations listed above, as well
as the many organizations that support them, have established comprehensive
training and education systems. Training takes place in the classroom as well
as in the field, culminating in regional exercises designed to simulate real-
world contingencies. Education comes in the form of seminars, workshops,

and symposia, expanding minds, sharing experience, and introducing new ways of solving problems. Training is all about standard operating procedures; education prepares individuals to deviate from SOPs in response to changing circumstances. Training is all about correct answers; education is about better questions. Both are needed for an effective and efficient maritime security government workforce.

Conclusion

Achieving comprehensive maritime domain awareness will always be more of a goal than an obtainable objective. However, as this chapter attempts to show, governments can greatly enhance their MDA by following a simple, step-by-step process to learn what a maritime nation needs to consider when it establishes a new maritime intelligence or domain awareness capability, or when it enhances an existing MDA center. It is essential that governments develop a deep understanding of their areas of responsibility, and then delineate manageable areas of interest. Few nations will have the ability to adequately monitor their entire AORs, much less their AOIs. However, governments need to do the best they can with what they have—identifying gaps and shortfalls, and knowing where they can get assistance.

Today's maritime challenges threaten all nations that rely on the global maritime commons for their prosperity if not their survival. This reality provides tremendous opportunities for interagency and multinational cooperation on MDA and other maritime security issues. Governments should not be intimidated or mesmerized by costly MDA technologies, since many of the best MDA systems are already available in the commercial sector. Some of them are simply individuals exchanging information and observations. Developing a common reporting language and procedures among agencies and regional neighbors is essential to the prompt and accurate dissemination of critical MDA data.

More than technology, however, nations must invest in the professionals who will man and operate the MDA "systems of systems," which are essential for success. All the intelligence, surveillance, and reconnaissance (ISR) assets in the world cannot compensate for a poorly trained or uneducated workforce. Education, training, and exercises can ensure these national and multinational collaborative MDA efforts are performed efficiently and effectively, generating essential trust among all participants in the process.

Notes

1. IMO MSC.1/Circ.1343, amendments to the *International Aeronautical and Maritime Search and Rescue (IAMSAR) Manual*, May 24, 2010, International Maritime Organization, Regulatory Guidance, available online at http://www.iadclexicon.org/maritime-domain-awareness (accessed November 11, 2014).

2. RADM Jonathan W. White, USN, "Advancing Maritime Domain Awareness (MDA) for the Fleet and Nation," *Navy Live*, January 16, 2014, available online at http://navylive.dodlive.mil/2014/01/16/advancing-maritime-domain-awareness-mda -for-the-fleet-and-the-nation (accessed October 20, 2014).

3. One major exception to the maritime intelligence's focus on enemy navies instead of transnational organized crime in the early twentieth century was the US Coast Guard's signals intelligence (SIGINT) and interdiction effort during Prohibition (1920–1933). During the so-called Rum War, the US Coast Guard developed advanced, radio direction-finding capabilities to help them locate smugglers of illegal alcohol at sea. See Donald L. Canney, "Rum War: The US Coast Guard and Prohibition," Coast Guard Bicentennial Series, available online at http://www.uscg.mil/history/articles/RumWar.pdf (accessed January 2, 2015).

4. John Keegan, *Intelligence in War: The Value—and Limitations—Of What the Military Can Learn About the Enemy* (New York: Vintage Books, 2002), 256–57.

5. Wyman H. Packard, Captain, USN (Ret.), *A Century of US Naval Intelligence* (Washington, DC: Department of the Navy, 1996). See also, Christopher Ford and David Rosenberg, *The Admiral's Advantage: US Navy Operational Intelligence in World War II and the Cold War* (Annapolis, MD: Naval Institute Press, 2005).

6. Office of Naval Intelligence, Piracy Analysis and Warning Weekly (PAWW) Report, December 30, 2014, available online at http://www.oni.navy.mil/Intelligence _Community/piracy/pdf/20141230_PAWW.pdf (accessed January 1, 2015).

7. The United States was among the nations that participated in the third United Nations Conference on the Law of the Sea, which took place 1973–1982, and resulted in the international treaty known as the United Nations Convention on the Law of the Sea (UNCLOS), and it also participated in the subsequent negotiations on modifications to the treaty 1990–1994. UNCLOS came into force in 1994. Although the United States now recognizes the UNCLOS as a codification of customary international law, the US Senate has yet to ratify the UNCLOS treaty, although successive administrations have abided by its provisions.

8. Roger Villar, *Piracy Today: Robbery and Violence at Sea since 1980* (London: Conway Maritime Press, 1985), 7.

9. The US Navy is the Department of Defense's Executive Agent for Maritime Domain Awareness. RADM Jonathan W. White, USN, http://navylive.dodlive .mil/2014/01/16/advancing-maritime-domain-awareness-mda-for-the-fleet-and-the -nation (accessed October 20, 2014).

10. The Shipping Law Blog, *The World's Top Ship Registries*, April 28, 2011, available online at http://www.theshippinglawblog.com/2011/04/article-worlds-top-ship -registries-flag.html (accessed November 11, 2014).

11. Lincoln Paine, *The Sea & Civilization: A Maritime History of the World* (New York: Alfred A. Knopf, 2013), 583.

12. Ibid., 585.

13. GCaptain, "CSCL's Second 19,100 TEU Giant Named and Delivered in South Korea," December 26, 2014, available online at http://gcaptain.com/cscls-second -19100-teu-giant-named-delivered-south-korea/?utm_source=feedburner&utm _medium=feed&utm_campaign=Feed%3A+Gcaptain+%28gCaptain.com%29 (accessed December 27, 2014).

14. Lincoln Paine, *The Sea & Civilization: A Maritime History of the World*, 586.

15. Michael S. Schmidt and Thom Shanker, "To Smuggle More Drugs, Traffickers Go Under the Sea," *New York Times*, September 9, 2012, available online at http:// www.nytimes.com/2012/09/10/world/americas/drug-smugglers-pose-underwater -challenge-in-caribbean.html?pagewanted=all&_r=0 (accessed November 11, 2014).

16. Daisy R. Khalifa, "The Next Playground for Hackers?" *Seapower*, November 2014, 12–14, available online at http://www.seapower-digital.com/seapower/ november_2014#pg14 (accessed November 11, 2014).

17. Ibid., 14–15.

18. The United States National Strategy for Maritime Security, September 2005, available online at https://www.ise.gov/sites/default/files/0509%20National%20 Strategy%20for%20Maritime%20Security.pdf (accessed November 23, 2014).

19. There are nine separate US agencies represented at JIATF-South from the Department of Defense, the Department of Homeland Security, Department of Justice, and the Central Intelligence Agency. The countries of Brazil, Canada, Chile, Colombia, the Dominican Republic, Ecuador, El Salvador, France, Mexico, the Netherlands, Panama, Peru, Spain, and the UK contribute liaison officers.

20. Evan Munsing and Christopher J. Lamb, "Joint Interagency Task Force-South: The Best Known, Least Understood Interagency Success," *Institute for National Strategic Studies Strategic Perspectives, No. 5.* (Washington, DC: National Defense University Press, June 2011).

21. The IMB's Piracy Reporting Centre, available online at https://icc-ccs.org/ piracy-reporting-centre (accessed November 15, 2014).

22. Keith Bradsher, "North Korean Ploy Masks Ships Under Other Flags," *New York Times*, October 20, 2006, available online at http://www.nytimes.com/2006/10/20/ world/asia/20shipping.html?fta=y&_r=0 (accessed November 23, 2014).

23 The Australian Border Protection Command's website, available at http:// www.customs.gov.au/aboutus/protectingborders/bpc/default.asp (accessed November 22, 2014).

24. Hugh Barkley, "Australia's Border Protection Command," *NMIO Technical Bulletin, Vol. 1* (National Maritime Intelligence-Integration Office: 2012), 4–5.

25. Angel Rabasa and Peter Chalk, *Non-Traditional Threats and Maritime Domain Awareness in the Tri-Border Area of Southeast Asia*, RAND National Defense Institute, Occasional Paper, 2012, 21–25.

26. Alexis Romero, "US Firm to Build Phl $18-M Coast Watch System," Philstar.com Headlines, August 26, 2013, available at http://www.philstar.com/head lines/2013/08/26/1135271/us-firm-build-phl-18-m-coast-watch-system (accessed December 14, 2014).

27. Ibid.

28. Camille Diola, *"Credible Defense Posture Within Noy's Term-Gazmin,"* Philstar.com Headlines, July 29, 2014, available at http://www.philstar.com/head lines/2014/07/29/1351649/credible-defense-posture-within-noys-term-gazmin (accessed November 22, 2014).

29. Nicolas Lim, LTC, Changi Information Fusion Centre, *NMIO Technical Bulletin,* Volume 1 (National Maritime Intelligence-Integration Office, 2012), 3.

30. Ibid., 3.

31. Dean Wingrin, "Navy to Establish Maritime Awareness Centres," *Defence-Web,* March 19, 2012, available at http://www.defenceweb.co.za/index.php?option =com_content&view=article&id=24437:navy-to-establish-maritime-awareness -centres&catid=51:Sea&Itemid=106 (accessed November 22, 2014).

32. Rajat Pandit, "India's Air and Maritime Shield Against Terror Stronger, but Gaps Persist," *Times of India,* September 6, 2014, available at http://timesofindia.india times.com/india/Indias-air-and-maritime-shield-against-terror-stronger-but-gaps -persist/articleshow/41827550.cms (accessed November 17, 2014).

33. Ibid.

34. Munsing and Lamb, 23.

35. Brian Santos and Levin Lunday, "Maritime Domain Awareness: International Involvement to Promote Maritime Safety and Security," *Naval Institute Proceedings,* Summer 2009, 24–28, available online at http://www.uscg.mil/proceedings (accessed December 23, 2014).

36. Petar Djokovic, "The Coastwatchers and Ferdinand the Bull," *Semaphore,* Sea Power Centre, Department of Defence, Australia, Issue 4, 2014.

37. Santos and Lunday, 25.

38. The Naval Oceanography Portal contains updated products of worldwide conditions produced by the Fleet Numerical Meteorology and Oceanography Center, the Joint Typhoon Warning Center, and other US Navy commands, available at http:// www.usno.navy.mil/FNMOC/meteorology-products-1 (accessed on November 5, 2014).

39. Joseph L. Nimmich and Dana A. Goward, "Maritime Domain Awareness: The Key to Maritime Security," in Michael D. Carsten, ed., *International Law Studies, Volume 82, Global Legal Challenges: Command of the Commons, Strategic Communications, and Natural Disasters* (Naval War College Press, 2008), 58.

40. Ibid., 60.

9 The Role of Institutional Leadership

Robert Schoultz

WHY BUILD A STRONG MARITIME SECURITY INSTITUTION? To what end? For what purpose? In his book, *Start with Why,* Simon Sinek eloquently makes the point that success is very often a function of the leader's commitment to purpose—the right purpose.[1] Given that this chapter is about building strong Maritime Security Institutions, it is important to start there. The textbook answer to the purpose of the institution may be "To protect maritime assets, resources, and infrastructure from threats internal or external," but there is an even more fundamental question: "What motivates the leader?" Leaders must ask themselves why they *want* to build strong Maritime Security Institutions. If your primary objective is to build a truly great institution, a great culture that has momentum that can sustain itself beyond your tenure, is extremely effective in conducting its missions, and reflects the best in your country and your government, then this chapter may give you some insights.

A Constellation of Maritime Security Institutions

Maritime security is a broad genre and is, by its nature, interagency within any government. It will include all branches of the military, though primarily naval and coast guard forces. It will also have a number of key stakeholders in local, regional, and national government institutions, as well as academic and research institutions. The rubric might also include nonprofits and nongovernmental organizations (e.g., coastal maritime environmental groups), as well as private contracting companies that perform maritime security functions for profit. Added to all that, maritime security has an important international component, requiring collaboration and information sharing with other nations, given that many or most threats come from and return to the international arena.

In the US government alone, the National Strategy for Maritime Security: National Maritime Domain Awareness Plan[2] includes in its list of key stakeholders in maritime security the Department of Transportation, Department of State, Department of Defense, Department of Commerce, Department of Homeland Security, and the US intelligence community (which includes a large number of organizations and institutions under the Director of National Intelligence), as well as a number of offices, advisory groups, and committees with functions specific to, or related to, maritime security. The US plan also includes in the list of stakeholders international partners and seeks "to unify and support efforts to enhance domain awareness, advance decision-making, and provide the best possible setting to make maritime information appropriately available to all members of the Global Maritime Community of Interest (GMCOI)."[3]

While most governments are smaller and less complicated than that of the United States, managing maritime security anywhere is an act of collaboration. Wherever an organization sits in a constellation of institutions, agencies, committees, and groups responsible for various pieces of the maritime security process, effective leadership is key to its success. Great leadership helps develop great organizations, which achieve great results. Leaders of maritime security institutions must take the extra step of getting all stakeholders to work as a team. Single institutions—and single governments—cannot do what is needed.

Leadership Versus Management

Managers focus primarily on process; it is very important that they ensure that the processes and the mechanics of running the institution function efficiently and well. But the *people* who carry out the processes are even more important—how they are motivated, inspired, trained, and held accountable.

And who are these people? They are military officers, civilian officials, and all their employees who execute any aspect of maritime governance, the functions of which are listed in Chapter 6.

The leader's key function within the institution is to create a climate that brings in good people and allows and inspires them to use processes already in place in the best interest of the institution. The leader should be like an orchestra conductor, managing the tempo, bringing the various sections in at the right times and with the proper intensity, to make beautiful music. The leadership function includes oversight over the managerial function, providing guidance and direction, while also ensuring that overzealous or incompetent managers don't undermine the vision of the leader, the morale of the institution, or the effectiveness of the institution's processes. Good people—inspired, motivated, and properly led—will make sure that a well-intentioned process doesn't get in the way of effectiveness in carrying out the mission. The leader has the key function of providing guidance and direction to the people in the institution and adjudicating between different perspectives that may be in conflict.

Because management is such a critical function and must be done well, the leader must guide the management of an institution. But to effectively lead the institution, the leader must let managers manage, remaining focused on the leadership function. Unfortunately, many leaders are promoted into leadership positions after having succeeded as managers, and when they get uncomfortable in the more nuanced, ambiguous and context-dependent dimensions of good leadership, they often default to performing management functions, where results are easily seen and measured. Circumstances sometimes do demand that leaders get very involved in management functions, but when they do, the leadership function suffers; connections are not made, relationships are not nurtured, reputations are not protected, opportunities are missed, and momentum is lost. Organizations that are managed instead of led progress slowly and cautiously, and only in directions that their internal processes allow.

The Sri Lankan Navy struggled for decades to defeat the Sea Tigers of LTTE until its leaders decided to do something different. As detailed in Chapter 12 of this volume, they went after the high-seas logistics support network that sustained the ground campaign. That is not something a manager would have done. Leaders seek to build and sustain *commitment* from the people within the institution to its mission and purpose. Managers focus more on *compliance* with the process and rules. Although a focus on both commitment and compliance would be ideal, leaders should concentrate on commitment, allowing managers to focus on compliance. Confusing or conflating these two functions can be devastating to an organization.

Taking Charge

All institutions can be improved through restructuring or reform. Long-serving and new leaders alike should do two things before imposing change: learn the truth about what is happening in the institution, and decide whom to trust—and how much.

Learning the truth about what is happening requires understanding the organization and how it works. Though much of this may be a management function, the leader must understand the basic processes in order to provide assistance and effective oversight and support to the institution's managers. Finding out what is really going on will take time and require listening to and balancing a number of different perspectives that will be given to the new leader. When listening, the leader will pay attention not only to what is being said, but also what is *not*. Leaders must stay positive, express confidence, and ask questions that help shape and inform their vision: "To take this organization to new levels, what do we need to do? What is my role? What do you need from me?"

Inefficient and counterproductive processes cause untold frustration in many institutions and inhibit creative and productive work. Coming to understand these processes often provides the reform-minded leader with the immediate opportunity to streamline and simplify procedures to free up the best people to contribute more. It can be helpful to ask three simple questions:

1. What are we doing that we shouldn't be doing?
2. What are we not doing that we *should* be doing?
3. What are we doing not nearly as well as we should be?

It is crucial that the leader hear the voice of the people at the lower end of the institution's structure. A reliable and trustworthy conduit for passing information as well as the awareness of contentious issues and dissatisfaction are key if the leader is to know what is going on. In military organizations, the Senior Enlisted Advisor, or Command Sergeant Major, ensures that the leader knows what the troops think and that the troops understand how the leader thinks. Institutions that do not have a person with this role are less effective, or even dysfunctional, because of miscommunication and misperceptions that result from the many filters in information flow from the top to the bottom and back. Leaders must determine, early on, how they will communicate with those at the bottom of the chain, and how they and their needs will be communicated to the leader, with as few filters as possible.

Deciding whom to trust is among the most important things leaders can do, especially in the early stages of their tenure as leaders of their institutions. Leaders who trust no one may be able to protect themselves for a while, but not indefinitely. All leaders need trusted confidants who they believe understand the leader's vision and goals, and who have the best interests of the leader and the institution at heart. Most people understand that the leader's trust is the most important currency within their organization; it is a source of power, and those who have it will sacrifice much to protect it. Once that trust is lost, it is difficult if not impossible to recover.

Leaders of dynamic institutions are always challenged when dealing with the inevitable "turf wars" of competitive subordinate leaders, aggressively promoting the importance of their role in fulfilling the mission of the institution. It frequently happens that subordinate leaders who are most aggressive, ambitious, and effective within the institution—or who had favored status with a previous leader—have gotten the most resources and attention. Rebalancing and synchronizing the institution's priorities with the leader's vision is a common challenge for all leaders and sets the tone for how they will lead their institutions.

One generalization applies to good leadership in any sector: it demands achieving objectives consistently and over the long run. "Over the long run" is key because it demands the support, full engagement, and buy-in of those who make up the institution, with the values, goals, and objectives of the institution and its leader. "Over the long run" requires consistency in application of fundamental principles and values of the institution. Poor and even toxic leadership may be able to coax or intimidate good results out of a group of people for a short while—but never (or rarely) over time.

Institutional Culture

Humans universally desire to be part of a great and strong tribe—and leaders of elite institutions use that tribal impulse to build a great organization. Great leaders seek ways to pull people together to build a strong sense of pride in themselves, their work, and each other while doing something important. As Peter Drucker famously quoted, "Culture eats strategy for breakfast, operational excellence for lunch, and everything else for dinner."[4] Every organization has its own culture—its own expectations, rituals, history, and momentum in how people work together. An organization with a poor or weak culture, at best bumbles along, no matter how well articulated its strategy may be, or how effective its processes may look on paper. A great institutional culture has its own momentum, and while no one individual makes the institution, the leader can have the greatest impact, positively or negatively, on the institution's culture.

But an *elite* institution has a special culture, one that others seek to emulate and in which people work effectively and confidently together and hold each other accountable to overcome a multitude of challenges and difficulties. Successful governments establish a climate within which all institutions wish to be considered "elite," but it takes the vision of the leader to actually create a sense of being elite within an institution. Creating a sense of being elite can be difficult in public-sector institutions, where government policies on hiring and retention and other personnel policies often serve as levelers, making it difficult for any one institution to develop policies, processes, and a culture that would allow them to stand out. And yet, with imagination, patience, time, and energy put into relationship and credibility building—and occasionally an effective hammer—the leader can shift the direction of an organization, up the level of commitment, and create a sense of being elite. Imaginative leadership finds a way to make average workers very good, very good workers great, and great workers truly exceptional.

A great culture consistently achieves its objectives over the long run, and that is what makes a great institution—not great strategy, operational excellence, or anything else. The US Navy SEALs are an example of consistent performance that has led to increased resources and a very strong institutional brand. The cultures of great institutions—whether recognized as elite or not—are characterized by an exceptional sense of purpose, trust, focus, and camaraderie.

Purpose (with Passion)

An elite culture has a strong sense of purpose that creates the energy and commitment to success that drives great institutions to succeed in spite of many obstacles. Articulating a compelling sense of purpose, and a vision for fulfilling it, is one of the most important early steps a leader must take. It gets everyone pulling in the same direction to create the momentum to carry the institution and the leader forward. The "with passion" modifier on "purpose" is important. The leader must regularly demonstrate passion for the purpose, and transmit that passion to others in the institution. Over time and with patience, and competent process building, the leader's passion becomes the institution's passion, and people within the institution hold each other accountable for how well they are fulfilling the purpose.

Simon Sinek's *Start with Why* makes the case that a strong sense of purpose (or "Why") creates energy and inspiration that drives the "How" and the "What" which are in the outer rings of what he calls his "Golden Circle." All are important, and the leader must be engaged in all three, but the leader's focus should be on reinforcing and sustaining the energy that comes from the "Why."[5] For private-sector businesses, the purpose is normally to provide a quality product or service that enhances life in the greater community, and to be well rewarded for it. For public-sector institutions, the purpose will similarly be about providing superb service to the government and the nation in the realm of the responsibility of the institution—in maritime security, for example.

The purpose of a maritime security institution is normally to protect the people and economy of the nation by aggressively pursuing a specific aspect of assuring the safety and security of the nation's maritime assets, resources, and infrastructure, in a manner consistent with the values of the nation's constitution. But a creative leader will find a more compelling and action-oriented expression of this purpose. Depending on the specific function of the institution, it might sound something like this: "We will protect our ports, ships, and facilities." "We will be the hardest targets for our enemies to attack." "We will do so in a manner that makes our nation proud of us!"

The sense of purpose must be articulated often and exemplified in the leader's behavior, actions, and decisions. The credibility of leaders is tied to their passion and effectiveness in fulfilling the institution's purpose, and the credibility of the purpose will likewise reflect on the leader. The leader must always be aware of the natural cynicism of those who distrust lofty goals, especially when, inevitably, the realities of politics or external factors force a temporary compromise between principles and purpose. In such cases, the leader must address his or her continued commitment to the purpose, for which compromise is occasionally necessary. Otherwise, the credibility of commitment to the purpose is compromised, and the leader gives fuel to the cynics who gleefully seek excuses to resist change.

To ensure success over the long run, the leader must stay out of the weeds, focused on the purpose, and ensure that the institution does the same. While people in the institution may be fighting over who owns which trees, the leader must constantly remind them of the forest, and of the fire that is coming over the next ridge.

Vision

A vision is the leader's guidance on *how* to fulfill the purpose. It is the guiding "How" that supports the "Why." Much has been written on organizational vision statements. One of the best articulations of the role of vision is *Built to Last*, in which the authors state that the vision must reflect the core ideology and the envisioned future of the institution.[6] Most public institutions have a legislated mission or purpose, further interpreted by a political leader in the statement of purpose. The institution's leader may rephrase that legislated mission or purpose, to give it emotional power and resonance.[7] The implementing vision should provide a reference point or anchor to guide decision-making. The following suggestions might be useful in developing the vision for a maritime security institution:

- Compose a rough draft with trusted members of your team, with representatives from all sectors of the institution.
- Request comment, seeking to determine whether the draft vision "resonates" or speaks to issues that are important to those most impacted by it. If you want honest feedback, the draft should be presented as an idea the leadership team is considering, rather than as the new leader's draft vision. Ensure that it includes input and feedback from those who do the most difficult physical work and take the greatest personal risks in maritime security. It should not work solely for the administrators and the bureaucrats.
- Make the vision simple and easy to remember; it should roll off the tongue easily and inject energy into the purpose of the institution.
- Make the vision speak much more to the *heart* than to the head.
- Tie specific changes planned in processes, direction, and priorities directly to the new vision, endowing them with immediate credibility.

- Have key leaders within the organization repeat the vision frequently, with passion and commitment, to those within the organization at all levels.
- Hold leaders accountable within their organizations for complying with the dictates of the vision. If a vision is violated for the sake of expediency, it loses its power and credibility. Therefore, leaders should plan to accept short-term losses in order to enhance the credibility of the vision, or if it must be violated, plan to explain why a particular circumstance required a somewhat different approach, but emphasize that the vision is still intact.

When I was the commander of the East Coast US Navy SEAL Teams, I had a four-point vision that gave guidance to my organization as to our values and priorities in how we fulfilled our mission. It also inspired passion and commitment. Four points were easy for me (and everyone else) to remember, and I believe it was key to my effectiveness as a leader. My vision was the following:

1. We run to the sound of the guns.
2. Our center of gravity is forward.
3. We excel in ambiguous environments.
4. We take care of each other and our families.

Simple and easy to remember, it articulated our organization's values and priorities. It also avoided corporate- or institution-speak. To be effective, a vision should inspire, guide, and ground your team—every day—and be constantly referred to by leaders and followers alike.

Trust

Elite organizations are characterized by a sense of trust throughout the organization, built upon the strength of commitment to the common purpose. The leader has a very important role in creating a climate of trust. Transparency in decision-making, to whatever degree circumstances permit, creates a climate of trust. If people in the institution feel that they are being kept in the dark and manipulated by their leaders, and that unknown processes and factors are determining their futures and fates, a climate of fear and distrust takes hold; employees will be watching their backs and spending an inordinate amount of time and energy taking defensive measures to protect themselves from exploitation. One simple formula that serves as a good foundation for creating an organization with a strong sense of trust is this: lead with humility, integrity, and transparency.[8]

The most important step leaders can take in developing a sense of trust in their organizations is to first be trustworthy themselves. Leaders should do what they say they will do, or explain why it wasn't possible. The second most important step is to pursue aggressively (with humility, integrity, and transparency) the institution's purpose, holding others accountable for doing so, even when costs are involved. When that happens, people see a different kind of leader, inspiring the best people to trust and follow. The leader should give credit to others at every opportunity, and not showboat or seek personal credit.

There are two fundamental rules for developing trust:

1. Pay constant attention. You have to keep working on building trust and never take it for granted.

2. When trust appears to be breaking down, see rule number 1.[9]

Focus

Purpose and trust require focus to accomplish their ends. Focus is more immediate, actionable, and measurable. Institutions have to get things done. Elite institutions create a track record of getting things done, and done well. To do this, individuals in the organization—and the organization itself—must focus their power, energy, and commitment on tasks, large and small, to achieve results consistent with the purpose. Futurist Joel Barker said, "Vision without action is merely a dream. Action without vision just passes the time. Vision *with* action can change the world" (italics added).[10] Focus is what puts the commitment into the purpose by putting into action those steps necessary to realize and fulfill it.

The ability to focus—to plan and execute effectively—distinguishes elite from other run-of-the-mill institutions. Focus is the operational excellence part of the elite equation. It represents the requirement for discipline, efficiency, and economy of effort to be as effective as possible in whatever the institution undertakes. A strong sense of purpose inspires the team to focus on fulfilling it, by prioritizing resources, efforts, and projects, and executing decisions efficiently and effectively. In the realm of focus, the leader is the driver, but the manager is the executor. Focus is the "How" and the "What" in Sinek's Golden Circle. The leader must stay engaged in these realms as well, while staying rooted in the "Why."[11]

Camaraderie

Camaraderie is an intangible that has to grow organically. It is not the same as friendship, which is also a complicated concept but on some levels can be similar. Camaraderie grows out of common fundamental values and trust that have been tested under stress—that is, with focus.

One of the best ways to develop camaraderie—as well as trust, purpose, and focus—is to share adversity. People under stress demonstrate a great degree of willingness to set aside personal comfort, preferences, and advantage for the good of the larger purpose, the mission, and the group as a whole—and this builds camaraderie. Leaders need to learn who the team players are and who, under stress, are the people clearly in it primarily for themselves. In military units, the camaraderie of those who have been together in combat is well known. Comrades may not be close friends, or choose to spend a lot of time together, due to different cultural values, backgrounds, or interests, but they are comrades based on having had to count on each other and not let each other down under the adversity of combat. Camaraderie that builds an institution's sense of being elite can also be developed in nonprofits, for-profits, and yes, even in public institutions with more administrative functions. It simply takes a bit of imagination.

Most institutional responsibilities don't include military combat, or a lot of physical adversity, but the work inherent in maritime security offers opportunities to share and appreciate the experiences of those doing the most challenging work in the most adverse environments. Creative leaders can find ways to build camaraderie through shared risk, adversity, and stress—physical and otherwise—through intense tabletop or command-post exercises or contingency-planning drills, which can also create the shared sense of overcoming adversity and other challenges to accomplish group goals. Such experiences not only build camaraderie but also help create a "no excuses" ethos in an organization.

The leader's demeanor and own willingness to work with people at all levels of the institution can be very effective in creating a sense of camaraderie in an institution. Camaraderie is often best built in small groups, in pockets within the institution. If managed properly, various groups that share a sense of camaraderie can create a broader sense of it within the whole institution. Remember, people's loyalty to the institution begins with their personal experience of that institution, featuring the people and teams with whom they work every day. And that is where camaraderie should begin.

Hiring and Firing

The most common complaint one hears from good people working in large institutions is that mediocre performance is routinely tolerated and becomes the accepted standard. People whose performance is mediocre or poor are seldom held accountable and often are even rewarded with a decreased workload. Excellent performers are then overburdened with work to overcome the deficit created by poor performers. When people are not held accountable for mediocre performance, great performers become demoralized and either leave or give up. Elite institutions do not tolerate those with a pattern of mediocre or poor performance.

Jim Collins, in his seminal work *Good to Great*, insists that the first and most important step to creating a great institution is to "get the right people on the bus"—even before creating a strategy, or a vision.[12] A maritime security institution may switch the metaphor to getting the right people "in the boat." Though new leaders may possess prerogatives to bring in their own people, it is much more important to the long-term success of the institution to assemble team players, people who are willing to subordinate personal agendas to the greater purpose of the institution. The ideal employee would be a team player with talent, but selecting team players with the capacity and willingness to learn is a much smarter move than seeking primarily talent and connections.

Taking care of the institution's best performers is very important. They need to be kept challenged and know that their work is appreciated; they need to know that they are making a difference. Dealing with those at the bottom of the competency and motivation spectrum is more challenging. Every institution has such people, and there are three fundamental steps in dealing with them. Seek to co-opt them into being more positively engaged with the team. If that doesn't work, isolate or marginalize them to the extent that they can at least contribute something without hurting the institution. If that doesn't work, take steps to move them on. Firing those who continue to provide poor or mediocre performance, or who are unwilling to step up to new challenges, is an unpleasant but often necessary step. Tolerating mediocre performance or employees who are pursuing their own agendas sends a message that the leadership is not serious about its purpose.

But the large majority of people in the institution will not be superstars, nor will they be the incompetent stallers who seek to get paid for as little work as possible. Those in the middle are the most interesting challenge. How do leaders tap into their potential and get them more engaged, more motivated, and more effective in their contribution to the team? The great leader's passion and example should move many of them in the direction of the super-performers. Daniel Pink's book, *Drive*, makes the point that most people are motivated to improve performance by three things: *autonomy*—the sense that they have some control over their work and its impact; *mastery*—the ability to become really proficient at their work; and *purpose*—a sense that what they are doing is important in a larger perspective.[13] The great leader considers how culture, climate, and process can be combined to inspire those in the middle and keep them from sliding into the sump of mediocrity that characterizes so many institutions.

Taking Risk

Good judgment and risk management are inherent in all leadership positions. Careful consideration of risk can help determine whether a plan or decision has a reasonable chance of success, and whether potential benefits justify likely, or even unlikely, costs. Having the wisdom, contacts, and credibility to seek and get advice in difficult cases is a very important leadership function. But an overemphasis on risk management can focus an organization on all that can go wrong, rather than on what should go well. Too much focus on risk can cause the institution to waver in its commitment to the bold action that is required to ensure success.

While risk management is clearly and always a function of leadership, great leaders maintain a bias for bold action. This bias keeps leaders and their teams looking for opportunities to advance the institution and its purpose. At the same time, risk management helps them recognize hidden dangers, prevent surprise, and mitigate negative, unintended consequences. Leaders should not, however, manage risk or take bold action on their own; others in the institution need to be on board. To succeed, managing risk and implementing bold action demand an intricate interaction and integration between the leader's goals and objectives and the personal biases, goals, and objectives of others in the institution. This balance is a team effort.

Looking Outside the Institution

This chapter has thus far primarily addressed building a great institution internally. Representing the maritime security institution effectively to important stakeholders external to the institution can be equally or more important to the institution's success.

Given the complex nature of the maritime domain, the multidimensional threats within it, and the many stakeholder functions involved in the security apparatus, no single institution can manage it all well. It is by its very nature multiagency and international in scope. Security in the maritime domain, where there is often no single institution or individual in charge, demands that institutional leaders collaborate extensively with other institutions and entities. Without a powerful enforcing authority, collaboration must be based upon trust and willing cooperation between institutions and individuals—built upon strong personal relationships and a common and unifying purpose. Collaboration skills are essential to the success of the leader of a maritime security institution.

Leaders of different maritime security institutions must work together to develop and coordinate issues of policy, establish common procedures for planning and coordinating operations, and develop procedures and mechanisms for sharing and using technology. They must develop simple, effective, and repeatable processes for working together in crisis prevention and response, and these processes must be regularly reviewed and tested. With no designated leader or authority to drive institutional interoperability, leaders must learn to influence and lead other institutions on the basis of a carefully developed credibility and a track record of success and competence. Successful collaboration demands that leaders and their subordinates be willing to adapt to and accommodate different institutional cultures and approaches to problem solving *to leverage the strengths of each, for the greater good of all.*

A program of effective and routine information sharing is absolutely essential for security institutions to work together successfully. This demands creative information technology (IT) mechanisms and processes that permit sharing of intelligence while avoiding compromise. Common IT protocols and regular exercises and meetings should facilitate sharing of technology, lessons learned, and best practices to improve the entire maritime security posture, both nationally and with international partners.

Regular, well-planned, and challenging tabletop exercises create opportunities for leaders and staffs of different institutions to communicate, build trust and relationships, test plans and processes, and identify and work through friction points before a crisis occurs. In order to build and maintain credibility with their partners, leaders must be ready to assume risk and trust others. Disagreements will always arise, and great leaders develop processes to work through friction points to find common ground and compromise solutions that permit progress to continue.[14]

The skill set required to be an effective leader in an interagency or cross-functional organization (whether ad hoc or standing) is somewhat different than what is needed to create an elite culture within an institution. Some leaders are natural networkers and network builders. For others, this task does not come naturally and can be challenging. Here are a few tips for the leader who may not be experienced at networking and bridge building with outside entities:

- Tap into the networks within your institution. Many of those individuals in networks within the institution will have established credibility and influence with key counterparts and stakeholders in other public- and private-sector entities. They will also have insights into the challenges of working with other institutions.

- Learn the personal histories and professional biographies of key leaders of institutions with whom you will be working. Finding areas of common interest outside of professional duties will facilitate trust and relationship building.

- Learn the cultures of the organizations that are key to the success of your institution. Learn their values and idiosyncrasies, and when possible, bend to them when dealing with those organizations. Whenever possible, meet them in their spaces and get a sense for who they are and how their people behave and treat each other.

- Seek to focus on areas where interests, values, and priorities overlap during discussions that reveal friction points on values, priorities, or directions. Without surrendering, seek to keep disagreements as low-key as possible, and do your best to keep the issues from becoming personal or undermining future opportunities for collaboration.

- Seek opportunities to do favors and help other institutions. New leaders should go out of their way to build equity with other organizations. This may require some convincing of others in the leader's own institution, but it is an effective strategy for building long-term alliances. For a great list of leaders who have achieved fabulous success by going out of their way to help others, without any explicit expectation in return, see Adam Grant's book *Give and Take*.[15]

Institutional Ethics

Often overlooked or taken for granted, ethics is a topic of major importance. The leader of any institution is driven to achieve desired results, but the ethical component of good leadership concerns *how* those results are achieved and how power and influence are exercised. Great leadership effectively and ethically exercises the power of influence apart from, but not independent of, position and other sources of power.[16] The ethical imperative of great leadership is to inspire and influence organizations to achieve great results using legitimate and ethical means, and actively seek to minimize any harm that may come from those means.

Below are several fundamental ethical considerations for the institutional leader: the example the leader sets, treating all with dignity; the difficult issue of special entitlements for the leader; and the even more difficult problem of corruption at the top. All these considerations come back to how great leaders influence and inspire ethical performance from those in their institutions.

Example

Leaders set the ethical tone within their organizations, more by how they behave than by what they say. *The leader's example and behavior are the most important tools the leader has to influence great and ethical performance.* People watch their leaders to find out what the "real" rules are, more so than listening to what leaders say about the rules. While the term and concept *leadership by example* has become something of a cliché, it is difficult to find leaders who actually strive to live and behave in a way that they want the people in their institution to emulate. Bad leaders make exemptions for themselves to rules that apply to the rest of the organization, and they justify such exceptions on the basis of their position and responsibilities. While sometimes this may indeed be justified, unless managed properly, when leaders make exceptions for themselves they undermine their own credibility as well as the rules they expect others to follow. What those within the institution see when they watch their leader is important, but what they *think* about what they see is critical.

Dignity

Respect for the human dignity of all people is a fundamental ethical value. It applies in simple cases of everyday conduct as well as to responses to egregious violations of ethical or other institutional protocols. This is not just a nice-to-have moral platitude; it is a good rule to follow for very practical reasons. A person who feels his or her dignity has been attacked or demeaned will often become an enemy forever. The rule of thumb is to attack the performance rather than the performer. Even those who have violated fundamental rules of the institution should be dealt with by those in authority in a manner that does not demean their personal dignity—and this includes during disciplinary processes, if or when dismissal is in order. As noted previously, the whole organization is watching, and apart from being the right thing to do, always respecting people's human dignity sets a high moral bar.

Entitlements

"Rank has its privileges" is an old saying in the military, often known by the shorthand RHIP. Many of the entitlements, perks, and privileges allowed for leaders of public institutions are statutory—that is, written into law or determined by instructions and guidance within the institution. Those lower in the organization understand and expect that those at the top who carry exceptional responsibilities associated with leadership should have certain privileges that help offset the additional stress that goes with the job. How extensive those privileges should be, and how they are perceived, varies not only according to the culture of the institution but also to the history and traditions of the nation the institution is serving. Cultures with a strong tradition of hierarchy and social class will usually afford more privileges to those in leadership positions than will those with more egalitarian traditions. Yet, in any environment, the leader who intends to build a culture of ethical service in a public institution will be careful to manage these privileges to ensure that they are perceived to clearly help the leader serve the mission of the institution as a whole and not merely the ego and pleasure of the leader.

The phenomenon of leaders believing they are entitled to privileges well beyond the moral or other authority of their position has recently become known as the *Bathsheba syndrome*, named for the biblical story of King David, who acted on a sense of entitlement to the wife of one of his officers.[17] Every culture and society has many examples of leaders who have acted on a sense of entitlement that went beyond what their positions warranted, with negative and occasionally tragic consequences for themselves and their organizations. When the perks and privileges assumed by those in leadership positions (especially those in public service) appear to exceed what reasonable people believe to be legitimate to their positions—and necessary to keep good people in positions of leadership—the credibility of the institution and its leaders erodes.

Corruption

The issue of entitlements is related to the difficult issue of government corruption, which plagues nearly all countries. What constitutes corruption varies from one country to another, but leaders should exemplify acceptable standards of behavior, always putting the best interests of their institution and its purpose ahead of personal gain or personal advantage. Leadership by example is critical here; if leaders are perceived to be profiting from their position in ways not sanctioned by law or culture, then the door is open for all to behave in similar ways. Not only is the leader compromised, but so are the institution and its purpose. Great leaders of great institutions do not tolerate corruption in their organizations.

Conclusion

Building a great maritime security institution is a long-term project that begins with an act of will by someone with passion and commitment. It takes time, intent, and patience, and it begins with commitment to the purpose of the institution, passion for that purpose, a vision for what is possible, and a belief in the ability of the people who make up that institution to fulfill a critical role for their nation. Protecting the nation's maritime assets, resources, and infrastructure from those who would either exploit them for personal gain or undermine them to harm the security of the nation is indeed a critically important role that needs to be done well every day. Maintaining that constant vigilance and focus requires an institution with a strong sense of purpose, internal trust, and—to sustain itself over the long term—camaraderie. For the leaders of maritime security institutions to succeed, it is imperative that they be effective at collaborating and coordinating with the many other institutions that work in the maritime security domain. An elite maritime security institution has its own forward momentum and drive—due in large part to the will, vision, and leadership of its leader. When the leader and the institution have generated positive momentum toward becoming a great culture and model institution in the service of the people, even the great leader will have to sprint to keep up. And the great leader never ceases to work hard, every day, to be worthy of being the leader of a great team.

Notes

1. Simon Sinek, *Start with Why-How Great Leaders Inspire Everyone to Take Action,* (New York, Penguin Group Inc., 2009), 6–7.

2. National Strategy for Maritime Security: National Maritime Domain Awareness Plan, Appendix B, available at https://www.hsdl.org/?view&did=747691 (accessed October 9, 2014).

3. Ibid., iv.

4. Peter Drucker was one of the most influential business management thought leaders of the twentieth century. This quote is often attributed to him, and some claim that it was made famous by Mark Fields, CEO of Ford Motor Company; yet, some dispute exists about whether he actually did say this—and if so, where and when. The point, however, is that the culture of an organization will prevail over strategy, operational excellence, and other basic business practices, and this perspective has gained wide acceptance. This quote is widely seen and used to make this point.

5. Sinek, op. cit., 37–47.

6. Jim Collins and Jerry I. Porras, *Built to Last: Successful Habits of Visionary Companies* (New York: Harper Collins, 1994), 220–36.

7. The purpose of a government institution is normally referred to as its *role*, defined as the continuing purpose for an organization.

8. For additional insight into the value of trust within an organization, see Stephen M. R. Covey, *The Speed of Trust: The One Thing That Changes Everything* (New York: Free Press, 2006).

9. James Kouzes' presentation to the National Council on Culture and Leadership, San Diego, CA, October 19, 2014. James Kouzes with Barry Posner wrote one of the most widely read books on leadership in the last twenty-five years: *The Leadership Challenge, 5th Edition* (San Francisco: Jossey-Bass, 2012).

10. Joel Barker, Futurist, Author, Lecturer, Film Maker, from his website at: http://www.joelbarker.com/perfect-quotes/vision-without-action-is-just-a-dream-action-without-vision-just-passes-the-time-vision-with-action-can-change-the-world/.

11. Sinek, op. cit., 137–43.

12. Jim Collins, *Good to Great* (New York: Harper Collins, 2001), 41–64. Collins notes that getting the right team in place will help create and get the right buy-in to the strategy and vision that the leader wants. Getting the right people "on the bus" begins creating the momentum that can take an organization "from Good to Great."

13. Daniel Pink, *Drive: The Surprising Truth About What Motivates Us* (New York: Riverhead Books, 2009).

14. Author interview, RADM Elizabeth Train, USN, Director, National Maritime Intelligence-Integration Office (NMIO), October 8, 2014.

15. Adam Grant, *Give and Take: Why Helping Others Drives Our Success* (New York: Penguin Books, 2013). In this book, Grant distinguishes between *givers* (give and help with no expectation of return), *matchers* (give with expectation of at least equal return), and *takers* (seek to win in every transaction). He elaborates on how givers succeed by seeking to provide value to others wherever they can, not primarily seeking value for themselves. In so doing, they develop great networks for collaboration and support.

16. Thomas Cronin and Michael Genovese, *Leadership Matters: Unleashing the Power of Paradox* (Boulder, CO: Paradigm, 2012), 101. This book is an excellent look at how good leadership is very much context dependent. The authors' discussion of leadership through history, and especially their treatment of Machiavelli, is particularly noteworthy.

17. Dean C. Ludwig and Clinton O. Longenecker, "The Bathsheba Syndrome," *Journal of Business Ethics*, April 1993.

10 The Maritime Legal Framework

Aubrey Bogle

T HE PREFACE TO THIS BOOK AND THOSE TO PREVIOUS
chapters have highlighted the complexity of the legal parts necessary to build the foundation for effective maritime security institutions. This
complexity exists in large part due to the elements that make up the legal regime, and thus define the rule of law in the maritime domain. These include
international law—in particular, the 1982 UN Convention on the Law of the
Sea (UNCLOS), UN Security Council resolutions, and other multilateral[1] and
bilateral treaties, including, in some circumstances, the Law of Armed Conflict and domestic laws (national constitutions, national/local statutes, and
regulations). The UNCLOS treaty is a monumental work that has been widely
praised. Reflecting the views of most nations, the Encyclopedia of Earth has
called it "one of the largest, and likely one of the most important, legal agreements in history."[2]

Notwithstanding its breadth and power, UNCLOS has not resolved all the
disputes arising from maritime claims. Many of these disputes arise from efforts to enlarge a State's internal waters (waters shoreward of the baseline over
which the State exercises full sovereignty) by drawing straight baselines or
claiming historic bays and other waters that other States argue do not comply
with the language and intent of the drafters of UNCLOS. One such claim is
China's assertion of authority over waters and islands in the South China Sea
encompassed by the "nine-dashed line." In the view of several countries in the
region, this claim infringes on waters and islands these countries are entitled

to under the provisions of UNCLOS, and has resulted in considerable turmoil in the region.

One of the central contributions of the UNCLOS treaty was to partition the global maritime domain in such a way that most governments agree to abide by zones of graduated sovereignty that reduce their legal authorities inversely to their distance from an established baseline. Once the baseline is determined (again, using rules outlined in the treaty), a State can expect others to observe a 12-nm territorial sea, a 24-nm contiguous zone, and a 200-nm exclusive economic zone. The treaty is flexible enough to allow for negotiated exceptions, but the relative certainty of maritime zones has permitted all governments to understand how much territory they must monitor, and the legal authority they may exercise in each zone. The universal acknowledgment of zoning has reduced much of the confusion around the fringe of what is commonly referred to as the high seas, where the original "global commons" dilemma challenges all governments.

The maritime domain[3] is vulnerable to a wide array of threats,[4] including illegal, unreported, and unregulated (IUU) fishing; environmental degradation; smuggling; human and narcotics trafficking; piracy; proliferation of weapons of mass destruction; and aggressive actions, including terrorism.[5] These maritime threats all have significant land-based dimensions, whether related to the origin of the threat, the locus of its effects,[6] or the land-based capabilities required for preventive or enforcement interventions. For example, the suicide boat attacks by al-Qaeda terrorists on the USS *Cole*, which was preparing to refuel while moored in Aden Harbor in 2000, and on the French flag petroleum tanker vessel MV *Limburg*, under way in the Gulf of Aden in 2002, were initiated shoreside.[7] This chapter will examine the legal aspects of maritime security and consider, to some degree, the land-based elements that must not be disregarded when developing a State's maritime security strategy.

International Law and Maritime Security

International law establishes the outer limits of the jurisdictional parameters of domestic law and regulations in the maritime domain. Stating this proposition another way, a State may establish jurisdiction to take action against terrorist acts, for instance, up to but not exceeding the limits established by international law. Thus, a comprehensive understanding of the relevant international law is a key aspect of building a domestic maritime security strategy firmly grounded in the rule of law.

The thirteen multilateral UN treaties and their protocols relating to international terrorism define offenses that involve or relate to violence that is already, or may be addressed by, appropriate governmental action, usually legislative, within a State's jurisdiction.[8] Terrorist acts by their nature are likely to cause serious injury or death. For this reason, many of the proscribed offenses involve conduct that may be criminal under many domestic legal systems (and therefore the creation of new criminal offenses in the implementing legislation is not always necessary).[9]

In the maritime domain, maritime law enforcement authority assigned to a State's maritime law enforcement agency (hereinafter called Coast Guard[10]) is an exercise of sovereignty by a State. The following discussion will use a model maritime terrorism law enforcement statute to identify the jurisdictional limits, geographic and otherwise, within which a State's maritime law enforcement authority—and therefore the Coast Guard's authority—may be exercised. As noted earlier, the outer boundaries of this authority are defined by international law.[11] The extent to which a State avails itself of this jurisdictional authority is a national decision made on the basis of its specific circumstances and objectives. These decisions are made on the basis of political priorities and reflected in domestic legislation and regulations. Ideally, they would also reflect the realities of the State's operational ability to conduct Coast Guard maritime law enforcement operations that would effectively enforce these laws and regulations.

Three basic international principles govern a State's ability to assert its maritime law enforcement authority or jurisdiction over a vessel, person, or area of water:

- First, under international law, the flag State (the State in which a vessel is registered) has the authority under UNCLOS to exercise its jurisdiction anywhere that vessel may be found in the world.[12] With this broad grant of jurisdictional authority, the flag State also has the obligation to regulate and ensure the safe and lawful operation of a vessel flying its flag.[13] The flag State also has the obligation to ensure that the vessel operates in a manner that is consistent with international law.[14]

- The second principle is that all nations have an equal right to navigate in and over international waters—that is, waters outside of any State's territorial sea. This freedom of navigation is often referred to as *high-seas freedoms of navigation and overflight* or, more simply, *high-seas freedoms*.[15] To ensure this principle of high-seas freedoms is respected, international law generally prohibits, with certain carefully delineated exceptions, any State from asserting jurisdiction over foreign vessels outside national waters. Thus, unless one of the few exceptions is applicable, a vessel in international waters is said to be subject to the exclusive jurisdiction of the flag State.[16]

- Finally, the third principle is that a vessel in the national waters of a State other than its flag State is ordinarily subject to the concurrent jurisdiction of the coastal State and the flag State; the nature and extent of the coastal State's jurisdiction vary with the particular circumstances. These principles are incorporated into the model maritime law enforcement (MLE) statute that follows.

The abbreviated model MLE statute that follows is presented as an example of how a specific maritime legal framework is worded. It utilizes the fictional State of Maritima, introduced in Chapter 3 of this book, in the section entitled "Protecting 'Maritima,'" as the hypothetical coastal State for which the Coast Guard is serving as the maritime law enforcement agency confronting maritime terrorism. References are provided within this chapter's model statute to provisions of the Law of the Sea Convention, where appropriate. In addition to the 1982 Law of the Sea Convention, there are several other Conventions relating to terrorism and piracy in the maritime domain. Because of limited space herein, the development of model MLE statutes for other maritime crimes is left to the reader.

Model Maritime Law Enforcement Statute for Maritime Terrorism Offenses in Maritima[17]

Article 1 Definitions
Vessel of Maritima. For purposes of this statute, the term "vessel of Maritima" means:

(A) A vessel granted the nationality of Maritima;

(B) A vessel owned in whole or part by:

    (1) Maritima or a territory, commonwealth, or possession of Maritima;

    (2) A political subdivision of Maritima;

(3) A citizen or national of Maritima; or

(4) A corporation created under the laws of Maritima or any political subdivision of Maritima, or any territory, commonwealth, or possession of Maritima; unless the vessel has been granted the nationality of a foreign nation in accordance with the laws of that State and Article 91 of the 1982 United Nations Law of the Sea Convention, and a claim of nationality or registry for the vessel is made by the master or individual in charge at the time of the enforcement action by an officer or employee of Maritima authorized to enforce applicable provisions of Maritima's law; and

(5) A vessel that was once granted nationality under the laws of Maritima and, in violation of the laws of Maritima, was either sold to a person not a citizen of Maritima or placed under foreign registry or a foreign flag, whether or not the vessel has been granted the nationality of a foreign nation.

(C) For purposes of this section, a *"vessel without nationality"* includes:

(1) A vessel aboard which the master or person in charge makes a claim of registry, which claim is denied by the flag nation whose registry is claimed;

(2) A vessel aboard which the master or person in charge fails, upon request of an officer of Maritima empowered to enforce applicable provisions of Maritima law, to make a claim of nationality or registry for that vessel;

(3) A vessel aboard which the master or person in charge makes a claim of registry and the claimed nation of registry does not affirmatively and unequivocally assert that the vessel is of its nationality; and

(4) A vessel aboard which the master or person in charge makes claim of registry under two or more States. A claim of registry under subparagraph (1) or (3) may be verified or denied by radio, telephone, or similar oral or electronic means. The denial of such claim of registry by the claimed flag nation is conclusively proved by certification of the Minister of Foreign Affairs or the Minister's designee.

(D) For purposes of this section, a *"claim of nationality or registry"* only includes:

(1) Possession on board the vessel and production of documents evidencing the vessel's nationality in accordance with Article 91 of the 1982 United Nations Law of the Sea Convention;[18]

(2) Flying a flag nation's ensign or flag; or

(3) A verbal claim of nationality or registry by the master or person in charge of the vessel.

Article 2 Duties and Prohibitions

(A) Terrorist acts

(1) An act or omission in or outside Maritima which constitutes an offence within the scope of a counter terrorism convention.

(2) Any person commits an offense who, by any means, unlawfully and intentionally, causes:

(a) death or serious bodily injury to any person; or

(b) serious damage to public or private property, including a place of public use, a State or government facility, a public transportation system, an infrastructure facility or to the environment; or

(c) damage to property, places, facilities, or systems referred to in paragraph (2) b) of the present article resulting or likely to result in major economic loss, when the purpose of the conduct, by its nature or context, is to intimidate a population, or to compel a Government or an international organization to do or to abstain from doing any act,[19]

(B) Recruitment

Whoever recruits another person to be a member of a terrorist group, or to participate in the commission of a terrorist act, shall be punished with [penalties which take into account the grave nature of those offenses].[20]

(C) Supply of weapons

Whoever supplies or offers to supply weapons to a terrorist group, a member of a group, or to another person to participate in the commission of a terrorist act shall be punished with [penalties which take into account the grave nature of those offenses].[21]

(D) Provision of support

Whoever provides support [as defined in national law or jurisprudence] to a group, a member of a group, or to another person to participate in the commission of a terrorist act shall be punished with [penalties which take into account the grave nature of those offenses].[22]

(E) Agreement to commit a terrorist act

(1) Whoever agrees with one or more persons to commit a terrorist act shall be punished with [penalties which take into account the grave nature of those offenses].

(2) [For the person to be punishable, one of the parties to the agreement must have undertaken an [overt] act in furtherance of that agreement.][23]

(F) Planning and preparation

Whoever makes plans or preparations with the intention or in the knowledge that such planning or preparation is for the purpose of committing a terrorist act shall be punished with [penalties which take into account the grave nature of those offenses][24]

(G) Incitement

Whoever distributes, or otherwise makes a message available to the public, with the intent to incite the commission of a terrorist act, where such conduct, whether or not directly advocating the commission of a terrorist act, causes a danger that one or more such acts may be committed, shall be punished with [penalties which take into account the grave nature of those offenses].[25]

(H) Relevance of commission of an act of terrorism

(1) For a conduct listed in sections (B) to (G) above to constitute an offense, it shall not be necessary that a terrorist act under section (A) be actually attempted or committed.

(2) A conduct constitutes an offense under sections (B) to (G) regardless of whether or not it is aimed at supporting, preparing, or instigating an offense in the same State.[26]

(I) Attempt

Whoever attempts to commit any of the offenses established in this Chapter shall be punished with [penalties which take into account the grave nature of those offenses].[27]

(J) Complicity and contribution

(1) To the extent not otherwise defined by law, the following acts defined as offenses in this Chapter shall be punished with [penalties which take into account the grave nature of those offenses]:

(a) participating as an accomplice in terroristic actions;

(b) organizing or directing others to commit such offenses;

(c) contributing to the commission of one or more such offenses by a group of persons acting with a common purpose, where such contribution is intentional and is made with the aim of furthering the criminal activity or criminal purpose of the group [in the knowledge of the intention of the group to commit such offense].[28]

(K) Liability of legal entities

    (1) Any legal person located in the territory of Maritima or organized under its laws is liable when a person responsible for its management or control has, in that capacity, committed an offense set forth in these Model Provisions.

    (2) The legal entities liable in accordance with para.1 of this section are subject to [effective, proportionate, and dissuasive criminal, civil, or administrative sanctions].

    (3) The application of para.1 of this section is without prejudice to the responsibility of those individuals as perpetrators of or accomplices to the offense.

Article 3 Jurisdiction and Prosecution

(A) The offenses defined in this Chapter shall be prosecuted if committed within the territory, internal waters, or territorial sea, and to the degree that the exercise of national jurisdiction is permitted by the 1958 Geneva Conventions on the High Seas and Contiguous Zone or the 1982 Convention on the Law of the Sea, within the exclusive economic zone, continental shelf, contiguous zone, or archipelagic waters, and on the high seas or in any place outside the jurisdiction of any State.

(B) The offenses defined in this Chapter shall also be prosecuted if committed:

    (1) On board or against a ship registered in or entitled to fly the flag of Maritima, wherever located; or

    (2) On or against a maritime structure licensed by or operating within the jurisdiction of the government of Maritima.

(C) Jurisdiction to prosecute shall also lie in the State apprehending or having custody of a person accused of committing an offense defined in this Chapter.

(D) Jurisdiction to prosecute shall also lie when the person accused of committing an offense defined in this Chapter is a citizen or national of the enacting State, or is a resident foreign national, or is a stateless person.

(E) Jurisdiction to prosecute shall also lie when an offense defined in this Chapter is committed against a person who is a citizen or national of, or is a foreign national resident in, Maritima, or is a stateless person.

(F) Jurisdiction to prosecute shall also lie when an offense defined in this Chapter is committed on board a foreign-flag ship, where:

   (1) The law enforcement or other public authority of the port or place where the ship is located has been requested to intervene by the State whose flag the vessel is entitled to fly, or by the ship owner, or the master or other person on board the ship; or

   (2) The commission of that act or a collateral act has disturbed the peace and tranquility of a port or place under Maritima jurisdiction.

Article 4 Extradition

(A) Where Maritima is a Party, or becomes a Party, to an International treaty listed in this Chapter, the offenses falling within the scope of that treaty are recognized as extraditable offenses in respect of another State that is also a party to the same treaty.

(B) Extradition of an alleged offender may take place when another State has jurisdiction over the offenses defined in this Chapter. The possession of jurisdiction by Maritima shall not preclude the extradition of an alleged offender to another State.

(C) If another State having a direct connection to the incident or other substantial interest claims jurisdiction with regard to an offense in this Chapter, and the alleged offender cannot or will not be promptly brought to trial in Maritima, the alleged offender shall be extradited to such requesting State. If multiple States with reasonable jurisdictional claims make requests for extradition in the absence of a trial in Maritima, the alleged offender shall be extradited to one of the requesting States.

(D) For the purpose of extradition, the offenses set forth in this Chapter shall not be regarded as political offenses, or as offenses connected with a political offense or offenses inspired by political motives.

Article 5 Enforcement

(A) Subject to the rights and limitations in International Law and Maritima domestic law and Maritime Law Enforcement Directives, an officer of the Coast Guard may at any time hail, stop, and board any vessel subject to Maritima jurisdiction and take all necessary action to enforce the provisions of Maritima law, this Chapter, and any directives issued under the authority of this Chapter, including detaining the vessel and diverting the vessel to a port, and execute any legal process issued by an officer or court of competent jurisdiction.

(B) With respect to a vessel that has the nationality of a foreign State, officers of the Coast Guard, when Maritima is authorized by the flag State, may:

    (1) Board the vessel;

    (2) Search the vessel; and

    (3) If evidence of involvement in illicit traffic is found, take appropriate action with respect to the vessel, persons, and cargo on board, to carry out these functions and any actions requested by the flag State.

(C) Officers of the Coast Guard are authorized to seize and secure any vessel, substances, merchandise, or contraband liable to seizure, and to arrest any person liable to arrest by virtue of violation of this Chapter, or customs or smuggling law or directive, and to use the minimum necessary force to seize or arrest the same. Vessels seized and persons arrested shall be turned over to the customs service or any other authorized Maritima agency for prosecution and disposition.

(D) In addition to enforcing the provisions of this Chapter and other related Maritima law and directives, the Coast Guard shall prepare the necessary documentation to support a violation or violations of this Chapter, Maritima law, or a directive, or to document action taken at the request of the flag State.

Article 6 Penalties

(A) Any person who commits an offense defined in this section shall be punished in accordance with the penalties set forth in the Maritima National Legal Code.

(B) Any vessel involved in violating provisions of this Chapter may be seized by an officer of the Coast Guard and, along with its cargo, forfeited to the Maritima National Treasury if:

    (1) It was built, purchased, outfitted in whole or in part, or held in Maritima or elsewhere for the purpose of being employed to smuggle a controlled substance into Maritima; or,

    (2) It is of Maritima registry and is, or has been, used or employed, or attempted to be used or employed, at any place, for any such purpose in violation of this chapter, and if not subsequently forfeited to

Maritima or to a foreign government, shall be seized and forfeited, along with its cargo.

(C) Any other property that is used, or intended for use, to commit, or to facilitate the commission of an offense under this Chapter shall be subject to seizure and forfeiture.

(D) Any vessel or property subject to seizure and forfeiture for violation of this Chapter shall be processed under the provisions of law relating to the seizure, summary and judicial forfeiture, and condemnation of property for violation of the customs laws, including the disposition of such property or the proceeds from the sale thereof.

Article 7 Interagency Coordination

Officers of the Coast Guard, in carrying out the responsibilities of this Chapter, are authorized to work with other governmental agencies and the Ministry of Defense, as provided for by Maritima law and directives.

Article 8 Designation of Competent National Authority[29]

(A) The Maritima Ministry of the Interior is designated as the authority to receive and respond to requests made pursuant to any bilateral or regional agreements to carry out Maritima mutual support obligations under these Model Provisions.

(B) Maritima Ministry of the Interior is designated as the authority to receive requests from relevant domestic authorities and assist in transmission of requests to foreign States.

(C) When a vessel of Maritima or a vessel flying its flag or otherwise claiming its nationality is reasonably believed to be engaged in actions in violation of any offense defined herein, Maritima may request the assistance of other States in suppressing its use for that purpose.

(D) The Maritima Ministry of the Interior is responsible for responding expeditiously to requests from other States to determine whether a vessel that is flying its flag is entitled to do so, and to requests for authorization to take appropriate measures in regard to that vessel.

(E) The Maritima Ministry of the Interior is to ensure the speedy and efficient consideration and execution of incoming requests and to oversee the quality and effectiveness of outgoing requests.

(F) In addition to the above functions, the Maritima Ministry of the Interior is authorized to provide information and advice to its counterparts in other States, and advise relevant domestic authorities concerning the requirements for authorization requests being submitted to foreign States, including provisional authorization and presumptive authority.

(G) When Maritima acts on behalf of a foreign State, the Maritima Ministry of Foreign Affairs shall make sure that the foreign State is promptly informed of the results of that act.

Conclusion

As evidenced by this small sample, the maritime legal framework is complicated. It is a panoply of domestic and international laws and treaties meant to underpin reasonable, ethical, and effective operations across the spectrum of institutions and governments acting together. The framework is complex because the global maritime domain itself is complex. Governments require rules to provide security and other services to their populations, and to guide negotiations over disputed interpretations of the law. Given the importance of legal considerations, it is not a surprise to discover that virtually all maritime security institutions find they need organic legal expertise to navigate smoothly. Good maritime governance and enhanced capacity would be largely unattainable without a legal framework with which to connect them to maritime security. Security in the maritime domain takes place in a legal context, and maritime law is framed in a security context. Much of this book deals with how governments enforce maritime laws. Those who enforce them must develop an understanding of where the laws come from, how they are formed, and why.

Notes

1. These multilateral treaties constitute the legal framework for much of the international effort against terrorism. They will be discussed in more detail later in this chapter.

2. United Nations Convention on the Law of the Sea (UNCLOS), 1982. The treaty can be found online at http://www.un.org/depts/los/convention_agreements/texts/unclos/unclos_e.pdf. Daniel Hollis, "United Nations Convention on Law of the Sea (UNCLOS), 1982," in Tatjana Rosen and Dawn Wright, eds., *Encyclopedia of Earth*, June 22, 2010, updated February 26, 2013, available at http://www.eoearth.org/view/article/156775/ (accessed December 16, 2014).

3. *Maritime domain* has been defined in many ways. One generally accepted definition is found in the US National Plan for Maritime Domain Awareness. In this plan,

maritime domain is defined very broadly to include: "all areas and things of, on, under, relating to, adjacent to, or bordering on the sea, ocean, or navigable waterway, including all maritime related activities, infrastructure, people, cargo, and vessels and other conveyances." *US National Plan for Maritime Domain Awareness, Plan for the National Strategy for Maritime Security,* December 2013, iv.

4. "The deliberate misuse of the maritime domain to commit harmful, hostile, or unlawful acts, including those against the maritime transportation system, remains an enduring threat to the safety and security of the American people, to wider US national security interests, and to the interests of our international allies and private sector partners." Presidential Policy Directive 18 (PPD-18): Maritime Security (August 14, 2012), 2.

5. A wide-ranging survey of maritime terrorism issues was provided by Peter Chalk in Chapter 2 of this volume.

6. See Thomas R. Mockaitis "The Mumbai Attacks," in Paul Shemella, *Fighting Back: What Governments Can Do About Terrorism* (Stanford, CA: Stanford University Press, 2011) 317–31, for an excellent discussion of the Mumbai attacks. For another account of the Mumbai attacks, see also David Kilcullen, *Out of the Mountains* (New York: Oxford University Press: 2013), 52–66. There were also numerous attacks against land targets in Sri Lanka by the Liberation Tigers of Tamil Eelam (the Tamil Tigers). The Tamil Tiger fighters often deployed from ships at sea to attack land targets in Sri Lanka during that country's lengthy civil war. A detailed account of that campaign can be found in Chapter 12 of this volume.

7. For an insightful discussion of the intelligence, policy issues, and political decisions leading to the use of Aden as a US Navy refueling port in spite of the known presence of terrorists in Yemen, see Raphael Perl, Specialist in International Affairs, et al., "Terrorists Attack on USS Cole: Background and Issues for Congress," *Congressional Research Service Report for Congress,* updated January 30, 2001 Order Code RS20721 (Washington, DC: Library of Congress).

8. Some of these treaties relate only to aviation issues, others are only peripherally related to the maritime domain.

9. In the 1970s, 80s, and 90s, prior to 9/11, relatively few national criminal laws explicitly defined terms such as *terrorism* or *terrorist crimes.* Rather, they implemented the earlier international terrorism conventions by creating specific offenses dealing with particular terrorist acts, such as hijacking, aircraft assaults, and hostage taking, or they determined that existing criminal law and procedure would sufficiently cover the offensive conduct of terrorism. Japan and South Korea, for example, rely heavily on the coverage of ordinary criminal law provisions rather than defining specific terrorism-related offenses or elements that convert traditional offenses into terrorism-specific offenses.

10. This chapter will use the commonly used term *Coast Guard* as a generic name collectively to refer to maritime forces such as navies, maritime police, customs agencies, border patrol, etc., and combinations of these agencies, tasked to accomplish maritime law enforcement missions. When a naval or a Coast Guard maritime force

performs maritime military defense functions, these forces utilize capabilities, personnel, and equipment to achieve a mission distinct from the law enforcement or revenue function associated with the civil and criminal authority functions.

11. Maritime terrorism, as the worst-case scenario within the spectrum of maritime threats, is profiled in the sample legal framework.

12. UNCLOS Article 94. As a matter of comity, a flag State does not exercise its jurisdiction in the territorial sea or internal waters of another State without that State's permission. Frequently this principle is incorporated in the maritime law enforcement statutes and regulations of the flag State.

13. UNCLOS Article 94.

14. UNCLOS Article 94.

15. UNCLOS Article 87 (1).

16. UNCLOS Article 92(1).

17. This abbreviated model MLE statute is largely drawn from the USCG Model Maritime Code (2008 Edition); *Maritime Criminal Acts: Draft Guidelines for National Legislation*, Legal Committee, International Maritime Organization LEG93/12/1, August 15, 2007; and *Model Legislative Provisions Against Terrorism* (draft), published by the UN Office on Drugs and Crime (Vienna, February 2009) and emphasizes the traditional law enforcement approach.

18. *Article 91: Nationality of ships*
   1. Every State shall fix the conditions for the grant of its nationality to ships, for the registration of ships in its territory, and for the right to fly its flag. Ships have the nationality of the State whose flag they are entitled to fly. There must exist a genuine link between the State and the ship.
   2. Every State shall issue to ships to which it has granted the right to fly its flag documents to that effect.

19. Source: Draft Comprehensive Convention Against International Terrorism, Appendix II to Letter from the Chairman of the Sixth Committee addressed to the President of the General Assembly. The full-text electronic version of the Commonwealth Secretariat's Model Provisions is available at: https://www.unodc.org/tldb/pdf/Commonwealth_modellaw_terr.pdf. This is only one of a number of possible definitions of terrorism. States with existing legal definitions of terrorism should, absent good reasons to the contrary, incorporate that definition into this provision in lieu of the language provided here.

20. The inclusion of a specific recruitment offense stems from Security Council Resolution 1373, which specifically requires States to "suppress recruitment of members of terrorist groups" (para. 2-a).

21. The adoption of a supply-of-weapons model provision stems from Security Council Resolution 1373, which specifically requires States to "eliminate the supply of weapons to terrorists" (para. 2-a).

22. This article is meant to contain a catchall provision, reflecting also a general requirement of Security Council Resolution 1373. For the sake of legal precision, it is for each State's laws or jurisprudence to identify exactly the types of support conducts

to be criminalized. In this context, the *Model Legislative Provisions on Measures to Combat Terrorism*, produced by the Commonwealth Secretariat, provides examples of such conducts (harboring of persons, provision of training and facilities, arrangements of meetings, etc.). The full-text electronic version of the Commonwealth Secretariat's Model Provisions is available at: https://www.unodc.org/tldb/pdf/Commonwealth_modellaw_terr.pdf. Also, legislative drafters may wish to refer to Article 7 of the Council of Europe Convention on the prevention of terrorism, which proposes its own definition of the offense of training for terrorism.

23. The language of this article draws in part from Article 5 (a)(1) of the UN Convention Against Transnational Organized Crime (TOC Convention).

24. This article contains another catchall provision. It differs from Article 18 (Provision of Support) in that the offense set forth in this article may well include plans for a terrorist act to be committed by the planner himself, whereas Article 18 covers support given to others, or for the benefit of a group.

The conducts set forth in this article are also distinct from the attempt to commit offenses: whereas an attempt is usually punishable on condition that the completed crime does not take place for reasons that are independent of the willingness of the person, the perpetrator of the planning conducts set forth in this article is punishable even when he voluntarily desists (for whatever reason) from the commission of the planned offense (for example, a person makes careful preparations with a view to committing a terrorist act, and then decides not to carry it out because he deems that the political climate is no longer appropriate, or because he receives instructions to cancel the operation).

The planning conducts set forth in this article are different from those set forth in Article 19 (Agreement to Commit an Offense), since the planning may well be committed by one individual only.

In principle, under the proposed approach, a person that plans to commit a terrorist act and subsequently carries it out (or at least attempts it), would be charged with both the planning conduct and the terrorist act. The concrete penalty applicable for a plurality of offenses committed by the same persons is then for each State to identify, in accordance with national rules concerning the calculation of the final penalty to be applied in case of cumulative offenses.

25. This proposed article takes into account requirements stemming from a series of universal legal instruments, notably:

- Security Council Resolution 1624(2005), Paragraphs 1(a) and 3 of which call upon States to "prohibit by law incitement to commit a terrorist act or acts" and "to counter incitement of terrorist acts motivated by extremism and intolerance."
- The International Covenant on Civil and Political Rights, Article 20, requires action to ensure that: "Any advocacy of national, racial or religious hatred that constitutes incitement to discrimination, hostility or violence shall be prohibited by law." While the covenant does not require that the prohibition of incitement be achieved by means of criminal law,

criminalization can certainly be considered an appropriate channel, as it is difficult to imagine non-penal sanctions being adequate to control the more extreme cases of incitement to violence.

- Letter dated September 14, 2006 from the Chairman of the Security Council Committee established pursuant to resolution 1373 (2001) concerning counter-terrorism addressed to the President of the Security Council containing the *Report of the Counter-Terrorism Committee to the Security Council on the Implementation of Resolution 1624* (2005), published in UN Security Council document S/2006/737, dated September 15, 2006, available online at http://daccess-dds-ny.un.org/doc/UNDOC/GEN/N06/520/37/PDF/N0652037.pdf?OpenElement.

- Apologie du terrorisme and "incitement to terrorism": Developments in the Case-Law of the European Court of Human Rights in connection with the cases concerning "apologie du terrorisme" and incitement to terrorism, Report of Council of Europe Committee of Experts on Terrorism, (Strasburg: Council of Europe Publishing, 2004). This report analyses the situation in member and observer States of the Council of Europe and their different legal approaches to the phenomenon of the public expression of praise, justification and other forms of support for terrorism and terrorists, referred to in this publication as "Apologie du terrorisme" and "incitement to terrorism."

26. Para.1 of this article clarifies that the offenses set forth in this section are punishable as *autonomous* criminal conducts—that is, regardless of whether or not they lead to the actual commission of a terrorist act. Also, the perpetrator of the support offenses should be distinguished from the accomplice, the latter of which is usually held criminally responsible on condition that the main offense take place, or is at least attempted. (Provisions relating to complicity are covered separately in Article 2(J) of the Model Statute.)

When accompanied by the appropriate investigative/procedural legal tools, para.1 has the potential to provide national authorities with the legal authority to disrupt ongoing preparations for terrorist offenses, without having to wait for the actual violence/damage to occur.

Paragraph 2 ensures that support/preparatory conducts are punishable even when the criminal plans are aimed to the commission of a terrorist act/offense related to terrorism abroad (e.g., if A recruits B in country X with a view of having him/her committing a terrorist offense in country Y, A has committed an offense under the laws of country X).

In doing so, para.2 reflects the broad requirement of Security Council Resolution 1373, calling upon States to "prevent those who finance, plan, facilitate or commit terrorist acts from using their respective territories [. . .] against other States or their citizens" (para. 2-d).

A practical implication of this principle among State Parties to the same Counter Terrorism convention includes the implementation of the *aut dedere aut judicare* principle (the obligation of a state party to extradite or prosecute criminal violators). This principle is reflected in Article 4 of the Model Statute.

27. The requirement to criminalize attempt is to be found in all of the international treaties, and it is reflected in this model provision accordingly. The notion of *attempt* is to be construed in line with the way in which the criminal laws and/or jurisprudence of each adopting State define it.

28. The requirement to criminalize participation as an accomplice (letter a) is found in all of the international treaties listed in the Definitions part of these model provisions.

The wording of para. b) and c) is taken from the Financing Convention, as reproduced in subsequent international treaties. Although previous conventions do not contain the same provision, for uniformity purposes it is proposed to extend its applicability to all the offenses set forth in these model provisions.

The *contribution* appearing in para. b) can either aim at furthering the criminal activities of the group or simply be made in the knowledge of the criminal intention of the group.

It is up to each State to interpret the notions set forth in this article (such as that of complicity) in line with their laws and jurisprudence applicable to the various degrees of participation in criminal offenses.

This model provision only covers accessory offenses before the act, as required by the conventions. Ancillary offenses after the act (*harboring* provision) may be introduced by national authorities. In some countries this may not be needed because of the existence of a catchall provision in the general part of the penal code.

29. One of the most effective and cost-efficient methods to execute missions is to avoid duplication of resources, yet ensure that all available resources and expertise can be used to address specific needs. To accomplish this objective, States need to authorize agencies to assist each other. Generally, there are two means through which agencies may assist with operations. First, other agencies may assist the Coast Guard while performing their own missions pursuant to their own organic authority to engage in the activity. Second, the Coast Guard may formally request assistance from other agencies and entities in carrying out its authority (such as providing an interpreter or logistical support). In addition to requesting and receiving assistance from other agencies and entities, the Coast Guard should be authorized to provide similar assistance to other agencies. In order to provide for oversight on the sharing of resources, it is beneficial to implement legal authority to provide guidance on requests for assistance from another agency, as well as on the circumstances under which assistance can be provided to other governments.

11 Managing Maritime Incidents

James Petroni

"**M**ARITIME INCIDENTS" HAVE OCCURRED EVER SINCE humans ventured forth onto the varied waters of the world. In the beginning, there wasn't much that could be done about such incidents, and the relatively few mariners were largely on their own if trouble occurred. Now, however, the seas are getting crowded, with the vast majority of the world's commercial goods moving on the water, and passenger vessels of all shapes, sizes, and kinds being more numerous than ever. The usual incident causes of storms and mechanical or human failure are still with us, but they are joined now by the resurgence of maritime criminal activity and the threat of terrorism in the maritime environment.

At the same time, our ability to respond to all these threats has increased substantially, with more vessels and other resources afloat and ashore, supported by technology undreamt of in years past. But with all these new threats and increased capabilities, we are still faced with the perennial problem of directing, managing, and coordinating a timely and effective response. Now, methodologies developed by land-based emergency responders are available and easily applied to the problem of managing maritime incidents. This chapter will provide ways and means for that end.

The Challenges of Maritime Incidents

The maritime environment presents a demanding set of challenges that are unique to security operations in this setting. First, it represents the coming together of a number of otherwise distinct security elements. There is the on-the-water environment, which can be anywhere from a small lake, river, or harbor to a vast sea or ocean, with security organizations ranging from huge sovereign navies to minimalist harbor or lake patrols. Where this water touches land (the shoreside environment), there is frequently an entirely separate and distinct regime of security operational elements, again covering the broad spectrum of actors from armies to local law enforcement. Above all this is the air space with a smaller set of actors to be sure, but nonetheless a distinct operational chain of command. And the water itself is ever-changing, sometimes placid and calm, but more often affected by weather and currents that combine to produce an operational context that demands constant attention from all those who operate upon it, requiring flexibility and adaptability in order to maintain their own security and safety as well as of those in peril.

Maritime incidents occur when some type of human maritime activity is being threatened or actually damaged. That threat to maritime activity may be as a result of nature, human error, equipment failure, or intentional malicious human act, but in all cases there needs to be an actual or potential risk to human activity for it to become an *incident*. For example, a storm, in and of itself, is not necessarily a problem, but when that storm threatens ships at sea or shoreside facilities and activities, it becomes an incident that requires a government response.

Problems in the Initial Response

In addition to maritime-specific complications of the physical environment and the multiplicity of agencies and jurisdictions, maritime incidents are not exempt from the common issues found in most incident responses. Typical issues that arise on most responses are lack of coordination, poor communication (both technical and intraorganizational), insufficient information about the actual incident dynamics, and failure to keep track of what everyone is doing. As a result, there is quite often a chaotic (and usually ineffective) phase as the event unfolds until the planned (or emergent) organization is able to grasp the scope of the situation and gain control of the responding forces. All too often, this chaos continues for far too long. Perhaps the worst example of this in recent US history was the response to Hurricane Katrina, during which failures related to the above-mentioned factors (along with many other issues) resulted in a protracted delay in reversing the damaging effects of the storm.[1]

When queried about the problems encountered in the early response to major incidents, many responders answer with "I didn't know who was in charge," and "I didn't really know what my job was." In other words, these valuable contributors to an effective response had no sense of where they were in the organization or to whom they needed to look for direction. Commanders in these responses, especially for incidents that occur with little or no warning, often state that they experience great difficulty gaining an understanding of the full scope of the event, and that they do not know what the different elements of the collective response are actually doing.

In a sudden-onset event, the command is often overwhelmed by the initial reports to a degree that promotes confusion regarding the full scope of the problem. Initial reports are usually urgent—often vivid—and understandably create a mental image of the event that is hard to displace. A flawed initial impression can lead to command decisions that may commit resources away from more important but not yet obvious problems. Nothing is more important than knowing exactly what is happening (commonly referred to as *situational assessment*, or SA, or the *common operating picture*, or COP). The accurate and complete picture required by all responders can be sharpened with an efficient organizational structure.

Changing Event Dynamics

Maritime incidents are not "set pieces." Incident dynamics are constantly changing, and the response must be altered to meet the new requirements. A reported grounding turns out be a major rescue (*Costa Concordia*), an oil platform fire turns into a massive oil spill (*Deepwater Horizon* platform), a hijacking turns into a hostage rescue (*Maersk Alabama*); and with each metamorphosis come new command requirements, new tactics, and often whole new response elements involved in the event. Rescue crews, security forces, salvage, or spill control teams may all be trying to operate on the same event; each comes with its own hierarchy and command structure, and all of their activities need to be coordinated and directed to best effect.

Changes also occur as a result of the actions taken to control the incident. An old adage in firefighting is that fighting fires is a series of errors corrected as you make them. For example, you approach a fire and decide how much water it will take to extinguish it. Upon applying that water one of two things (or "errors") will occur. If the fire goes out, the error is that there is now too much water flowing and you must reduce it. If the fire doesn't go out, the error is that there is not enough water and you must apply more. This principle is generally applicable to all control operations, whether military, law enforcement, firefighting, or medical. You take an action, you see the consequences, and then you alter your actions, as necessary, to achieve your control objectives. This is usually accomplished by periodic operational assessment and planning efforts during the response, the outcome of which is typically a recommended new plan or *course of action* (COA). This COA, when approved by the command, becomes the new operational plan—until the situation changes again.

A specific emergency incident can usually be seen as having different phases over its life cycle, and the transitions between these phases are often problematic if not anticipated and prepared for. There may be the *imminent response* phase, during which no actual damage is occurring but the threat is clear (such as an approaching storm). A second possibility is the *immediate response* triggered by a serious emerging incident. Either of these may become an *extended* or *sustained* phase of the emergency response, lasting days, weeks, or even months as damage is still occurring (e.g., during an uncontrolled pollution event). All this is inevitably followed by a *recovery* phase, still further broken down into short-, mid-, and long-term subphases that may continue for years. Each of these phases comes with a transitional period between them, sometimes well defined and possibly abrupt, and other times barely noticeable and protracted. But these transitions often necessitate a shift of command responsibilities and personnel and, if not handled smoothly, they can be detrimental to the effectiveness of the overall effort.

The Need to Manage and Command

An effective response to any maritime incident needs to be well *managed* as well as being properly *commanded*. The two terms are clearly related but not synonymous. *Command* refers to the ability to direct (and redirect, as necessary) response forces to mitigate the damaging effects of the event. Command implies that the commander has the enforceable authority to cause these actions. *Manage* describes actions that must be taken to ensure that all elements of the organization that support the response forces are functioning as needed. This support could include intelligence and information management; logistics; personnel; and finance or other administrative functions.

While oversight of these activities clearly requires a certain authority, it is usually performed in a more collaborative and persuasive (versus directed) manner.[2]

A traditional military maxim is that "amateurs think of tactics; professionals think of logistics." This holds true for maritime incidents, especially complex or extended-duration events. One of the great lessons learned on the logistical requirements of maritime incidents came from the *Exxon Valdez* oil spill of 1989 which required nearly 300 vessels and over 2,500 personnel to operate in a sparsely inhabited and difficult-to-access area of Prince William Sound, Alaska.[3] The *Exxon Valdez* incident and many others since then have underscored the need for a robust and efficient logistical support organization to support the response forces. Ensuring that such a logistic effort succeeds is typical of the management function; if commanders have to worry about it, they will not be able to focus their full attention on command.

Coordination Is Key

It is safe to predict that almost every after-action report, every critique of a response, will mention the need for improved or greater coordination. Lack of coordination is the most often cited failure in large responses. It is an especially dominant theme in those events that involve a wide number of different services or agencies. Interagency coordination can certainly be reduced through preparation and planning. Real-time response coordination, however, has been a constant problem. The maritime operational environment, with its wide range of potential actors from the government, civilian, military, and private sectors, poses a significant coordination challenge.

A complex maritime incident that required close coordination under nighttime conditions with a large number of responders was the shipwreck of the *Costa Concordia* with 4,229 passengers on board. The impressive response had, at its peak, 14 merchant vessels, 4 tugboats, 26 patrol boats, and 8 helicopters on scene. In addition to those forces afloat and airborne, there were onshore command centers; rescue and medical personnel and vehicles; victim reception organizations; pollution control organizations; and a massive media operations component. All in all, 28 government agencies were involved in the incident. The total response, from immediate rescue to removing the wreck, lasted for nearly two and a half years. It was a very large coordination problem, to say the least.[4]

The Beginnings of a Solution

The solution to maritime incident management in the United States has its origins in a nonmaritime series of disasters in the late 1960s and early 1970s. The "trigger" was a series of nearly 800 wildland fires in Southern California that burned nearly 600,000 acres, destroyed over 700 homes, and killed 17 people. Wildland fires that burn into inhabited areas are not unusual in California, but the intensity and number of these fires underscored a problem that had been building for years. The problem was not only the phenomenon of fire, but also how the fire services of the entire United States were organized to fight fires.

There is no truly national firefighting agency in the United States. There are federal fire departments, such as the US Department of Agriculture's Forest Service, a specialized agency focused on the management and control of fires in national parks and forests. But the Forest Service has very little contact with municipal fire agencies and has no operational control over them. The fifty states each have their own fire agencies, but they too rarely, if ever, have operational control over the other fire departments in their respective states. In fact, there are over 30,000 independent fire departments in the United States, with over a million firefighters, but each department operates independently under its own command structure.[5]

This largely unstructured system works reasonably well under normal conditions. It is not terribly efficient, but it allows each jurisdiction to create and maintain the level of fire protection that it desires and can afford; overall, it has served to create a vast amount of firefighting resources nationwide. This arrangement works well enough for most fires, in that the individual fire departments can bring enough resources to bear to successfully control and extinguish the normally expected incidents. But the large fire that is beyond the capabilities of any single department, or that affects several jurisdictions at the same time, requires operational and tactical coordination between these independent agencies.

The fires of 1970 underscored this problem to a degree not seen in prior events. Recognizing the potential of these regularly occurring large fires, California had long ago developed a system to bring in other fire departments to support the fire departments who were experiencing catastrophic fires. This system, referred to as Fire Mutual Aid, is predicated on a master mutual-aid agreement in which all fire departments volunteer to support others who, in turn, will reciprocate. This has always worked extremely well and routinely results in amassing as many as 10,000 firefighters from hundreds of different departments to fight one particular major fire.

The fire events of 1970 painfully revealed the problem of coordinating the operations of all these different fire departments. Often the "victim" fire department requesting this mutual aid assistance was relatively small, frequently without much experience in managing major events, and the very fact that they were requesting assistance meant that they were overwhelmed. Plus, each department would arrive with equipment of varying capabilities, with variable staffing; each one brought its own communications frequencies and command organization. This meant that effective and efficient command and control were highly problematic, and the fires took longer to control, usually with much more damage as a consequence.

The 1970 fire disaster acted as a catalyst to bring together a comprehensive review of the overall problem. The summary report from that gathering described six key areas of needed improvement. First, the lack of a common organization on the fireground was cited as a tremendous problem. Second was the poor on-scene communication between the various agencies and tactical elements. Poor joint planning, both before and during the firefight, was the third. Fourth was poor intelligence about the scope and potential spread of the fires. The fifth area for improvement was resource management, as the responding fire agencies had to take care of their own support functions. Sixth and finally, there was the very limited ability to predict fire behavior.

As a result, the fire agencies got together to deal with these problems. It is important to note that this was a local, or what is referred to as a *grassroots*, initiative. The effort was not in response to a federal or state (of California) mandate; it was done because the individual fire departments simply had to fix the problem or face the prospect of more damaging fires.

However, the group quickly got support from both the US Congress and the State of California, and in 1971 the organization known as FIRESCOPE (Firefighting Resources of Southern California Organized for Potential Emergencies) came into formal existence. Its mission was to "create and implement new applications in fire service management, technology, and coordination with emphasis on incident command and multi-agency coordination."[6]

The Incident Command System

The establishment of FIRESCOPE led to the development of a "neutral" command and control architecture, one that was eventually agreed to by all

Southern California fire agencies. This initial group of concerned fire suppression experts spent considerable time defining desired key attributes of the
new system, design elements that remain absolutely valid today. In fact, those
key attributes first elucidated in the early 1970s are still included virtually ver-
batim in the contemporary training materials. The desired functions and objectives of the new system were listed as follows:

- Unity of command
- Modular and adaptable
- Common objectives
- Joint operational coordination
- Span of control
- Comprehensive resource management
- Incremental action planning
- Common terminology

The product of these deliberations was a new way of commanding and
managing large-scale firefighting. Called the Incident Command System
(ICS), it was "owned" by no single agency, but "bought into" by all of them.
It took only a few years until it became the fully accepted and normally practiced method for managing major fire emergencies. Confusion was greatly reduced, the efficiency (and the safety) of the firefighting forces was improved,
and the investment of time and money to fully implement the program was
relatively minimal.[7]

Soon other sectors of the response community beyond the fire service
saw the benefits of ICS as they realized it could be used by many different
disciplines and for many different events other than its original fire-related
applications. It was quickly adapted by different levels of government for
multidisciplinary responses to natural and technological emergencies. In the
1980s, the ICS was also being used for other than tactical field commands, as
it was found to have great utility in more complex, higher-echelon emergency
operations centers.

Another catastrophic fire in 1991 ultimately resulted in the State of California mandating ICS as the uniform statewide organizational response for all
agencies and for all major emergencies, calling it the Standardized Emergency
Management System. While the principal component of this system was the
ICS, it also included a number of state reporting structures and information
systems. Within a few years, it was fully implemented statewide, and the ex-

perience was overwhelmingly positive, with tremendous benefit gained by having all 58 counties and well over 500 separate cities all using a common command and control architecture. What California saw when it mandated this system in the entire state, throughout local governments, was an immediate improvement in interagency and interjurisdictional coordination, both vertically within the government hierarchy and horizontally across disciplines and neighboring communities. Common titling for crucial functions in all jurisdictions across the state—even with the initial training in performing those functions—improved overnight the transfer rate for critical information.

ICS in the Maritime Domain

In the maritime sector, the United States Coast Guard (USCG) experienced its own version of the fires of 1970 when the previously mentioned oil tanker *Exxon Valdez* hit a reef in Prince William Sound in Alaska in 1989 and spilled massive amounts of oil in what had been a pristine and sensitive environment. The response to contain and clean up the spill necessitated the employment of thousands of workers and hundreds of vessels, large and small. In the aftermath, the Coast Guard realized that the requirements for coordinating this complex, widespread, and long-term event were beyond its expertise. Within a few short years, the institution adapted a federal firefighting version of the ICS (the National Interagency Incident Management System) to the requirements of managing a maritime oil spill.[8]

The ICS has also spread globally since its inception. It is recognized by the fire service in most countries and is the recommended standard for wildland firefighting by the United Nations. It is the *de facto* worldwide standard for maritime oil spill response and is used by many agencies to coordinate maritime SAR events. Several countries in addition to the United States recognize the benefits of this system, having already adopted or considered it as a national standard for emergency response to all major incidents.[9] The adoption of such an easily adaptable and flexible system on a nationwide basis has considerable benefits, especially in its inherent ability to blend different resources and reduce much of the typical early response confusion.

A Flexible Structure

Let us examine the ICS in detail and imagine how it can assist us in managing complex maritime incidents. It is a deceptively simple, task-oriented organizational structure that has proven to be infinitely adaptable and readily expandable. The system can be implemented on a wide range of incident types, from the initial response of a single individual to the full organizational requirements of many different agencies, hundreds of units, and thousands of personnel. It can be considered as a shell structure, filled as necessary to blend the resources of many diverse entities into a single mission response.

The Basic Organization

The ICS is derived from the traditional military staff structure used by most Western nations, with a simplified staff structure comprising four main sections under a command element. Each section can be expanded as the requirements of the incident dictate. The four main sections under the Commander are Operations, Plans/Intelligence, Logistics, and Administration/Finance, with any number of subordinate elements, as required (see Figure 11.1). A key part of the success of the ICS is that it simplifies expansion (or contraction) of the response organization as the dynamics of the incident change. One of the basic principles built into the system is maintaining a realistic span of control. Experience suggests that from three to a maximum of seven elements reporting to a supervisor is ideal. If the number of subordinate elements exceeds that number, a further subdivision is easily created.

Assigning Position Titles

The emerging response organization also comes with its own position titles. This allows for the incorporation of personnel from many different organizations to be blended into the ICS structure without confusion. It also facilitates the assignment of the most qualified individuals to their appropriate positions. The rank structure of an individual's parent organization is

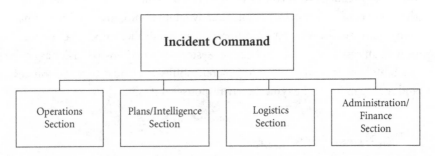

FIGURE 11.1 Basic Incident Command System structure

"checked at the door." The environment of neutrality gives a response organization its own identity and fosters closer cooperation.

ICS-specific titling means that personnel from widely differing organizations can be blended together without confusion. Consider, for example, the use of the rank of Captain. The captain of a vessel, whether a giant tanker or a simple fishing craft, is the highest authority on board. But in most armies and air forces, a captain is only a middle-rank officer. In many Western police agencies, a captain is a senior commander over many personnel, while in the fire service a captain is usually a first-line supervisor with command of fewer than ten firefighters. So, using the rank of Captain in a mixed-agency response would simply not work.

Individuals in leadership positions are called Section Chiefs. Subordinate elements of the ICS are also clearly defined by function or task, and each type of subelement has its own titling or rank nomenclature. In order to reinforce this, and to facilitate the instant recognition of key individuals, members normally wear a simple lightweight vest (a high-visibility safety vest works well) with the specific ICS position boldly displayed on the back (see Figure 11.2).

FIGURE 11.2 Meeting of the Incident Command team
SOURCE: US Coast Guard file photo.

Basic Functions of the Primary Sections

Command

The Command Section is the element ultimately responsible for the outcome of the incident. It develops the overall strategy and objectives for the response and oversees the other elements of the organization. It is usually a single individual, but it may be a unified or joint command comprising several individuals. In order to be effective, the Command Section must always be seen as a single, unified entity by the rest of the organization. It selects the chiefs of the subordinate sections. When appropriate, the Command Section is supported by several staff sections, referred to collectively as the Command Staff. These staff positions typically perform advisory or liaison roles, such as media relations and legal advice. The heads of all the sections are known as the General Staff.

Operations

This section is where the mission of the organization is accomplished, be it Search and Rescue (SAR), firefighting, managing the consequences of a terrorist attack, or pollution control. The Operations Section is where operational coordination occurs, missions are assigned, and tasks are deconflicted. The operational authority for all responding elements must be represented in this section. Subelements of the section can be organized by function or geography, or a combination of the two. The structure of the Operations Section should be extremely flexible and highly modular. In order to accommodate the dynamic nature of an incident, it must be the most adaptable piece of the entire structure. The Operations Section is capable of managing and directing the actions of dozens of agencies and thousands of responders, blending diverse resources into an organization with common objectives.

Most organizations work well within their own chains of command but have much resistance to being directed by "outsiders." When organizations are thrown together in an emergency response, their cultural and operational differences can lead to complications. Military units typically resist taking orders from civilian field commanders, and vice versa. The same goes for fire agencies working with law enforcement, medical, or other dissimilar organizations. The ICS overall, and the Operations Section in particular, recognizes this problem. Under Operations, the organization can be structured to respect the different chains of command of the agencies under its operational control. The Operations Section Chief may task organizations with missions, but leaves it up to the tasked organizations to execute those missions.

Plans/Intelligence

A critical and often underappreciated element of the ICS, this section manages all information relevant to the event. It provides a number of information and intelligence products to the rest of the organization, such as situation assessment and analysis, resource status tracking, event documentation, and other such services as may be required. This section is also responsible for producing, in collaboration with other sections, the periodic Incident Action Plan for the Incident Commander's approval.

Logistics

The Logistics Section provides all support and services needed by the rest of the organization. It acquires additional response resources as requested by the Operations Section and all other resources (including response or staff augmentation) needed by the other sections. This may include facilities; communications and IT equipment and services; and food and housing for the responder organization.

Administration/Finance

Usually, the last section to be staffed and often only activated in large-scale events, this element performs critical administrative and financial services for the rest of the organization. It is the purchasing and accounting entity for the organization and performs cost analysis for the ICS as required. It is often also tasked with the overall personnel management function for the ICS.

The Incident Command System can appear complicated if one first examines a fully fleshed out organizational chart. In order to simplify the explanation of how such a system would work in the real world, the ICS is often described as follows:

> Imagine you are first on the scene of a small but growing fire. You're *everything* at that time; you're in charge, so therefore you're the Incident Commander. And if you're trying to extinguish or control the fire, you're Operations too. As you try to figure out how big the fire is and where it will go if you can't extinguish it, you're also Plans, and if you're looking around for more water or calling for more resources, you're also Logistics. You're all those things until others arrive and you're either relieved of some of those duties or you delegate them to someone else.

Expanding the ICS

Although the ICS can be implemented by just one person, one of the most practical benefits it brings to operational responses is the ability to expand and adapt to a growing incident. The primary way it does this is by creating subelements that reflect either the need to limit the span of control or to accommodate different functions or agencies. In the ICS, these subelements have become somewhat formalized, with specific unit titles for different levels of the organization.

The following are subordinate organizational elements found in the ICS below the section level, along with their leadership titling. The chart shown in Figure 11.3, taken from the ICS training materials provided by the US Federal Emergency Management Agency, shows the organizational relationships of these elements.

- *Branch.* Used to distinguish between functional, geographical, or jurisdictional responsibilities, such as a Fire Branch or Spill Control Branch. The individual in charge is called a Branch Director.
- *Division.* Used in large incidents to identify a geographic area of responsibility and led by a Division Supervisor.
- *Group.* Used within the Operations Section to identify a particular functional element and led by a Group Supervisor. Examples would be an Air Operations Group or a Mass Fatality Management Group.
- *Unit.* An organizational element having specific functional responsibility under the Plans, Logistics, or Administration/Finance Section and led by a Unit Leader. Examples would be the Situation Status Unit under Plans, or the Communications Unit under Logistics.

Application to Maritime Scenarios

Using all of the above as background, the application of the ICS to expected maritime incidents makes sense. Indeed, given the complexity of the maritime domain, the absence of such a system would complicate even the simplest response. Notional incident vignettes will be illustrated below, using the notional country of Maritima, as described in Chapter 3. In that chapter, Paul Shemella uses a number of hypothetical targets to introduce a method of comparative targeting analysis, imputed to terrorists wishing to attack the

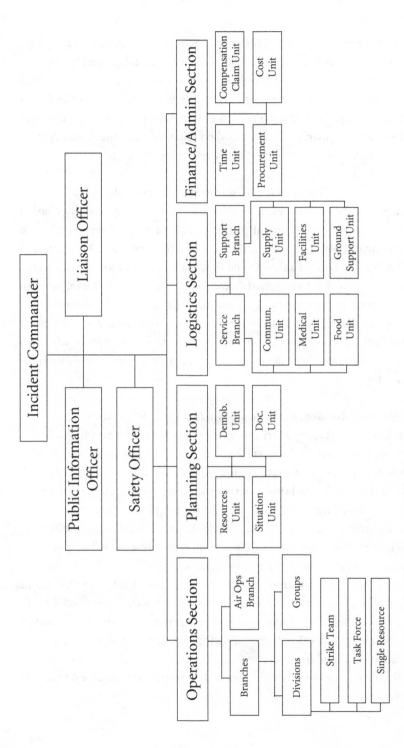

FIGURE 11.3 Expanded Incident Command System structure
SOURCE: ICS 402-IG, US FEMA.

country's maritime interests. This exercise will focus on three of those pieces of maritime infrastructure to provide just enough background to imagine how the government response could be structured using the ICS. We suggest that readers extend the scenarios beyond the text presented here and then draw the appropriate ICS organization charts. After that, readers are invited to substitute their own scenarios, based on potential maritime infrastructure in their own countries that could lead to major incidents.

Incident #1: Offshore Oil Platform Delta

An oil platform supply vessel (PSV) suffered an engineering casualty, causing an allision with the offshore oil platform. This caused a fire and explosion and an uncontrolled oil spill that threatens the fragile coast of Maritima and its neighbor country. In an event like this, the ICS could provide the mechanism to allow for Joint or Unified Command at the Command level between maritime and environmental agencies, and then facilitate the coordination of the government and private-sector resources across a wide geographic area for the containment and cleanup (for a more detailed example of what this might look like, see later information in this chapter on the *Deepwater Horizon* incident).

Incident #2: Shoreside Incident at Power Plant #1

Terrorists have attacked Maritima's Power Plant #1. The attack involved a bomb explosion and a subsequent fire at the power plant. Small arms fire has been heard onshore at the facility, and it is presumed that terrorists are still active on site. Additional threat information suggests that additional terrorists from a vessel near shore are approaching the power plant from the sea. Agencies involved in the response include the coast guard, navy, fire service, and shoreside law enforcement. In an event such as this, an ICS response organization could be very useful to coordinate shoreside and waterside law enforcement activities within the Operations Section. Under the Operations Section, it might be necessary to set up a Perimeter Security or Force Protection element (Branch, Unit, or Group as appropriate) to focus on that aspect of the problem while other elements are focused on controlling the active terrorists within the plant site. The Plans/Intelligence Section could integrate real-time situation analysis with internal and external intelligence on the perpetrators and their intentions.

Incident #3: Water City Ferry Fire at Sea

The Water City Ferry, *Maritima*, the flagship of the fleet, has suffered an on-board explosion. The vessel is in international waters, and the explosion has resulted in a loss of all power. The ship is rapidly taking on water. The captain reports that his damage-control teams are unable to maintain the ship's stability, and he may need to issue the order to abandon ship. Weather conditions in the area are poor and getting worse, with winds in excess of twenty knots and a rising sea state. Because of this, the ferry captain is very reluctant to put his passengers in the water. One of your patrol vessels is nearby and heading toward the stricken vessel, as are several other commercial and fishing vessels. In an incident like this, once the responding vessels come on scene, actions would include attempting to keep the ship afloat while preparing for the rescue of the passengers and crew should the ferry sink. Who has command of this event? The captain of the ferry? The captain of the response ship? How do you coordinate the tactical operations of damage control and rescue? The flexibility and adaptability of the ICS would allow you to have a Joint Command overall, as well as an Operations Section that could coordinate the efforts and interaction of other vessels and oversee the rescue and damage-control operations.

The *Deepwater Horizon* Incident: ICS in the Real World

On April 20, 2010, the dynamically positioned oil well drilling unit *Deepwater Horizon* was engaged in drilling the exploratory well in the Macondo Prospect oil field, some 41 miles off the Louisiana coastline, in approximately 5,000 feet of water. A series of events resulted in a massive explosion and fire, killing eleven crewmen on the drilling unit. The fire was uncontrollable, and on April 22, the *Deepwater Horizon* capsized and sank, leaving the ruptured well at the seafloor spewing huge amounts of oil into the ocean. The rupture continued for 87 days until the well was finally capped. The total amount of oil spilled is estimated to be in the range of 4.9 million barrels (210 million US gallons or 780,000 cubic meters).[10]

Before the *Deepwater Horizon* went down, the US Coast Guard had fully adopted the ICS and trained its personnel to apply the system in a wide variety of situations.[11] As the lead US agency responsible for maritime oil spills, the Coast Guard was placed in overall command of the disaster response. It was the worst oil spill on record. The Coast Guard had to manage disparate efforts to contain the spill, control the leak, and remove as much of the oil from the environment as possible. Because of the vastness of the area affected, which included the coastlines of several US states, the Coast Guard used the guidelines of ICS to establish five Incident Command posts under the Incident Commander. Through this emergent organization, the Coast Guard managed and directed the efforts of more than 47,000 federal, state, and local responders. A vast armada of vessels, including 835 specialized oil-skimming craft, 6,100 response boats, and an additional 3,190 vessels of opportunity responded together, supported by more than 120 aircraft. Using these resources, 34.7 million gallons of oily-water mix were recovered and over 11 million gallons of oil were removed from the ocean using *in situ* burning. Figure 11.4 shows the ICS organization employed by the State of Florida sector of the response.[12]

Supporting Materials and Implementation Aids

One of the other benefits of using the ICS is the wealth of supporting materials that are openly available to emergency management officials worldwide. In the process of refining and implementing the ICS over the past decades, a wide range of training materials (including instructor and student manuals, along with presentations), individual position descriptions, checklists, forms, field handbooks, planning guides, and much more are available in the public domain. These materials make it very easy to implement this system and will be of great value in developing customized training and/or certification programs. Much of this is available on the Internet and can be downloaded from the United States Department of Homeland Security's Federal Emergency Management Agency (US DHS FEMA) website.[13]

Summary

Effectively managing major maritime incidents is a serious challenge, but not an insurmountable one. The wide range of incident types, the unique mix of participating organizations (both civil and military), and potentially complex jurisdictional issues, along with the ever-changing nature of the maritime environment itself, require a flexible and adaptable approach. The increasing use of the maritime environment for transportation, natural resources development, recreation, and other activities has created an expanded potential for

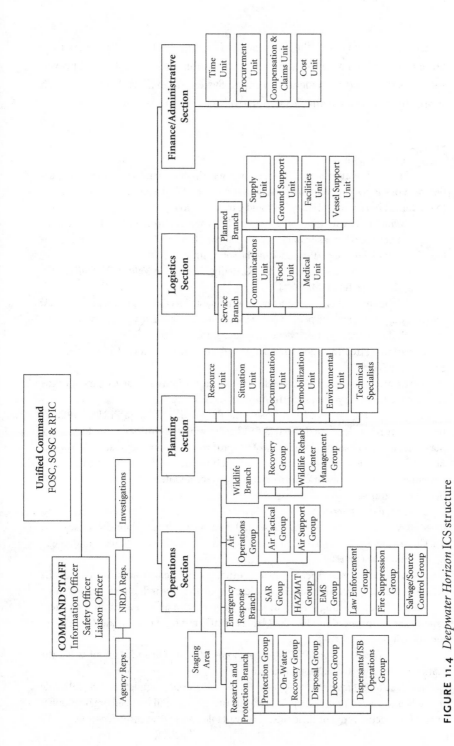

FIGURE 11.4 *Deepwater Horizon* ICS structure

SOURCE: Report of the Effectiveness of the Use of the Incident Command System in the *Deepwater Horizon* Incident, November 2, 2012.

industrial accidents, and the resurgence of criminal activity in the maritime domain has added a new dimension to the problem. But helpful and proven solutions such as the Incident Command System do exist and, with so much supporting material available, are relatively easy to implement.

Notes

1. Many of the after-action reports mention this problem. For an excellent assessment of the Katrina response, see Robert Block and Christopher Cooper, *Disaster* (New York: Times Books, Henry Holt and Company, 2006).

2. *Command* is usually typified as the issuance of direct orders to initiate or change an action, whereas *management* is a form of oversight and guidance that allows for a more flexible performance by the subordinate.

3. Samuel K. Skinner and William K. Reilly, *The* Exxon Valdez *Oil Spill* (PDF), National Response Team, May 1989.

4. See the comprehensive report on this incident, *The Costa Concordia Shipwreck: Summary of Emergency Response Management,* David Fabi, Dipartimento della protezione civile—Ufficio gestione delle emergenze, 2012.

5. National Fire Protection Association website, www.nfpa.org, *United States Fire Service Fact Sheet.*

6. For more information about the Fire Service origins and development of the Incident Command System, see http://www.firescope.org.

7. Through the 1970s and early 1980s, the fire service, through FIRESCOPE, refined and further developed the ICS until it became the ordinary way to manage major fire emergencies throughout most of California. Supporting materials, such as field guides and position descriptions, were published, and a wealth of training was developed, ranging from brief introductions to very detailed, position-specific certification programs.

8. See the latest version of the *US Coast Guard Incident Management Handbook,* dated May 2014, available as a PDF in several languages at https://homeport.uscg.mil/ics. Go to "Library > Incident Command System ICS > Job Aids > Incident Management Handbook (IMH)."

9. Determining the exact number of other governments that have adapted the ICS, or something derived from it, would be a worthy research effort. During more than ten years of teaching foreign officials, we have seen great interest in the system (and heard many anecdotes like "yes, we use that") but have never undertaken a systematic study.

10. *"On Scene Coordinator Report, Deepwater Horizon Oil Spill,"* submitted to the National Response Team, September 2011.

11. The USCG *Incident Management Handbook* is a very complete and useful guide to the ICS, with position descriptions, checklists, guides, and detailed organizational charts for specific types of incidents. It is available as a PDF at http://www.uscg.mil/

hq/cg5/cg534/nsarc/2014%20USCG%20Incident%20Management%20Handbook%20
(English).pdf).

12. *Report 2: An analysis of the Effectiveness of the Use of the Incident Command System in the* Deepwater Horizon *(DWH) Incident,* Florida Commission on Oil Spill Response Coordination, 2012.

13. The FEMA website is http://training.fema.gov/EMIWeb/IS/ICSResource/ index.htm. There is additional maritime-supporting information at the United States Coast Guard's website, https://homeport.uscg.mil.

III CASE STUDIES

12 Defeating the Sea Tigers of LTTE

Rohan Gunaratna

AFTER THIRTY YEARS OF FIGHTING, THE SRI LANKAN government militarily defeated the Liberation Tigers of Tamil Eelam (LTTE), one of the world's most ruthless terrorist and guerrilla groups, in May 2009. The game changer in the defeat of the LTTE was the destruction of the LTTE's brown- and blue-water capabilities. The blue-water fleet transported arms, ammunition, explosives, and other supplies to Sri Lankan exclusive economic zone (EEZ) or territorial waters. Until the Sri Lankan government, especially the Sri Lankan navy, interdicted the LTTE supplies and destroyed their logistics chain, the LTTE sustained the fight.[1]

Working with their US, Australian, and Indian security and intelligence counterparts, both the Sri Lankan navy and its military and national intelligence services mapped the LTTE fleet. Until the Sri Lankan navy, in collaboration with their domestic and international counterparts, detected, disrupted, and dismantled the LTTE fleet of ships, the LTTE replenished their losses and wastage. In parallel, the Sri Lankan navy and the Sri Lankan air force destroyed the LTTE brown-water fleet that linked oceangoing ships to shore.

In contemporary history, there is no non-state actor that built either a brown- or a blue-water capability as extensive, versatile, and powerful as the LTTE. The LTTE provided the current template for maritime terrorism, guerrilla operations, and support activities.[2] The study of the LTTE maritime organization, both its offshore and deep-sea assets, provides an insight into the maritime terrorist capabilities, roles, and technologies of an insurgent group. This chapter will analyze Sri Lanka's defeat of the maritime forces of the LTTE, revealing new information gleaned from interviews with former insurgents.

Context

Founded by Velupillai Prabhakaran,[3] the LTTE wanted to create an ethnically pure enclave in the north and the east of Sri Lanka. Originally established as the Tamil New Tigers (TNT) in 1974, the group evolved into the Liberation Tigers of Tamil Eelam (LTTE) on May 5, 1976. After Prabhakaran murdered Alfred Duraiappa (the then Tamil mayor of Jaffna on July 27, 1975), he fled to India by boat. When the pressure on Prabhakaran reduced, he returned to Sri Lanka, again by boat, and continued to engage in robberies and killings. To raise funds for his group and activities, the LTTE committed its first bank robbery on August 31, 1977. The LTTE committed the first murder of a policeman in Jaffna on December 14, 1977, and it also killed the policemen involved in the investigations into LTTE crimes. Determined to disrupt the civil and political administration, the LTTE mostly killed Tamils associated with or who were part of the government. In the initial phase, the LTTE had no boats of their own, so they used the boats of the smugglers plying between Sri Lanka and India for transport.

In response to the escalating violence by the LTTE, the Sri Lankan army was summoned to assist the police to maintain law and order in the predominantly Tamil north. On October 25, 1981, the LTTE killed the first soldier, and on July 21, 1983 it activated the first landmine in Jaffna, killing thirteen soldiers. In response, Sinhalese mobs in the south retaliated and attacked Tamil households and places of work in the south. With the deterioration of security conditions, several tens of thousands of Tamils living in the south either fled to the north and east or traveled overseas. This watershed event changed the complexion of the conflict for two reasons. First, the anger, resentment, and suffering of the Tamil territorial, migrant, and diaspora communities were harnessed by the LTTE and several other Tamil militant groups. Second, over geopolitical and electoral pressures both the national government of India and the state government of Tamil Nadu started to support the LTTE and other Tamil groups. The LTTE broad-based its organization and increased its recruitment drive, both in the military and in the political wing.

Due to the strained relationship between a pro-US Sri Lanka and a pro-Soviet India, India, especially Tamil Nadu, emerged as its principal support base. The LTTE used the smuggling boats to move between Sri Lanka and India. Due to geopolitical and geostrategic differences, New Delhi covertly assisted the LTTE and, due to ethnic differences, Tamil Nadu governments supported the LTTE. After the ethnic riots of July 1983, the Indian authorities, including its navy, coast guard, police, and intelligence services, either turned a blind eye or facilitated LTTE, including its maritime activities, between India and Sri Lanka. After the LTTE grew in strength, size, and influence, the LTTE could no longer be controlled by the Indian government. After the LTTE and India had a falling out, fighting started between the LTTE and the Indian Peace Keeping Force (IPKF). Nonetheless, the LTTE boat movement was constrained. However, the movement by sea between Sri Lanka and India, the principal source of supplies to fight the IPKF, continued.

Origins of the Sea Tigers

The Sea Tigers wing of LTTE was founded in 1991 by Soosai, who led the organization until 2009. The LTTE had a modest maritime capability throughout the 1980s. From 1987 through 1991, the Sea Tigers did not exist. Raheem, the LTTE spokesperson in the 1980s who left the LTTE in 1990 said, "There was no Sea Tigers during my time."[4] The LTTE always had a senior cadre in charge of the boat movement between India and Sri Lanka. At one point, Pottu Amman, who later became the intelligence chief of the LTTE, was based in Vedaranium, Tamil Nadu, and was in charge of the boat movement. He was later to use that knowledge to plan a seaborne infiltration to assassinate Rajiv Gandhi. Before the creation of the Sea Tigers, the LTTE had a few boats and a team of cadres who had limited expertise in navigation. The boats traveled between India and Sri Lanka, enabling the flow of supplies and transit of people.

A former LTTE cadre, Janarthana Nallanathan (alias Nathan), is credited for conceiving the term *Sea Tigers*. After the second iteration of training by India's foreign intelligence service, Research and Analysis Wing (RAW), in Himachal Pradesh in north India, he relocated to Vedaranium to travel to Sri Lanka and serve in the LTTE. While in Vedaranium in 1984, he took a piece of chalk and wrote on a boat "Sea Tigers."[5] He belonged to the first group that operated in Mannar under Marcelline Fuseless (alias Victor). Most of the second-batch LTTE-trained cadres served in Mannar and participated in the Anuradhapura massacre, where they attacked the sacred Buddhist city. Later, Nathan died fighting the Indian Peacekeeping Force (IPKF). Contrary to stories that the name *Sea Tigers* was coined by the LTTE leadership, it was Nathan—a former student of Central College, Jaffna (where his father was a dispenser)[6]—who named the group.

To build maritime capacity in the early stages, the LTTE relied on fishermen and mariners. A cadre with maritime expertise, Rasakumar, known by his LTTE name, David, was an expert boat driver who originated from the coastal village of Velvettithurai, a smuggling den. Under the orders of Pottu Amman, David traveled from Sri Lanka to India to collect Sivarasan, the operational commander of the Rajiv Gandhi assassination. On the way, he suffered a freak accident when his boat cracked open. Together with Sivarasan, David was involved in the Pathmanabha murder in June 1990, an event that preceded the Gandhi assassination. However, the Indian government did not take appropriate action after the Pathmanabha killing to deny Tamil Nadu sanctuary for LTTE operations. Prabhakaran subsequently established a Sea Tiger base in David's name in Jaffna. It was only after the LTTE assassinated Gandhi that the Indian government disrupted the LTTE support network in Tamil Nadu. Nonetheless, since the defeat of the LTTE in Sri Lanka in May 2009, the support base in Tamil Nadu has been reconstituted.

Sea Tiger Capabilities

As the coastal communities in the north and east engaged in fishing, all material to construct boats was available in market. The Sea Tiger boats were made of fiberglass and did not require much sophistication to construct. The boats were made using a mold. A single mold was capable of producing many boats. The Sea Tiger capabilities evolved starting in the 1990s, building from simple boats to complex craft with designs from overseas, notably from Australia.

The Sea Tigers organization had twelve sections as of 1995:

1. Sea battle regiments
2. Underwater demolition teams
3. Sea Tiger strike groups
4. Marine engineering and boat-building unit
5. Radar and telecom unit

6. Marine weapons armory and dump group

7. Maritime school and academy

8. Recruiting section

9. Political, financial, and propaganda section

10. Exclusive economic zone–marine logistics support team

11. Reconnaissance team and intelligence section

12. Welfare and registry

While the sea battle regiments fought out at sea, the Sea Tiger strike groups protected the logistics and supplies from overseas. The exclusive economic zone-marine logistics support team (EEZ-MLST), supported by the recce team and intelligence section and radar and telecommunications unit, received the supplies from tankers and ships. Marine weapons armory and dump group stored the weapons and other supplies on land. Underwater demolition teams attacked ships anchored or berthed. While the political, finance and propaganda section and the recruiting section generated the manpower, maritime school and academy trained the Sea Tiger leadership. While the welfare section cared for the families of dead and injured cadres, the registry maintained all records. The marine engineering and boat building section manufactured boats. These boats were categorized into four types, according to roles. Throughout the 1990s and 2000s, the Sea Tigers used attack craft, logistic craft, suicide craft, and modified craft.

The attack craft, which were fitted with medium caliber guns ranging from 14.5 mm to 23 mm, were used to fight with naval units. They were also supported by several mounted weapons on either side. They carried RPG and other assortments of small arms. The LTTE maintained a fleet of two to three dozen attack craft from about the late 1990s until about 2007. Known LTTE Sea Tiger attack craft were:[7]

1. *Murali*
2. *Adiman Oscar*
3. *Prashanth*
4. *Amuda Surawi*
5. *Kanendran*
6. *Vankadi* (or *Vangawi*)
7. *Sudarshana*
8. *Oviya*
9. *Idayan*
10. *Raj Mohan*
11. *Udaya Chelvi*
12. *Shriral*
13. *Mayuran*
14. *Indumathi*

15. *Madhu* (or *Madawi*)   20. *Roja*

16. *Cheliyan*   21. *Ilaneela*

17. *Parandaman*   22. *Wannila*

18. *Paradi Dasan*   23. *Kadal Rasa*

19. *Dahai Cheliyan* (or *Aga*   24. *Kadal Arasan*
    Cheliyan)

The Sri Lankan navy damaged or destroyed the fleet of attack craft. A few, such as *Indumathi*, were captured on June 19, 2007. Due to the disruption of the supplies, the Sea Tigers could not replenish the losses and wastage.

The logistics craft were designed to carry goods from one place to another. They were armed with 12.7-mm guns and carried items without exposing them to sea sprays, thus protecting items. The suicide craft varied from *theppums* to multi-day-fishing trawlers. The Sea Tigers built custom-made stealth-type suicide boats to carry out suicide attacks. These low-profile boats were virtually undetected by radar. The big suicide boats, powered by four outboard motors (OBMs), were designed to attack steel-hull ships in deep seas. Suicide boats had ramming horns in the front part of the boats, and explosives were packed in them. The modified craft varied for the purpose. The Sea Tigers used normal fiberglass dinghies with false bottoms to ferry items, disguising themselves as fishermen and becoming "human torpedoes" to carry out suicide attacks in harbors. Powered by gasoline-driven OBMs, the boats were equipped with radar, GPS, and communication equipment. These boats were about 14 meters in length and appeared to be sleek and low profiled. According to the role, they had about twelve to fourteen men manning the guns and equipment. The fiberglass hull is mixed with isocyanates (a type of compound that gives a shining surface and improves resistance in water; South Africa is the world's number-one supplier) to improve the quality of load bearing, fatigue absorption, and speed. The purpose of the brown-water fleet was to support the movement of supplies from overseas to Sri Lanka. The Sri Lankan navy targeted both the blue- and brown-water fleets simultaneously.

The Development of LTTE Power

The fighting power of the LTTE grew between July 1983 and July 1987, but the LTTE reached its peak, both in size and capability, in 2000. The LTTE envisioned a four-phase strategy in Sri Lanka:

1. Disruption of State's Intelligence System in the Tamil homeland by eliminating the persons working for them and their civilian informants, identified as traitors.

2. Launch of an armed campaign aimed at paralyzing the police, civil & political administrative systems in Tamil Eelam, with guerrilla attacks.

3. Ambushes and direct engagements with the armed forces.

4. Conversion of its guerrilla forces into a revolutionary people's army, with the participation of the Tamil masses.[8]

To secure logistics support to Sri Lanka, the LTTE adopted land and maritime guerrilla and terrorist tactics. With Sri Lanka's ceremonial military overreacting to LTTE attacks resulting in civilian deaths and injuries, Tamil support and sympathy for the LTTE grew. Until the LTTE assassinated Rajiv Gandhi on May 21, 1991, a segment of the Tamil population who were exposed to LTTE propaganda regarded the LTTE as freedom fighters. Nonetheless, the LTTE continued to kill civilians to put pressure on the Sri Lankan government, a practice Prabhakaran continued until the very end. The LTTE staged its first suicide attack on May 7, 1987 at Nelliady in Jaffna; LTTE cadre Vasanthan (alias Captain Miller) launched a suicidal attack on the security forces using a vehicle laden with explosives. Due to the attack, seventeen personnel were killed and twenty-one were injured.

To create an ethnically pure north and east in Sri Lanka, the LTTE built an influential lobby in Tamil Nadu and later in New Delhi. Thereafter, the LTTE acquired their own fleet of boats and ships. The boats were used to transport recruits, personnel, weapons, and other supplies between Sri Lanka and India. The Sea Tiger wing and the shipping network were under the military wing. While Soosai controlled the Sea Tigers, Prabhakaran personally controlled international procurement and the shipping network. The transportation of supplies from the ships and trawlers to land was controlled by the Sea Tigers and led by Soosai. In a letter to the suicide "Black Sea Tigers" Prabhakaran said,

Geographically, the security of Tamil Eelam is interlinked with that of its seas. It is only when we are strong on the seas and break the dominance of the enemy that we will be able to retain the land areas we liberated and drive our enemies from our homeland.[9]

The LTTE pursued a strategy of fighting and negotiating to achieve its goal of an independent Tamil State. With the assistance of India, Norway, and the international community, the LTTE and the Sri Lankan government engaged in several rounds of peace talks. However, LTTE leader Prabhakaran's uncompromising stance of creating an independent Tamil State prevented a resolution. The talks strengthened the LTTE and created opportunities to build their land and maritime capabilities. The LTTE emerged as the undisputed world leader in suicide terrorism,[10] including maritime terrorism; LTTE technology inspired and influenced other groups to copy its tactics from maritime suicide operations to human-borne suicide attacks.[11]

The LTTE International Network

The LTTE international organization originated as a network. The maritime capability enabled the steadfast rise of the Tamil militant movement, which originated in Velvettiturai, a fishing village in Jaffna renowned for smuggling between India and Sri Lanka. The links between the smugglers in Sri Lanka and India are well established. One of India's most notorious smugglers of gold, narcotics, and electronic goods, Vakil Kandasamy, supported and worked with the LTTE. The LTTE created an office of overseas purchases (OOP), and Prabhakaran appointed Selvarajah Pathmanathan (alias Kannadi Pathmanathan, alias K.P.), as its leader. In the early days, he was "arrested in India for smuggling gold from Singapore to Bombay"[12] but Indian state patronage enabled him to be a free man. In an interview with the author, K.P. said, "Travelling between Singapore and India, Vakil Kandasamy purchased walkie-talkies for the LTTE."[13] While the Central Bureau of Investigations of India alleged that K.P. was involved in smuggling drugs, he denied he was personally involved.[14] However, K.P. did say that LTTE received contributions from those engaged in drug trafficking. When the author asked the then LTTE leader in France, Illango Nadarajah, why they accepted monies from narcotics traffickers, he said, "When a contribution was made [for the LTTE], we had no right to ask for the source of the funds."

The LTTE built a maritime capability to support a state-of-the-art international network essential to sustain its campaign in Sri Lanka. Appointed by Prabhakaran, Selvarasa Pathmanathan (alias Tharmalingam Shanmugam Kumaran, alias Kumaran Pathmanathan, alias K.P.), born on April 6, 1955 in Kankasanthurai, Sri Lanka, was the head of LTTE's international finance, procurement, and shipping network from 1984–2003. He was reappointed and served briefly in 2009 until he was arrested in Malaysia and deported to Sri Lanka.

While the LTTE in Sri Lanka focused on propaganda, recruitment, training, and fighting both on land and at sea, the LTTE international organization focused on propaganda, fundraising, procurement, and shipping. LTTE propagandists and fundraisers overseas played a pivotal role in supporting the terrorist activities in Sri Lanka. Their aboveground activity was carried out through LTTE fronts such as the Canadian Tamil Congress, Illankai Tamil Sangam in the US, Tamil Sydney, etc. They supported the LTTE umbrella, the Global Tamil Forum, led by Father S.J. Emmanuel, the *de jure* leader and Nediyawan, the *de facto* leader. To continue the fight for separatism—the end goal—the LTTE through GTF and its country affiliates engaged Western politicians to make statements that promoted their cause. Some politicians, susceptible to constituency pressure, were lured into supporting LTTE by votes and campaign funds. The politicians exercised pressure on government bureaucracy not to act against the LTTE infrastructure and their operations. Furthermore, through LTTE owned and operated media such as TamilNet and human rights groups such as Human Rights for Tamils (HURT), the LTTE sought to influence the mainstream media and human rights groups.

In the wake of military defeat, what remains of LTTE continues to generate funds from criminal activity. To legitimize LTTE's international criminal activities, the LTTE political networks in the diaspora canvass host-country support. The traditional nexus between these two structures continues at the time of this writing. LTTE shipping, procurement, and facilitation units that traditionally provided the logistics and supplies have reorganized themselves to engage in commercial and criminal activity. As human smuggling is highly profitable, both the procurement officers and ship managers engage in it to profit either themselves or the group. They include Ravishankar Kangarajah in Canada, Shanmugasundaran Kanthaskaran in the UK, Chandran in the Netherlands, Ponniah Anandarajah in Thailand, Kandiahpillai Bakerathan (alias Bhavi, alias Bahi, alias Khan) in Indonesia, and others. They take instructions from Nediyawan, the LTTE leader in Norway.

Human Smuggling: Then and Now

The illegal movement of Sri Lankans in the postconflict phase is no longer driven by the conflict. Human smuggling constitutes a major challenge for host governments, with the most favored transit countries including

Indonesia, Malaysia, Thailand, Philippines, Singapore, and East Timor, and destination countries including Australia, Europe, and Canada. As in the past, the role of the LTTE in human smuggling is limited, but it is very significant. The motive is both to move its own members for regrouping and to raise funds. Until May 2009, the focus on the LTTE ships was to move arms, ammunition, explosives, and other supplies to sustain the fight. The ships transported out LTTE cadres wishing to travel overseas—both to serve the LTTE logistical network in Indonesia, its main base outside Sri Lanka, and to relocate to other countries to support the fight. Currently, according to Sri Lankan law enforcement, security, and intelligence services, the direct involvement of the LTTE in human smuggling is limited. However, the LTTE is quite capable of operating through criminal groups—both Sinhalese and Tamils—in Sri Lanka without showing its hand. Traditionally, smuggling of Sri Lankans is mostly conducted by economically motivated Sri Lankan individuals and very small groups with linkages to networks in Southeast Asia and beyond. With the end of the conflict in Sri Lanka, the LTTE is using its extant organized crime network of cells and assets (from front companies to ships) overseas to move people.

Since the LTTE was dismantled in Sri Lanka in May 2009, this network has morphed. The LTTE campaign in Sri Lanka was fought largely by locally recruited youth with funds generated outside of the country. Although the LTTE raided military camps for weapons in the early stages, subsequently the LTTE procured most of its weapons from North Korea and dual-user technologies from East Asia, especially Singapore, Japan, China, and Australia. Asia has remained the key theater for LTTE activities, even after its defeat. The LTTE international network harnessed its robust infrastructure for raising funds, procuring, and shipping supplies to support its economic and political survival. Rather than dismantling the infrastructure, the current LTTE leadership is exploiting it to advance its aims and objectives.

While some individuals are now driven by economic motives, the main body of LTTE international is still political. However, the criminal faction of the group is still engaged in human smuggling. Furthermore, the LTTE has infiltrated and established control over other individuals and their networks. The LTTE-influenced networks are disciplined, clandestine, and resilient. In many ways, the capabilities inherent in the LTTE are now percolating into the criminal domain more generally. Compared to other Sri Lankan criminal networks, however, the LTTE controlled or influenced networks are the hardest to dismantle. It will require significant investment of resources by several government agencies to study and map the network. Furthermore, considerable coordination and collaboration is necessary to detect, disrupt, and dismantle this network. As a highly disciplined and secret organization, the LTTE criminal network presents the biggest threat. It draws LTTE members from both underground and aboveground networks.

Arms Procurement

Starting in 1984, K.P. was responsible for building LTTE's arms-procuring network from Lebanon, Bulgaria, Ukraine, and North Korea to sustain LTTE's guerrilla and terrorist campaigns. Until the LTTE structure was defeated, it functioned in northern Sri Lanka; key decisions were made by Prabhakaran, and LTTE headquarters in Sri Lanka gave instructions overseas. The center of gravity of LTTE procuring and shipping operations moved from the Middle East to Eastern Europe and then to East Asia. Although Southeast Asia, especially Thailand, remained an important theater for LTTE procurement, North Korea became the key country for LTTE procurement after 1996. Indonesia was the main center for coordinating procurement and shipping operations.[15] The very first detection of an LTTE arms consignment was by the Malaysian Customs in Penang on December 13, 1990. Malaysia detained the LTTE ship MV *Sunbird*, which was transporting a consignment of arms, ammunition, and dual technologies. According to the Malaysian Special Branch, the ship was transporting:

1. 2,600 rounds of Blank Ammo
2. 3 Large Speed Boats
3. 8 Johnson & Yamaha Outboard Engines
4. 324 Transceiver Base Stations
5. 440 Walkie-Talkies (Hand Held Sets)
6. 6,000 Batteries

The Malaysian Special Branch also raided LTTE safe houses in Malaysia and recovered financial and other documents that provided an insight into the LTTE international network—both into its bank accounts and its operatives. The documentation that was recovered revealed, among other information, how the LTTE was operating through front organizations in the West, and how they had a budget to penetrate human rights groups and the UN.[16] On November 18, 1991, the Indian navy detained the LTTE ship MV *Tongnova*, carrying a consignment of military equipment.

In August 1994, the LTTE successfully procured and transported 60 metric tons of high explosives (RDX and TNT) from Ukraine on board the LTTE ship MV *Baris*. The World Tamil Movement, the premier LTTE front in Canada, provided the funds to procure this consignment through a bank account in Hong Kong–Shanghai Bank in Vancouver.[17] Among other attacks, the LTTE used these explosives to conduct suicide attacks on the Central Bank in Colombo on January 31, 1996 and on the Hotel Galadari in Colombo on October 15, 1997. The latter target was selected by the LTTE because the intended target, the newly inaugurated World Trade Centre, could not be successfully attacked.[18]

On February 13, 1996, the Sri Lankan navy and air force sank the LTTE ship MV *Horizon*, which was carrying a consignment of explosives and other military equipment. On March 3, 1999, Sri Lankan and Indian navies sank the LTTE ship MV *Mariama*, which was carrying a large consignment of military equipment in the Mullaitivu seas. On April 9, 2000, the Marine Police raided the LTTE boatbuilding yard in Phuket and recovered among other items:

1. Submersible/Mini-Submarine
2. Water Scooter
3. Speed Boats

In October 2003, the LTTE delegation that traveled for talks with the government in October 2003 brought equipment for the LTTE in Colombo from Ireland as personal items, as follows:

1. 10 or 12 Radars for Sea Tigers Boats
2. 2 Kenwood VHF Sets
3. 3 or 4 Walkie-Talkies

The LTTE Shipping Network

The LTTE maintained a shipping network unrivalled by any other threat group in history. As the LTTE was a large secret organization, no one single person knew the entire structure, processes, and assets of the group. As the lifeline to the LTTE was considered to be its shipping network, this component of the LTTE was perhaps the most secretive. Over the years, LTTE ships, procurement officers, captains, and ships came to the attention of law enforcement, military, intelligence, and other government agencies. The ships from 1984–2001 included:

1. MV *Cholan*, the first ship purchased by the LTTE from Singapore in 1984
2. MV *Illiyana*, purchased and operated in Asia
3. MV *Sunbird*, detained by the Malaysian authorities
4. MV *Golden Bird*
5. MV *Ahat*, destroyed by Indian navy as MV *Yahata*
6. MT *Showamaru*, a Japanese merchant tanker
7. MV *Omiross*
8. MV *Emerald*
9. MV *Swene*, also operated as MV *Bari*
10. MV *Akatsu*, Japanese-built
11. UV *Blue Hawk*, a 96-seat passenger ferry, but used as a utility vessel for transporting cargo; Japanese-built with a US engine
12. MV *Satsuma*, Japanese-built
13. MV *Orion 1*
14. MV *Horizon*
15. MT *Mariama*, Japanese-built
16. MV Daishin, Japanese-built
17. MV *Seishin*, Japanese-built
18. UV *Magamai*, Japanese-built
19. UV *Rakuy*, Japanese-built
20. MV *Matsushima*, Japanese-built
21. MT *Shoshin*, Japanese-built
22. MT *Manyoshi*, Japanese-built
23. MV *Shinwa*, Japanese-built
24. MV *Seiko*, Japanese-built

After 2001,

25. MT *Seyo*, Japanese-built
26. MT *Koshia*, South Korean–built

27. MT *Kyoi*, Japanese-built

28. MT *Koi*, Japanese-built

After K.P. was sidelined in 2003, the procurement and shipping operations were separated. While Aiyyah was entrusted with the responsibility for overall procurement, Kandiahpillai Bakerathan (alias Bhavi, alias Bahi, alias Khan) was entrusted with the overall responsibility for managing the shipping network. This network has been mapped on the basis of debriefings of those who were a part of the network, including captains, crew members, and procurement officers. In addition to the chief of communication of the EEZ-MLST, Arulananthan Nishantha (alias Illankottuwan), this included others who developed their knowledge from listening to the secret communications between LTTE HQ and the ships.[19]

The LTTE built a strong relationship with North Korea to procure armaments, starting in 1996. The transactions demonstrate that by 1996 the LTTE relied on North Korea extensively. On May 3, 1999, immediately after MV *Shinwa* was purchased by the LTTE, both *Shinwa* and *Matsushima* went to North Korea in the span of one week. While MV *Matsushima* was loaded with ten 82-mm mortar weapons, ten PK LMG rifles, and other small weapons, MV *Shinwa* was loaded with 120-mm machine guns and 20,000 shells. While Rajendram Karunakaran (alias Pradeepan) from the war materials production unit traveled to the equator south of Sri Lanka on this ship with Captain Kamal, Nathan from Point Pedro remained in North Korea.[20] In the second half of 1999, MV *Shinwa* traveled to North Korea to transport 5,000 130-mm shells, 50 tons of TNT, and 25 tons each of RDX and C-4 explosives. In March 2000, MV *Matsushima* transported six 130-mm machine guns, 10,000 shells for 130-mm guns, ten 82-mm mortar weapons, and 10,000 mortar barrels. Both Nathan and Kamal traveled from North Korea to Sri Lanka. Around August 2000, Pradeepan traveled on the ship MV *Seiko*, the largest ship owned by the LTTE, to North Korea to transport another weapons consignment. The shipment included ten 120-mm mortar weapons, 10,000 shells, ten 17.5-mm weapons, and 3,000 shells for 107-mm weapons. Pradeepan remained in North Korea. The ship MV *Shinwa* arrived in North Korea around January 7, 2001. The ship was loaded with nine 152-mm weapons and 10,000 shells.

Destruction of the LTTE Fleet

For much of the conflict, LTTE vessels smuggling arms, ammunition, and other supplies to northern Sri Lanka turned the battle in favor of the LTTE.

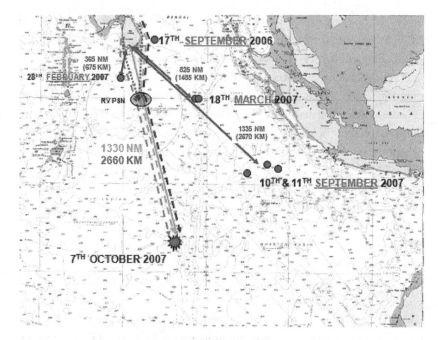

MAP 12.1 Locations of Sea Tiger ships destroyed by the Sri Lankan navy
SOURCE: Sri Lankan navy.

After September 11, 2001, however, LTTE's international isolation increased as the world community became more focused on eradicating terrorism. As a result, a number of countries increased military cooperation with Sri Lanka, especially in the area of intelligence.[21] Map 12.1 of the Indian Ocean region shows locations for some of the LTTE ships destroyed. A chronology of success after 2001 follows:

• The LTTE MT *Koi Maran*, captained by Lt. Col. Silappasan (alias Silambarasan, alias Ranjan), was destroyed on March 10, 2003. The tanker was transporting 3,000 120-mm shells, 3,500 82-mm shells, and 1,500 130-mm shells. When the LTTE was in the process of unloading matériel from the ship, the Sri Lankan navy destroyed it about 180 nautical miles off the Mullaitivu coast.

• The LTTE MT *Shoshin*, captained by Maj. Nirmalan, was destroyed on June 14, 2003. The vessel was transporting 300,000–500,000 liters of fuel; 25,000 artillery and mortar shells; 4 artillery guns; 20 mortar guns; 25 Yamaha 250 and 25 Suzuki outboard motors; 10,000 kg of C-4, RDX, and TNT; 5,000 kg of food; and 5,000 meters of cloth. The vessel was interdicted off Mullaitivu by the Sri Lankan navy and the Sri Lankan air force. During the attack on LTTE MT *Kioshi*, the captain, Stephen, escaped. Arrested and released by the Indonesian authorities, Stephen continued to serve on board LTTE ships.

- The LTTE procured the bulk of their weapons from North Korea. However, for certain specialized weapons such as surface-to-air missiles (SAMs) essential to turn the battle in LTTE's favor, they turned to the United States for procurement. Bold and willing to accept the risk, the LTTE financiers and procurement officers tried to bribe US government officials and procure from them. The LTTE decision to procure weapons in the US led the West to share their intelligence on the LTTE procurement and shipping network with Sri Lanka and its counterparts. The FBI in the US mounted operations against two dozen LTTE procurement officers and others attempting to purchase SA18 missile launchers, AK 47 rifles, and other weapons on US soil in August and September 2006.

- As some LTTE operatives operated across borders, the RCMP and FBI co-investigated and mounted joint operations. The British and Australian law enforcement and intelligence agencies worked with their US and Canadian counterparts, leading to the uncovering of the LTTE fundraising, procurement, and shipping network. Thavarasa Pratheepan (alias Sampras Thavaraja, alias Tambi Sampras) was arrested by Indonesian police when he was on a flight bound for Malaysia on January 4, 2007 and handed over to the FBI for further investigation. He was involved in the abortive purchase of SAMs for the LTTE. As exemplified below, the sharing of specific intelligence led to the detection and disruption of the LTTE shipping network by the Sri Lankan navy. Other governments, including India, assisted with both the intelligence and the interdiction. With the improved quality of intelligence, the Sri Lankan navy developed the capacity to go out at sea and strike. With the destruction of the bulk of the LTTE fleet in 2006, 2007, and 2008, the LTTE could not replenish its matériel losses.

- The LTTE vessel captained by Stephen (alias Lt. Col. Maniyan) was transporting weapons from the equator to the north and was destroyed on September 17, 2006. Both the Sri Lankan navy and the Sri Lankan air force targeted this Indonesian-built fast vessel off Kalmunai in eastern Sri Lanka.

- The LTTE vessel *Marudu* was destroyed by the Sri Lankan navy on September 26, 2006. The vessel, 35 nm off Arippu on the west coast, was transporting weapons.

• LTTE MT *Kioshi*, captained by Murugan with sixteen crew members, was destroyed off Dondra by the Sri Lankan navy on February 28, 2007. The ship transported about 600 120-mm shells, 150 130-mm shells, and 25 barrels of aircraft fuel. The LTTE ship was 185 nm off Dondra in the southern seas.

• An Indian trawler, *Sri Krishna*, hijacked by the LTTE, was transporting weapons when interdicted by the Maldivian coast guard on May 17, 2007. The coast guard sank the trawler, rescued the Indian engineer, and captured the LTTE crew. The debriefing, carried out jointly by US, Australian, and Indian intelligence, provided insights into where the LTTE warehouses were floating.

• The LTTE MT *Eyoshi*, a new tanker, captained by Lt. Col. Issaikon, was destroyed on March 18, 2007. The tanker carried T56 guns; 130-mm and 152-mm artillery guns; 130-mm, 120-mm, and 85-mm mortar guns; as well as 130-mm, 152-mm, 122-mm, 120-mm, and 81-mm shells. In addition to oil, grease, and a heavy electric engine and cloth to stitch military uniforms and shoes, the ship also carried outboard engines—Suzuki, Yamaha, Johnson 250 hp. The vessel was destroyed by the Sri Lankan navy in the seas southeast of Arugam Bay.

• The LTTE MT *Koshia*, captained by Amman, was destroyed together with two other ships in the seas southeast of Dondra by the Sri Lankan navy on September 10–11, 2007. The ship, also known as MV *Goishin* (alias MV *Joishin*, alias MV *Jeishin*), had the IMO No. 8518948. In addition to transporting 29,000 artillery rounds (152-mm and 122-mm) and artillery guns,[22] the ship was transporting 9,000 82-mm shells, 1,500 130-mm shells, 50,000 152-mm shells, and an unknown quantity of aviation fuel.

• LTTE MV *Seishin*, captained by Sobithan, was destroyed in September 2007. Also known as MV *Mann*, the old cargo vessel with the IMO No. 8312825 was transporting mortar launchers, 60-mm and 120-mm shells, artillery guns, 2.7-mm and 14.5-mm guns, 40–50 barrels of air fuel, and 7,000 rolls of cloth for uniforms.[23] The ship was destroyed together with two other ships in the seas southeast of Dondra by the Sri Lankan navy on September 10–11, 2007.

• LTTE MT *Manyoshi*, captained by Senpakavenan (alias Senpgaselvan, alias Semba), was destroyed together with two other ships in the seas southeast of Dondra by the Sri Lankan navy on September 10–11, 2007. The ship, with the IMO No. 8106513, was transporting a bulletproof vehicle, radars, GPS, uniform cloth materials, small arms, and ammunition.[24] MT *Manyoshi* was anchored off Indonesia and maintained a floating armory. Bahi in Indonesia provided the food and fuel.

• LTTE MV *Matsushima*, captained by Kapilan (alias Kabilan), was destroyed by the Sri Lankan navy on October 7, 2007. The ship, with IMO No. 8221571, was transporting 2,000 130-mm shells, 1,000 152-mm shells, 700 140-mm shells, boat engine parts, HF sets, 3 aircraft, one Land Cruiser Jeep, one bulletproof Land Cruiser Jeep, torpedoes, torpedo launchers, sonar, jet skis, diving equipment, swimmer-delivery vehicles, and water scooters.[25]

Despite these reversals, the LTTE was determined to maintain its supplies. The LTTE MT *Koshia*, captained by Kamal, transported 50 tons of C-4, 10,000 T-56 weapons, 100 thousand rounds of ammunition, and 120-mm mortar shells in November 2004. LTTE MV *Shinwa*, captained by Kamal and Vinod, transported 20,000 120-mm shells, 500 AK 47 weapons, 300 pistols, four antitank weapons, and 100 PK weapons (35-mm cannon) between 2005 and 2006. The LTTE MV *Shinwa* transported 5,000 130-mm shells, 50 tons of TNT, 25 tons each of RDX and C-4 explosives from North Korea to Sri Lanka in late 2007. As of May 2009, the ship was anchored in the seas off Indonesia.

In May 2009, the LTTE leadership was isolated in Mullaitivu. The LTTE leaders and members could not escape because the army had cordoned off the area from the land and the navy by sea. Although 11,500 cadres surrendered and were rehabilitated, most of the leaders committed suicide or were killed. The LTTE brown-water capability was nonexistent, but a few of its ships remained overseas. On July 30, 2009, Sri Lanka's State Intelligence Service reported to the Security Council of Sri Lanka that two LTTE captains remained overseas. As captain of MV *Princess Easwary*, Captain Kamalraj Kandasamy attempted to transport the last consignment of arms, ammunition, and explosives from North Korea to Sri Lanka in early 2009. As the EEZ MLST logistic support team was dismantled and there was no other way for him to move the weapons to the LTTE land forces, he dumped the weapons in the sea and returned to Indonesia. After renaming his ship MV *Ocean Lady*, Captain Kamalraj Kandasamy and his crew transported to Canada LTTE members, LTTE family members, and Sri Lankan Tamils who paid for their voyage. Second, Captain Vinod, who was captain of *Matsushima* and *Kio*, remained back in Southeast Asia to transport other LTTE members. With the disruption operations carried out by the Canadian, Australian, and other local law enforcement and intelligence services, Captain Vinod's plan to transport another group of LTTE and non-LTTE Tamils from Indonesia-Thai-Malaysian waters to Canada was shelved. Vinod traveled to Scandinavia and claimed asylum.

Conclusion

The decline of the LTTE was driven by four factors. One was the destruction of the LTTE shipping fleet. The other three were the defection of Karuna (the overall military commander and eastern commander of the LTTE, over a disagreement with Prabhakaran), the increase in Sri Lankan military strength that enabled the military to fight in multiple theaters, and the aggressive LTTE conscription and taxation that led the public to turn away from the LTTE. The LTTE persisted, but only a handful of shipments reached their ground forces. With ever-better government intelligence, the LTTE failed to replenish its material wastage by sea.

The maritime capabilities of the LTTE enabled them to survive and wage a sustained campaign, as well as enabling and empowering them to successfully fight against two standing armies—the Indian peacekeeping force and the Sri Lankan security forces—for three decades. The Sri Lankan naval innovation and operations led by Admiral Wasantha Karannagoda to dismantle the LTTE blue- and brown-water capabilities was a game-changer in defeating them.

The LTTE has been defeated, but the Sri Lankan navy has to play a frontline role in collecting intelligence and engaging the vulnerable communities to prevent a resurgence. The Naval Research Wing was initiated by Admiral Jayanth Collambage in 2003 to systematically document the history of the LTTE maritime organization and operations. Although the bulk of the Sea Tigers have been rehabilitated and lead normal lives in Sri Lanka, a few dozen engage in crime to survive overseas. The Sri Lankan navy has yet to engage the rehabilitated and un-rehabilitated LTTE cadres to ensure they do not return to violence or share their expertise with other threat groups as they have done in the past. According to Mumbai Police Commissioner Rakesh Maria, who investigated the Mumbai terrorist attacks of November 26–29, 2008, the LTTE trained the Allah Tigers, an elite maritime wing of Lashkar-e-Taiba (LeT). The seaborne infiltration of ten suicide attackers of LeT created a new threat landscape in India and beyond.

As the expertise on the LTTE, including that of the Sea Tigers, very much rests with the Sri Lankan security forces that defeated the LTTE, it is paramount for the Sri Lankan navy, especially its Special Boats Squadron, to share their experience and expertise with the rest of the world. Furthermore, there is a need to invest in expanding Sri Lankan naval intelligence capabilities that will secure Sri Lanka, the region, and the world from the LTTE as the organization continues its attempts to revive.

Notes

1. The LTTE did not simply disappear after its military defeat. Remnants of the force continue to operate through political action, fueled by organized crime.
2. Jeffrey H. Norwitz, ed., *Armed Groups: Studies in National Security, Counterterrorism and Counterinsurgency* (Newport: US Naval War College, 2008).
3. John F. Burns, "Asia's Latest Master of Terror: A Sri Lankan Evokes Pol Pot," *New York Times*, May 28, 1995.
4. Interview, Srikumar Kanagaratnam (alias Raheem), former LTTE spokesperson, relocated to Canada, June 7, 2012.
5. Ibid.
6. Ibid.
7. Interview, Commodore Y.N. Jayaratne, Sri Lankan navy, 2004.
8. LTTE diary of combat.
9. This letter can be seen at the Naval Museum in Trincomalee, Sri Lanka.
10. Robert A. Pape, "The Strategic Logic of Suicide Terrorism," *American Political Science Review*, Vol. 97, No. 3, August 2003.
11. After al-Qaeda's USS *Cole* attack in Yemen in October 2000, Sea Tiger Chief Soosai said, "I think in Yemen, they used our strategy of targeting the hull of their suicide attack to blow up an American ship USS Cole. This is exactly what we used to do." *BBC*, March 19, 2003.
12. "Profile: Meet K.P.," *Sunday Leader*, Sri Lanka, May 31, 2009, available at http://www.thesundayleader.lk/20090531/profile.htm. Contrary to press reporting that Vaithyalingam Soranalingam (alias Shankar) was responsible for setting up the LTTE's office of overseas purchases (OOP), K.P. said in an interview with the author that it was he who established LTTE's procurement office. Interview with K.P., North-East Rehabilitation and Development Organization, Kilinochchi, Sri Lanka, December 20, 2012.
13. Interview with K.P., North-East Rehabilitation and Development Organization, Kilinochchi, Sri Lanka, December 20, 2012.
14. Subramanian Swamy, *Assassination of Rajiv Gandhi: Unanswered Questions and Unasked Queries* (New Delhi: Konark Publishers, 2000). The Central Bureau of Investigation's Special Investigation Team (SIT Folder No/XV Part II) MADRAS is comprehensive. During 1983 K.P. was arrested for smuggling gold worth Rs 40 lakhs from Singapore to Bombay in collusion with Vakil Kandasamy. He was then operating under the name of Kutti (alias Padmanabha). He was arrested again for smuggling in 1984.
15. LTTE Procurement from Indonesia, FBI Report, New Delhi.
16. LTTE International Organization, Malaysian Special Branch, December 1990.

17. Government of Canada, confidential source.

18. A team from the Bureau of Alcohol, Tobacco, Firearms and Explosives, US Department of Justice, visited Sri Lanka and analyzed the explosives residue. The ATF report conclusively links the explosives used in the attacks to the consignment procured by the LTTE in Ukraine.

19. Myles, a communications officer, identified 26 ships. Debriefing in December 2009.

20. Nathan's family, including parents—naturalized citizens of Canada—lived in Canada. To study navigation, Nathan subsequently left for Canada. Nathan's cousin was Charles, a well-known leader in TOSIS who masterminded several bombings and assassinations.

21. The US State Department designated the Liberation Tigers of Tamil Eelam (LTTE) a foreign terrorist group on October 8, 1997. After the September 11, 2001 terrorist attacks in the US, and the Bush administration's subsequent "Global War on Terror," the US became more active in its political, military, and intelligence support of the Sri Lankan government. See the US State Department's list of foreign terrorist organizations. http://www.state.gov/j/ct/rls/other/des/123085.htm (as of February 2, 2015).

22. Commodore Ravindra Wijegunaratna, *Importance of Securing Regional Waters*, Sri Lankan navy, October 2007.

23. Ibid.

24. Ibid.

25. Ibid.

13 Suppressing Piracy in the Strait of Malacca

Lawrence E. Cline

ALTHOUGH NOT RECEIVING THE POPULAR ATTENTION THAT piracy off the coast of Somalia did in recent years, the Malacca Strait has had, for a considerable period, a significant number of piracy and other seaborne crimes.[1] Because the Strait of Malacca represents one of the world's major shipping routes—and likewise is a potential choke point—developments in this waterway have significant impact. This chapter is intended to survey the overall security issues surrounding the strait, and the efforts that have been taken to improve the security environment along its waters.

Geography and Importance of the Malacca Strait

The Strait of Malacca (or Melaka in Malay) represents one of the key trade routes in the world. It is about 805 kilometers long, beginning in the north between Malaysia and Thailand and stretching along the Malay Peninsula and the Indonesian island of Sumatra. It is somewhat funnel-shaped, with an average width of about 250 kilometers in the north, narrowing to 65 kilometers in the south. At its narrowest point, the Phillips Channel, to the south of Singapore, the strait narrows to only 2.8 kilometers wide, creating a major choke point. It is relatively shallow, with its shallowest portion only about 25 meters deep, reducing its usefulness for some of the larger oil tankers. Even though this reduces some economy-of-scale advantages, the time-distance factor still gives the strait economic advantages over other routes:

> The voyage of a tanker from an Arabian Gulf port to Yokohama in Japan would be about sixty-five hundred nautical miles in length using the Straits of Malacca but well over seventy-five hundred nautical miles using the Lombok-Makassar route. For a supertanker moving at a typical cruising speed of fifteen knots, this would add about three days to the journey.[2]

The political geography of the strait is rather complex. The Phillips Channel creates an area of the strait that lies completely within the territorial waters of Singapore and Indonesia. Likewise, at its eastern outlet into the South China Sea, it lies within claimed Malaysian and Indonesian waters. Each of the three countries bordering the major part of the Malacca Strait— Indonesia, Malaysia, and Singapore—has varying claims to the strait based on internal waters, territorial seas, contiguous zones, and exclusive economic zones. Even though not all these claims are internationally recognized, they create a rather complex legal environment.[3] As will be discussed later, all of this leads to some significant diplomatic, operational, and practical issues in providing security for the strait.

The Malacca Strait is the main shipping channel between the Pacific and the Indian Oceans. Equally important, it is also the shortest sea route to the South China Sea. Even though, as noted earlier, it is too shallow for the largest tankers, it is the critical route for oil supplies to Japan, Indonesia, and China, with an estimated flow of 15.2 million barrels a day in 2011.[4] Although firm figures are difficult to establish definitively, the most common midrange estimate is that:

> Over 60,000 vessels use the Straits annually, including large tankers and cargo carriers proceeding from Europe and the Middle East to East Asia, as well as smaller vessels on local voyages. Around 30 per cent of world trade and 50 per cent of world energy needs pass through the Straits each year.[5]

As noted, the strait is particularly important in energy transport: "In terms of energy transport, more than two-thirds of the world's liquefied oil and natural gas passes through the busy sea-lanes. This is three times more than the oil and gas cargo passing through the Suez Canal and fifteen times more than the fuel traffic transported via the Panama Canal."[6] Combined with the movement of other goods, and the importance of contiguous waters as major fishing grounds and for local trade, the economic impact of the Strait of Malacca continues to be internationally important.

Piracy in the Strait

Historically, the Strait of Malacca has been known as a haven for pirates and seaborne criminals.[7] This certainly extended into the 1990s and early 2000s. Piracy attacks have involved robberies, vessel hijackings, and kidnappings for ransom. The largest number of attacks has been robberies. For several years (although apparently now not a significant problem) there has also been an issue with "ghost ships," in which (usually smaller) vessels have been hijacked and then used for fraudulent trade. Although details are not always available, the most common weapons used by the pirates have been *parangs* (the local equivalent of machetes) or knives. Generally, the level of violence has been relatively limited, and ransom demands for kidnapped crewmembers and seized vessels quite "reasonable" by international standards.[8] Typical pirate crews number between five and ten, with most attacks occurring at night.

During this period, international attention increasingly became focused on the piracy threat in this area. Statistics from the International Maritime Organization (IMO) on crimes against vessels and their crews in the Malacca Strait, depicted in Table 13.1, suggest the scope of the issue.

Unfortunately, there are a number of complications with actually determining the true scope of the problem. The first is simply how piracy is defined and reported. As noted elsewhere in this volume, analysts have used two principal definitions, one by the IMO and the other by the International Maritime Bureau (IMB). These definitional issues result in some very different figures for piracy. Further complicating the picture is that various national estimates also differ at times. The regional reporting system, the Information Sharing Centre, has provided yet other figures.[9] Even using only the IMO standards in the case of the Strait of Malacca can be problematic. Owing to the overlapping territorial waters of the bordering countries, the "high-seas" requirement may not apply to a considerable length of the strait.

Other issues also complicate the picture. In common with other piracy-prone areas of the world, it is quite likely that the ship operators and shipping companies simply do not report the full extent of either piracy or other seaborne crimes. In some cases, this has been the result of being unwilling to

TABLE 13.1 Crimes against vessels in the Malacca Strait

	1996	1997	1998	1999	2000	2001	2002	2003	2004	2005	2006	2007	2008	2009	2010	2011	2012
LOCATION																	
International waters	4	2	3	16	75	12	10	8	20	8	5	4	2	0	0	5	0
Territorial waters	5	4	3	13	25	13	6	3	3	2	3	1	0	0	0	14	2
Port	3	2	0	8	12	11	8	4	12	0	8	1	0	0	0	2	0
STATUS																	
Steaming	3	4	5	22	76	17	12	11	22	8	4	1	2	0	0	9	1
At anchor or at berth	7	4	1	15	34	19	10	3	13	2	7	3	0	0	0	8	1
Not stated	2	0	0	0	2	0	2	1	0	0	5	2	0	0	0	4	0

SOURCE: International Maritime Organization Data for Piracy Incidents in the Straits of Malacca (Extracted from Annual Reports, International Maritime Organization, London).

face the prospect of increased insurance costs. Reporting also ties up ships in lengthy postattack investigations, which means they are not moving goods and, hence, not making money. In other cases, ship operators—particularly of smaller regional vessels operated locally—may have found through experience that little is to be gained from reporting. Clearly, the nonreporting, for whatever reason, is not subject to firm estimates, but also has to be factored into the overall picture.[10]

The reason that the "baseline" numbers matter is that without an accurate picture of the true environment, it is virtually impossible to measure whether or not various initiatives are in fact succeeding. In general, however, some fairly rough trend lines can be determined. The overall trajectory of the numbers indicates that the Malacca Strait (and associated territorial waters) began having a spike in piracy in 1999, reaching crisis proportions in 2000. After 2000, it then began dropping again from 2001 to 2003, with somewhat of a spike in 2004, although nowhere near as bad as 2000. It once again dropped significantly beginning in 2005, reaching zero reported cases in 2009–2010. As profiled in Figure 13.1, there was an increase in 2011, but the numbers dropped again in 2012.

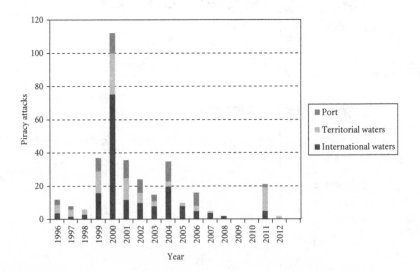

FIGURE 13.1 Piracy statistics for Strait of Malacca
SOURCE: International Maritime Organization Data for Piracy Incidents in the Straits of Malacca (Extracted from Annual Reports, International Maritime Organization, London).

Although decidedly not the thrust of this chapter, brief mention should be made about a possible associated threat, that of terrorism. A number of analysts have argued that the Malacca Strait is a very logical target for terrorism due to its geographical characteristics, its importance to global commerce, and issues surrounding adequate regional security.[11] All these factors, of course, can be combined with the fact that a number of terrorist groups are operating in Southeast Asia (albeit none around the Strait of Malacca), most notably Jama'at Islamiya, Abu Sayyaf Group, the Moro Islamic Liberation Front, and affiliates of al-Qaida. To date, however, there has been little concrete evidence of terrorist groups targeting the strait. Thus far, in fact, there have been only two major threats noted publicly. The first was noted by the Indonesian Chief of Intelligence, who stated, "Jemaah Islamiah terrorists now in detention have admitted that attacks on the Malacca shipping lane have been contemplated in the recent past."[12] The second was the reported involvement by members of the Free Aceh Movement (GAM) in a kidnapping for ransom, but these cases are murky at best.[13] Despite the very limited evidence of terrorist operations around the Malacca Strait, in 2005 Lloyd's of London temporarily designated the strait an Area of Enhanced War Risk, raising insurance costs for shipping companies; this designation was lifted in 2006.

Worldwide, there have been some international maritime terrorism attacks, including the 1985 hijacking of the *Achille Lauro*; the 2000 bombing of the USS *Cole* in Aden Harbor; the 2002 attack on the French oil tanker *Limburg* in the Gulf of Aden; and several attacks in inshore waters in the Philippines against ferries and other small craft. It would seem logical that some terrorist movements in the area would look to the strait for operations, given its criticality. Thus far, however, this has not seemed to be a focus for terrorist groups, either in the area or elsewhere. At least in part, this might simply be a function of terrorist "comfort zones": most groups have appeared to be much more land-focused. None of this obviates completely the threat of terrorist attacks, but many of the counterpiracy efforts already in place can serve double-duty as counterterrorism measures.

Regional Countries' Capabilities for Countering Piracy

One practical issue for the three countries most directly involved in providing security for the strait is that of the basic capability of their respective naval forces. The Indonesian navy has two submarines, six frigates and destroyers, twenty-three corvettes, seven missile craft, fourteen offshore patrol craft, and thirty inshore patrol craft.[14] Clearly, only some of these vessels are suitable for counterpiracy operations. Moreover, both the quality and age of the ships have degraded actual capabilities. Operational status of the equipment has remained problematical; one author cites a 30 percent operational ready status in 2004–2005, with a more recent estimate of a 50 percent readiness status.[15] Indonesia has announced a major military restructuring and modernization program under the rubric of the *minimum essential force* to be completed by 2024.[16] Even if these plans reach fruition, many of the purchases planned for the Indonesian navy are more suited for conventional naval battles than for counterpiracy or counterterrorism operations.

Likewise, both Malaysia and Singapore are equipped for major naval operations, although Singapore does have more strength in actual patrol vessels and has demonstrated that providing security in its territorial waters is a major priority. Malaysia has two submarines, two frigates, ten corvettes, eight missile craft, and six inshore patrol vessels. Singapore's naval inventory includes six submarines, four large amphibious vessels (a cross between transports and helicopter carriers), six frigates, six corvettes, and twenty-four patrol vessels.[17] As with Indonesia, Malaysia has announced a modernization program, apparently with both lesser aspirations and at considerably less cost.[18] Singapore might be described as being in perpetual modernization, but has focused on gradual buildup of its naval forces.

The role of coast guard–type forces is at least as critical as naval forces for counterpiracy operations; two of the three regional countries have the functional equivalent of a coast guard. Malaysia has the Malaysian Maritime Enforcement Agency (the MMEA or APMM). This service is equipped with about eighty-eight vessels of various classes, together with some 163 small boats, two amphibious planes, and six helicopters.[19] It should be noted, however, that many of these vessels are over thirty years old, with some of them being received as used equipment from other ministries such as Fishing or Customs. The MMEA also operates a chain of radar sea surveillance systems along the strait, both for safety and security. The service has claimed a "significant number of successful interdictions" as a result of this system.[20] The MMEA is a relatively new service, not officially launched until March 21, 2006. Its formation was based on a 1999 government study that found that maritime "enforcement was not effective because too many agencies were involved that resulted in overlapping functions, overlapping jurisdiction, and uneconomical use of resources."[21] The stated missions of the MMEA look virtually identical to any nation's coast guard.

The Singapore service also has a relatively short history. Singapore had a long-standing marine police force that was upgraded to the police coast guard on February 13, 1993. The police coast guard's stated missions tend to be very inshore-oriented: "joint operations with the Republic of Singapore Navy (RSN), anti-illegal migrant operations, handling foreign government vessel intrusions and guarding Horsburgh Lighthouse in the Singapore Straits."[22] The mission statement also notes search and rescue operations. Singapore has had an active program to regularly upgrade their vessels, so establishing exact numbers of active patrol craft is difficult, but Singapore has about fifty coastal vessels of various classes currently being operated.[23]

Indonesia is somewhat the "odd man out." Although it has several agencies that deal with various aspects of maritime security, as of at least February 2013 it did not have a unified coast guard. According to the *Jakarta Post*, although a coast guard was intended to have been established in 2011, "The [Transportation] ministry's director general for sea transportation, Leon Muhammad said in Jakarta last week the drafting of the regulation had been slow as several sections of the regulation had to be changed due to resistance from a number of institutions involved in maintaining maritime safety and security."[24]

The three countries have national coordination bodies for developing national-level policies for maritime security. Indonesia formed the Maritime Security Coordinating Board (Bakorkamla) in 1972. Its missions include establishing general policies, coordinating operations, and increasing institutional capacity. Membership comprises civilian ministries, the military, police, and intelligence services. It also supervises the Maritime Security Policy Preparation Center and the Maritime Security Operations Coordination Center.[25] As one report notes, however, Bakorkamla "possesses the authority to coordinate existing institutions via a 2005 presidential regulation, but only at a 'planning level' and it cannot give directives in the field."[26]

In Singapore, the Maritime Security Task Force is organized under the Singapore armed forces. It comprises three groups: the Comprehensive Maritime Awareness Group (which is intended to work closely not only with other government agencies, but also with the shipping community); the Operations Group, which is completely military; and the Inter-Agency Coordination Group, which incorporates representatives of the "Police Coast Guard (PCG), the Maritime and Port Authority of Singapore (MPA), the Immigration & Checkpoints Authority (ICA), and the Singapore Customs (Customs)."[27]

Malaysia formed the National Maritime Enforcement and Coordination Centre (NMECC) in 1985. This actually preceded the formation of the Malaysian Maritime Enforcement Agency, and as one senior Malaysian officer noted, this

> did not solve the problem of enforcement as each agency was still engulfed with its own priorities and interests particularly in managing its assets and human resources. Besides this, NMECC also lacked command and control functions over the agencies while the assets assigned to her were meant to meet specific duties only.[28]

The problems associated with NMECC in fact were directly responsible for the creation of the MMEA, which reportedly has solved many of these difficulties.

Regional Cooperative Responses to Piracy

Regional operational coordinated efforts began in July 2004, with the launch of the Malacca Strait Security Patrols. On September 13, 2005, Malaysia, Singapore, and Indonesia launched the Eyes in the Sky (EiS) initiative—later joined by Thailand and the Philippines—incorporating long-range aircraft patrols along the strait. Each patrol aircraft was intended to have officers from each of the countries on board. The three initial countries followed this in April 2006 with the Malacca Strait Sea Patrol [MSSP; initially called the MALSINDO (Malaysia-Singapore-Indonesia) naval patrols]. Each naval vessel in these patrols is intended to have a team with officers from each of the countries on board to facilitate operations. A joint coordinating committee coordinates both programs, serving as a means to coordinate intelligence and operational procedures.

These two efforts became institutionalized as the Malacca Strait Patrol (MSP). Initially conducted by the three countries, Thailand then joined in September 2008. Along with the MSP, the three nations (later joined by Thailand) formed the MSP Intelligence Exchange Group to support the deployment of the patrols. This group developed an information-sharing system called the Malacca Strait Patrols Information System. This is a secure web-based platform that enables real-time information and intelligence reporting among all the deployed regional assets.

Although more broadly based than merely focusing on the Malacca Strait itself, the Regional Cooperation Agreement on Combating Piracy and Armed Robbery Against Ships in Asia (ReCAAP), signed in 2004 and implemented on September 4, 2006, has also had an important role.[29] Nineteen countries, both Asian and European, have signed this agreement.[30] All signatories to ReCAAP have to have statutes on their books that criminalize the act of piracy. Significantly, however, neither Indonesia nor Malaysia has ratified membership in the organization, although both reportedly maintain *de facto* coordination with the system. Parenthetically, it might be argued that these two countries' relationship with ReCAAP might be analogous to the US's official attitude of abiding with the provisions of the United Nations Convention on the Law of the Sea despite not having formally ratified it. Although not an official government position, a statement in the *Jakarta Post* likely summarizes the underlying logic of the Indonesian reluctance to participate:

> [T]he weaknesses of the multilateral maritime security cooperation regimes in fighting non-traditional threats provides a greater incentive for Indonesia not to rely on them and to start building a more comprehensive naval capability.[31]

This go-it-alone attitude—although moderated by less formal forms of cooperation and coordination with regional countries—and deep concerns over national sovereignty likely will continue to impact both Indonesia's and Malaysia's willingness to expand formal cooperative measures. At the same time, however, both countries in fact have continued to expand cooperation with neighbors, such as the Philippines, with measures such as information sharing agreements.

Perhaps the most significant contribution of the ReCAAP has been the Information Sharing Centre (ISC), located in Singapore. The official roles of the ISC are to

- serve as a platform for information exchange with the ReCAAP Focal Points via the Information Network System (IFN); facilitate communications and information exchange among participating governments to improve incident response by member countries; analyze and provide accurate statistics of the piracy and armed robbery incidents to foster better understanding of the situation in Asia;

- facilitate capacity-building efforts that help improve the capability of member countries in combating piracy and armed robbery in the region; and
- cooperate with organizations and like-minded parties on joint exercises, information sharing, capacity-building programs, or other forms of cooperation, as appropriate, and agreed upon among the contracting parties.[32]

One important aspect of the ISC is that it has liaison officers from ten countries working there full time.[33] The ISC has a round-the-clock tracking and reporting capability. It also has communications and reporting links with agencies in about twenty-five countries, enabling better coordination. Among other groups, ReCAAP and the ISC coordinate the International Association of Independent Tanker Owners (INTERTANKO), Asian Ship Owners Forum (ASF), the Baltic and International Maritime Council, the NATO Shipping Center, and INTERPOL. At a somewhat lower level, at least according to the Singapore Police Coast Guard website, there has been active cooperation between its service and the Royal Malaysian Marine Police and the Indonesian Navy.[34]

Another coordinating mechanism is the Heads of Asian Coast Guards Meeting. This initiative began with the first meeting held in Tokyo in June 2004, and has been held throughout the region every year except 2005. It involves seventeen countries, including all the Malacca Strait littoral countries.[35] More broadly, the ASEAN Ministerial Meeting on Transnational Crime, established in 1997, meets every two years, with piracy being one of the regular topics for discussion. Piracy has also become a relatively common topic for other regional conferences and meetings.

Contributions from other countries in antipiracy efforts should also be noted. Although Indonesia and Malaysia in particular have been reluctant to cooperate too closely with outside countries, some cooperative programs have been implemented. Japan in particular has been active in trying to support cooperative efforts. The Malacca Strait is critical to Japan, because some 50 percent of its energy resources and about 90 percent of its oil are from the Middle East, almost all of which is transported through the strait. Most Japanese support to the littoral countries thus far has involved holding conferences, coordinating model action plans, deploying survey teams to the area, conducting joint exercises and, of course, providing funding.

The Indian navy has carried out joint antipiracy exercises with both the Singapore navy and Indonesia. In 2002, the Indian and US navies were also permitted to jointly escort vessels transiting the strait carrying high-value American cargo. In May 2013, the Indian government also announced that it was planning on using long-range aircraft from an airbase in the Andaman and Nicobar Islands to patrol the strait.[36] The third major Asian power to have significant reliance on the Strait of Malacca is China. It has provided some rather minor training and assistance to the strait countries, but generally has not gotten too directly involved. In large measure, this likely can be ascribed to the larger geopolitical issues of greater Chinese assertiveness in the South China Sea and beyond. The trust level of Indonesia—and Malaysia in particular—toward China is not high, and Beijing may feel that overly activist initiatives probably would be rebuffed, even if offered.[37]

Not surprisingly, the United States has had considerable interest in enhancing security in the strait. Some proposals for increased US involvement, however, have been stillborn. Perhaps the most ambitious proposal was by Admiral Thomas B. Fargo, then commander of the United States Pacific Command. He offered a plan under the rubric of the Regional Maritime Security Initiative in testimony to Congress on March 31, 2004. In his statement, he said, "we're looking at things like high-speed vessels, putting Special Operations Forces on high-speed vessels to conduct effective interdiction in, once again, these sea lines of communication where terrorists are known to move about." He included the Strait of Malacca in this plan.[38] Both Malaysia and Indonesia quickly (and perhaps unsurprisingly) vetoed the concept. Despite this setback, the US has since been very active in an advise-and-assist role. Both the US Coast Guard and Navy have provided training missions to all three strait nations, and US funding has been provided for improvements such as additional coastal surveillance radar systems along the strait.

Effectiveness of Counterpiracy Operations

Information from the International Maritime Bureau (IMB) said piracy in the Southeast Asian region had decreased by 70 percent due to the implementation of the joint patrol between Indonesia, Malaysia, and Singapore in the Malacca Strait from 2004 to 2011.[39] Another source cited an IMB conclusion that the maritime security patrols have been "directly attributable to keeping the overall number of incidents in this important strategic choke point down."[40] This type of assessment of the tri-national (and, more recently, four-nation) cooperation system has become somewhat conventional wisdom. It might be useful, however, to broaden the discussion to incorporate potential weaknesses of some aspects of the regional cooperative framework and some other possible factors for the reduction in piracy in the Malacca Strait.

There have been some criticisms of the tri-national cooperative efforts at the practical level. One author noted several operational issues in making these measures significantly effective. In particular, these include the aircraft range versus area to be covered by the EiS patrols; problems in actually detecting the small vessels the pirates use; and maintaining operational restrictions owing to the individual countries' insistence on maintaining sovereignty over their declared three-mile maritime limits.[41] Focusing on the EiS missions, Raymond stated, "It is estimated that seventy sorties per week need to be carried out by the aerial patrols in order to monitor the strait effectively, 24/7. However, currently only eight are flown."[42] Likewise, flights reportedly are flown only during daylight hours; since many, if not most, pirate attacks have occurred at night, this clearly limits full effectiveness. Also, the patrols are best described as coordinated rather than truly joint. In large measure, this is the result of legal constraints in apprehending pirates in other countries' territorial waters. At least as of 2008, according to one source, the aerial patrols "cannot go within three miles of the other littoral states' territorial coastlines when in pursuit of pirates."[43] Likewise, the 2001 proposal for a tri-national information-sharing center has not progressed due to disputes over where it would be located.[44]

Full cooperation among the regional countries has also been constrained by national political sensitivities. As Malaysian Deputy Prime Minister Najib Razak explained, "you don't enter each others' territorial waters. No sharing of vessels, no hot pursuit. We have to respect the cardinal principle of national sovereignty."[45] More recently, however, efforts have reportedly been made for a qualified right of hot pursuit or at least a handover of the target between countries. Likewise, when the US mooted the prospects of using American military forces to provide security in the Malacca Strait, Razak stated, "control of the Strait is the sovereign prerogative of Malaysia and Indonesia, and US military involvement is not welcome."[46] One telling comment by a senior Malaysian naval officer in a conference presentation provides one argument for why the Malaysian government is so concerned about maintaining a reasonably stable security environment in the Malacca Strait: the "lack of enforcement portrays lack of display of authority and eventually, sovereignty . . . In fact, the absence of an effective law enforcement mechanism invites intervention by the security forces from other States."[47]

There is a broader split among attitudes by the governments in the region that would seem to underlie their attitudes toward cooperation. This is described well by J.N. Mak:

> The primary and overarching problem was the clash of interests between the key littoral states of Malaysia and Indonesia, which are essentially coastal states with coastal interests on the one hand, and the international users of the Straits . . . Singapore occupies a unique position in Straits cooperation, being geographically a littoral state, but in terms of interests and perceptions, more inclined to adopt the worldview of a maritime state.[48]

Public statements by regional leaders can give a flavor of these differences in attitudes. In response to the plan proposed by Admiral Fargo mentioned earlier, the Malaysian prime minister, Abdullah Ahmad Badawi, remarked, "I think we can look after our own area."[49] In contrast, during a conference in 2004, the then Deputy Prime Minister of Singapore Tony Tan stated, "It is not realistic to unilaterally confine such patrols only to countries in this part of the world. . . . [W]e can do more if we galvanize the resources of extra-regional players."[50]

It is difficult to discuss regional counterpiracy cooperation without factoring in larger transnational disputes that create disincentives to full cooperation. A number of territorial disagreements continue to fester. Although the majority of these involve conflicts between Malaysia or Indonesia and other Asian countries, Malaysia and Indonesia have a long-standing dispute over the potentially oil-rich Ambalat sea block off the coast of Indonesia. Although limited largely to a continuous stream of diplomatic notes, small-scale naval incursions occurred in 2005 and 2009.[51] Likewise, there are long-standing antipathies between Malaysia and Singapore after the latter's expulsion from the Malay Federation in 1965, together with continued territorial disputes.

Larger issues in driving piracy itself must also be incorporated in analyzing the prevalence of piracy and the reasons for increases or decreases. There is no space to address root causes in detail, but economics clearly play a major role. One author notes the importance of piracy to local villagers and fishermen as essentially a supplement to their (frequently uncertain) income.[52] The extreme spike in piracy in 2000 arguably may have been a result of the Asian financial crisis in 1997. Economies throughout the region were crippled, taking several years to recover. Although there was a time lag between 1997 and 2000, this could have been the result both of amateur pirates becoming more skillful at piracy and a certain bandwagon effect in which fishermen and villagers began seeing the success of others.

Likewise, local government corruption and problems with fisheries likely have been driving factors in the rates of piracy.[53] Although never conclusively proven, there have been multiple reports of Indonesian security forces (particularly the military and customs) being implicated either in direct involvement or in support of piracy.[54] Certainly, the overall corruption environment in Indonesia—with Transparency International ratings of 85th of 90 countries in 2000, 133rd of 145 in 2004, and despite some increased governmental reform efforts, 114th of 175 countries in 2013—provided an environment conducive to either direct or indirect support of criminality. Even beyond pure economics, larger seemingly extraneous factors can play a role. For example, Phaovisaid argues that in "2005, pirate attacks in the Malacca Strait declined by 29 percent because the Asian tsunami destroyed ships that were perhaps used by pirates."[55]

Improved security efforts by shipping companies and the ships' crews themselves also almost certainly have played a role in reducing successful attacks. In many cases, these have been the result of either recommendations or requirements instituted by the IMO or IMB. For example, as of July 2004, the IMO required all ships over 300 tons (albeit the minority of vessels using the strait) to install the Ship Security Alert System for rapid reporting of attacks.[56] These technical means should not be overstressed—only a minority of vessels is required to have them, and their use likely is spotty even then—but they may serve as a deterrent to some pirates. Almost certainly more significant, the information-sharing process, especially through the IMB and the ReCAAP systems, has improved greatly. This additional sharing structure between information centers and shipping companies and individual ships enables the captains to be better prepared for secure passage through the strait.

Conclusion

Although problems in measurement complicate a fully accurate assessment, the security situation in the Strait of Malacca has improved significantly since the early 2000s. Suggesting a mono-causal explanation is too simplistic.

Issues such as larger economic trends, along with improved communications and coordination between civilian ships and various coordination centers, have played their roles. Having said that, however, the major improvements in coordinated efforts by the regional countries have played a key role. Beyond this, pressures (both overt and tacit) by regional countries on one another to improve security in their individual territorial waters have increased over time. Although a number of impediments to a true integrated regional counter piracy structure remain, the Malacca Strait countries are much further advanced in regional cooperation against piracy than are most regions. As such, the cooperative systems along the Strait of Malacca deserve study both for their successes and their weaknesses.

Notes

1. The author would like to thank Dr. Peter Chalk for his very valuable comments on the manuscript.

2. Donald B. Freeman, *The Straits of Malacca: Gateway or Gauntlet?* (Quebec: McGill-Queen's University Press, 2003), 119.

3. For details on some of the legal claims and issues surrounding them, see Sam Bateman, Catherine Zara Raymond, and Joshua Ho, *Safety and Security in the Malacca and Singapore Straits: An Agenda for Action* (Singapore: Institute of Defence and Strategic Studies, May 2006), 9–12. Also, Robert C. Beckman, "Combatting Piracy and Armed Robbery Against Ships in Southeast Asia: The Way Forward," *Ocean Development & International Law* 33 (2002), 317–41.

4. US Energy Information Administration, "World Oil Transit Chokepoints," last updated August 22, 2012, available at http://www.eia.gov/countries/regions-topics.cfm?fips=wotc&trk=p3 (accessed 29 December 2013).

5. Bateman et al., *Safety and Security*, 8.

6. Felipe Umaña, *Threat Convergence: Transnational Security Threats in the Straits of Malacca* (Washington, DC: Fund for Peace, 2012), 5.

7. For an historical survey of piracy in the Malacca Strait, see Freeman, *Gateway or Gauntlet?*, 174–88.

8. Stefan Eklof Amirell, "Political Piracy and Maritime Terrorism: A Comparison Between the Straits of Malacca and the Southern Philippines," in Graham Gerard Ong-Webb, ed., *Piracy, Maritime Terrorism and Securing the Malacca Straits* (Singapore: Institute of South East Asia Studies, 2006), 55.

9. For example, for 2009 and 2010, when IMO figures do not show any attacks, ReCAAP reported six actual and three attempted attacks in 2009, and five and three respectively in 2010. ReCAAP Information Sharing System, *Annual Report January–December 2012: Piracy and Armed Robbery Against Ships in Asia* (Singapore: ReCAAP, 2013), 12.

10. One author has cited a nonreporting rate of attacks as possibly being up to 50 percent; Darin Phaovisaid, "Where There's Sugar, the Ants Come: Piracy in the Strait of Malacca," *International Affairs Review* 14/2 (Fall 2005), 93.

11. For example, see Tammy M. Sittnickt, "State Responsibility and Maritime Terrorism in the Strait of Malacca: Persuading Indonesia and Malaysia to Take Additional Steps to Secure the Strait," *Pacific Rim Law & Policy Journal* 14/3 (June 2005), 743–69; Yun Yun Teo, "Target Malacca Straits: Maritime Terrorism in Southeast Asia," *Studies in Conflict & Terrorism* 30/6 (2007), 541–61.

12. Mark J. Valencia, "The Politics of Anti-Piracy and Anti-Terrorism Responses," in Graham Gerard Ong-Webb, ed., *Piracy*, 88.

13. Ibid., 85.

14. Extracted from Global Security at http://www.globalsecurity.org/military/world/indonesia/alri-equipment.htm (accessed December 26, 2013).

15. Tammy M. Sittnickt, "State Responsibility," 754. Ristian Atriandi Supriyanto, "Naval Modernisation: A Sea Change for Indonesia?" *Nation*, January 30, 2012, available at http://www.nationmultimedia.com/opinion/Naval-modernisation-A-sea-change-for-Indonesia-30174719.html (accessed December 28, 2013). A third analyst suggests a readiness rate of 25 percent; Umaña, *Threat Convergence*, 10.

16. For details of the MEF, see "Indonesia's Military Modernization," *Asian Military Review*, November 1, 2012, available at http://www.asianmilitaryreview.com/indonesias-military-modernization/ (accessed December 30, 2013).

17. Figures from http://www.globalsecurity.org (accessed December 28, 2013).

18. "Malaysian Defence Modernisation," *Asian Military Review*, March 1, 2013, available at http://www.asianmilitaryreview.com/malaysian-defence-modernisation/ (accessed December 27, 2013).

19. Figures from attendee at MMEA briefing.

20. First Admiral Maritime Zulkifli bin Abu Bakar, "Enhancing Maritime Security: Law Enforcement in Malaysia," 24th Asia-Pacific Roundtable, Kuala Lumpur, June 7–9, 2010.

21. "MMEA's Background," Malaysian Maritime Enforcement Agency, available at https://www.mmea.gov.my/eng/index.php/en/about-us/background (accessed December 24, 2013).

22. Singapore Police Force website at http://www.spf.gov.sg/abtspf/pcg.htm#dept (accessed December 21, 2013).

23. Estimate based on reporting on the Singapore Police Force website, available at http://www.spf.gov.sg/ (accessed December 23, 2013).

24. "Uncertainty Still Clouds Formation of Coast Guard," *Jakarta Post*, February 4, 2013, 14.

25. Indonesian Maritime Security Coordinating Board website, available at http://bakorkamla.go.id/en/ (accessed December 24, 2013).

26 "Uncertainty Still Clouds Formation of Coast Guard," *Jakarta Post*, February 4, 2013, 14.

27. Ministry of Defense, "MINDEF Singapore Fact Sheet," Singapore, February 23, 2009, 2.

28. Bin Abu Bakar, "Enhancing Maritime Security."

29. The full details of the organization and operations of the ReCAAP are at ReCAAP Information Sharing Centre, "Regional Cooperation Agreement on Combating Piracy and Armed Robbery Against Ships in Asia," undated.

30. The countries involved are Australia, Bangladesh, Brunei, Cambodia, the People's Republic of China, Denmark, India, Japan, Republic of Korea, Laos, Myanmar, the Netherlands, Norway, the Philippines, Singapore, Sri Lanka, Thailand, United Kingdom, and Vietnam.

31. Syafiq Al Madihidj, "Indonesia to Avoid Reliance on Maritime Security Regime," *Jakarta Post,* June 16, 2013, available at http://www.thejakartapost.com/news/2013/06/16/indonesia-avoid-reliance-maritime-security-regime.html (accessed January 20, 2014).

32. "Background Information About the Regional Cooperation Agreement on Combating Piracy and Armed Robbery Against Ships in Asia (ReCAAP), and the ReCAAP Information Sharing Centre (ISC)," ReCAAP, available at http://www.recaap.org/AboutReCAAPISC.aspx (accessed December 11, 2013).

33. As of April 2011, these include Australia, France, India, Malaysia, the Philippines, Thailand, New Zealand, United Kingdom, United States, and Vietnam, with "[s]everal more countries . . . expected to deploy ILOs [international liaison officers] later in 2011." LTC Nicholas Lim, "The Information Fusion Centre (IFC): A Case for Information Sharing to Enforce Security in the Maritime Domain," *Pointer: Journal of the Singapore Armed Forces,* April 2011, 7.

34. Singapore Police Force website, available at http://www.spf.gov.sg/abtspf/pcg.htm#dept (accessed December 28, 2013).

35. For a full list, see "Friends of WMU Japan" website at http://www.wmu.sof.or.jp/newsletter41.pdf (accessed December 28, 2013).

36. Kalyan Ray, "Indian Aircraft to Keep an Eye on Straits of Malacca," *Deccan Herald,* May 13, 2013, available at http://www.deccanherald.com/content/332462/indian-aircraft-keep-eye-straits.html (accessed December 24, 2013).

37. For a fuller discussion, see Chen Shaofeng, "China's Self-Extrication from the 'Malacca Dilemma' and Implications," *International Journal of China Studies* 1/1 (January 2010), 1–24.

38. Catherine Zara Raymond, "Piracy and Armed Robbery in the Malacca Strait: A Problem Solved?" *Naval War College Review* 62/3 (Summer 2009), 35. This proposal was part of a larger US strategy, the Regional Maritime Security Initiative. For a more complete examination of this plan and regional reaction to it, see Yann-huei Song, "Security in the Strait of Malacca and the Regional Maritime Security Initiative: Responses to the US Proposal," *International Law Studies* 83 (2006), 97–156.

39. Embassy of the Republic of Indonesia, Washington DC, "US Supports Tripartite Malacca Straits Security Arrangements," January 18, 2011, available at http://www.embassyofindonesia.org/news/2011/01/news079.htm (accessed December 26, 2013).

40. Ian Storey, "Calming the Waters in Maritime Southeast Asia," *Asia Pacific Bulletin,* East-West Center 29, February 18, 2009, 2.

41. Graham Gerard Ong-Webb, "Introduction," in Graham Gerard Ong-Webb, ed., *Piracy*, xxxii. In what perhaps might be construed as a "glass half full" attitude, Raymond notes that this at the very least means that the joint aircraft are permitted within the twelve-mile territorial limits claimed by the respective countries. Raymond, "Piracy and Armed Robbery," 37.

42. Raymond, "Piracy and Armed Robbery," 38.

43. Caroline Vavro, "Piracy, Terrorism and the Balance of Power in the Malacca Strait," *Canadian Naval Review* 4/1 (Spring 2008), 14.

44. Ibid.

45. Cited in J. N. Mak, "Unilateralism and Regionalism: Working Together and Alone in the Malacca Straits," in Graham Gerard Ong-Webb, ed., *Piracy*, 155.

46. Ibid.

47. Bin Abu Bakar, "Enhancing Maritime Security."

48. Mak, "Unilateralism and Regionalism," 135.

49. Raymond, "Piracy and Armed Robbery," 35.

50. Ibid.

51. Tang Siew Mun, "Malaysia's Security Outlook and Challenges," in Eiichi Katahara, ed., *Asia Pacific Countries' Security Outlook and Its Implications for the Defense Sector* (Tokyo: National Institute for Defense Studies, 2010), 30.

52. Eric Frecon, "Piracy and Armed Robbery at Sea Along the Malacca Straits: Initial Impressions from Fieldwork in the Riau Islands," in Graham Gerard Ong-Webb, ed., *Piracy*, 73. In his chapter, he offers an excellent field study of a pirate den and the economics surrounding it, 68–83.

53. Roderick Chia, Pau Khan Khup Hangzo, and Kevin Punzalan, "Maritime Predations in the Malacca Straits: Treading New Waters," *NTS Insight*, August 2009, 1–13.

54. For treatments of this issue, see Stefan Eklöf, *Pirates in Paradise: A Modern History of Southeast Asia's Maritime Marauders* (Copenhagen: NIAS Press, 2006), 141–42; Peter Chalk, *The Maritime Dimension of International Security Terrorism, Piracy, and Challenges for the United States* (Santa Monica: RAND, 2008), 16.

55. Phaovisaid, "Where There's Sugar," 88.

56. As an aside, some of the technical requirements for ship operations in fact may have been somewhat counterproductive. A prime example of this is the Automatic Identification System (AIS) that ships are required to operate. Frecon (78–79) notes that pirates have monitored the AIS channels, and in fact, at least one unidentified ship captain said that he made a point of shutting off the system when in the strait to avoid being tracked by pirates.

14 Maritime Violence in the Sulu Sea

Thomas R. Mockaitis

F OR MOST OF THE MODERN ERA, CONCERN FOR MARITIME security during peacetime has focused on the perennial problem of piracy. Attacks upon shipping in coastal waters, on the high seas, and in ports by privateers seeking plunder have plagued every seafaring nation since oceanic commerce began. This preoccupation with piracy has influenced how individual states and the international community view maritime terrorism, leading them to a preoccupation with attacks upon shipping as the primary threat posed by extremist groups within the maritime environment. To take just one example, a July 2012 article on maritime terrorism noted that while the incidence of attacks had been small, the potential threat was great. The author, however, conceptualized maritime terrorism almost entirely as a threat to shipping and commerce. "Hijacking and using a ship as a weapon or to sink and close a major shallow chokepoint such as the Strait of Malacca or the Suez Canal could have significant economic implications for the global economy," Donna Nincic concluded. "Similarly, an improvised explosive device (IED), chemical or biological weapon, or other weapon of mass destruction discovered in a container could have dramatic economic repercussions."[1]

As serious as economic threats to ports and shipping certainly are, they do not constitute the sole, the most likely, or perhaps even the most serious threat to international security. Maritime security must focus, not only on ports, sea lanes, and waterways, but also on the coasts surrounding them. The US Navy's new *maritime domain awareness* concept recognizes this more expansive understanding of the maritime domain. "[The US] Navy has recognized for some time that its operational focus was broadening from primarily blue water to include the littorals," the document concludes."[2] Foremost among the potential threats within the new maritime domain are terrorist attacks on coastal cities launched from the sea. Amphibious landings are as old as warfare itself, but seaborne infiltration by terrorist teams or insurgent units to terrorize a city is relatively new.

Such an attack paralyzed Mumbai, India for three days in November 2008. A well-trained commando team of ten Lashkar-e-Taiba terrorists that trained in Pakistan with the help of the Pakistani Inter-Services Intelligence Department journeyed by freighter to Indian waters, captured a fishing vessel to take them within range of Mumbai, and landed in a coastal slum using small boats. They then split up into pairs and conducted a series of well-coordinated attacks at multiple locations. Before Indian security forces finally neutralized them (killing nine and capturing one), the terrorists had killed 173 people (including twenty-eight deliberately targeted foreign nationals) and wounded 308. They also did extensive damage and cost the city millions of dollars in lost revenue.[3]

The Mumbai incident should have heightened awareness of threats to coastal cities. Few analysts, however, interpreted the incident as an act of maritime terrorism. Instead, they contextualized it as part of the local struggle between India and Pakistan over Kashmir, and/or many set it within the global context of jihadist terrorism. Then in 2013, David Kilcullen published his groundbreaking book, *Out of the Mountains*, which challenges the way global terrorism has been conceptualized. His analysis includes a reassessment of the Mumbai attacks as maritime domain incidents. "Mumbai," Kilcullen concludes, "represents the current state of the art in urban littoral terrorism."[4] He argues that the attack succeeded precisely because the terrorists operated effectively in a complex maritime environment. "The attackers exploited networks of connectivity within and between the two coastal megacities of Karachi and Mumbai."[5] The terrorists operated in coastal waters used for a variety of licit and illicit activities and landed in a coastal slum, taking advantage of these linked, loosely governed spaces.[6] The extent of such unstable environments around the world increases the likelihood that more Mumbai-style attacks will occur. As of 2012, 80 percent of the world's population lives within sixty miles of the sea, many of them in the vast urban slums of coastal megacities.[7]

Kilcullen's analysis of Mumbai highlights the need for further consideration of maritime domain threats that go beyond attacks upon shipping. Case studies can provide a highly effective way of understanding terrorist threats. Analyzing past incidents can provide valuable lessons on how to prevent and, if necessary, respond to future attacks. While the world's oceans and coastlines provide a vast incident-rich environment from which to draw relevant examples, one region in particular commends itself for closer examination. The Sulu Sea region bordered by the Philippines and Malaysia has been the site of terrorist and insurgent activities for decades. Much of this violence has been associated with the movement conducted by various groups to achieve independence from the Philippines for the Muslim population of Mindanao and the Sulu Archipelago. In that long struggle, the year 2013 was particularly violent, with two Mumbai-style attacks, one against the Malaysian region of Lahad Datu and the other against Zamboanga City on the island of Mindanao. Analysis of these attacks within the context of the larger insurgent terrorist conflict to which they belong may provide valuable lessons on the nature of maritime domain threats and how to combat them.

Sulu Sea Region

The Sulu Sea is a section of the southwest Pacific Ocean bounded by Sabah (the Malaysian province on the northeast of the island of Kalimantan/Borneo) on the southwest, the island of Palawan on the west and northwest, the island of Mindoro on the north, the Visaya Islands on the northeast, the island of Mindanao on the east, and the Sulu Archipelago on the southeast, all belonging to the Philippines. Extending approximately 490 miles north–south and 375 miles east–west, the sea covers an area of 100,000 square miles.[8] The population of Palawan, western Mindanao, and the Sulu Islands (the area most affected by terrorist/insurgent violence) numbers 14,350,000.[9] Mindanao (particularly its central region and the Zamboanga Peninsula) and the Sulu Archipelago are home to most of the 5,127,084 Philippine Muslims.[10] Most Philippine Muslims belong to the Moro or Bangsamoro ethnic group, which consists of numerous subgroups.

The Sulu Sea is a complex geopolitical region that is not so much an ungoverned space as a space subject to contested governance. Providing security in such an environment with its hundreds of islands and thousands of miles of coastline, extensive migration across porous borders, and areas claimed by more than one littoral country is, to the say the least, incredibly challenging. Pirates have long plied these waters. A broad separatist movement has plagued the southern Philippines for decades. To help resolve the conflict, the government of the Philippines in 1996 created the Autonomous Region of Muslim Mindanao, comprising the western coast of Mindanao (excluding the Zamboanga Peninsula) and the Sulu Archipelago. To further complicate matters, Sabah in Malaysia contains several million people who migrated from the Philippines over the past half century (including thousands of illegal immigrants), making it an ideal staging area for insurgents and terrorists opposing the government of Manila.[11]

Insurgent and Terrorist Organizations in the Southern Philippines

The Philippines has been plagued by intermittent violence since it received independence following World War II. During the last three decades, most of the violence has been focused in the south, although groups from that region have conducted attacks as far away as Manila. Ethnic separatism intensified by religious ideology has motivated the three main groups that opposed the government in Manila on behalf of Filipino Muslims. The Muslim population of Mindanao and the Sulu Archipelago has long been marginalized in the predominantly Christian country. They had actually resisted being incorporated into the Philippines when it got independence from the United States in 1946.[12] Not only did the Moro fail to gain independence or even autonomy, they suffered victimization by Filipino immigrants from the north who legally and illegally appropriated much of their land.[13] Poverty exacerbated ethnic tensions. From 1987 to 1991, to take a single example, unemployment in western Mindanao was 14% higher than the national average of 22 percent.[14] These tensions led to the creation of three distinct but related separatist groups (and several subgroups) beginning in the early 1970s.[15]

The Moro National Liberation Front (MNLF) grew out of intercommunal violence between Christian and Muslim gangs in the 1960s. In 1968, Governor Datu Udtog Matalam of Cotabato Province formed the legal Muslim Independent Movement. From 1969 to 1974, some 477 of its members received paramilitary training from British advisors in Sabah, Malaysia.[16] The British no doubt thought that fomenting unrest in the Philippines would make it harder for Manila to assert its claim on Sabah in Malaysia, a close British ally. At its peak in 1975, the MNLF had an estimated strength of 30,000.[17] The Philippine government dealt with the MNLF through a combination of force and negotiation. Conflict between the insurgents and the Philippine government cost 50,000 lives.[18] The MNLF entered into negotiations with Manila and, in 1976, signed the Tripoli Agreement. In 1987 the insurgents agreed to the Jakarta peace accord, abandoning their demand for independence in return for local autonomy, and in 1996 they signed a "final" peace accord that called for the integration of 7,500 of their 17,000 fighters into the Philippine armed forces and police.[19] Thereafter, the MNLF declined in numbers and importance. By 2010, it had an estimated membership of just 5,800.[20] While the MNLF ceased to be the major insurgent group fighting for Moro rights, it maintained bases in Sulu, and a rogue faction of the group would reemerge to conduct a devastating attack in 2013.

Peace between the MNLF and the government in Manila did not, however, mean peace for the Sulu Sea region. As frequently happens in the southern Philippines, when one group gives up the armed struggle, another, more radical one emerges to take its place.[21] Formed in 1977, the Moro Islamic Liberation Front (MILF) operated as a group within the MNLF and maintained its own camps in Mindanao. The Philippine government did not consider the MILF a major threat until after the Jakarta Accord.[22] The group had not approved the deal, and disillusionment over the failure of the Philippine government to deliver benefits the agreement had promised led many MNLF members to defect to MILF.[23] As its name suggests, the group has a religious as well as an ethnic-nationalist focus, which distinguishes it from its more secular predecessor. By most estimates, MILF has 12,000–15,000 fighters, supported by a much larger sympathetic population.[24] Because it has generally confined itself to attacking the armed forces of the Philippines, most analysts consider MILF an insurgent movement rather than a terrorist organization. The United States has not placed the group on its terrorist watch list. Like MNLF, MILF has pursued a dual path of armed resistance and negotiations. Talks began in 1997, but the Philippine government and MILF did not reach a definitive settlement until October 2012. The Framework Agreement grants expanded autonomy to Bangsamoro (the Moro autonomous region), addressing many of the shortcomings of the 1987 and 1996 accords. While implementation needs to be worked out, all signs indicate that MILF has put the gun on the shelf.

Both MNLF and MILF had members who had fought in the Afghan jihad against the Soviets during the 1980s, and MILF received training from al-
Qaeda operatives in the Philippines during the 1990s.[25] Jemaah Islamiah (JI),
the Indonesian terrorist group, also had camps in the southern Philippines.
JI's 2000 attack on the residence of the Philippine ambassador in Jakarta has
been interpreted as a "thank you" to the MILF for allowing the terrorist group
to use Moro territory as a logistics and staging area.[26] MILF has also been accused of cooperating with the radical Islamic group Abu Sayyaf, a charge that
MILF denies. Despite these connections, MNLF and MILF have maintained
sufficient distance from al-Qaeda and its affiliates to preserve their identity
as ethnic separatist insurgent movements rather than being designated mere
terrorist organizations.

The third and most virulent group active in the southern Philippines
could not as easily claim to be an insurgent organization. During the early
1980s, approximately 300–500 Moro Mujahedeen journeyed to Afghanistan
to fight the Soviet-backed government in Kabul.[27] Ustadz Abubaker Janjalani
soon emerged as their leader and returned home committed to waging jihad
in the Philippines.[28] In 1991 Janjalani founded the Abu Sayyaf ("the sword
bearer") Group (ASG). He continued to travel to and from Peshawar, Pakistan to recruit fighters and received training and funds from al-Qaeda.[29] ASG
was always the smallest of the three Moro organizations, numbering between
200–500 members at any given time.[30] As the word *group* suggests, it was
not a unified movement, but a cluster of factions. Neither its small size nor
its factionalism, however, impeded it from being a very destructive terrorist
organization. While the MNLF and MILF targeted the police and military,
Abu Sayyaf killed ordinary civilians, especially Christian clergy and laity.

The United States targeted ASG aggressively after 9/11 because of its connection to al-Qaeda. Building on *Balikatan* ("shoulder to shoulder"), an annual joint US-Philippine military exercise conducted from 1991 to 1995 and
then from 1999 to the present, the US increased counterterrorism support to
the Philippines in the form of Operation Freedom Eagle, launched in 2002.
Subsumed into the larger global struggle against terrorism as Operation Enduring Freedom–Philippines, the mission included 1,200 advisors from Special Operations Command Pacific. In 2003, the Pentagon announced that US
forces would participate in joint operations against ASG.[31] These operations
reduced the group to 100 members by 2012, after which it behaved more like a
criminal gang than a terrorist organization.[32]

Maritime Violence

The Sulu Sea region is by its very nature a complex maritime environment. That environment does not, however, in and of itself mean that all insurgent and terrorist groups operating in the region engage in maritime attacks. The MNLF (until 2013) and MILF certainly moved men and supplies by sea, but they mounted essentially land-based operations. In February 2005, for example, the MNLF conducted a ten-day assault on the Armed Forces of the Philippines (AFP) base on the island of Jolo in the Sulu Archipelago. During this conventional battle, they attacked fixed positions with mortars and heavy machine guns while the AFP responded with artillery and airstrikes.[33] In August 2007, the insurgents ambushed an AFP unit on Jolo, killing sixty people.[34]

MILF attacks have generally followed a similar pattern, albeit on a smaller scale. In January 2005, the group carried out an attack against government troops in Maguindanao that killed twenty-three. Another attack against a Marine unit in Basilan in July 2007 killed eleven.[35] MILF did, however, carry out one devastating maritime terrorist attack. On February 25, 2000, the group placed bombs on two buses and detonated them aboard the ferry *Our Lady of Mediatrix* as it was about to dock at Ozamiz City, Mindanao. The attack killed thirty-nine people, wounded forty-one, and left twelve people missing.[36] This incident appears to have been atypical of MILF violence, however, as the group's other attacks have taken place on land.

ASG, on the other hand, has made extensive use of maritime terrorism. For this terrorist group the maritime environment (seas, waterways, and littorals) is not merely a transit zone and supply route but an operational area. The group has conducted numerous kidnappings from boats on the open water and in amphibious assaults on coastal resorts and towns. These kidnappings demonstrate the interrelationship between crime and terrorism in the Sulu Sea region. Most of the victims were ransomed, but some were murdered, including two Jehovah's Witnesses beheaded after their August 2002 abduction. ASG employs the highly effective technique of raiding coastal resorts using speedboats. On September 30, 2000 ASG terrorists captured three Malaysians from a resort in Sabah, releasing them in April 2001 after the Philippine government paid a ransom of US $15 million.[37] The success of this mission no doubt emboldened ASG, which conducted another hostage-seizing raid within a month of releasing the Malaysian captives. On May 27, 2001 the terrorists seized seventeen Filipinos and three Americans from the Dos Palmas resort on the Philippine Island of Palawan. They murdered several, including two of the Americans, one of whom they beheaded.[38] These and other brazen raids illustrate how vulnerable coastal towns are to raids by small groups of terrorists.

ASG's most infamous attack occurred on February 27, 2004 when the terrorist group bombed *Super Ferry 14* on route to Bacolod in the central Philippines. The explosion and subsequent fire killed 116 of the 900 people on board. As with other ASG operations, the bombing may have had a criminal as well as a terrorist objective. Investigators suspect that the group targeted the ferry because its owners refused to pay $1 million in protection money demanded by ASG in 2003.[39] ASG cooperated with Jemaah Islamiah and the Rajah Sulaiman Movement (a small Islamist terrorist group comprising Christian converts to Islam) to conduct the attack, which cost $400 to mount and took two months to plan.[40] The incident provides yet another example of how few resources it takes to produce such a devastating effect. Fortunately, the *Super Ferry 14* bombing may have been the last such attack ASG could conduct. The group's international terrorist ties made it a target for stepped-up US-Philippine counterterrorism efforts after 9/11. By 2012 ASG had been broken up into small groups capable of little more than criminal acts of piracy.[41] This criminal activity could, however, still prove quite lethal. On November 15, 2013 suspected ASG members raided a resort in Sabah, killing a Taiwanese man and abducting his wife.[42]

The Mumbai Paradigm and the Sulu Sea

For the past three decades maritime violence in the Sulu Sea region has conformed to a consistent pattern blending traditional piracy with terrorist and insurgent goals. Bombing ferries kills large numbers of people, causes considerable economic damage, and spreads fear. Seaborne kidnappings force governments to pay ransom and discourage tourism. So long as such activities remain confined to the southern Philippines conflict, which is being steadily resolved by negotiations, they represent more of a nuisance than a serious threat to international or even regional security. Two incidents in 2013, however, deserve closer examination, not because they achieved any long-term results, but because they conform to the pattern of the Mumbai attacks and thus provide further examples of the new style of terrorist activity that Kilcullen finds so ominous.

Lahad Datu Incident

Lahad Datu is a Malaysian town and district on the coast of Sabah, in Borneo. The province has a large Philippine population and once belonged to a medieval entity known as the Sultanate of Sulu, which also included the Sulu Archipelago. Based upon this history and the province's ethnic makeup, the Philippines laid claim to the territory in the 1960s, a claim that Malaysia successfully refuted. While the Philippines had not relinquished its claim to the territory, neither had it pressed the matter in some time when a bizarre episode took place in early 2013. Jamalal Kiram III, a descendant of the Sultan of Sulu, asserted his claim to the title and territory. The attack may have had more to do with contemporary events than ancient history. The attack began on the very day that the Philippine government, in cooperation with the MILF, launched the Sajahatra Bangsamoro Program, a health, education, and economic development effort in the Bangsamoro (Moro autonomous region).[43] The timing of the attack gives credence to the theory that the "Sultan of Sulu" represented disgruntled elements angry at being left out of the peace process.[44] The invaders may also have received help from Filipino expatriates unhappy about their treatment by the Malaysian government.[45]

The incursion took the Malaysian and Philippine governments as well as local authorities by surprise. On February 11, 2013 the world learned that a force of approximately 200 men, claiming to be part of the "Royal Sulu Army," led by Kiram's brother, had invaded Lahad Datu to reclaim the area as part of their ancestral home. Most accounts maintain that they arrived in small boats on February 9, but one source claims that they landed over several days, beginning on February 3.[46] Only thirty of the intruders appear to have been armed with light weapons.[47] Like the Mumbai terrorists, the invaders blended into the normal oceanic traffic to enter the target area undetected until they had landed at Tanduo beach. The insurgents then broke into groups and moved to Kampung Tanduo, a small village of fifteen houses and twenty families,[48] and Kampungs Kunak and Semporna. Because the "invasion" posed no serious threat to Malaysia, the government in Kuala Lumpur tried to resolve the situation peacefully. They cordoned off the occupied area and offered to negotiate an end to the crisis.

The incursion turned violent on March 1, when terrorists attempting to break out of Tanduo engaged police at a checkpoint. The gun battle, which killed twelve intruders and two policemen, ended the hopes for a peaceful resolution. On March 3, a group of the intruders believed to number fewer than ten ambushed a police unit near Semporna; six police and seven insurgents reportedly died in that engagement. The situation had clearly escalated beyond what the local police could handle, so Kuala Lumpur had little choice but to call in the military. On March 5, three F-18s and five Hawk jets carried out airstrikes around Tanduo, killing thirteen insurgents. The Malaysian army followed up the airstrikes with a ground sweep to clear the town house by house as part of Operation Daulat ("sovereignty"), which lasted from March 15 to June 29. The military then handed responsibility for security to the newly created Eastern Sabah Security Command. Sixty-eight people died in the Lahad Datu incident: fifty-six Sulu insurgents, nine members of the Malaysian security forces (army and police), and six civilians.[49] The rest of the insurgents were either captured or they fled.

The entire episode would have been farcical had it not cost so many lives and caused so much disruption. The 200 poorly trained insurgents stood no chance of accomplishing their romantic goal of rebuilding the Sultanate of Sulu. The local population did not rise to support them, and their "Sultan" died later in the year without ever being invited to discussions on the future of the region. Rather than come to blows, Malaysia and the Philippines cooperated during the crisis with the Philippine navy deploying ships to prevent further infiltration from its territory into Sabah. Philippine President Benigno Aquino III has made it abundantly clear that he will pursue diplomatic and legal but not military options to resolve the Sabah dispute.[50]

The futility of the endeavor notwithstanding, thirty poorly trained, lightly armed insurgents with about 170 followers managed to cause a great deal of damage. The village of Tanduo has been permanently closed, and 1,500 Philippine residents of Sabah had to seek refuge in the Philippines.[51] The attack did untold economic damage to the region's palm oil industry and probably adversely affected tourism as well. Had all 200 of the intruders been armed, the loss of life and damage to property would have been much greater. A better trained unit of the same size or even smaller might have done considerably more harm. The sheer irrationality of the attack underscores the difficulty of preventing such incidents. Marginalized people who believe they have nothing to lose and do not mind dying for a cause, no matter how desperate, are very unpredictable. When they belong to an ethnic group that lives on both sides of a maritime border, which they commonly transit, they can move from one country to attack another with considerable ease. Their ability to operate in a complex maritime environment with thousands of miles of littoral containing many potential targets compounds the security challenge they pose.

Zamboanga City Attack

The Lahad Datu incursion was not, unfortunately, the only such incidence of maritime insurgency in the Sulu Sea region during 2013. In September a rogue faction of the MNLF infiltrated Zamboanga City by sea and engaged police and military forces for three weeks, causing considerable loss of life, extensive damage to property, and a serious refugee crisis. Like the Sabah incursion, this incident occurred because a disgruntled leader feeling left out of and/or unhappy with the peace accord between the MILF and the government of the Philippines could tap into deeper discontent among his people. On August 12, the founder of the long-quiescent MNLF, Nur Misuari, declared an independent Bangsamoro Republic from his Talipao region on the island of Jolo in the Sulu Archipelago. Even though he had signed the 1996 peace accord and been appointed a regional governor, Misuari soon became disillusioned with the deal. Some of his fighters attacked Philippine forces soon after the agreement was signed. Misuari fled to Malaysia, but the government in Kuala Lumpur sent him back to the Philippines, where he was placed under house arrest until 2008. Once released, he opposed the peace process with the MILF. All efforts at reconciliation proffered by the Philippine government had failed to placate him.[52]

Misuari laid claim to a vast area, including Sarawak and Sabah in Borneo as well as the Sulu Archipelago and parts of Mindanao for his new republic. To assert this claim, he launched a daring but futile assault on Zamboanga City, Mindanao. The MNLF website insists that its followers had merely gathered for a peaceful demonstration on September 9, 2013, when Philippine security forces attacked them, and that MNLF supporters in the city rose to their defense: "The oppressive provocation led the MNLF members in Zamboanga City to arm themselves so as to aid and rescue the beleaguered MNLF members that spontaneously started the AFP-MNLF battle in the city."[53] The evidence does not support this claim. The MNLF made an armed incursion into the city and unleashed three weeks of mayhem to little effect.

The episode began just before midnight on September 8. Philippine Navy Special Forces on a routine patrol encountered approximately 200 armed insurgents from what the Philippine government aptly calls the *MNLF-MF*

(MNLF-Misuari Faction) in the coastal town of Rio Bangay Hondo.[54] These and other troops in the city may have been deployed because the government had intelligence that an armed group would try to enter Zamboanga City and raise the Bangsamoro Republic flag.[55] After landing in one of the city's coastal slums in one large motorboat and eight smaller vessels, the intruders killed a member of the naval forces and proceeded to the city.[56] Accounts vary as to how many insurgents/terrorists took part in the attack, with estimates ranging from 200–600. Open sources do not clearly indicate whether all those involved in the attack came by sea or whether some were already on the island. The armament of the intruders, their engagement with the Philippine navy on the previous night, and their behavior once in the city indicate MNLF-MF's hostile intent. The Philippine military later captured a 50-caliber machine gun as well as fifteen other "high powered firearms," and numerous smaller-caliber weapons—hardly equipment necessary for peaceful demonstrations.[57] The crisis continued to worsen in the hours and days ahead. Around 4:30 a.m. on September 9, the invaders again clashed with government troops and took twenty hostages, a pattern that would continue until the afternoon, by which time they held 300 people captive.[58] By the end of the day, thousands of people had fled their homes, and the city had come to a standstill.

Over the next week the AFP recouped the situation, although at a terrible cost. The intruders had ensconced themselves in five villages, but by September 16, security forces had evicted them from 70 percent of the coastal territory they occupied. The security forces employed helicopter gunships and limited strikes by fixed-wing aircraft against the rebels. The fighting destroyed 850 homes and caused 82,000 to flee the conflict zone. One week after the incident began, approximately 100 intruders holding 100 or so hostages remained.[59] It would take the security forces another three weeks to clear Zamboanga City of all the terrorists and free the remaining hostages.

By the time the government declared the crisis over on September 28, the incident had taken a terrific toll. The security forces had killed 183 members of MNLF-MF and captured 292 at the cost of twenty-three of their own and twelve civilians killed.[60] Beyond this loss of life, the attack seriously disrupted social and economic life. Fighting in the city had destroyed 10,000 homes.[61] Nearly 120,000 people had fled, many of whom remained displaced for months after the crisis had ended.[62] The conflict also led to the loss or disruption of 46,000 jobs.[63] The incursion necessitated a significant humanitarian relief effort, and its full economic cost has yet to be calculated.

The Zamboanga City incident was remarkable both for its futility and for its destructiveness. Other than the intent to raise their national flag, the intruders seem to have had no operational plan. Had they been better organized and led, they would have killed many more soldiers and civilians. Their strategic objectives were equally unclear. They had no hope of seizing the city or of disrupting the peace process. The MILF quickly disavowed the violent actions of MNLF-MF. Far from bringing their leader into new discussions with the Philippine government, the attack made Nur Misuari the country's most wanted man. Such rational considerations, however, clearly did little to counter the powerful emotive force of ethnic nationalism tinged with religious extremism.

Lessons of the Lahad Datu and Zamboanga City Incidents

The Lahad Datu and Zamboanga City attacks have received surprisingly little attention from terrorism analysts. Scholars of the conflict in the southern Philippines may consider the incidents of little significance in a conflict that has already claimed 150,000 lives over the past half century. Those who study terrorism more broadly might understandably dismiss the attacks as the last-gasp efforts of extremists resisting a successful peace process. Insurgent violence often intensifies just before a conflict is resolved, as those opposing a settlement try to keep the conflict going. The two incursions did little but serve the fantasy ideology of narcissistic leaders trying to stall a very successful peace process.[64] Thus, in and of themselves, the incidents would not be worthy of detailed study.

Seen within a larger context, however, Lahad Datu and Zamboanga City illustrate the emerging pattern of terrorism that Kilcullen describes in such frightening detail. In both cases, disenfranchised, arguably desperate people were willing to die in a hopeless cause that empowered them, however briefly. Both incursions took place in a complex maritime environment of seas, islands, and littorals. The Lahad Datu invaders blended into normal seaborne traffic that allowed them to escape detection until they had landed in Sabah. There they could operate within a sympathetic Filipino population living as second-class citizens in Malaysia. Even though the invaders had little strategic guidance and no clear operational plan, the Malaysian armed forces had to exert considerable effort to neutralize them. It took five Malaysian battalions (perhaps as many as 6,000 troops) supported by five aircraft to kill or capture 200 insurgents in over a month of operations.[65] A better-trained and better-led force with clearer objectives would have caused far greater loss of life and destruction.

The Zamboanga City attackers also escaped detection until they came ashore, even though the Philippine military had intelligence that a group of MNLF-MF members would try to raise their flag over the town hall. Small boats moving amid a steady stream of interisland traffic proved very difficult to detect. Once the intruders had landed and dispersed in five of the villages attached to the city, it took 5,000 troops, including the army's elite Scout Ranger unit supported by the air force, to kill or capture them.[66] Government forces needed three weeks to clear the city and, in some cases, they engaged in house-to-house fighting with the enemy "as close as one wall away."[67] The presence of hostages and the desire of Philippine President Benigno Aquino III to capture as many of the insurgents as possible further complicated an already challenging operation.[68] The perpetrators caused far fewer casualties than the ten highly trained Mumbai terrorists, but their numbers made neutralizing them more difficult and resulted in far more destruction. Had they been as well trained and focused as the Lashkar-e-Taiba fighters, the results would have been disastrous.

Countering Maritime Threats

Analyzing terrorist attacks after the fact is always easier than anticipating them. Any case study should, therefore, conclude with consideration of what can be learned from it to help prevent future incidents. Even when such lessons have been identified, however, implementing improved security measures can be difficult and costly. While terrorism can no more be eradicated than organized crime, it can be reduced significantly. The experience of the past two decades suggests how security in the Sulu Sea region in particular and maritime zones in general can be improved.

The first requirement for improved security is improved governance. One analyst describes the Sulawesi-Mindanao arc (an area that includes the Sulu and Celebes Seas and the lands bordering them) as an ungoverned space in which "no historical or cultural basis for the separation of the populations around the Sulu Sea among different nations" exists.[69] It might, however, be more accurate to describe the region as a "loosely governed" or "alternatively governed space," an area in which non-state actors exercise *de facto* local autonomy while challenging the sovereignty of the nation-state in which they reside. The Bangsamoro Republic is a case in point. Mindanao and the Sulu Archipelago also suffer from lack of "state penetration," the failure of Manila or the Autonomous Region in Muslim Mindanao (ARMM) to build reliable institutions of justice and government to regulate social life and resolve disputes.[70] Poor infrastructure and lack of economic development add to the region's problems. To take a single example, in 2000, 92 percent of the population of Jolo in the Sulu Archipelago fell below the poverty level.[71] When compounded by strong ethnic and religious loyalties, such poor living conditions breed insurgent and terrorist groups. Neither the Bangsamoro Republic nor MNLF-MF had any difficulty recruiting angry young men to take part in their forlorn incursions into Lahad Datu and Zamboanga City, respectively.

Security also depends on regional and international cooperation. The old adage that there are no purely national solutions to the problem of international terrorism is doubly true for the maritime realm. International waters are quintessential ungoverned spaces in which no nation or even the international community exercises meaningful sovereignty. The territorial waters in which many maritime terrorist incidents occur are often contested. The South China Sea provides the most extreme example of a complex maritime domain dispute among several nations, but similar zones of contention exist around the world. The Sulu Sea is one such region. Cooperation between Malaysia and the Philippines has been hampered by a dispute over the province of Sabah, in North Borneo, now a part of Malaysia but claimed by the Philippines. Although Manila has not aggressively asserted its claim in several years, the problem remains unresolved. The presence of legal and illegal Filipino immigrants working in Sabah further complicates matters. Malaysia has periodically deported illegal immigrants back to the Philippines, often treating them harshly in the process.[72] From January to November 2013, the Malaysian authorities deported 9,414 Filipinos from Sabah and were holding others in detention centers.[73] These complex migration patterns and the international tensions they caused not only facilitated the terrorist operation, they also hampered cooperation between the two nations affected.

Cooperation between Malaysia and the Philippines has improved since the Lahad Datu incident, at least in principle. During the crisis, the Philippine navy had deployed vessels to interdict further incursions. In February 2014 the chief of the Philippine navy visited his Malaysian counterpart, Tan Sri Abdul Aziz Jaafar, to discuss joint training exercises, bilateral discussions, and intelligence sharing. "The visit of the Chief of Navy of the Philippines will impact positively on the national defence [sic] diplomacy," Jaafar observed, "especially in strengthening and boosting bilateral ties and regional cooperation in maritime security for both nations."[74] Whether the meeting will lead to meaningful cooperation, and in turn reduce maritime violence in the region, remains to be seen.

International cooperation in the Sulu Sea has fared somewhat better regionally. The Philippines has long received significant US military aid. Counterterrorism assistance to fight Abu Sayyaf increased after 9/11, and the "rebalancing to the Pacific" aimed at countering Chinese expansionism in East Asia promises to benefit Manila even further. On April 28, 2014, the two countries signed an Enhanced Defense Cooperation Agreement to supplement the Mutual Defense Treaty of 1951. The agreement gives US military and civilian contractors access to certain designated locations in the Philippines and promises to assist Manila "by addressing short-term capabilities gaps, promoting long-term modernization, and helping maintain and develop additional maritime security, maritime domain awareness, and humanitarian and disaster relief capabilities."[75] The bases are intended to counter the Chinese threat, but they will undoubtedly benefit Philippine security in other ways as well, including securing the Sulu Sea region.

While maritime security requires regional and international cooperation, a threatened state must also improve its ability to patrol territorial waters and protect littorals from infiltration. Ironically, the Philippines had taken such steps just prior to the Zamboanga City attack. In 2008, it created the Coast Watch System (CWS), an integrated Maritime security system linking the Navy, Coast Guard, National Anti-Terrorism Task Force, and various bureaus and agencies responsible for a range of activities, including fishing and maritime commerce. The CWS has three key functions:

1. to develop a common operating picture of the maritime domain in the Philippines;

2. to collect, consolidate, and integrate all data relevant to maritime security; and

3. to provide real-time information for the purposes of cueing (providing range and bearing), locating, interdicting, apprehending, and prosecuting those who engage in illegal maritime activities.[76]

The program calls for creating twenty offshore platforms with surveillance and interdiction capability, twelve of which were operational at the time of the

2013 incidents, including eight in the Sulu Sea region.[77] Far from being an indictment of CWS, the successful infiltrations into Sabah and Zamboanga City illustrate the incredible difficulty of securing littorals. Terrorists, insurgents, and pirates who blend in with normal maritime traffic in heavily traversed areas are very hard to find until they mount an attack. Improved maritime security measures can help, but they are no panacea.

Conclusion

A few important conclusions can be drawn from this Sulu Sea case study. First, it confirms Kilcullen's conclusion that attacks upon underdeveloped, densely populated, and loosely governed littorals represent a major threat to international security. This threat is more prevalent and potentially more serious than threats to transoceanic shipping. It is also much harder to counter. Cargo ships can be escorted, but thousands of miles of coastline cannot be protected from incursions by terrorists using small boats, especially in waters plied by dense, largely unregulated maritime traffic. Although an important security measure, the Philippine CWS did not prevent the 2013 incursions.

The difficulty of instituting truly effective coastal security measures points to the second conclusion to be drawn from the Sulu Sea case: attacking the root causes of unrest remains the most effective way to fight insurgency and terrorism on land and sea. The lack of infrastructure and extreme poverty of the region made it much easier for the Sultan of Sulu and Misuari to recruit followers to carry out their suicidal plans. A population filled with poor, young men who have little hope of a better future is a fertile terrorist recruiting ground. The temporary empowerment of being able to strike a blow for a cause may be sufficient reward for the hopeless to sacrifice their lives in a lost cause. In light of that reality, the Philippine government might achieve greater maritime security by building roads, schools, and hospitals in underserved areas of its territory than by acquiring more naval vessels to patrol its waters.

Notes

1. Donna K. Nincic, "Maritime Terrorism: How Real Is the Threat?" *Fair Observer* (online), July 16, 2012, available at http://www.fairobserver.com/region/north _america/maritime-terrorism-how-real-threat/, accessed July 29, 2014.

2. *Navy Maritime Domain Awareness Concept* (Washington, DC: Department of the Navy, 2007), 2.

3. For details and discussion of the attacks, see Thomas R. Mockaitis, "The Mumbai Attacks," in Paul Shemella, ed., *Fighting Back: What Governments Can Do About Terrorism* (Stanford, CA: Stanford University Press, 2011), 317–31.

4. David Kilcullen, *Out of the Mountains: The Coming of Age of the Urban Guerrilla* (New York: Oxford University Press, 2013), 75.

5. Ibid., 71.

6. Ibid., 75.

7. Ibid., 40.

8. "Sulu Sea," *Encyclopaedia Britannica* (online), available at http://www.britannica.com/EBchecked/topic/573066/Sulu-Sea, accessed August 1, 2014.

9. Angela Rabasa and Peter Chalk, *Non-Traditional Threats and Maritime Domain Awareness in the Tri-Border Area of Southeast Asia: The Coast Watch System of the Philippines* (Santa Monica, CA: RAND, 2012), 5. Figures are from 2008.

10. *The Philippines in Figures* (Manila: Republic of the Philippines National Statistics Office, 2014), 27.

11. Rabasa and Chalk, *Non-Traditional Threats*, 5.

12. Mark Turner, "Terrorism and Secession in the Southern Philippines: The Rise of the Abu Sayyaf," *Contemporary Southeast Asia*, Vol. 17, No. 1 (June 1995), 9.

13. Ibid.

14. Ibid., 12.

15. Although the New People's Army, the military wing of the Communist Party of the Philippines, is a major threat and does have a presence in Mindanao, it is not a major player in the separatist movement, nor has it conducted significant operations in the Sulu Sea region. It does not, therefore figure in this study.

16. "Moro National Liberation Front (MNLF)," *Institute for the Study of Violent Groups*, available at http://vkb.isvg.org/Wiki/Groups/Moro_National_Liberation_Front_%28MNLF%29, accessed August 5, 2014.

17. "Moro National Liberation Front," Stanford University, *Mapping Militant Organizations* (website), available at http://web.stanford.edu/group/mappingmilitants/cgi-bin/groups/view/379#cite11, accessed August 5, 2014.

18. "Moro National Liberation Front (MNLF)," Federation of American Scientists (FAS) website, available at http://fas.org/irp/world/para/mnlf.htm, accessed August 6, 2014.

19. *The Philippines: Dismantling Rebel Groups* (Brussels: International Crisis Group, 2013), 4.

20. "Moro National Liberation Front," Stanford University, *Mapping Militant Organizations* (website), available at http://web.stanford.edu/group/mappingmilitants/cgi-bin/groups/view/379#cite11, accessed August 6, 2014.

21. Turner, "Terrorism and Secession in the Southern Philippines," 11.

22. *Southern Philippines Backgrounder: Terrorism and the Peace Process* (Brussels: International Crisis Group, 2004), 5.

23. Ibid.

24. "Moro Islamic Liberation Front," Stanford University, *Mapping Militant Organizations* (website), available at http://web.stanford.edu/group/mappingmili tants/cgi-bin/groups/view/309?highlight=MILF, accessed August 6, 2014.

25. Zachary Abuza, "Tentacles of Terror: Al-Qaeda's Southeast Asian Network," *Contemporary Asia*, Vol. 24, No. 3 (December 2002), 438.

26. Ibid., 439.

27. Ibid., 440.

28. Ibid.

29. Ibid.

30. "Abu Sayyaf," *Mapping Militant Organizations* website, available at http://web.stanford.edu/group/mappingmilitants/cgi-bin/groups/view/152?highlight =abu+Sayyef, accessed August 9, 2014.

31. Details on US CT aide to the Philippines from "Operation Enduring Freedom—Philippines," GlobalSecurity.org, available at http://www.globalsecurity.org/military/ops/enduring-freedom-philippines.htm, accessed August 9, 2014.

32. Rabasa and Chalk, *Non-Traditional Threats*, 10.

33. Soliman M. Santos, Jr., et al., *Armed Groups and Human Security Efforts in the Philippines* (Geneva: Small Arms Survey, 2010), 336.

34. "Moro National Liberation Front," Stanford University, *Mapping Militant Organizations* (website), available at http://web.stanford.edu/group/mapping militants/cgi-bin/groups/view/379#cite11, accessed August 12, 2014.

35. Details on the two attacks from "Moro Islamic Liberation Front," Stanford University, *Mapping Militant Organizations* (website), available at http://web.stanford.edu/group/mappingmilitants/cgi-bin/groups/view/309?highlight=MILF, accessed August 12, 2014.

36. Lino de la Cruz, "Victims of Ozamis [sic] Ship Blast Cry for Justice," *Philippine Star* (online), February 27, 2003, available at http://www.philstar.com/nation/196938/victims-ozamis-ship-blast-still-cry-justice, accessed August 12, 2014.

37. Rommel C. Banloi, "Maritime Terrorism in Southeast Asia: The Abut Sayyaf Threat," *Naval War College Review*, Vol. 58, No. 4 (Autumn 2005), 72.

38. Ibid.

39. "Bomb Caused Philippine Ferry Fire," BBC News online, available at http://news.bbc.co.uk/2/hi/asia-pacific/3732356.stm, accessed August 13, 2014.

40. Rabasa and Chalk, *Non-Traditional Threats*, 12.

41. Ibid., 18.

42. International Center for Political Violence and Terrorism Research (Singapore: Nanyang Technological University), *Counter Terrorism Trends and Analysis*, Volume 6, Issue 1 (January/February 2014), 12.

43. *Swords to Ploughshares: The Sajahatra Bangsomoro Program*, government of the Philippines website, available at http://www.gov.ph/sajahatra-bangsamoro -program/, accessed August 14, 2014.

44. Khor Lu Yeng, "The Sabah Sulu Crisis Threatens the Palm Oil Supply," *Perspective*, No. 12, March 6, 2013 (Singapore: Institute of Southeast Asian Studies), 3.

45. Ibid., p. 2.

46. Ibid.

47. "Statement of His Excellency Benigno S. Aquino III, President of the Philippines, on the Sabah Incident," February 26, 2013, available at http://www.gov.ph/2013/02/26/statement-of-president-aquino-on-the-sabah-incident-february-26-2013/, accessed August 15, 2014.

48. Sandra Sokial, "Kampong Tandu Permanently Closed," *Borneo Post* (online), March 29, 2013, available at http://www.theborneopost.com/2013/03/29/kampung-tanduo-permanently-closed/, accessed August 14, 2014.

49. Details of incursion and military operations against it from Najiah Najib, "Lahad Datu Invasion: A Painful Memory of 2013," *Astro Awani* (English; online), December 31, 2013, available at http://english.astroawani.com/news/show/lahad-datu-invasion-a-painful-memory-of-2013-27579, accessed August 14, 2014.

50. "Sabah Not on Aquino's Agenda in Malaysia Visit," *Borneo Insider* (online), February 20, 2014, available at http://borneoinsider.com/2014/02/20/sabah-issue-not-aquinos-agenda-in-malaysia-visit/, accessed August 15, 2014.

51. "Crisis in Sabah After Malaysia's Standoff with Armed Filipinos," *Global Voices* (online), March 26, 2013, available at http://globalvoicesonline.org/2013/03/26/crisis-in-sabah-after-malaysias-standoff-with-armed-filipinos/, accessed August 15, 2014.

52. Background on Misuari from Bryony Lau, "The Southern Philippines in 2013: One Step Forward, One Step Back," *Southeast Asian Affairs 2014* (Singapore: Institute of Southeast Asian Studies, 2014), 268.

53. "AFP Burning of Zamboanga," available at http://mnlfnet.com/Articles/BYC_05Oct2013_Burning%20of%20Zambo%2010,000%20Houses.htm, accessed August 19, 2014.

54. "NFWM [Naval Forces Western Mindanao] on Zamboanga Crisis," *Philippine Navy Today*, October 27, 2013, available at http://www.navy.mil.ph/news.php?news_id=1196, accessed August 20, 2014.

55. "Philippines Say Zamboanga Crisis Is Over," *Voice of America* (online), September 28, 2013, available at http://www.voanews.com/content/all-hostages-freed-inphilippines-rebel-fight/1758902.html, accessed August 23, 2014.

56. "More Rebels Attack Zamboanga City," *Star* (online), September 9, 2013, available at http://www.thestar.com.my/News/Nation/2013/09/09/Manila-Moro-Zamboanga/, accessed August 20, 2014.

57. PCinsp Ariel T. Huesca, "Public Advisory on Zamboanga City Crisis (Update 1)," September 16, 2013, available at http://pro9.pnp.gov.ph/index.php?view=article&catid=79%3Apress-release&id=1904%3Apublic-advisory-on-zamboanga-city-crisis-september-16-2013&format=pdf&option=com_content&Itemid=132, accessed August 23, 2013.

58. Andrei Medina, "Timeline: Crisis in Zamboanga," *GMA News* (online), September 10, 2013, available at http://www.gmanetwork.com/news/story/325855/news/regions/timeline-crisis-in-zamboanga-city, accessed August 23, 2014.

59. Details on operations and their impact from Associated Press, "Gov. Forces Retake 70% of Rebel-Held Villages in Zamboanga City," *Inquirer* (online), September 16, 2013, available at http://newsinfo.inquirer.net/488789/govt-forces-retake-70-of-rebel-held-villages-in-zamboanga-city#ixzz2f5yjo8oF, accessed August 25, 2014.

60. "End to Zamboanga Threat, but Concern for Philippines Displaced," *ABC Radio Australia* (online), available at http://www.radioaustralia.net.au/international/2013-09-28/end-to-zamboanga-threat-but-concern-for-philippines-displaced/1197246, accessed August 26, 2014.

61. United Nations Office for the Coordination of Humanitarian Assistance (OCHA), *Zamboanga and Basilan Emergency: Situation Report No. 5* (as of 30 September 2013) (Manila: OCHA, 2013), 2.

62. Ibid., 1.

63. Ibid., 3.

64. The term *fantasy ideology* is most associated with the writings of Lee Harris. See Lee Harris, *Civilization and Its Enemies* (New York: Free Press, 2004).

65. "Intrusion of Filipino Rebels in to Lahad Datu, Sabah," *Malaysia Factbook* [sic] (online), April 24, 2014, available at http://malaysiafactbook.com/Intrusion_of_Filipino_rebels_into_Lahad_Datu,_Sabah, accessed August 26, 2014.

66. Greg Cahiles, "Troops in High Morale as Zambo [sic] Siege Ends," *9 News Philippines* (online), September 30, 2013, available at http://www.9news.ph/news/regional/2013/09/30/troops-in-high-morale-as-zambo-siege-ends#.UlLGWNIjxfY, accessed August 26, 2014.

67. Colonel Teodora Llamas, quoted in ibid.

68. Ibid.

69. Angel Rabasa, "Case Study: The Sulawesi-Mindanao Arc," in Angel Rabasa, et al., *Ungoverned Territories: Understanding and Reducing Terrorism Risks* (Santa Monica, CA: RAND, 2007), 111.

70. Ibid., 117–19.

71. Ibid., 118.

72. Helen E.S. Nasadurai, "Malaysia's Conflict with the Philippines and Indonesia over Labor Migration: Economic Security, Interdependence and Conflict Trajectories," *Pacific Review*, Vol. 26, No. 1 (2013), 89–113. Nasadurai notes that Malaysian relations with the Philippines are better than those with Indonesia owing to the former's ability to advocate on behalf of its expatriates.

73. "11,992 Illegals Repatriated from Sabah Between January and November, Says Task Force Director," *Malay Mail* (online), November 22, 2013, available at http://www.themalaymailonline.com/malaysia/article/11992-illegals-repatriated-from-sabah-between-january-and-november-says-tas, accessed August 28, 2014. Most of the remaining deportees were Indonesian.

74. "Malaysia, Philippines to Boost Defence Relations," *Borneo Post* (online), February 21, 2014, available at http://www.theborneopost.com/2014/02/21/malaysia -philippines-to-boost-defence-relations/, accessed August 28, 2014.

75. *Agreement Between the Government of the Philippines and the Government of the United States of America on Enhanced Security Cooperation*, April 28, 2014, 2, available at http://www.gov.ph/2014/04/29/document-enhanced-defense-coope ration-agreement/, accessed August 30, 2014.

76. Rabasa and Chalk, *Non-Traditional Threats*, 21.

77. Ibid., 22–23.

15 Maritime Crime in the Gulf of Guinea

Peter Chalk

THE GULF OF GUINEA—A COASTAL ZONE THAT EXTENDS FROM Senegal in the north to Angola in the south—provides an economic lifeline to both littoral and land-locked states in West Africa and is of strategic importance to the rest of the world in terms of trade links, especially with regard to energy. Unfortunately, the region is beset with a major and proliferating problem of maritime crime and violence, which has steadily expanded from the Niger delta to affect the territorial waters of Benin, Cameroon, the Ivory Coast, Ghana, Guinea, Togo, and Gabon. This chapter examines the scope and dimensions of illicit seaborne activity in the Gulf of Guinea (GoG), focusing on armed maritime crime (AMC), oil bunkering, and drug trafficking, all manifestations of what we have called *maritime violence.* The chapter identifies some of the key causal factors behind these challenges; delineates the implications they carry for local and international security; and considers some of the main measures that have been instituted to enhance maritime domain awareness and stability in this part of the world.

Armed Maritime Crime

Between 2009 and June 2014, 265 acts of armed maritime crime occurred in the Gulf of Guinea.[1] The region has now decisively surpassed the Horn of Africa (HoA) in terms of attack levels and during the first half of 2014 accounted for nineteen incidents (compared to just four in the Gulf of Aden/

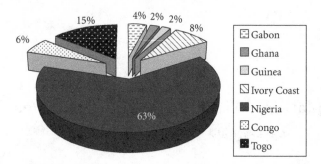

FIGURE 15.1 Actual and attempted armed maritime attacks in the GoG, 2013
SOURCE: International Maritime Bureau.

GoA).[2] The most dangerous waters lie off Nigeria, which in 2013 saw thirty-one attacks (actual and attempted), just under two thirds (63.2 percent) of which occurred in the wider GoG coastal belt (see Figure 15.1).[3]

In common with many other parts of the world, the true magnitude of piracy and maritime robbery afflicting the Gulf of Guinea is undoubtedly far higher than these figures suggest, largely because the majority of attacks—possibly as many as 50 percent—are never recorded. This is because ship owners are generally unwilling to alert authorities to all but the most egregious assaults on their vessels, on account of the costs that subsequent investigations and delays will necessarily entail (which are borne by the companies themselves) as well as due to a fear that acknowledging incidents will merely serve to raise maritime insurance premiums. In many cases the combined magnitude of these losses would outweigh those resulting from a seaborne attack, meaning that there is a strong economic incentive *not* to report.[4]

Most attacks in the Gulf of Guinea occur in national or coastal waters and generally take the form of ship boarding with the aim of stealing equipment, money, and other portable valuables that are immediately transferred to a secondary skiff or barge for transfer to land. Outright hijackings also take place. However, unlike in the Horn of Africa, where perpetrating groups would attempt to extort ransoms for both the captured vessel and its crew, the main objective in the Gulf of Guinea is the theft of cargo that is then sold on the black market.[5] All types of freighters are targeted, although it is tankers carrying petroleum products that are especially favored, on account of the value of their payload.

Because gangs operating in these waters are not concerned with leveraging hostages for money, accompanying levels of violence tend to be high, again eclipsing anything that has been witnessed in the Gulf of Aden.[6] Lethality has been further fueled by the abundance of combat weaponry in West Africa, which includes everything from Beretta AR-70 light machine guns to AK-47, G3, FNC and FAL assault rifles, antipersonnel mines, and rocket-propelled grenades (RPGs). Most of these munitions are procured from leftover stocks in war-ravaged parts of the subregion (notably Sierra Leone and Liberia), illicit arms traders, or corrupt members of the security forces.[7]

Apart from attacks on ships, there have been numerous strikes against offshore oil platforms, particularly in and around the Niger delta. These attacks are typically carried out by organized militias and generally justified under the rubric of promoting social, political, and economic change. In most cases raiders use powerful, highly maneuverable speedboats—often equipped with onboard cannons—to quickly surround and overcome preselected targets in succession. These swarm-based tactics are aimed at full-system disruption, either by forcing the complete shutdown of production or by delaying/halting ongoing repairs.[8]

Global maritime organizations have viewed the incidence of AMC in the Gulf of Guinea with growing concern. In 2011 the Joint War Committee (JWC), which represents insurers from both Lloyd's of London and International Underwriting Association (IUA) company markets, extended a war-risk zone for Nigerian waters up to 200 nautical miles offshore.[9] Since then, Benin and Togo have also been added as listed areas where extra premiums apply for transiting vessels.[10] Although the number of attacks in the region showed a decline in the first half of 2014 (compared to the same period in 2013), nineteen incidents still occurred, prompting the International Maritime Bureau (IMB) to warn that the area remained risky for international shipping, especially the vicinities off the Port of Lagos in Nigeria.[11]

Oil Bunkering

Bunkering—a process that entails tapping oil pipelines and extracting their contents onto barges for resale—is an activity that almost exclusively takes place in Nigeria's Niger delta. Initially a relatively small-scale enterprise, this has since developed into a thriving "business," generating windfall profits that are both augmenting the threat potential of armed militias and depriving the state of a vital source of revenue.

In its original form, bunkering merely entailed siphoning off small amounts of liquid petroleum fuel oil (LPFO) from sabotaged pipelines that were then shipped to industry customers in large commercial centers such as Lagos. In most cases, gangs operated on demand-only basis, eschewing large-scale extractions due to problems associated with storage. The scale and so-phistication of illegality changed, however, with the opening up of a market in crude oil and associated opportunities to sell to refineries. The greater profit margins that could be yielded have since led to the development of an orga-nized bunkering system composed of several independent "owners," which while acting as ostensibly independent businesses, are part of one interlinked criminal system. Numerous communities participate in the illegal trade, in-cluding the Ajagbodudu, Abitoye, Egborode, Egwa I, Egwa II, Obodobodo, Odidi, and Ubeji. However, it is Ijaw and Itsekiri warlords who undertake the most concerted activities, acting as the effective "kingpins" of much of the theft that is presently taking place in the delta region.[12]

The actual mechanics of bunkering is a complex affair that starts in the marshlands of the delta and culminates in the coastal waters of Nigeria's ex-clusive economic zone (EEZ). The first stage involves the siphoning of oil. This is achieved by drilling a small hole in a section of pipeline that is used to house a tube with a two-way valve that is, in turn, connected to a barge. When turned on, this junction diverts the pressurized oil upwards onto the holding boat, where it is stored. Once the required volume of oil has been ex-tracted, the valve is switched off, allowing the petroleum to resume its normal course through the pipeline. Next, a tugboat tows the collection vessel to one of many illegal refineries in Delta State, where the tapped crude is processed. The barge is then taken to a preassigned delivery point, where its contents are off-loaded onto a third coastal transport ship. Finally, the refined petro-leum is taken to a super-freighter anchored in the EEZ, where it is sold for an agreed price (often with the tacit approval of corrupt officials), exchanged for weapons, or both.[13]

To ensure safe passage, the transport vessels are accompanied by an armed protection cordon, which is either privately contracted on a fee-for-service basis or provided by co-opted senior officers from the Nigerian navy who al-legedly levy a "security tax" on every liter of oil that is being transferred. The entire operation thus involves several players: those who drill and maintain the valves; those who own the storage barges; those who run the tugboats; those who operate the coastal delivery vessels; those who provide the secu-rity for these ships; and those who arrange and broker the terms for the final sale of the crude to the super-freighters. As noted, although each acts as an independent venture, they all ultimately come together to form one extended criminal enterprise.

The scale of illegal oil theft taking place in the delta is difficult to quantify, given the covert nature of the enterprise, official corruption, and the lack of consistent reporting data. James Ibori, the former governor of Delta State, believes as much as 300,000 barrels per day (bpd) of crude are lost every day as a result of organized theft. Multinationals operating in the region reject this as an overestimation, but still approximate an overall robbery rate of between 150,000 and 200,000 bpd. Other analysts put the figure closer to 100,000 bpd.[14] Whatever the case, the extent of the problem is clearly enormous, cutting deeply into Nigeria's average output of two million bpd and costing the government and oil companies heavily in lost revenue.

Concerted sweeps by the Nigerian navy in the delta region in recent years have disrupted the organization of the bunkering system and helped to uncover the depth of corruption in the navy. However, these actions have not eliminated oil theft—they have merely caused it to become far less centralized and disaggregated. Today, a variety of militias and crime gangs continue to run diversion junctions along pipelines, contracting out to their own barge/tugboat operators. Oil is sold both for profit and to procure weapons that are then used to protect their respective business patches. In some instances, rather than tap from pipelines, bunkerers have also gone straight to wellheads that have been abandoned by oil companies as a result of militant attacks, smuggling crude to neighboring states such as Ivory Coast, Benin, and Togo.[15]

Drug Trafficking

Drug trafficking in the Gulf of Guinea centers on the international cocaine trade. The region has emerged as an increasingly important transshipment hub for Latin American drug syndicates seeking to diversify from an almost exclusive focus on the United States to consumers in Europe. The growing emphasis on the latter reflects higher street prices (see Table 15.1) as well as shifting demand patterns toward cocaine and highly addictive derivatives such as crack. Within Europe, the United Kingdom constitutes the principal market for these drugs, with usage so common that traces of benzoylecgonine—the metabolized form of cocaine once it has passed through the body—have actually been found in Britain's water supply.[16]

TABLE 15.1 Comparative estimated values of Latin American cocaine exports to consumers in North America and Europe

Region	Estimated value (US$ millions)
North America: Low estimate	15
North America: High estimate	23
Europe: Low estimate	30
Europe: High estimate	45

SOURCE: Beau Kilmer and Rosalie Liccardo Pacula, *Estimating the Size of the Global Drug Market: A Demand-Side Approach: Report 2* (Santa Monica, CA: RAND, 2009), 70.

While certain amounts of cocaine are trafficked directly to European ports such as Barcelona, Lisbon, Antwerp, and Rotterdam, the more common route runs via Sierra Leone, Guinea, Ghana, Senegal, and especially Guinea-Bissau. All these countries have weak judicial institutions, lack the resources for effective (or even rudimentary) coastal surveillance, and are beset by rampant corruption—traits that make them ideal as transfer points for moving narcotics out of Latin America. According to estimates from the United Nations Office on Drugs and Crime (UNODC), at least 50 tons of refined cocaine worth US $2 billion pass through the GoG en route to Europe every year.[17] In the words of Antonio María Costa, the former executive director of UNODC, the illicit trade has become so endemic that it has now effectively turned the "Gold Coast into the Coke Coast."[18]

Most of the cocaine that is trafficked to the GoG is exported from Venezuela. Consignments follow what has colloquially become known as "Highway 10"—a reference to the 10th degree of latitude that connects the northern part of Latin America with its closest point on the African continent across the Atlantic.[19] The drugs are then shipped overland to the Maghreb, entering Europe across the Mediterranean Sea via traditional hashish smuggling routes.

Within the GoG, Guinea-Bissau forms the apex of smuggling activity—so much so that the country is now generally considered to be the world's first genuine narco-state. The value of drugs that pass through this West African nation rivals that of its official economy, while complicity in the trade extends to the very highest levels of the military and governing civil bureaucracy.[20] In 2013, the head of Guinea-Bissau's armed forces, General Antonio Injai, was indicted in absentia by a New York court on cocaine and weapons trafficking charges that directly tied him to the criminal enterprises of the

Revolutionary Armed Forces of Colombia (FARC).[21] Two weeks earlier, the former chief of the navy, Rear Admiral José Américo Bubo Na Tchuto, was arrested in a Drug Enforcement Agency (DEA) sting operation during which he admitted to undercover agents that he could arrange for the storage and transfer of Colombian cocaine at a rate of US $1 million for every 1,000 kilograms brought into the country.[22]

Facilitating Factors

Several factors serve to drive illicit violent maritime activity in the Gulf of Guinea. First is a lack of coastal surveillance. The region encompasses a huge swath of territory—the Niger delta alone covers an area of 20,000 square kilometers within wetlands of 70,000 square kilometers[23]—that is well beyond the capacity of the littoral states, either singularly or collectively, to monitor.[24] One recent study estimated that the combined maritime forces of the region comprise less than twenty-five large security vessels.[25] While smaller patrol boats are higher in number, even in the case of relatively advanced coast guards, such as that of Nigeria, they are generally antiquated, in need of repair, and in some instances have not been decked in more than three decades.[26] The resultant enforcement void has created a plethora of opportunities that illicit organizations have been quick to seize upon.

Second is corruption. As noted, official complicity in cocaine trafficking has directly contributed to the GoG's degeneration into a narcotics transshipment hub for Latin American cartels. Corruption has also directly availed oil bunkering—in Nigeria it is estimated that a fifth of the country's refined petroleum is sourced from illegally diverted supplies in the Niger delta[27]—and has provided the necessary "lubrication" for piracy and maritime theft to thrive. In the latter case, state involvement has embraced everything from providing accurate intelligence on ship locations and the types of cargo they carry to assisting with the rapid discharge of stolen commodities once they reach land.[28]

Third, weak criminal justice structures have lowered the risk threshold of engaging in maritime crime, dramatically altering the cost-benefit ratio when determining whether or not to embark on such a course of action. This has been particularly evident with respect to piracy/armed theft, where the lack of a clear system for passing suspected criminals at sea to appropriate law enforcement agencies on land has led to a *de facto* policy of "catch and release."[29]

The resultant absence of legal deterrence (very few prosecutions of alleged pirates/maritime criminals have ever taken place) has spurred youths otherwise deprived of legal employment opportunities to join with syndicates that can "net" a sizable return for a single successful attack.

The fourth facilitating factor is poverty and lack of economic opportunity. Piracy and other crimes are among the few financially rewarding occupations in the Gulf of Guinea, largely because the two main employers in the region—fishing and agriculture—have been decimated by the combined effect of maritime poaching (which has seriously depleted offshore protein stocks) and irresponsible oil extraction practices (which have poisoned both soil and water).[30] Willful government neglect has merely compounded matters—something that finds particular expression in the Niger delta. Here, unemployment rates hover around 70 percent, with nearly three quarters of the region's 40 million people lacking access to electricity, proper sanitation, potable wells, and special medical care.[31] Under such circumstances the appeal of "quick return" crime becomes understandable, especially when the prospect of imprisonment is so low.

Finally, and perhaps most importantly, is the emergence of organized tribal militias in the Niger delta who remain at the forefront of illicit maritime activity throughout the Gulf of Guinea. The Ijaw constitute the bulk of the population in this region, most of whom live in abject poverty. This is despite the fact that the majority of Nigeria's oil wealth—which makes up 80 percent of the country's GDP and 95 percent of its foreign exchange earnings—is pumped out of the rivers and delta states.[32] Over the past decade, several groups have taken up arms to fight for a more equitable share of the region's oil wealth and have since devolved into straight crime syndicates. Prominent examples include the Movement for the Emancipation of the Niger Delta (MEND) and its subsidiary groups,[33] the Niger Delta People's Volunteer Force (NDPVF), the Niger Delta Vigilantes (NDV), and the People's Liberation Force (PLF).[34]

National, Regional, and International Implications

Illicit violent maritime activity holds real dangers for the countries of the Gulf of Guinea and their dependency on the resources and commerce originating from this part of the world. Attacks on shipping have detracted from the

GoG's status as a safe, oceanic trading corridor, with vessel owner-operators exhibiting a growing reluctance to pay the higher insurance premiums that are now required for transiting the region's waters. This has cost West African states in terms of lost landing and anchorage fees (60 percent of Benin's GDP is derived from its port)[35] and hindered dynamic commercial trade—stymieing in the process the ability of GoG governments to attain their development goals.[36]

Rampant corruption engendered from organized oil theft and drug trafficking has further encouraged and entrenched what was already a serious problem of official graft, undermining popular confidence and trust in elected officials, members of the armed forces, and law enforcement officials. As previously discussed, issues of this sort have been glaringly evident in Guinea-Bissau, where the custodial functions of the state have been systematically exploited to avail personal profiteering by those supposedly charged with ensuring and protecting the interests of their constituents.

Militias in the Niger delta have had a profound impact on the domestic stability of Nigeria, the political anchor for both the Gulf of Guinea and West Africa more generally. Not only have groups such as MEND, NDV, and NDPVF helped to normalize violence as an accepted form of social action, their criminal activities have directly impacted oil output. According to Rear Admiral Oyagha, Director of the Nigerian Navy's Transformation Office, the state lost an average of 1,656,281 barrels a month to oil theft in 2013. Based on prevailing market rates for crude oil, this translated into a deficit of almost US $20 billion.[37] For a country held hostage to acute economic externalities that show no sign of abating (at least in the near term), costs of this magnitude are something that the government can ill afford.

Besides its fiscal effects, illicit bunkering is contributing to the proliferation of light weapons, many of which are becoming increasingly sophisticated and lethal, in Nigeria as well as the wider GoG region.[38] Not only are these munitions radically expanding the range of attack options available to pirates, criminals, and militias, they are also tearing at the fabric of society by encouraging violent responses to unresolved problems. Just as importantly, this flood of armaments is undermining the efforts of those seeking to develop and employ peaceful mechanisms for addressing internal challenges.

Beyond its national and regional effects, maritime crime in the Gulf of Guinea has relevance for broader international security. The region is now a critical node in the global cocaine trade, which is both boosting the insurgent war chest of FARC[39] and "feeding" growing addiction and drug-related crime problems in Western Europe.[40] Equally as important, the activities of pirates and militias are disrupting oil production in an area that accounts for around 4 percent of the world's total petroleum output. Most of these products are ultimately destined for either Europe or the United States, with the former receiving approximately 40 percent of its oil from the GoG. The US share of 29 percent is expected to rise further as Washington progressively moves to reduce the country's dependence on traditional supplies from the Middle East.[41] On top of these issues, maritime crime is contributing to a lack of governance across a wider geographic space that hosts or lies proximate to two prominent zones of terrorist activity: Boko Haram in northern Nigeria/Cameroon and al-Qaeda in the Islamic Maghreb (AQIM) in the Sahel.[42] Both of these organizations stand to benefit from the instability that is being engendered in the Gulf of Guinea—if not directly through access to money, weapons, and recruits, at least tangentially in terms of being able to leverage favorable operating settings that are typically a by-product of weak state structures.[43]

Responding to Maritime Violence in the Gulf of Guinea

Steps have been taken to address the prevalence of maritime crime in the Gulf of Guinea. Nationally, the region's littoral states have moved to conclude agreements for the acquisition of more advanced and effective patrol vessels. Nigeria has been at the forefront of these efforts, "inking" deals with China, France, and Singapore. The navy has additionally sought government approval to buy up to forty-nine ships and forty-two helicopters over the next ten years, which will be used to monitor both the country's territorial waterways and the wider gulf more generally.[44] In addition, moves have been made to bolster the strength of regional coast guards. The 2013 establishment of Ghana's Marine Police Unit, whose training is being supported by the United States, is one case in point.[45]

At the collective level, naval forces from Ghana, Gabon, Equatorial Guinea, Togo, and Benin participated in an American-led multilateral exercise in 2012, which was designed to enhance coordinated response and intelligence capabilities for combating piracy, trafficking, and other sea-based crimes. Joint antipiracy patrols have also become more evident and now involve Benin, Nigeria, Cameroon, Togo, Gabon, Equatorial Guinea, and São Tomé.[46]

More promising were the results of a two-day summit in 2013 that took place in Yaoundé, Cameroon. Attended by representative governments of the Economic Community of West African States (ECOWAS), the Economic Community of Central African States (ECCAS), and the Gulf of Guinea Commission (GGC),[47] the meeting was instrumental in driving two major outcomes: (1) the creation of an Inter-Regional Coordination Center on Maritime Safety and Security for Central and West Africa (to be headquartered out of Yaoundé); and (2) the adoption of a Code of Conduct on the Prevention and Repression of Acts of Piracy, Armed Robbery Against Vessels, and Illicit Activities in the West and Central African Domain. Combined, these initiatives could have a significant impact in fostering common action to mitigate illicit maritime activity (the aim is to have a common strategy in place by the end of 2014), especially as they have the strong backing from ECOWAS, ECCAS, and the GGC—the region's key intergovernmental bodies.[48]

Finally, various outside actors are playing a role in helping to bolster maritime domain awareness in the Gulf of Guinea:

- The European Union (EU), which has a particular interest in securing energy supplies from West Africa, is contributing to capacity-building efforts in the region, in addition to acting as a useful bridge between the Anglophone and Francophone component elements of ECOWAS and ECCAS.[49]

- The International Maritime Organization (IMO) is working to promote whole-of-government strategies for mitigating maritime threats by running tabletop exercises (TTX) that bring together national authorities responsible for such areas as environmental protection, oil, finance, aviation, coastal policing, and justice.[50]

- The United States is providing joint antipiracy training for GoG states through its Africa Partnership Station (APS)[51] and has supplied over $35 million to support local gulf forces in countering sea-based threats in their respective territorial waters.[52] Washington is also in the process of establishing an offshore rapid response Marine Corps capability to fend off piracy and other maritime threats in the Gulf of Guinea. The force will fall under the command of a larger Spain-based crisis-containment unit that the service set up in 2013 to deal with emergencies in North Africa that currently includes 550 troops and six MV-22B Osprey helicopters.[53]

Conclusion

Despite efforts taken at national, regional, and international levels, maritime violence and crime remain a significant threat in the Gulf of Guinea. This state of affairs reflects some important gaps in the current suite of mitigation measures. Aside from the lack of any meaningful (i.e., visible) presence in the territorial waters of the GoG—a function of the littoral states' chronic lack of surveillance and patrol assets—one major problem is the absence of effective protocols for coordinating joint search and rescue patrols, much less anything approaching a codified right of hot pursuit. It is conceivable that a GoG-focused version of the proposed African Union's Common Exclusive Maritime Zone for Africa (CEMZA) could be applied to help promote greater collaboration and MDA among the GoG states. However, the AU's concept is very nascent (it is part of a wider continent-wide integrated maritime strategy) and there has been no guidance as of yet on how it might be implemented.[54]

In addition, many GoG countries are not in full compliance with the IMO's International Ship and Port Security (ISPS) Code, which has triggered warnings from American authorities that any shipping line wishing to do business in the United States may be prohibited from entering or leaving a gulf terminal. Finally, the Suppression of Unlawful Acts (SUA) Convention is effectively in abeyance, as several states in the Gulf of Guinea have yet to accede to the accord, including Angola, Cameroon, DRC, Gabon, and Sierra Leone.[55]

Perhaps the biggest problem, however, is that the various initiatives that have been instituted to secure the GoG proceed from the assumption that threats can best be dealt with at sea. This is at odds with the basic reality that the main drivers for maritime violence and crime in the gulf stem from land—notably, economic marginalization, social deprivation, poverty, and corruption. Until comprehensive moves are made to mitigate these root causes—particularly in the Niger delta, which constitutes a main source for many of the sea-based threats currently afflicting the region—issues such as armed maritime crime, oil theft, and drug trafficking will remain an enduring feature of the wider Gulf of Guinea landscape.[56]

Notes

1. International Maritime Bureau (hereafter referred to as IMB), *Piracy and Armed Robbery Against Ships: Report for the Period 1 January–31 March 2014* (London: IMB, April 2014), 5.

2. IMB, *Piracy and Armed Robbery Against Ships: Report for the Period 1 January–30 June 2014* (London: IMB, July 2014), 5–6.

3. IMB, *Piracy and Armed Robbery Against Ships: Report for the Period 1 January–31 December 2013* (London: IMB, January 2014), 5.

4. See, for instance, Ryan Cummings, "The Rise and Rise of Piracy in the Gulf of Guinea," *Think Africa Press*, July 18, 2013. It is the financial liability that is incurred by delays to onward journeys (known as demurrage costs) that hurt ship owners the most. The extent of these losses—which can run to between $20,000–$30,000/day—are especially great in countries where police authorities are either inefficient or lacking in professionalism, both of which can result in investigations that take weeks or even months to complete.

5. Adjoa Anyimadu, *Maritime Security in the Gulf of Guinea: Lessons Learned from the Indian Ocean* (London: Chatham House, Africa Paper 2013/02, July 2013), 3; Cummings, "The Rise and Rise of Piracy in the Gulf of Guinea." Unlike the HoA, the GoG does not lie proximate to any state that has collapsed to the same extent that Somalia has, with all littoral countries retaining an ability to exert at least a semblance of control over their national territory. As such, there is no equivalent opportunity for a syndicate to hold a seized freighter for extended periods of time while ransom negotiations—that usually last at least 45 days and possibly as long as a year—proceed.

6. P.K. Ghosh, *Waiting to Explode: Piracy in the Gulf of Guinea* (New Delhi: Observer Research Foundation Occasional Paper #46, September 2013), 16; IMB, *Piracy and Armed Robbery Against Ships: Report for the Period 1 January–31 December 2013*, 21; Jessica Lincoln, "Thinking Globally: Countering Piracy in West Africa," *Current Intelligence—Analysis*, June 8, 2012, available online at http://www.currentintelligence.net/analysis/2012/6/8/thinking-globally-countering-piracy-in-west-africa.html, as of July 23, 2013.

7. Shedrack Gaya Best and Dimieari Von Kemedi, "Small-Arms Proliferation Rises in Nigerian Rivers and Plateau States," *Jane's Intelligence Review* (October 2005), 37–38; Lincoln, "Thinking Globally."

8. "Nigeria's Shadowy Oil Rebels," *BBC News*, April 20, 2006, available online at http://news.bbc.co.uk/go/pr/fr/-/2/hi/africa/4732210.stm, as of February 13, 2008; "Intelligence Brief: M.E.N.D. Escalates Instability in Nigeria," *Power and Internet News Report*, April 27, 2006, available online at http://www.pinr.com/report, as of February 13, 2008.

9. David Rider, "Piracy's Emerging Market: The Gulf of Guinea," *gCaptain*, August 8, 2011, available online at http://gcaptain.com/piracys-emerging-market-gulf/, as of July 23, 2014.

10. Joint War Committee, "Hull War, Piracy and Related Perils Listed Areas," JWLA/021, June 12, 2013; "Togo Added to Piracy Risk Areas List: Lloyd's Maritime Association," *Platts*, June 14, 2013.

11. IMB, *Piracy and Armed Robbery Against Ships: Report for the Period 1 January–30 June 2014*, 19–20.

12. See, for instance, Augustine Ikelegbe, "The Economy of Conflict in the Oil Rich Niger Delta Region of Nigeria," *Nordic Journal of African Studies*, 14/2 (2005), 215–16; and Adekunbi Ero, "We Are Making Progress," text of Interview with Brigadier Wuyep Rimtip, Commander, Joint Task Force in the Niger delta, reproduced in *Tell Magazine* (May 26, 2008), 28.

13. Author interview, Abuja, September 2008. For a detailed overview of the oil bunkering process see Stephen Davis, Dimieeari von Kemedi, and Mark Drennan, "Illegal Oil Bunkering in the Niger Delta," n.d.a., available online at http://www .legaloil.com/Documents/Library/Pas%20Paper%20Illegal%20Oil%20Bunker ing%20210406.pdf, as of July 23, 2014.

14. Ikelegbe, "The Economy of Conflict," 222; Human Rights Watch, *The Warri Crisis: Fueling Violence*, Human Right Watch Report 15/18A (2003), 17–18; Kenneth Ehigiator, "Oil Smugglers Accused of Fueling Warri Crisis," *Vanguard Newspaper*, August 21, 2003; Neil Ford, "In Deep Water," *Jane's Intelligence Review* (August 2008), 56; Lincoln, "Thinking Globally"; "Nigeria Losing a Fifth of Revenue to Oil Theft—Report," *Reuters*, May 15, 2012.

15. Human Rights Watch, *The Warri Crisis*, 19–20.

16. "Cocaine Use in Britain So High It Has Contaminated Drinking Water, Report Shows," *Independent* (UK), July 23, 2014. Overall, between 700,000 and 1.2 million people in the UK are thought to use cocaine every year.

17. *West Africa Coast Initiative* (New York: UNODC, 2013), available online at https://www.unodc.org/westandcentralafrica/en/west-africa-coast-initiative.html, as of July 23, 2013.

18. Antonio María Costa, cited in Andy Webb-Vidal, "Cocaine Coasts: Venezuela and West Africa's Drug Axis," *Jane's Intelligence Review* (February 2009), 47.

19. Joseph Kirscjhke, "The Coke Coast: Cocaine's New Venezuelan Address," *World Politics Review* (September 11, 2008). In an effort to stem these flows, several European governments established a dedicated intergovernmental counternarcotics organization in 2006. Known as the Maritime Analysis and Operations Centre (MAOC) and headquartered out of Lisbon, this body has the remit to disrupt cocaine shipments sent from Latin America in an arc stretching 12,000 kilometers that extends from Iceland to the Cape of Good Hope in South Africa. MAOC blends law enforcement and military units, fusing and disseminating intelligence to avail coordinated drug interdiction by seven participating states: France, Ireland, Italy, the Netherlands, Portugal, Spain, and the UK (Germany, Canada, and Europol all hold observer status). See Andy Webb-Vidal, "Secret Weapons," *Jane's Intelligence Review* (April 2009), 58.

20. Anyimadu, *Maritime Security*, 6.

21. Adam Nossiter, "US Indicts Guinea-Bissau's Military Chief in Drug Case," *New York Times*, April 19, 2013. At the time of writing, Injai remained free in Guinea-Bissau.

22. Adam Nossiter, "US Sting That Snared African Ex-Admiral Shines a Light on the Drug Trade," *New York Times*, April 16, 2013.

23. Ghosh, *Waiting to Explode*, 10.

24. See, for instance, Francois Vreÿ, "Bad Order at Sea: From the Gulf of Aden to the Gulf of Guinea," *African Security Review* 18.3 (2009), 25.

25. James Carafano, "Oil and Gas Attract Pirates to Gulf of Guinea," *Maritime Executive*, November 15, 2013, available online at http://www.maritime-executive.com/article/Oil-and-Gas-Attract-Pirates-to-Gulf-of-Guinea-2013-11-15, as of July 23, 2014.

26. Author interviews, Abuja, September 2008.

27. "Nigeria Losing Fifth of Revenue to Oil Theft—Report."

28. See, for instance, Rider, "Piracy's Emerging Market"; and "Combating Piracy and Oil Theft in Nigeria," *Lookout*, May 28, 2012, available online at http://lookout newspaper.com/combating-piracy-and-oil-theft-in-nigeria/, as of July 23, 2014.

29. Anyimadu, *Maritime Security*, 6; Lincoln, "Thinking Globally." The term "catch and release" refers to situations in which suspected pirates apprehended by naval patrols are simply set free because no jurisdiction is available to prosecute them. This was a particular problem off the HoA and was only ameliorated by the conclusion of pirate-transfer agreements with several East African states (Kenya, Tanzania, Seychelles, Mauritius) that were prepared to take in, try, and incarcerate detained pirates.

30. The Niger delta has been described as one of the most contaminated regions on the planet. According to the United Nations Environment Programme (UNEP), it will take up to thirty years of intensive cleanup efforts to restore the region.

31. Ghosh, *Waiting to Explode*, 9; "Combating Piracy and Oil Theft in Nigeria."

32. One of the main reasons for this economic marginalization is that under a constitutional provision first enacted in 1979, state governors possess title to land, which deprives the people who live on it of its material benefits. Another problem is that while a formal requirement exists for the monthly disbursement of federal funds to state governments, no specific mechanism exists for accounting how these monies are spent.

33. These include the Federated Niger Delta Ijaw Communities (FNDIC), the Outlaws, "General" Boyloaf, and the Niger Delta Strike Force (NDSF).

34. Jean Herskovits, "Nigeria's Rigged Democracy," *Foreign Affairs* (July/August 2007), 123–25; Ford, "In Deep Water," 57; Ghosh, *Waiting to Explode*, 11–13; "The Rise and Rise of Piracy in the Gulf of Guinea"; Tomas Malinas, "Militancy in Niger Delta," Matthew B. Ridgway Center for International Security Studies, University of Pittsburgh, n.d.a, available online at http://www.ridgway.pitt.edu/Ridgway Research/Issues/InternationalPeaceSecurity/BackgroundersIPS/tabid/552/smid/1686/ArticleID/646/reftab/497/t/Militancy-in-the-Niger-Delta/Default.aspx, as of July 23, 2013.

35. "Piracy: Benin in the Firing Line," Port Management Association of West and Central Africa, October 2011, available online at http://www.pmawca-agpaoc.org/news.php/11/piracy-benin-in-the-firing-line.html, as of June 8, 2012.

36. Vreÿ, "Bad Order at Sea," 24; Raymond, "Enhancing Maritime Security in the Gulf of Guinea," *Strategic Insights* VI/1 (January 2007), 5.

37. "Nigeria Loses US$20 Billion Annually to Crude Oil Theft—Rear Admiral Oyagha," *Vanguard*, May 30, 2014, available online at http://allafrica.com/stories/201405300250.html, as of July 24, 2014.

38. See, for instance, Gilpin, "Enhancing Maritime Security," 3; *Topical Seminar on Energy and Security in Africa: Program Highlights* (Washington, DC: Africa Center for Strategic Studies, 2005).

39. FARC is estimated to earn between US $200 and $300 million from the cocaine trade. See, for instance, Bilal Saab and Alexandra Taylor, "Criminality and Armed Groups: A Study of FARC and Paramilitary Groups in Colombia," *Studies in Conflict and Terrorism* 32/6 (2009), 455–75; and Alexandra Guaqueta, "The Colombian Conflict: Political and Economic Dimensions," in Karen Ballentine and Jake Sherman, eds., *The Political Economy of Armed Conflict: Beyond Greed and Grievance* (Boulder, CO: Lynne Rienner Publishers, 2003), 73–106.

40. For more on the wider social, political, economic, public health, and security implications stemming from the global cocaine trade, see Peter Chalk, *The Latin American Drug Trade: Scope, Dimensions, Impact and Response* (Santa Monica, CA: RAND, 2011).

41. Patrice Sartre, *Responding to Insecurity in the Gulf of Guinea* (New York: International Peace Institute, July 2014), 3; Rider, "Piracy's Emerging Market"; Moki Edwin Kindzeka, "US, African Countries Team Up to Tackle Piracy in Gulf of Guinea," *Voice of America*, April 23, 2014, available online at http://www.voanews.com/content/us-african-countries-team-up-to-tackle-piracy-in-gulf-of-guinea-/1899510.html, as of July 25, 2014.

42. N.R. Jenzen-Jones, "Maritime Security in West Africa: An Industry-Based Approach," *Current Intelligence—Analysis*, June 5 2012, available online at http://www.currentintelligence.net/analysis/2012/6/5/maritime-security-in-west-africa-an-industry-based-approach.html, as of July 25, 2014.

43. For a detailed analysis on how weak states can avail terrorist designs see Angel Rabasa, Steven Boraz, Peter Chalk, Kim Cragin, Theodore W. Karasik, Jennifer D.P. Morioney, Kevin A. O'Brien, and John E. Peters, *Ungoverned Territories: Understanding and Reducing Terrorism Risks* (Santa Monica, CA: RAND 2007).

44. Ghosh, *Waiting to Explode*, 22–23; Will Ross, "Nigeria Celebrates First Home Made Warship," *BBC News*, June 7, 2012, available online at http://www.bbc.co.uk/news/world-africa-18300358, as of July 24, 2014; "Offshore Energy and Piracy in the Gulf of Guinea," *Recorded Future*, July 17, 2012, available online at https://www.recordedfuture.com/offshore-energy-and-piracy-in-the-gulf-of-guinea/ as of July 25, 2014.

45. Anyimadu, *Maritime Security*, 7.

46. Ghosh, *Waiting to Explode*, 23–24; "Joint Imperialists: African Military Exercise in Gulf of Guinea," *Pan African News*, February 21, 2012, available online at http://panafricannews.blogspot.com/2012/02/joint-imperialists-african-military.html, as of July 25, 2014; "Nigeria-Benin Anti-Piracy Patrols 'Successful,'" *DefenceWeb*, October 18, 2011, available online at http://www.defenceweb.co.za/index.php?option=com_co

ntent&view=article&id=20172:nigeria-benin-anti-piracy-patrols-successful&catid=
51:Sea&Itemid=106, as of July 25, 2014.

47. Observers from Belgium, Brazil, China, France, Germany, Japan, Russia, Spain, the United Kingdom, the United States, the European Union, the International Maritime Organization (IMO), the Africa Center for Strategic Studies, AFRICOM, and the Maritime Organization for West and Central Africa were also in attendance. The specific wording of the Memorandum of Understanding (MOU) that resulted from the summit meeting can be accessed at http://www.ecowas.int/publications/en/maritime_security/mou.pdf, as of September 12, 2014.

48. Sartre, *Responding to Insecurity in the Gulf of Guinea*, 9; Carafano, "Oil and Gas"; Anyimadu, *Maritime Security*, 13, 15; Ghosh, *Waiting to Explode*, 25–26; Kindzeka, "US, African Countries"; "UN Security Council Urges Comprehensive Approach to Counter-Piracy in Gulf of Guinea," *UN News Center*, August 14, 2013, available online at http://www.un.org/apps/news/story.asp?NewsID=45625#.U9 LruajB3lo, as of July 25, 2014.

49. Anyimadu, *Maritime Security*, 12.

50. Sartre, *Responding to Insecurity in the Gulf of Guinea*, 9; Anyimadu, *Maritime Security*, 12.

51. The APS is an initiative that falls under AFRICOM and which aims to encourage engagement between a range of partner African coastal states and relevant nongovernmental organizations (NGOs) to improve collective maritime professionalism, infrastructure, integration, and domain awareness. For more on the program, see "About Africa Partnership Station," AFRICOM, available online at http://www.africom.mil/Newsroom/Photo/10193/africa-partnership-station, as of July 25, 2014.

52. Anyimadu, *Maritime Security*, 6; Ghosh, *Waiting to Explode*, 25; Jenzen-Jones, "Maritime Security in West Africa," 3.

53. Dan Lamothe, "Meet the Marines' New Pirate-Hunting Team," *Foreign Policy*, November 5, 2013.

54. For more on the CEMZA and integrated maritime strategy, see Africa Union, "2050 Africa's Integrated Maritime Strategy," available online at http://au.int/maritime, as of September 12, 2014.

55. Sartre, *Responding to Insecurity in the Gulf of Guinea*; "Bad Order at Sea: From the Gulf of Aden to the Gulf of Guinea," 25; Magnus Addico, "Maritime Security Threats and Responses in West and Central African Sub-Region/Gulf of Guinea," presentation given before the United Nations Open-Ended Informative Consultative Process on Oceans and the Law of the Sea—Maritime Security, New York, June 23–27, 2008, available online at http://www.un.org/Depts/los/consultative_process/documents/9_magnusaddico.pdf, as of May 22, 2009; Anyimadu, *Maritime Security*, 8.

56. Cummings, "The Rise and Rise of Piracy"; "Combating Piracy and Oil Theft in Nigeria."

16 Yemen

The Case for a Coast Guard

Aubrey Bogle

YEMEN HAS DAUNTING, MULTIPLE, AND UNIQUE MARITIME security issues. The country has a coastline of 1,760 km (approximately 1,100 miles), strategically located on the Arabian Sea, Gulf of Aden, and Red Sea, between Oman and Saudi Arabia. In an interview conducted by Sue A. Lackey, associate editor, *Navy League* magazine in March 2005, Captain Robert Innes, US Coast Guard (referred to later in this chapter), offered the following insights into the importance of the maritime domain to Yemen and some of its challenges:

> Yemen's internal road connections are virtually nonexistent. Its door to the outside world is its ports; that is also its line of defense. There has been a traditional sea route through 5,000 years of recorded history that moves from Pakistan, down the Omani coast and Yemen and then turns south to the Horn of Africa. Separating out the actual density of who's who—refugees, bad guys [commercial traffic, etc.]—we're still trying to sort that out. This is the first time ever that anyone has tried to analyze what has been a traditional sea route. . . .
>
> My job here is not to build the US Coast Guard or the US Navy. My job is to build a maritime force that they (the Yemenis) can live with. It may end up being in the long run very different from what it started out to be, but it will be capable, it will be functional and it will also be cooperative. They are going to adopt and adapt.[1]

In the 1990s, Yemen was virtually defenseless from terrorist and other criminal activity originating within its maritime domain.[2] Its navy was essentially incapable of conducting any maritime security operations either along the coast or in internal waters. Its ships were largely derelict and incapable of getting underway.[3] It had no coast guard and had never had one. The most effective maritime law enforcement organization was probably the Yemeni port police in Aden Harbor, however its authority to act was limited to Aden Port.[4]

Yemen's coastline is the most porous border in the region. It is the ancestral homeland of the bin Laden family, and nearly one-third of Osama bin Laden's original recruits were Yemeni. Many of the hard-line mujahideen who fought beside bin Laden against the Russians in Afghanistan returned to Yemen. Bin Laden maintained a training camp there until 1992, and Palestinian militant groups have long established offices in Sanaa, the capital and largest city.[5] General Anthony Zinni, Commander of US Central Command, and his senior staff generally knew this situation. However, there was a sense that al-Qaeda would not "soil its nest" in Yemen by conducting terrorist attacks in Yemen.[6] Thus, in 1998 Gen. Zinni moved the US Navy refueling operations from Djibouti to Aden.

Due to a lack of funds, and perhaps because of bureaucratic differences at the highest levels of the Yemeni government, the planned formation of a Yemen Coast Guard was delayed until 2002. The suicide bombing of the *Cole* (DDG-67) during a refueling stop in Aden on October 12, 2000, the bombing of the French merchant vessel *Limburg* in October 2002, and pressure from the West, however, prodded the government of Yemen to face its own growing maritime threat.[7] The need to establish a coast guard service quickly prompted Yemen's President Ali Abdullah Saleh to send a request for aid to the US Embassy for assistance. In partial response to this request, the US Coast Guard selected Capt. Robert Innes, USCG, an officer with more than three decades experience in the creation of coast guard and naval units for foreign governments, to assist in the creation of the Yemen Coast Guard.[8]

An interview of Brigadier General Ali Ahmed Ras'ee,[9] then Commander of the Yemen Coast Guard, was conducted by Hasan al-Zaidi (*Yemen Post* staff) in May 2008.[10] During this interview Brig. Gen. Ras'ee described the missions of the Yemen Coast Guard as follows:

> The tasks of coast guard forces are stipulated in the establishment decree, and these tasks are varied. The coast guard forces have security and not military

functions, including keeping order in Yemeni ports and launching patrols in Yemeni coasts and regional waters. Other tasks are limiting illegal immigration, protecting national waters against indiscriminate fishing, protecting environment against pollution, fighting piracy, rescue and search activities.

Subsequently, during the same interview, Brig. Gen. Ras'ee characterized illegal immigration as "one of the biggest problems we face." He also highlighted the importance of international cooperation in coping with maritime security issues.[11]

More recently, Commodore Asif Khaliq, Pakistan Navy, who is currently the Commander of Combined Task Force (CTF) 150, met Brigadier General Fouad S. Basuleman, Acting Chairman Yemen Coast Guard at the Yemen Coast Guard Headquarters. In a report dated October 1, 2013, Brig. Gen. Basuleman echoed these same concerns. Following this meeting Brig. Gen. Basuleman said:

> During recent times, the political situation in the Arab countries in general and Yemen has had an impact on Yemen and the Yemen Coast Guard. Drug trafficking, human smuggling and weapon smuggling from Africa to Yemen, piracy and other crimes remain the major issues for the Yemen Coast Guard."[12]

He emphasized the joint efforts to curb this menace and provided assurance that Yemen would continue its cooperation with the Combined Maritime Force (CMF).[13]

Illegal smuggling and trafficking of migrants from Somalia is greatly facilitated by the geographic proximity of Somalia to Yemen. The 1,300-km coast of Somalia on the Gulf of Aden, and the remainder of the Horn of Africa, are directly opposite the coast of Yemen on the Gulf of Aden. None of these countries, especially Somalia, have sufficient resources to adequately patrol their maritime borders. When asked about the human smugglers during his interview, Brig. Gen. Ras'ee observed that:

> First of all, Somali smugglers are inhuman and they are criminals in the true sense of the meaning. They transport immigrants in old and wrecked boats, and they do not commit themselves to their capacity. A boat that holds 10 will be loaded with 30 and one that holds 40 will be amassed with 100. Second, when there is overload, they force people on board to jump into the sea under the threat of arms . . . (We) can't let these smugglers practice their dirty jobs, and we have to protect our regional waters.[14]

The UN High Commissioner for Refugees (UNHCR), in a report dated October 17, 2014, reported on the increasing numbers of illegal immigrant deaths at sea and attributed at least some of these deaths to cruelty by the smugglers.[15]

The trend in illegal immigration from the Horn of Africa has generally been upward for a number of years; however, recently, with the internal conflict in Yemen, the rate has increased greatly. In September 2014—the most recent month for which statistics have been released—the Nairobi-based Regional Mixed Migration Secretariat (RMMS) reported 12,768 arrivals, predominantly from Ethiopia. It was more than double the figure for September 2013 and represented the single largest monthly influx on record.[16]

However, there is a more sinister aspect to illegal immigration flowing to Yemen from the Horn of Africa. The newspaper *Yemen Times* reports that al-Qaeda terrorists from Somalia are passing through the Port of Shuqra "to fight on the side of Ansar Al-Sharia in Abyan and Shabwa governorates, located in the east and south of Yemen."[17] Between March 2012 and February 2014, more than 500 Somali fighters were reported to have come into Yemen, according to the Interior Ministry. The *Yemen Times* reported that the Somali Embassy in Sanaa said this figure might increase.[18]

As early as 2008, Brig. Gen. Ras'ee recognized that the illegal immigration problem was an international issue and beyond the scope of the Yemen Coast Guard to cope with alone. In his 2008 interview he offered the following:

> (I)llegal immigration does not target our country as 70 percent of those who cross Gulf of Aden go to the Gulf and European countries as well as America. *There should be joint cooperation with Gulf countries and European countries like France, Britain and Italy to curb such a phenomenon.* The European Union has supported Spain to fight illegal immigration, though it is a rich country and not poor like Yemen.[19] (Emphasis added)

The smuggling of humans from the Horn of Africa is not the only maritime security issue created by smuggling facing Yemen. Other forms of maritime smuggling, especially drugs, small arms, and commodities smuggling, also pose national security threats. The threat from these sources is reported to be increasing.[20] Arms smuggling, both into and out of Yemen, has proved a growing problem. In 1992, the UN passed an embargo against the trade of small arms to Somalia, and it was repeatedly violated. In 2003, the UN convened a panel of experts to investigate violations of this embargo. What they found was a strong distribution network of weapons and ammunition that supplied the different warring groups. The panel determined that these weapons originated from neighboring countries in the Horn of Africa and the Middle East but "Yemen remains the most important source of commercial arms transfers to Somalia." Arms trafficking is entrenched in Yemeni government and society, making it difficult to eradicate. The lack of economic development and a weak central government facilitated the creation of an illicit weapons trade stretching from the Gulf of Aden through the Horn of Africa.

In a 2012 paper by Kathryn Corbi, the author takes a pessimistic view of the Yemeni illegal arms trade in the absence of decisive action by the Yemeni government. Ms. Corbi writes:

> The Yemeni government has failed to adequately address the trafficking problem with Somalia, and the longer it continues, the more difficult it becomes for the government to enforce laws regulating arms trade. Now that Al-Qaeda has set up a new base in Yemen, "Al-Shabab [Islamic militant organization in Somalia] has declared its intention to support and supply weapons to Al-Qaeda." While Yemen plays a major role in supplying arms to Somalia and exacerbates the conflict in that country, Somalia will likewise play an increasing role in the deteriorating security situation in Yemen. Although the Yemeni government is making efforts to expel Al-Qaeda from the country, if it does not address the arms trade with Somalia, the likelihood that its efforts will be successful is slim.[21]

> To combat the arms trade, the Yemen Coast Guard has become more active in the waters between the Gulf of Aden and Al Mukalla (located on the Yemen coast). While this has had some impact on the arms trade from ports in these areas, the Coast Guard is unable to monitor the entire area, particularly east of Al Mukalla, the northern coast of Puntland, and Somaliland. This means that the arms trade continues from these unpatrolled areas. Authorities in these areas have also confirmed that Yemen remains their largest single source of arms.[22]

Unfortunately, with the social unrest and governmental instability created by the al-Houthi rebellion in the north, and the presence of al-Qaeda in Yemen's southern mountains, the chance that the arms trade from Yemen will decline in the near future is remote. As noted by Kathryn Corbi in her paper:

> The Yemeni government must take action to stabilize the state as a means to curb the arms trade.[23]

The new government must also focus on the application of rule of law. President Saleh's connections to tribal groups in the north contributed to the lack of rule of law in the state. It is not enough to merely create laws; they must be adequately enforced and continuously monitored. Yemen's government must reform its judicial system and military to ensure it is capable of enforcing laws against the arms trade.[24]

Narcotic and psychotropic drugs have become a serious national security threat. For many years, khat and hashish have been the most common substances that were abused in Yemeni society. These substances are either produced domestically or enter Yemen from its southern coast, unlike weapons, which enter from the west.[25] However, this situation has changed dramatically for the worse in the last few years. "Drug abuse is a huge problem in Yemen and has become a bigger problem since 2011, especially synthetic drugs as they are more available and [at] cheaper prices," said Golala Ruhani, a development consultant who recently worked on community outreach projects on drugs in Yemen.[26] The deterioration in security inside Yemen has made it easier to sell drugs on the streets.

Meanwhile, increased insecurity along Yemen's borders with Saudi Arabia and Oman—key destinations for both illicit drugs and smuggled pharmaceuticals in the past—has led to a glut in supply and falling prices. Quoting a former addict, "The problem began in 2011, with the revolution . . . Drugs started out with the pharmacies but they started appearing in the streets, for free. As much as you want. Some areas of the revolution were out of government control. The dealers used the squares [where protests were held]. The people got addicted there; the problem started there."[27]

The primary source of these drugs has been reported to be from Africa.[28] There is also a reported nexus between drug smuggling and human trafficking. This is not surprising, given that many smuggling operations combine different cargoes, including drugs, arms, and East African migrants looking for asylum, employment opportunities, or both, in Yemen or in the neighboring gulf states. Recently, traffickers have been opening up new channels of distribution by offering migrants the chance to pay off debts or make money by transporting drugs into Taiz, Yemen and distributing them on the streets.[29]

The Yemen Coast Guard has made considerable contributions to the success of reducing the continuing piracy threat along its Red Sea and Arabian Sea coast. The Yemen Coast Guard is uniquely positioned to contribute to defeating piracy in the region.[30] In a 2012 interview with a correspondent from alShorfa.com, Brig. Gen. Ras'ee confirmed this point:

> Yemen is qualified to fight piracy if it has the necessary resources, based upon several factors, including the fact that Yemen is the only country that faces Somalia [across the Gulf of Aden], and it has the longest coastline on the Gulf of Aden and the Arabian Sea. Moreover, the shipping lanes now run closer to Yemen after the International Maritime Organisation moved them closer to Yemen and farther away from the dangers posed by Somali pirates.
>
> I believe Yemen is qualified to fight piracy because of the coastal monitoring centres that were built for the coast guard, which would limit piracy and drug and weapons trafficking considerably if countries in the region would cooperate with each other and Western countries would provide the necessary support. And I stress here that support for the Coast Guard means support for national and international economies.[31]

During this same interview, Brig. Gen. Ras'ee commented on the importance of resolving the social and economic problems in Somalia, domestic support from the Yemeni government, and international support and cooperation as elements to reach a final solution to the piracy issue.

> Fundamental solutions to the piracy phenomenon can only be achieved by finding a solution to problems in Somalia, which has not had a government in 20 years. The acts of piracy that can occur on a daily basis, such as robberies and threats, are linked directly to the situation in Somalia.
>
> We need co-operation from the Yemeni government, wherein it would provide complete support for the Coast Guard Authority so it can perform its duties. That will be accomplished by activating the coastal monitoring centres the coast guard established, providing the necessary resources to operate them, and providing an actual budget, because the coast guard supports the nation's economy.
>
> We also need co-operation from foreign countries and regional support for the coast guard, especially from Saudi Arabia given its massive resources. The international community would then recognise the effort that is being made and provide us with support because fighting piracy is a global issue that is in the international community's interest, not just in Yemen's interest alone.
>
> There is co-operation, exchange of information, and support for the Yemen Coast Guard . . . especially in combating drug trafficking and the fight against

piracy. The international forces that have been in the region [for several years now] help to protect merchant ships and respond to distress calls.[32]

Somali piracy peaked in 2009 and 2010, when forty-six and forty-seven vessels were hijacked respectively, according to the European Union Naval Force. Hijackings dropped to twenty-five in 2011, five in 2012, and zero as of July 2013.[33] With Somali piracy having fallen on hard times, former Somali pirates are now reported to be providing protection to illegal fishing vessels and are "also trafficking in arms, drugs and humans, according to a report published this month by the UN Monitoring Group on Somalia and Eritrea."[34] One current pirate said he did not know about pirates providing protection to foreign fishing vessels, but he said some pirates are using Yemeni fishermen to smuggle weapons into Puntland. "That's our current money-making business because ship hijackings have failed," a pirate commander who goes by the name Bile Hussein said by phone from Garacad, a pirate lair in central Somalia. "If you drop one business, you get an idea for another."[35]

Fisheries are an important national resource for Yemen, providing for around 3 percent of its GDP, with some 500,000 people (or approximately 2.9 percent of the population) being directly or indirectly dependent on the fishing industry for their livelihood in 2003. Of this number, an estimated 50,000 people were directly involved in catching fish. The country possesses significant fish stocks, among them valuable species such as lobster, shrimp, and cuttlefish.[36]

Illegal fishing in Yemeni waters has also posed a national security threat. Presently, Yemen is facing illegal industrial fishing along the Yemeni coasts of the Red Sea, the Gulf of Aden, and the Arabian Sea. These waters are wasted, destroyed, and looted, thus jeopardizing the country's fisheries. As per the available information, there are sixty active multinational fishing vessels, some of which are unlicensed, operating in Yemeni waters. These "fish pirates" often use explosives to force fish outside their habitats.[37] The Yemen Coast Guard has been increasingly active in addressing the fisheries issues. A recent report reflects these activities. On October 14, 2014, the *Arab Today* website reported that the Yemen Coast Guard had seized three Egyptian fishing vessels fishing in the Red Sea in Yemeni waters.[38]

The general consensus in the international community is that the Yemen Coast Guard has achieved remarkable operational capabilities in a very short period of time. It has established three operational districts: the Red Sea District, the Gulf of Aden District, and the Arabian Sea District. It has also created a training institute in Aden.[39] This Institute conducts training in a variety of subjects including: Operations (Navigation, Communication, and Radar); Port Security (Sentries, Weapon Specialist, and Boarding); Electrical Engineering; Seamanship; and Logistics.[40] In 2009 with assistance from Italy, Yemen installed a coastal surveillance radar system centered in Aden.[41] Finally, the Yemen Coast Guard has been an active contributor to Combined Task Force 150 operations.[42] Capt. Innes, during his 2005 interview, commented that "We have an excellent reputation; so much so that the Yemen model is being duplicated elsewhere, to include Iraq."[43]

However, all has not been smooth sailing for the Yemen Coast Guard. During the interview of Brig. Gen. Ras'ee cited earlier, he said that international aid had been a disadvantage in the Yemeni government budget process because of the Yemeni bureaucratic intransigence and perhaps ignorance. During the interview he stated:

> It is of disadvantage because people as well as high-ranking officials believe that coalition countries provide us with unlimited support even at the level of budget. When we ask for our budget from the Ministry of Finance, they tell us that we are a supported institution, therefore, we neither receive support from foreign countries nor a budget from the government as others. I again assure that our administration has been established with Yemeni resources and we receive limited support from some friendly countries and we thank them for that.[44]

Yemen Coast Guard personnel have also been targets of terrorist attacks. The most recent was an al-Qaeda attack, killing four personnel working in a coast guard camp overlooking the Gulf of Aden in January 2014.[45]

In 2010 and early 2011, it was widely reported that the Yemen Coast Guard was providing security services for hire to vessels transiting in Yemeni waters. Security packages typically included a team of up to nine armed, uniformed personnel and heavily armed patrol vessels, for fees of up to $55,000 for a detail of about three days. Some if not all of these forces had been trained by the US Coast Guard, and at least some of the armed vessels used as escorts had been provided by the US Coast Guard. Use of the vessels in this manner is in violation of US regulations prohibiting the use of these vessels in private transactions, and has been the subject of US Congressional hearings.[46]

Further complicating the maritime law enforcement picture for the Yemen Coast Guard is the Yemeni maritime commercial enterprise and law enforcement culture that views what is considered "unlawful" very differently than would most Western law enforcement officials or citizens. Perhaps Capt. Innes said it best during his 2008 interview:

> There are some things I've learned the hard way . . . One is to be very circumspect about the idea of corruption, and the other is to be very careful with the word smuggling. It's only smuggling if it's against the law; otherwise it's enterprise. Here is a society that for thousands of years has prided itself on being traders and engaging in commerce. It's only been within the last few decades that all these things that have grown from thousands of years of enterprise have now become "smuggling."[47]

Innes also said these are cultural obstacles to overcome, and, even though the Yemen Coast Guard is based on North American and Western European models, it is unique.[48]

Conclusion

An effective maritime law enforcement organization is a critical element of national security. The Yemen experience highlights this fact. A maritime law enforcement organization may take one of many forms. Maritime operations, whether traditional naval military forces or coast guard law enforcement, are costly both in terms of capital and in highly trained personnel. Many countries have chosen to employ their navies in the maritime law enforcement role. Others, like Yemen, have established a separate organization in a ministry other than the Ministry of Defense.[49] These organizational choices both have their own unique advantages and disadvantages.

In addition to highly specialized training, law enforcement requires an entirely different mindset from military operations in war in terms of the use of force. The US Coast Guard has a use-of-force policy that specifies only that "minimum force necessary to compel compliance (with the orders of the Coast Guard law enforcement officer)" will be used in carrying out a law enforcement operation. Use of deadly force is generally limited to self-defense situations. This standard is consistent with international law. Use of force during military operations in time of war (armed conflict) is subject to the international Law of Armed Conflict (LOAC) and a state's Rules of Engagement (ROE).

During an armed conflict, lawful combatants are protected by LOAC when they engage in the killing of enemy combatants and destroying military objects—conduct that would otherwise be unlawful during peacetime. ROE usually contemplate overwhelming force may be used to defeat the enemy during an engagement. A highly trained "war fighter" may find it difficult to scale back his use-of-force orientation during a law enforcement mission. Correspondingly, it may be difficult for a well-trained law enforcement officer to adapt to the much higher level of force required when engaging the enemy during an armed conflict. Consequently, when a maritime force is called upon to carry out both the law enforcement and military operations missions, training must be more extensive, complex, and costly.[50]

There is no single right way to organize a Coast Guard. The Yemenis seem to have gotten it right for their country.[51] Notwithstanding enormous maritime security challenges and domestic internal conflict, Yemen has been able to establish an effective coast guard in a short period of time. States wishing to enhance their coast guard or establish one may find it useful to draw on the Yemeni experience.[52]

Notes

The author of this chapter served as the US Coast Guard liaison officer and Maritime Interception Operations officer on the Fifth Fleet/US NAVCENT staff forward deployed to Manama, Bahrain. He served under Vice Admiral Charles "Willie" Moore, Commander Fifth Fleet/Commander US Naval Central Command in the late 1990s. During this time, he accompanied VADM Moore on several visits to Sanaa and Aden, Yemen, for meetings with high-level Yemeni government officials, including President Abdullah Saleh, his prime minister, his minister of defense, and his minister of interior. Meetings were also held with the US Ambassador, Barbara Bodine, who fully supported the establishment of a Yemen Coast Guard. These meetings were intended to lay the foundation for the creation of the Yemen Coast Guard. This case study draws upon this personal experience as well as documentation relating to the bombing of the destroyer USS *Cole* in the Port of Aden on October 12, 2000 and events subsequent to establishment of the Yemen Coast Guard in 2003.

1. Sue A. Lackey, associate editor, "Yemen After the Cole," *Seapower,* March 2005.

2. This comment is based on personal observation and on the lack of any operational engagement by the Yemeni navy with any operational navy in the region, including the US Navy.

3. The Yemeni navy was primarily equipped with Soviet-era warships. Many of these ships were sunk/damaged and their armaments destroyed during the 1990 and 1994 revolutions.

4. Based on personal observation. However, it should be noted that the Aden Port police failed to discover or intercept the suicide boat attacks on the USS *Cole* and the MV *Limburg.*

5. Lackey, "Yemen After the Cole."

6. Personal knowledge of the author.

7. In December 1999, al-Qaeda had attempted a similar attack against USS *The Sullivans* (DDG-68). The attack failed when the suicide boat sank before reaching the USS *The Sullivans* because it was overloaded with explosives.

8. Lackey, "Yemen After the Cole."

9. As an agency with primarily law enforcement missions, the Yemen Coast Guard is an agency assigned to the ministry of interior, however it has adopted the land-force rank structure for its personnel. As is common with Arab names translated into English, there are many different spellings of any given name, especially surnames. Brig. Gen. Ras'ee's name is spelled differently in almost every publication he is referenced in. I have chosen to use the spelling found in his interview with the *Yemen Post* referenced below.

10. Hasan al-Zaidi, "Interview with Commander of Yemeni Coast Guard Forces Ali Ahmed Ras'ee," *Yemen Post*, February 9, 2008, available at http://www.yemenpost .net/28/InvestigationAndInterview/20081.htm (accessed 5 November 2014).

11. Ibid.

12. "CTF 150 Meeting with Acting Chairman Yemen Coast Guard," October 1, 2013, available at http://combinedmaritimeforces.com/2013/10/01/ctf-150-met-with -acting-chairman-yemen-coast-guard/ (accessed on December 7, 2014); also participating in the meeting were Dr. Diyar Khan, Ambassador of Pakistan, Colonel Amen A.S. Alansei, Director Yemen Military Cooperation, and several senior officers from the Yemen Coast Guard.

13. Ibid. The meeting also afforded an opportunity to emphasize the need for close coordination between Combined Maritime Forces (CMF) and the Yemen Coast Guard, and all parties agreed that the challenges to maritime security in the region could be better addressed through cooperation among regional countries and CMF. Combined Maritime Forces is a multinational naval partnership that exists to promote security, stability, and prosperity across approximately 2.5 million square miles of international waters, which encompass some of the world's most important shipping lanes.

CMF's main focus areas are defeating terrorism, preventing piracy, encouraging regional cooperation, and promoting a safe maritime environment.

CMF counters violent extremism and terrorist networks in maritime areas of responsibility; works with regional and other partners to improve overall security and stability; helps strengthen regional nations' maritime capabilities; and, when requested, responds to environmental and humanitarian crises.

It comprises three task forces: CTF-150 (maritime security and counterterrorism), CTF-151 (counterpiracy), and CTF-152 (Persian Gulf—or Arabian Gulf in accordance with current US doctrine—security and cooperation).

There are thirty member nations: Australia, Bahrain, Belgium, Canada, Denmark, France, Germany, Greece, Italy, Japan, Jordan, Republic of Korea, Kuwait, Malaysia, the Netherlands, New Zealand, Norway, Pakistan, Philippines, Portugal,

Saudi Arabia, Seychelles, Singapore, Spain, Thailand, Turkey, UAE, United Kingdom, United States, and Yemen. See: http://combinedmaritimeforces.com/about/.

14. Al-Zaidi, "Interview with Commander of Yemeni Coast Guard."

15. "There's been a sharp increase this year [2014] in the number of migrants and asylum seekers losing their lives in attempts to get to Yemen, mainly from the Horn of Africa, with more deaths in 2014 than in the last three years combined. In the latest tragic incident on Oct 2, 64 migrants and three crew members died when their vessel, sailing from Somalia, sank in the Gulf of Aden. With five additional deaths since, this brings the number of dead this year to 215, exceeding the combined total for 2011, 2012 and 2013. It's also the largest single loss of life since [earlier] sinkings [in 2014] in June, when 62 people died; March, when 44 people lost their lives; and another in April, with 12 people dead.

"There have been frequent reports of mistreatment, abuse, rape and torture and increasingly cruel measures being adopted by smuggling rings that seem to account for the increase in deaths at sea. Boats crossing to Yemen are overcrowded, and smugglers on numerous occasions have reportedly thrown passengers overboard to prevent capsizing or avoid detection. Search-and-rescue officials say the practice has resulted in hundreds of undocumented casualties in recent years." Quoted from UN High Commissioner for Refugees (UNHCR) report, "2014 Becomes the Deadliest Year at Sea off Yemen," October 17, 2014, available at http://www.refworld.org/docid/54588d234.html (accessed December 6, 2014).

16. Integrated Regional Information Networks (IRIN), "Yemen Crisis a Boon for People Smugglers," November 20, 2014, available at http://www.refworld.org/docid/546f32cd4.html (accessed December 5, 2014).

17. Mohamed al-Samei and Muaad al-Maqtari, "Yemen: Coasts Without Protection," *Yemen Times*, May 24, 2012, in News, available at http://www.yementimes.com/en/1575/news/883/Yemen-Coasts-without-Protection.htm, (accessed December 6, 2014).

18. Ibid.

19. Al-Zaidi, "Interview with Commander of Yemeni Coast Guard."

20. See a discussion of the recent growth of smuggling, especially drugs and small arms, into Yemeni ports in [author's name withheld by the publisher for the safety of the correspondent], an *al-Monitor* Correspondent in Yemen, "Yemen Faces Increasing Weapons, Drugs Smuggling Problems," *al-Monitor*, Translator(s) Rani Geha, posted March 14, 2014, available at http://www.al-monitor.com/pulse/originals/2014/03/yemen-smuggling-drugs-weapons-human-ml##ixzz3L9GUoT63 (accessed December 6, 2014).

21. Kathryn Corbi, "Small Arms Trafficking in Yemen: A Threat to Regional Security and Stability," *New Voices in Public Policy*, Volume VI, Winter 2011/2012, George Mason University, 13.

22. Ibid.

23. Ibid., 15.

24. Ibid., 16.

25. *Al-Monitor*, "Yemen Faces Increasing Weapons, Drugs Smuggling Problems."

26. "Increasing Drug Use Strains Yemen's Services," June 30, 2014, IRIN, Humanitarian News and Analysis, a service of the UN Office for the Coordination of Humanitarian Affairs, available at http://www.irinnews.org/report/100272/increasing-drug-use-strains-yemen-s-services (accessed on December 7, 2014).

27. Ibid. Mohammed (not his real name), a former addict, reported that drug dealers were increasingly lacing their products with more dangerous substances. For example, marijuana, which has long been available in Yemen, is now mixed with sleeping pills and hallucinogens. Among the most common substances sold are strong sleeping pills, painkillers—including varieties that contain opiates—antidepressants, and anxiety-relief drugs. It has recently become popular for substance abusers to inject Tramadol, a strong prescription painkiller.

28. *Al-Monitor*, "Yemen Faces Increasing Weapons, Drugs Smuggling Problems." Read more: http://www.al-monitor.com/pulse/originals/2014/03/yemen-smuggling-drugs-weapons-human-trafficking.html#ixzz3LFoVd4JO.

29. Ibid.

30. See article by Brig. Gen. Ali Ahmed Rasaa (Ras'ee)/Former Chairman, Yemen Coast Guard "Yemen's Strategic Role in Maritime Security" *Unipath, United States Central Command (CENTCOM)*, available at http://unipath-magazine.com/yemens-strategic-role-in-maritime-security/ (accessed December 7, 2014).

31. Faisal Darem, "Coast Guard Official: Yemen Well Positioned to Fight Piracy," January 24, 2012, al-Shorfa.com, http://al-shorfa.com/en_GB/articles/meii/features/main/2012/01/24/feature-01 (accessed December 7, 2014).

32. Ibid.

33. Abdi Guled, Associated Press, "Somali Pirates Now Protecting Illegal Fishing Ships, Says UN Report," *Fox News*, July 25, 2013, available at http://www.foxnews.com/world/2013/07/25/somali-pirates-now-protecting-illegal-fishing-ships-says-un-report/ (accessed December 7, 2014).

34. Ibid.

35. Ibid.

36. Gary Morgan, FAO Consultant, Fishery Policy and Planning Division, Fisheries Department, "Review of the State of World Marine Capture Fisheries Management: Indian Ocean. . . . Country Review: Yemen," UN Food and Agriculture Organization, Fisheries and Aquaculture Department, July 2004, available at http://www.fao.org/docrep/009/a0477e/a0477e0v.htm (accessed December 8, 2014).

37. *Yemen Times*, "Yemen Faces Illegal Fishing in Its Waters," worldfishingtoday.com, February 5, 2008, available at http://www.worldfishingtoday.com/news/default.asp?nyId=315 (accessed December 8, 2014).

38. "Three Egyptian Boats Seized in Yemen Waters for Illegal Fishing," *Arab Today*, October 14, 2014, available at http://www.arabtoday.net/geygef-geyqhk/3%20Egyptian%20boats%20seized%20in%20Yemen%20waters%20for%20illegal%20fishing.html (accessed December 8, 2014). See also the report in *Yemen Times* dated October 30, 2014, found at http://www.yementimes.com/en/1829/report/4514/

Sixty-six-Egyptian-fishermen-held-in-Hodeida.htm. This report includes additional information on the apprehension of the illegal Egyptian fishermen. The *Yemen Times* reports that the Egyptians were initially detained by Yemeni fishermen and then turned over to the Yemen Coast Guard for legal processing. This cooperative arrangement had been carefully coordinated for some time prior to the apprehension of the Egyptian fishermen.

39. Yemen Coast Guard presentation at the ninth meeting of the UN open-ended Informal Consultative Process on Oceans & the Law of the Sea, available at http://www.un.org/depts/los/consultative_process/documents/9_sahel_presentation.pdf (accessed October 3, 2015).

40. Captain Abdullah Alqadhi, YCG director of OPS control room, Briefing slides, "Maritime Security and Human Migration," available at http://www.un.org/depts/los/consultative_process/documents/9_sahel_presentation.pdf (accessed December 8, 2014).

41. Muaad al-Maqtari, "Coastal Security Equipped Through International Support," *Yemen Times*, June 21, 2012, available at http://www.yementimes.com/en/1583/news/1021/Coastal-security-equipped-through-international-support.htm (accessed December 9, 2014).

42. "CTF 150 Meeting with Acting Chairman Yemen Coast Guard." For example, coast guard personnel have served as ship riders on CTF 150 warships to provide local knowledge to vessels patrolling in the vicinity of Yemen, the coastal radar network has provided cueing information to CTF 150 vessels, and Yemen Coast Guard vessels have controlled cooperatively with CTF 150 units.

43. Lackey, "Yemen After the Cole."

44. Al-Zaidi, "Interview with Commander of Yemeni Coast Guard."

45. Associated Press, "4 Yemen Coast Guard Members Killed in al-Qaida Attack in a Southern Town," *Fox News*, January 12, 2014, available at http://www.foxnews.com/world/2014/01/12/4-yemen-coast-guard-members-killed-in-al-qaida-attack-in-southern-town/ (accessed December 9, 2014).

46. Margaret Coker, "US Military Aid Is Available for Hire in Yemen," *Wall Street Journal* (online), January 4, 2011, available at http://www.wsj.com/articles/SB10001424052970204204004576049660513491614 (accessed December 9, 2014). Four Yemeni officials familiar with the private security details said they are done for profit and involve high-ranking officials in the Ministry of Interior and the nation's Coast Guard Authority, which falls under the ministry.

47. Lackey, "Yemen After the Cole."

48. Ibid.

49. Even countries that have established a separate coast guard may draw on navy personnel to staff the coast guard and man coast guard vessels, as Yemen does. Others, such as the Egyptian coast guard, will regularly rotate personnel from the navy to the coast guard and back.

50. In terms of numbers of vessels and personnel, the US Coast Guard is one of the twelve largest navies in the world. In terms of area, the US Exclusive Economic

Zone is the largest in the world, and the US Coast Guard is the agency that has been designated as the primary law enforcement organization to enforce US law in that region. By law, the US Coast Guard is both a military and a law enforcement organization. It may be incorporated as part of the US Navy during an armed conflict, as it was during World War II. US Coast Guard units and personnel have also participated in every US armed conflict since World War II. In this regard, it is unique in the US government. To maintain its naval military readiness, it regularly conducts naval warfare training and exercises with the US and foreign naval forces. The costs associated with equipping Coast Guard vessels for naval warfare and this training are paid out of the US Navy budget. However, one of the hidden costs associated with the naval warfare mission is that fewer Coast Guard resources are available to accomplish the law enforcement mission.

51. No doubt the ancient maritime tradition of Yemen was a significant benefit in the establishment and development of their coast guard.

52. The following is a personal note from the author of this chapter: *Tragically, the security situation that has developed in Yemen since this chapter was originally written has deteriorated to the point that all indications are that the Yemen Coast Guard operations have been seriously impaired. I can no longer communicate with my friends in the Yemen Coast Guard by e-mail or telephone. Notwithstanding the current situation, I have every confidence that Yemen will endure this tragedy, and the Yemen Coast Guard will be even stronger and more capable after the current violence subsides.*

17 Conclusion

Paul Shemella

W E HAVE DISCUSSED MARITIME VIOLENCE IN THE BROADEST possible way because we believe that all its manifestations are interconnected. Maritime violence is, in fact, an ecosystem populated by individuals and small groups who wish to exploit the murkiness of the maritime domain for selfish financial and political gain.[1] The challenge for governments is to channel all citizens into licit forms of behavior that help consolidate rather than divide society. It is sometimes said that politics is what separates us, while culture is what brings us together. Where maritime subcultures lie at the fringes of society, governance is a matter of finding ways to incorporate them into the whole; nations created from islands and archipelagos should have a head start on national cohesion, but they are among the poorest of the world's countries.[2] In either case, economic insecurity is a common root cause of most maritime violence.[3]

Ironically, the maritime domain is rich in natural resources. Coastal geography provides the basis for the commercial infrastructure needed to bring additional resources from around the world. Europe and North America were blessed with the right geography and got an early development lead. The continent of Africa, generally, was not endowed with favorable coasts and rivers, but it is catching up with maritime infrastructure development. Policies that provide a central role for the generation of national and personal wealth can help governments find hidden opportunities that accompany the challenges of the maritime domain. Maritime industries, from energy extraction to commercial fishing to international trade, have the potential to transform poor nations into rich ones. But directing resources to where they are needed obliges governments to go beyond the rhetoric of policy to develop comprehensive strategies and action plans for all their maritime institutions. As we have shown, high-capacity, clean, and well-led institutions are the instruments democratic governments use to get things done.

But sustainable development in the maritime domain is not possible without security. At least some of a government's resources must provide the climate within which maritime commercial activity can thrive. The key question is "how much?" As we have shown in this volume, the complex process of developing strategy helps provide the answer. And that answer will be different for each government. Some countries begin with more wealth (Brazil) or a smaller maritime domain to protect (Benin); many do not have enough resources even to monitor what is going on in their maritime spaces. It is these countries that must determine how to share the exclusive economic zones they "own" and pool the resources they have.[4] Even if they do that, they will need the assistance of great maritime powers like the United States, China, India, and the European Union.

Built on a foundation of political will, the two main pillars of maritime security are governance and capacity. Good maritime governance can create a climate of security, but only increased capacity can sustain it. Wealthy governments can help their under-resourced brethren in both areas. The two levels of assessment introduced in Chapter 6 provide all governments with a framework for enhancing the whole (undertaken with or without foreign assistance). Great maritime powers, however, find it much easier to help build capacity than to help developing nations improve maritime governance (boats, radars, and exercises are easier to count). As explained in Level Two, *having* a strategy is different than being able to implement it. But the opposite is also true—having the capacity without a *strategy* is a recipe for failure. Governance and capacity, assisted by others or not, must be enhanced in parallel. They are bookends for the maritime strategy library.

That library will have to contain many volumes. Managing maritime violence is a "wicked" problem set that does not have a definitive or lasting solution. Most nonsocial problems are "tame" in that they lend themselves to scientific hypotheses that can be tested until a consensus develops around one particular solution that can be proven. Wicked problems can only be solved for one array of myriad variables (extant in the maritime domain). Although maritime threats share many characteristics, the resolution for one unique situation is not transferrable (intact) to another problem. Because operational success can lead to strategic failure, wicked problems are best addressed at the highest possible level. That makes political-level strategies the key to producing the best possible outcomes relative to maritime violence. Given the inevitability of unintended consequences, strategists can never be sure they are on the right path. Strategy, as suggested in Chapter 5, must be continually measured and adjusted.[5]

For the chronic problems of maritime smuggling and sea robbery, for instance, governments know they will fail to achieve total eradication (those trying to smuggle illicit cargos at sea have always had the advantage over those trying to stop it). For the prevention of terrorist attacks and industrial accidents, they will not get a second chance. We have suggested ways that governments can obtain the best possible outcomes, given the complexity with which they must deal. They face multiple forms of maritime violence, unique circumstances with each situation, and the uncertainty of knowing which actions will solve the problem (and which will make it worse). Adding resource constraints to that mix is enough to discourage any strategist. But strategists have two things in their favor: imagination and judgment. We also suggest they consider the following precepts to guide the pursuit of that illusive set of desired outcomes.

Understand the problem set. Use every individual and institutional resource available to achieve total awareness of root causes and maritime threats. Consult with regional governments and act together with them to achieve maximum maritime domain awareness. Find common centers of gravity that point the way toward broad strategic approaches. Create a network of maritime security institutions that relies on education, encourages coordination, and fosters debate. Greater understanding of the context is a direct result of education, not training.

Investigate alternative solutions. Study other cases, from national history and international experience, but use them for learning, and do not apply the same exact remedies. Imagine the unintended consequences of all government actions, especially at the operational level. In just one glaring example, the provision of mosquito nets to African governments has resulted in the decimation of critical fresh-water animal populations, as villagers use them as fishing nets. Maritime security officials must also be prepared for failure, both tactical and strategic, and be ready to explain that to their populations.

Find the connections. Cooperation between terrorists, pirates, smugglers, and other criminals has been observed or alleged for a long time. While strategic interests differ greatly, tactical marriages of convenience certainly thrive. If it is discovered that criminal groups are sharing resources, focus on disrupting that cooperation. The prospect that the so-called Islamic State could infiltrate terrorists into southern Europe by hiding them in cargoes of refugees boarded in Libya reminds us that such connections must be anticipated.[6]

Identify institutional roles and resources. Maritime security institutions must have clear (and written) roles to reduce inefficient overlaps and balance resource distribution. Roles and resources must be synchronized. Roles without resources are just paper; resources without clear roles are a recipe for waste. Defined roles allow institutions to prepare for expected missions by developing the necessary capabilities. But capabilities are not enough; institutions need additional resources to build the capacity to execute emerging missions day in and day out. And they need training.

Promote the right people. Too often, governments place individuals in positions of leadership on the basis of politics and personal relationships rather than merit. Promoting officials from within can isolate an institution, or make it greedy, breeding destructive competition among institutions. Leaders of single institutions should have experience in several different institutions before they begin making strategic decisions. They should also understand how to get the most from their institutions. Creativity is maximized at the edge of chaos; leaders must learn to cultivate a climate of free-flowing ideas without allowing institutions to go over the edge.

Think globally. The maritime domain is vast, but there are a lot of nations in, on, and around it. International cooperation can shrink the field of play; competition and conflict can make it seem bigger. No single government has the resources to master its own piece of the maritime domain, but governments acting together, sharing the high seas—and even EEZs—will steadily grow the global capacity to reduce maritime violence. Perhaps Admiral Mike Mullen's vision of a "Thousand-Ship Navy" can be realized after all.[7] We are going to need it.

Use the maritime domain to increase national wealth. For most of this volume, we have characterized the maritime domain as an adversary. Governments that view their maritime spaces as sources of sustainable wealth make the investments necessary to protect critical infrastructure, the environment itself, and the people who live there from harm. They must balance commerce and security. Rising standards of living across the whole society are still the best measure of good governance.[8]

Clean up the neighborhood. Maritime domain awareness is a crucial precursor for effective security. Low-level maritime crime is rampant in most national maritime domains. This suggests that governments can reduce the level of crime and improve MDA at the same time. An important part of developing the operational strategy is to decide whether to spread out scarce MDA assets to mop up petty crime, or to hold them in reserve for worst-case scenarios. Every government will have a different solution to this puzzle.

Craft comprehensive strategies. The family of strategies against maritime threats should incorporate the ideas and capabilities of all maritime security institutions, properly resourced, educated, and trained. Other institutions—for example, the ministries of education, information, and foreign affairs—are called on for critical support. Governments must target root causes, threats, and their own vulnerabilities, all at the same time. Institutions must be made to work together, and then work with their counterparts in neighboring countries. Diverse threats require a diversity of operational strategies, all adjustable as the situation changes. Strategy is what makes it all come together.

Exercise good maritime governance. As with terrestrial security, the key to maritime security is good governance. Maritime governance, for all its unique characteristics, is different than governance more generally. The fundamentals, however, are the same: create an inclusive and cohesive society; strike the proper balance between security and liberty; and demonstrate that the government cares about its people. When asked why he became an "evil" pirate, a Somali youth responded, "When evil is the only option, you do evil." Government is about creating opportunity. The maritime domain can nurture good behavior or bad, but people need options to be good.

Notes

1. The ecosystem analogy rests on the fact that most maritime violence activities benefit from the same climate of insecurity in regions remote from government presence. Insurgents, terrorists, smugglers, and other criminals coexist, perhaps even in symbiosis, as they do what is necessary to survive.

2. Not all island nations share a maritime identity. The author was surprised to find that government officials in Madagascar do not consider themselves part of a

maritime society. To be sure, Madagascar is a very large island with abysmal road infrastructure, but with a maritime domain of more than one million square kilometers, this extremely poor country could derive enormous economic benefits from adopting a maritime orientation.

3. Root causes operate across a whole society. They do not necessarily result directly in a manifestation of maritime violence, but widespread conditions like poverty certainly contribute to maritime criminal activity.

4. The 2050 AIM Strategy, developed by the African Union, calls for a "shared EEZ" among Gulf of Guinea nations. This goal could become a goal for other regions facing large EEZs and scarce resources.

5. For a fascinating discussion of wicked problems, see Horst W. J. Rittel and Melvin M. Webber, "Dilemmas in a General Theory of Planning," *Policy Sciences* 4 (1973), 155–69. Rittel and Webber, professors at the University of California, Berkeley, first coined the phrase.

6. See James Stavridis, "Defending Italy from the Islamic State," *Washington Post*, March 12, 2015, http://www.washingtonpost.com.

7. Admiral Michael G. Mullen, US Navy, address to the *Seventeenth International Seapower Symposium*, US Naval War College, Newport, RI, September 19, 2005. Text available online at https://www.usnwc.edu/getattachment/a56bf61f-f637-4391-a9d1 -7e261146b3ed/ROP-17th.aspx.

8. The new president of Indonesia, Jokowi Widodo, has expressed a desire to recover the strong maritime roots of his nation's ancestors. His early speeches call for reviving the maritime economy and for using security forces to protect the fishing industry. Mr. Widodo has articulated, perhaps better than we could, why it is so important for governments to manage maritime violence holistically. See, "Fishing Trips," *Economist*, January 3, 2015, 29.

Index

Abidjan, Port of, 94

Abu Sayyaf Group (ASG), 132, 248–50; assault planning by, 16–17; counter-terrorism assistance in fighting, 258; Southeast Asia operations, 229; *Super Ferry 14* bombing, 17, 48n27, 250

Accessibility, as target-assessment criterion, 33, 34. *See also* CARVES target analysis model

Accountability and oversight subfunction, 99

Achille Lauro hijacking, 112, 229

Administration, in ICS, 191

AEOs (authorized economic operators), 116, 123n32

Africa: containerized freight inspection in, 21; CSI at ports in, 114; Gulf of Guinea case study, 265–76; maritime infrastructure development in, 298; mosquito nets as fishing nets in, 300; vetting of ferry personnel in, 16

African Union (AU), 85, 276

Africa Partnership Station (APS), 275, 281n51

Aircraft, as surveillance tool, 90

AIS (Automatic Identification System), 90, 136, 242n56

Aiyyah (Sea Tigers), 216

al-Basra oil terminal, 19, 27n33

Allah Tigers, 221

al-Qaeda: economic destabilization as goal of, 18; explosives transport and weapons smuggling by, 22; ISPS Code and, 112; Moro organizations and, 248; in Southeast Asia, 229; USS *Cole* suicide boat attacks, 163; in Yemen, 283, 285; Yemeni Coast Guard attack by, 290

al-Qaeda in the Arabian Peninsula (AQAP), 23–24

al-Qaeda in the Islamic Maghreb (AQIM), 1, 2, 274

al-Shabaab, 23–24

Alternative solutions, investigating, 300–301

AMC. *See* Armed maritime crime

Amman, Pottu, 205

Anandarajah, Ponniah, 211

AOI (areas of interest), 134

AOR (areas of responsibility), 134

APMM (Malaysian Maritime Enforcement Agency), 230–32
APS (Africa Partnership Station), 275, 281n51
AQAP (al-Qaeda in the Arabian Peninsula), 23–24
AQIM (al-Qaeda in the Islamic Maghreb), 1, 2, 274
Aquino, Benigno, III, 132, 252, 256
Areas of interest (AOI), 134
Areas of responsibility (AOR), 134
Armed maritime crime (AMC), 2, 49–62. *See also specific types of crime, e.g.*: Piracy; anchorage thefts of ships at harbor, 50, 51; armed robbery in territorial waters or on high seas, 51; dangers associated with, 52–53; defined, 49; drivers for, 62; factors in contemporary rise of, 53–57; in Gulf of Guinea case study, 265–67; hijackings, 51–52; private security companies in countering of, 57–62; scope and dimensions of, 50–52; terrorism and, 24
Armed robbery at sea, 1, 2; Code of Conduct on the Prevention and Repression of Acts of Piracy, Armed Robbery Against Vessels, and Illicit Activities in the West and Central African Domain, 275; criminal justice structures and, 271–72; in Gulf of Guinea, 266; IMB Piracy Reporting Centre, 131; in Malacca Strait, 226; off Horn of Africa, 50; Regional Cooperation Agreement on Combating Piracy and Armed Robbery Against Ships in Asia, 233–34; in territorial waters or on high seas, 51
Armed robbery of ships at harbor, 50, 51
Arms procurement (Sea Tigers of LTTE), 213–14
Arms proliferation, rise of armed maritime crime and, 57

Arms smuggling/trafficking (Yemen), 285–86
Arms trade to Somalia, UN embargo against, 285–86
ASEAN Ministerial Meeting on Transnational Crime, 234
ASF (Asian Ship Owners Forum), 234
ASG. *See* Abu Sayyaf Group
Ashdod, Port of, 22
Asia. *See also* Southeast Asia; *specific countries*: armed maritime crime in territorial waters of South Asia, 49; containerized freight inspection in, 21; CSI at ports in, 114; LTTE in, 212; migration of manufacturing from North Asia, 107; rice crisis in, 64n17; vetting of ferry personnel in, 16
Asian financial crisis (1997), 237–38
Asian Ship Owners Forum (ASF), 234
Assessing maritime governance, 88–102; Level I examination, 89–96; Level II examination, 95–101
ATS (Automated Targeting System), 115
AU (African Union), 85, 276
Australia: Border Protection Command, 131–32; coast-watcher network in, 136; and defeat of LTTE in Sri Lanka, 203; human smuggling and, 212; LTTE weapons and, 212, 218; maritime domain awareness of, 126
Aut dedere aut judicare principle, 177–78n26
Authorized economic operators (AEOs), 116, 123n32
Automated Targeting System (ATS), 115
Automatic Identification System (AIS), 90, 136, 242n56
Autonomous criminal conducts, 177n26

Bab el-Mandeb, Strait of, 23, 65n21
Badawi, Ahmad, 237
Bahamas, 51

Bakerathan, Kandiahpillai (Bhavi, Bahi, Khan), 211, 216
Baltic and International Maritime Council (BIMCO), 117, 123n33, 234
Baltic Sea, 17
Bangladesh, 53
Bangsamoro Republic, 253–54, 257
Baris, MV, 214
Barker, Joel, 151
Basuleman, Fouad S., 284
Bathsheba syndrome, 159
Belgium, 17, 130
Belize, 51
Benin, 274, 299
BIMCO (Baltic and International Maritime Council), 117, 123n33, 234
Bin Laden, Osama, 18, 283
Biometric SIDs, 117
"Bleed-to-bankruptcy" strategy, 18, 24
Boko Haram, 274
Border Protection Command (BPC; Australia), 131–32
Border security, 4, 283, 287
Bosphorus Strait, 65n21
Boston, Massachusetts, port of, 109
BP (British Petroleum), 53
BPC (Border Protection Command; Australia), 131–32
Brazil, 53, 299
Bridges, target analysis for, 41–42, 44
British Petroleum (BP), 53
"Broken windows" strategy, 81–82
Brookings Institution, 118
Built to Last (Collins and Porras), 149
Bunkering, 267. *See also* Oil bunkering

Cabotage laws, 121n10
California: Standardized Emergency Management System in, 186–87; wildfires in, 184–86
Camaraderie, in institutional leadership, 152–53
Cameroon, 126, 274

Canada, 212, 214, 218
Capability(-ies), 77; critical, 99, 101; of terrorists, 86n12
Capacity, 77, 83–84, 299; governance and, 102; of terrorists, 86n12
CARVER target-analysis process, 33–34
CARVES target analysis model, 34–46; end product of, 42–45; prioritized list of targets from, 39–42; public security in, 36–37; tactics and tradecraft in, 37–39; weighting factors in, 35–36
Case studies: defeating Sea Tigers of LTTE, 203–22; Gulf of Guinea maritime crime, 265–76; maritime violence in Sulu Sea, 243–59; suppressing piracy in Strait of Malacca, 224–39; Yemen Coast Guard, 282–92
Casualties. *See also individual incidents*: in armed maritime crime, 52; civilian, of LTTE, 209; deaths of migrants and asylum seekers, 295n15; from ferry accidents, 17; mass causalities as terrorist goal, 13, 15–18; public security in target assessment, 36–37
Catastrophe management. *See* Managing maritime incidents
CBP (Customs and Border Protection) officers (United States), 114
CEMZA (Common Exclusive Maritime Zone for Africa), 276
Centers of gravity, in net assessment, 74–75
Chandran (Sea Tigers), 211
China: corruption in, 53; LTTE weapons from, 212; and Malacca Strait security, 235; migration of manufacturing to, 107; Nigeria's agreement with, 274; oil supply for, 225; phantom ship frauds in, 52, 63n10; on South China Sea authority, 162–63
China Shipping Container Lines, 129

Chinese fishing vessels, Ivory Coast impoundment of, 2
Choong, Noel, 57, 63n4
CIA *World Factbook*, 120–21n3
"Closed" flag registry, 107–8
CMF (Combined Maritime Forces), 293–94n13
COA (course of action), 182
Coastal radar, integrated, 135–36
Coastal regions: as focus in maritime security, 243; as power centers, 102n3; subcultures of citizens in, 88
Coastal surveillance, in Gulf of Guinea, 271
Coastal waters, criminal maritime incidents in, 50
Coast Watch System (CWS; Philippines), 132, 258–59
Code of Conduct on the Prevention and Repression of Acts of Piracy, Armed Robbery Against Vessels, and Illicit Activities in the West and Central African Domain, 275
Cold War, 126–29
Cole, USS, 163, 229
Collambage, Jayanth, 221
Collins, Jim, 153
Combined Maritime Forces (CMF), 293–94n13
Command: defined, 182; in ICS, 190 (*see also* Incident Command System); in initial incident response, 181; management vs., 182–83, 198n2
Commercial activities, in anti-violence strategy, 73
Commodities trade, 107
Common Exclusive Maritime Zone for Africa (CEMZA), 276
Common operating picture (COP), 181
Commonwealth Fusion Center (Massachusetts), 111
Communication, by governments, 46, 84

Connections between criminal groups, 301
Construction of vessels: cruise liners, 15, 25n9; free-surface effect, 26n16; passenger ferries, 17, 26n16; and requirements for sinking vessels, 27n29
Contacts of interest, reporting standards for, 137
Container complex, 13
Containerized trade, 107; cargo inspections, 129; CSI for, 114–15
Container Security Initiative (CSI), 114–15
Container ships, 28n29, 28n30; locks on containers, 21; point-of-origin inspections for, 21–22; terrorist infiltration of, 21
Coordination activities: closing gaps in, 110; in incident management, 183
COP (common operating picture), 181
Corbi, Kathryn, 286
Core strategy, 77
Corporations, 86n9
Corruption: armed maritime crime and, 53; drug trafficking and, 270; in Gulf of Guinea area, 271, 273; leadership and, 159; piracy rates and, 238
Cost: of aircraft surveillance, 90; economic, of armed maritime crime, 52–53; of policing EEZs, 93; of PSCs, 60–61; and return on investment, 91
Costa, Antonio María, 270
Costa Concordia, 91, 183
Course of action (COA), 182
Crews. *See* Workforce of seagoing personnel
Criminal justice structures, maritime crime and, 271–72
Critical infrastructure, 31–32; analyzing target potential of (*see* Target-analysis model); attacks on, 47n5; cyberattacks on, 47n5; as hard targets, 31; information technology

systems as, 118; ISPS Code for, 112–14; maritime, 32; port facility security plan, 112–13; sabotage of, 19–20

Criticality, as target-assessment criterion, 33, 34. *See also* CARVES target analysis model

Cruise liners/ships, 15, 16, 25n8, 25n9

CSI (Container Security Initiative), 114–15

C-TPAT (Customs-Trade Partnership Against Terrorism), 115

Culture: institutional, 146–47; maritime subcultures, 298

Customs: assessing enforcement of, 92–93; Customs-Trade Partnership Against Terrorism, 115; SAFE Framework, 115–16

Customs and Border Protection (CBP) officers (United States), 114

Customs-Trade Partnership Against Terrorism (C-TPAT), 115

CWS (Coast Watch System; Philippines), 132, 258–59

Cyberattacks, 2; on critical infrastructure, 47n5; on information systems, 118

Cybersecurity threats, 117–18, 130

Cyprus, 51

Deepwater Horizon oil spill, 53, 195–97

Defensive strategy, 77–81

Dignity, leadership and, 158

Diplomacy, in anti-violence strategy, 72

Diplomatic and foreign affairs support, 97

Directions of Trade Statistics Yearbook (IMF), 120n1

Disaster management. *See* Managing maritime incidents

Disaster response, assessing, 94

Domain awareness. *See* Maritime domain awareness (MDA)

Dover, Port of (England), 16

Drive (Pink), 154

Drucker, Peter, 147, 160n4

Drug smuggling/trafficking: European cyberattack in, 118; in Gulf of Guinea, 269–71, 273–74; Joint Interagency Task Force—South, 130–31; by LTTE, 210; *Pong Su,* 131; in Yemen, 287, 295n27

Dry cargoes, 107

Ducting, 136

Duriappa, Alfred, 204

East Asia, LTTE weapons from, 212

East Timor, 212

Ebola virus, 2

Economic Community of Central African States (ECCAS), 275

Economic Community of West African States (ECOWAS), 275

Economic destabilization, as terrorist goal, 18–20

Economic means, in anti-violence strategy, 73

Economic opportunity, maritime crime and, 272

Economies: cost of armed maritime crime to, 52–53; international trade and, 106; maritime terrorism's impact on, 243

Ecosystem: of maritime governance functions, 89; of maritime violence, 1, 2, 298, 302n1

ECOWAS (Economic Community of West African States), 275

Education, of MDA workforce, 137–38

EEZs. *See* Exclusive economic zones

Effect(s), as target-assessment criterion, 34, 35. *See also* CARVES target analysis model

EiS (Eyes in the Sky) initiative, 232, 236

Elba Island, Georgia LNG terminals, 17

Elite institutions, 147. *See also* Institutional leadership

Emergency management, in anti-violence strategy, 73–74
Emergency response phases, 182
Emmanuel, Father S.J., 211
Employees. *See* Workforce of seagoing personnel
Ends, in maritime strategy development, 76–78
Energy security, maritime, 48n28
Energy transport, through Malacca Strait, 225
Entitlements, leadership and, 158–59
Environmental disasters: from AMC attacks, 53; oil spills, 53, 91, 111, 183, 187, 195–97; prevention of, 95
Environmental pollution, 2; in Niger delta, 279n30; seaborne trade and, 107; from vessel fuels, 121n7
Equatorial Guinea, 274
Estonia sinking, 17, 91
Estuaries, lack of surveillance of, 11
Ethics, institutional, 157–59
EU (European Union), 275
Europe: CSI at ports in, 114; cyberattack in, 118; as drug market, 269, 270, 274; geography of and development in, 298; human smuggling and, 212; intergovernmental counternarcotics organization in, 278n19; migration of manufacturing from, 107
European Commission, 115
European Union (EU), 275
Everett, Massachusetts LNG terminals, 17
Example, leading by, 157–58
Exclusive economic zones (EEZs): cost of policing, 93; overlapping governments in, 3; sharing, 299; UNCLOS obligations for protecting, 127; of United States, 296–97n50; vessels capable of operation throughout, 90
External stakeholders: institutional leadership and, 155–57; in maritime security, 142–43

Exxon Valdez oil spill, 91, 183, 187
Eyes in the Sky (EiS) initiative, 232, 236
Eyoshi, MT, 219

FARC (Revolutionary Armed Forces of Colombia), 271, 274, 280n39
Fargo, Thomas B., 235, 237
FBI, LTTE weapons procurement efforts and, 218
Federal Emergency Management Agency (FEMA), 196
Ferries, 15–17, 26n16; incident management for, 194; target analysis for, 41–42, 44–45
Fields, Mark, 160n4
Finance, in ICS, 191
Financial damage, from maritime terrorism, 19
Financial means, in anti-violence strategy, 73
Firefighting (US), 184–85; California wildfires in, 184–86; UN-recommended standard for, 187
FIRESCOPE, 185–86, 198n7
Firing, institutional, 153–54
Fisheries: AIS for, 90; Yemeni, 289
Fishing. *See* illegal fishing
Flags of convenience (FoC), 51, 61, 108, 129
Flag state, 107–8. *See also* vessel flag registry
FoC (flags of convenience), 51, 61, 108, 129
Focus, in institutional leadership, 151–52
Foreign trade. *See* International foreign trade
France, 274
Free Aceh Movement (GAM), 229
Freedom, balancing security and, 45
Free-surface effect, 26n16
Fuel bunkering, 1, 2, 267–69, 273
Fuseless, Marcelline (Victor), 205
Fusion centers (intelligence), 111

Gabon, 274

GAM (Free Aceh Movement), 229

Gandhi, Rajiv, 205, 206, 209

GGC (Gulf of Guinea Commission), 275

Ghana, 270, 274

"Ghost ships," 226

Gibraltar Strait, 18, 65n21

Girone, Salvatore, 60

Giuliani, Rudolph, 81

Global container complex, 13

Global Maritime Community of Interest (GMCOI), 143

Global port security, 104–20; characteristics of modern ports, 109–10; closing gaps in, 110–11; Container Security Initiative, 114–15; Customs-Trade Partnership Against Terrorism, 115; cybersecurity threats, 117–18; IMO's role in, 111–12; international foreign trade and, 105–7; ISPS Code provisions for, 112–14; SAFE Framework, 115–16; technology in, 118–19; vessel flag registry, 107–8; workforce of seagoing personnel and, 116–17

GMCOI (Global Maritime Community of Interest), 143

GoA. See Gulf of Aden

GoG. See Gulf of Guinea

Goishin, MV (Joishin, Jeishin), 219

Good to Great (Collins), 153

Governance, 298; ashore, 88; capacity and, 102; maritime governance vs., 302 (see also Maritime governance)

Governments: challenge for, 298; communication resources investment by, 46; corporations' adversarial relationship with, 86n9; maritime security role of, 2–3; maritime strategy development toolkit for, 72–74; net assessment of, 74–76; prioritization of defensive efforts by, 30–32, 39–42; safety laws and regulations of, 91–92;

strategy guidance from, 83; surveillance platforms of, 90; terrorist target analysis by, 33–34

Grant, Adam, 161n15

Great Britain: inspections in, 25n11; and LTTE weapons procurement efforts, 218; naval intelligence in, 127; personal freedom concerns in, 37

Guinea, 270

Guinea-Bissau, 270–71, 273

Gulf of Aden (GoA), 12; attack level in, 265, 266; as choke point, 65n21; international naval patrols in, 54; MV Limberg incident, 19; naval flotillas in, 64n12; piracy and terrorist activity near, 23–24

Gulf of Guinea (GoG): armed maritime crime around, 49; case study of maritime crime in (See Gulf of Guinea maritime crime [case study]); regional efforts in, 85; strategic importance of, 265

Gulf of Guinea Commission (GGC), 275

Gulf of Guinea maritime crime (case study), 265–76; armed maritime crime, 265–67; drug trafficking, 269–71; factors facilitating, 271–72; national, regional, and international implications of, 272–74; oil bunkering, 267–69, 273; responding to, 274–75

Gulf of Mexico, 53

Gulf of Thailand, 85

Hamas, 22

Harbor entities, 109

Hard targets, 31

Hart Group, 66n37

Heads of Asian Coast Guards Meeting, 234

Herald of Free Enterprise, 17

High seas, 11, 126; as anarchic, 88–89; ransacking of vessels on, 51; search

High seas (*continued*)
and rescue on, 94; vessel flag registry
and, 107
High-seas freedoms of navigation and
overflight (high-seas freedoms), 165
Hijackings, 38, 50–52, 229; of *Achille
Lauro*, 112, 229; economic implica-
tions of, 243; as insurance fraud,
63n7; in Malacca Strait, 226; phan-
tom ship phenomenon, 51–52; and
PSC protection of ships, 59; ransoms
paid for, 54–57; in Somalia, 289
Hiring, institutional, 153–54
HoA. *See* Horn of Africa
Hobbes, Thomas, 11
Holistic strategies. *See* Maritime strat-
egy development
Homeland Security, US Department of,
31, 110, 196
Homeland security systems, 54
Honduras, 51
Hormuz, Strait of, 18, 65n21
Horn of Africa (HoA): armed maritime
crime around, 49, 54; hijackings and
robberies off, 50; illegal emigration
to Yemen from, 284, 294n15; PSC
protection of ships off, 57–59, 61–62
Human security, 92
Human smuggling/trafficking, 119,
211–12; drug smuggling and, 287;
from Horn of Africa, 285; by LTTE,
211, 212; in Yemen, 284–85
Hussein, Bile, 289
Hyundai Heavy Industries, 129

Ibori, James, 269
ICS. *See* Incident Command System
ICU (Islamic Courts Union), 24
IFC (Information Fusion Centre; Singa-
pore), 132–33
Illegal, unlicensed, and unregulated
(IUU) fishing, 93, 103n11

Illegal fishing, 1, 2; in Gulf of Guinea,
272; in Ivory Coast waters, 2; in Yemeni waters, 289
Illegal immigration (Yemen), 284, 285,
294n15
Illegal maritime trafficking, 1. *See also*
Maritime smuggling/trafficking;
specific types of trafficking/smuggling
Imaging devices, 119
IMB. *See* International Maritime Bureau
IMF (International Monetary Fund),
120n1, 122n22
IMO. *See* International Maritime Organization
Incident Command System (ICS): expansion and adaptation of, 192, 193;
flexible structure of, 187–89; functions of primary sections, 190–91;
in maritime domain, 187; maritime
scenario applications of, 192, 194–97;
overview, 185–87; supporting materials and implementation aids for, 196
Incident management: maritime (*see*
Managing maritime incidents); in
the United States, 184–85
Incident(s), 50; emergency response
phases for, 182; IMB definition of, 50;
maritime, 179–82 (*see also* managing
maritime incidents)
India: coastal security measures in,
133–34; corruption in, 53; and defeat
of LTTE in Sri Lanka, 203–5, 209,
210; Malacca Strait joint antipiracy
exercises, 235; migration of manufacturing to, 107; Mumbai attacks
(2008), 22–23, 28n47, 244, 250; smugglers of, 210
Indonesia, 303n8; armed maritime crime
in, 50; claims to Strait of Malacca,
225; corruption in, 53, 238; counterpiracy capability of, 229–31; human
smuggling and, 212; MDA of, 126; oil

supply for, 225; regional cooperative responses to piracy, 232–37

Information, in anti-violence strategy, 72

Information Fusion Centre (IFC; Singapore), 132–33

Information sharing: among security institutions, 155–56; closing gaps in, 110; on Malacca Strait piracy, 238

Information Sharing Centre, 226, 233–34

Information technology (IT), 117–18, 155–56

Infrastructure: coastal geography and, 298; critical (see Critical infrastructure); for ports and terminals, 104, 110

Injai, Antonio, 270–71

Innes, Robert, 282, 283, 290, 291

Inspections: of containers, time required for, 119; at destination ports, 20; detection challenges in, 129–30; point-of-origin, 21–22

Institutional culture, 146–47

Institutional ethics, 157–59

Institutional jurisdictions, inside territorial seas, 3

Institutional leadership, 142–60; camaraderie in, 152–53; external stakeholders' importance to, 155–57; focus in, 151–52; hiring/firing and, 153–54; institutional culture and, 146–47; institutional ethics and, 157–59; and management vs. leadership, 143–45; prerequisites to imposing change, 145–46; purpose (with passion) in, 147–49; risk taking in, 154–55; trust in, 150–51; variety of maritime security institutions, 142–43; vision in, 149–50

Institutions. See also Maritime Security Institutions: disaster response and legitimacy of, 94; elite, 147; maritime agency organization, 97; for maritime governance, 89

Insurance: and Gulf of Guinea shipping, 266, 273, 277n4; and Nigeria's war-risk zone, 267; and PSC protection of ships, 59, 66n37

Insurgency, 1; piracy blended with, 250; in Sulu Sea region (see Sulu Sea violence [case study]); terrorism vs., 6n3

Integrated coastal radar, 135–36

Integrated strategies. See Maritime strategy development

Integrated weather prediction data, 136

Intelligence. See also Maritime intelligence: in defeat of Sea Tigers, 218; in ICS, 191; intelligence gathering, 90, 110; regional intelligence fusion centers, 111

Interagency approach, 135, 155

Interagency process, 83

Interdependency, trade and, 106

International Association of Independent Tanker Owners (INTERTANKO), 234

International Convention for the Safety of Life at Sea (SOLAS), 91, 111, 113–14, 136

International cooperation: on maritime security issues, 284, 288–89; in search and rescue, 94; in Sulu Sea area, 257–59

International foreign trade: global port security and, 105–7; seaborne, 64n20, 106, 121n6; SLOC closures and, 18–19; value of, 106

International Labor Organization, 117

International law. See also Legal framework; Maritime law; specific laws: for AIS, 90; for maritime security, 163–65; on ship registry, 107

International Maritime Bureau (IMB): incident definition of, 50; piracy definition of, 49, 50; on piracy in

International Maritime Bureau (IMB) (*continued*)
Southeast Asia, 235–36; Piracy Reporting Centre, 131; and PSC protection of ships, 59; on shipping in Gulf of Guinea, 267

International Maritime Organization (IMO), 111; and domain awareness in Gulf of Guinea, 275; ISPS Code and, 114; on Malacca Strait crimes, 226, 227; MDA defined by, 125; port security role of, 111–12; safety function of, 91; Ship Security Alert System required by, 238; SIDs databases of, 117; SOLAS, 91, 111, 113–14, 136

International maritime transport system, 20; terrorists' exploitation of, 22–23; vulnerability of, 20–22

International Monetary Fund (IMF), 120n1, 122n22

International Safety Management (ISM) Code, 91

International Ship and Port Facility Security (ISPS) Code, 112–14; biometric SIDs mandated by, 117; Gulf of Guinea countries non-compliant with, 276; port facility security assessment, 112; port facility security plan, 112–13

International shipping system, 19. *See also* Sea-lanes of communication (SLOCs)

International supply chain, 115, 117

International Trade Yearbook (United Nations), 120n2

International trading system, 11

INTERPOL, 234

Inter-Regional Coordination Center on Maritime Safety and Security for Central and West Africa, 275

INTERTANKO (International Association of Independent Tanker Owners), 234

Iran, 22

Iraq oil terminal strikes, 19, 27n33

Islamic Courts Union (ICU), 24

Islamist militants, Somali pirates' training of, 23

Island nations: maritime identities of, 302–3n2; poverty in, 298

ISM (International Safety Management) Code, 91

ISPS Code. *See* International Ship and Port Facility Security Code

Israel, 22

Issaikon, Lt. Col., 219

IT (information technology), 117–18, 155–56

IUU (illegal, unlicensed, and unregulated) fishing, 93, 103n11. *See also* Illegal fishing

Ivory Coast, 2, 94

Jaafar, Tan Sri Abdul Aziz, 257–58

Jakarta Accord, 247

Jama'at al-Tawhid wa'a-Jihad, 19

Jama'at Islamiya, 229

Janjalani, Ustadz Abubaker, 248

Japan: LTTE weapons from, 212; and Malacca Strait security, 234; oil supply for, 225

Jemaah Islamiah (JI), 14, 132, 229, 248

JHOCs (joint harbor operations centers), 110–11

JI (Jemaah Islamiah), 14, 132, 229, 248

JIATF-South (Joint Interagency Task Force—South), 130–31, 134–35, 140n19

Jihadi moral code, 24

Johnson, David, 57

Joint harbor operations centers (JHOCs), 110–11

Joint Interagency Task Force—South (JIATF-South), 130–31, 134–35, 140n19

Jordan, 126

Jurisdictions: closing gaps in, 110; of flag States, 164, 165; high seas and,

11; international law for, 163–64; overlapping, 3; at ports, 95; under UNCLOS, 163

Kamal, Captain (Sea Tigers), 216, 220
Kandasamy, Kamalraj, 220
Kandasamy, Vakil, 210
Kangarajah, Ravishankar, 211
Kanthaskaran, Shanmugasundaran, 211
Kapilan (Kabilan; Sea Tigers), 220
Karannagoda, Wasantha, 221
Karuna (Sea Tigers), 221
Karunakaran, Rajendram (Pradeepan), 216
Katrina, Hurricane, 180
Khaliq, Asif, 284
Khor al-Amaya oil terminal, 19, 27n33
Kidnappings: by ASG, 249–50; in Malacca Strait, 226, 229; for ransom, 226, 249
Kilcullen, David, 244–45, 259
Kioshi, MT, 218, 219
Kiram, Jamalal, III, 251
Kline, Jeff, 90
Koi Maran, MT, 217
Koshia, MT, 219, 220

Lackey, Sue A., 282
Lahad Datu incident, 251–53, 255–56
Lashkar-e-Taiba (LeT), 22–23, 221, 244
Latin America: CSI at ports in, 114; drug trafficking from, 269–71
Lattore, Massimiliano, 60
Law enforcement. See also Maritime law enforcement (MLE): assessing, 92–93; use-of-force policy in, 291–92
Law of Armed Conflict (LOAC), 291–92
Leadership. See also Institutional leadership: informing, in Level II assessment, 96–97; management vs., 143–45; promoting the right people, 301
Lebanon, 126

Legal framework, 162–73; international law for maritime security, 163–65; model maritime law enforcement statute for terrorism offenses, 165–73; protection of natural resources and, 93; for use of PSCs, 60
Legitimacy: armed maritime crime and, 53; disaster response and, 94
LeT (Lashkar-e-Taiba), 22–23, 221, 244
Liberation Tigers of Tamil Eelam (LTTE), 203–4. See also Sea Tigers of LTTE (case study); arms procurement of, 213–14; declared as terrorist group, 223n21; fighting power of, 208–10; human smuggling and, 211–12; international network of, 210–11; Sea Pigeons, 22; shipping network of, 214–16; supply lines for, 220
Liberia, 51, 129
Limburg attack, 19, 163, 229
Liquefied natural gas (LNG) tankers, 17–18
Liquid bulk cargoes, 107
Lithuania LNG terminals, 34, 47n13
LNG (liquefied natural gas) tankers, 17–18
LNG terminals: in Lithuania, 34, 47n13; as terrorist targets, 17–18
LOAC (Law of Armed Conflict), 291–92
Locks on containers, 21, 41, 42, 44
Logistics: in ICS, 191; LTTE, 209; of Sea tigers, 207
Long Beach terminal (United States), 22
LTTE. See Liberation Tigers of Tamil Eelam
Luttwak, Edward, 33

Madagascar, 302–3n2
Major bulk cargoes, 107
Mak, J. N., 237
Malacca Strait, 18, 65n21, 85, 224–26, 229
Malacca Strait Patrol (MSP), 232

Malacca Strait Patrols Information System, 232

Malacca Strait piracy (case study), 224–39; effectiveness of operations against, 235–38; geography and importance of Strait, 224–26; history of, 226, 227; problems in determining scope of, 226, 228–29; regional cooperative responses to, 232–35; regional countries' capabilities for countering, 229–32

Malacca Strait Sea Patrol (MSSP), 232

Malaysia: claims to Strait of Malacca, 225; counterpiracy capability of, 230–31; dispute over Sabah, 247; human smuggling and, 212; Lahad Datu incident, 251–53, 255–56; and LTTE arms procurement, 213; regional cooperative responses to piracy, 232–37

Malaysian Airlines Flight 370 search, 124

Malaysian Maritime Enforcement Agency (MMEA, APMM), 230–32

Malta, 51

Management: command vs., 182–83, 198n2; leadership vs., 143–45

Managing maritime incidents, 179–98, 299–302; challenges of, 179–80; changing event dynamics and, 181–82; coordination as key to, 183; expanding ICS for, 192, 193; flexible ICS structure for, 187–89; functions of primary ICS functions, 190–91; ICS application to maritime scenarios, 192, 194–97; ICS in maritime domain, 187; ICS overview, 185–87; initial response problems in, 180–81; need for command and, 182–83; origin of solution for, 184–85; strategies for (see Maritime strategy development); supporting materials and implementation aids for ICS, 196

Mann, MV, 219

Manyoshi MT, 219

MAOC (Maritime Analysis and Operations Centre; Europe), 278n19

Maria, Rakesh, 221

Mariama, MV, 214

"Maritima" example: defensive strategy in, 78–81; maritime incident management in, 192–95; model maritime law enforcement statute for terrorism offenses, 165–73; target analysis in, 39–45

Maritime agency organization, 97

Maritime agency outreach and stakeholder coordination, 99

Maritime Analysis and Operations Centre (MAOC; Europe), 278n19

Maritime crime, 2. See also specific crimes; armed (see Armed maritime crime [AMC]); in Gulf of Guinea (see Gulf of Guinea maritime crime); history of maritime intelligence, 126–30

Maritime critical infrastructure, 32

Maritime domain: definitions of, 85n1, 173–74n3; governing the, 89; in increasing national wealth, 301–2; UNCLOS partitioning of, 163

Maritime domain awareness (MDA), 124–38, 302; assessing, 89–91; building blocks for, 134–37; changing maritime threat environment and, 127–30; coastal areas in, 243–44; defined, 89–90, 125; history of, 126–27; institutional solutions for, 130–34; in strategy development, 84; training and education in, 137–38; use of term, 124–25

Maritime energy security, 48n28

Maritime governance, 88–89, 298, 299, 302; assessing (see Assessing maritime governance); defined, 89; disaster response, 94; enforcement of customs and maritime law, 92–93; lack of, 3; of low-level activities, 81; maritime domain awareness, 89–91; maritime safety, 91–92; maritime search and rescue, 93–94; port operations and security, 94–95; protection of natural resources, 93; traditional maritime security, 92

Maritime incidents, 179–82. See also Managing maritime incidents

Maritime intelligence. See also Maritime domain awareness (MDA): in anti-violence strategy, 73; history of, 126–30; intelligence gathering, 90; monitoring and surveillance in, 90–91

Maritime law, 97. See also International law; Legal framework; specific laws; in anti-violence strategy, 72–73; assessing enforcement of, 92–93

Maritime law enforcement (MLE): in anti-violence strategy, 73; assessing, 92–93; broken-window approach for, 82; as exercise of sovereignty, 164; model statute for terrorism offenses, 165–73; naval power vs., 92; by Yemen Coast Guard, 290–91

Maritime mission, 97

Maritime policy, 97

Maritime professionals, 99

Maritime programs, 99

Maritime safety: assessing, 91–92; subfunctions of, 91

Maritime search and rescue: assessing, 93–94; ICS in, 187

Maritime security, 142–43. See also Port security; energy security, 48n28; focus on coasts in, 243–44; governments' role in, 2–3; institutions for, 142–43, 148, 301; international law for, 163–65; private security companies, 57–62; for sustainable development, 299; traditional, assessing, 92; Yemen Coast Guard provision of, 290

Maritime Security Coordinating Board (Bakorkamla; Indonesia), 231

Maritime Security Institutions: identifying roles in and resources of, 301; leadership of (see Institutional leadership); purpose of, 148; variety of, 142–43

Maritime Security Sector Reform (MSSR) Guide (USAID), 94

Maritime Security Task Force (Singapore), 231–32

Maritime smuggling/trafficking, 1, 300. See also Arms smuggling/trafficking; Drug smuggling/trafficking; Human smuggling/trafficking; of crude oil, 269; Indian and Sri Lankan networks for, 210; by TCO submersible submarines, 129–30; in Yemen, 284–87, 294n20

Maritime strategy development, 71–85; "broken windows" approach to, 81–82; ends, ways, means, and measures in, 76–78; government toolkit for, 72–74; illustration of, 78–81; net assessment in, 74–76; successful, prerequisites for, 82–84

Maritime targets: Malacca Strait as, 229; nature of, 13; for terrorism, 15–18 (see also Target-analysis model)

Maritime terrorism, 2, 11–24; al-Qaeda in the Islamic Maghreb, 1, 2; by ASG, 249–50; countering, 256–59; defined, 25n3; economic destabilization as goal of, 18–20; incidence and nature of, 12–13; mass casualties as goal of, 13, 15–18; model maritime law enforcement statute for, 165–73; movement of terrorist weapons and personnel, 20–23; Mumbai attacks as, 244; nature of threat, 243; notable incidents and prevented incidents of,

Maritime terrorism (*continued*)
13, 14; piracy and, 23–24; recent spike
in, 13, 14; targets for, 15–18 (*see also*
Target-analysis model)
Maritime trade, 64n20, 104. *See also*
International foreign trade; Port
security
Maritime trafficking. *See* Maritime
smuggling/trafficking
Maritime violence, 298–302. *See also*
specific types of threats; defined, 1, 71;
as ecosystem of related threats, 1, 2,
298, 302n1; rise of, 1–2; Sulu Sea case
study, 243–59
Marshall Islands, 129
Marudu, 218
Massachusetts Port Authority (MASS-
PORT), 109
Mass casualties: public security in target
assessment, 36–37; as terrorist goal,
13, 15–18
MASSPORT (Massachusetts Port Au-
thority), 109
Matalam, Datu Udtog, 246
Matsushima, MV, 216, 220
McArthur escort vessel, 66n33
MDA. *See* Maritime domain awareness
Means, in maritime strategy develop-
ment, 76–78
Measures: in maritime governance as-
sessment, 99–101; in maritime strat-
egy development, 76–78
MEND (Movement for the Emancipa-
tion in the Niger Delta), 19, 20, 272
Middle East, CSI at ports in, 114
MILF (Moro Islamic Liberation Front),
229, 247–49, 255
Military forces: in anti-violence strat-
egy, 73; use of force by law enforce-
ment personnel vs., 291–92
Mindanao, 245; Autonomous Region of
Muslim Mindanao, 246; as loosely-
or alternatively-governed area,

256–57; MILF camps in, 247; Zambo-
anga City attack, 253–56
Mission: maritime, 97; of Yemen Coast
Guard, 283–84
Misuari, Nur, 253, 255
MLE. *See* Maritime law enforcement
MMEA (Malaysian Maritime Enforce-
ment Agency), 230–32
MNLF (Moro National Liberation
Front), 246–49, 253–55
*Model Legislative Provisions on Measures
to Combat Terrorism,* 176n22
Moro Islamic Liberation Front (MILF),
229, 247–49, 255
Moro National Liberation Front
(MNLF), 246–49, 253–55
Movement for the Emancipation in the
Niger Delta (MEND), 19, 20, 272
Movement of terrorist weapons and per-
sonnel, 20–23
MSP (Malacca Strait Patrol), 232
MSP Intelligence Exchange Group, 232
MSSP (Malacca Strait Sea Patrol), 232
*MSSR (Maritime Security Sector Reform)
Guide* (USAID), 94
Mullen, Mike, 301
Multinational approach, 135
Mumbai attacks (2008), 22–23, 28n47,
244, 250
Murphy, Martin, 17–18, 37–38, 89
Murugan (Sea Tigers), 219
Muslims, Filipino, 245–47

Nadarajah, Illango, 210
Nallanathan, Janarthana (Nathan), 205,
206, 216, 223n20
National flag registry, 107–8
National identity, 97
National Interagency Incident Manage-
ment System, 187
National Maritime Enforcement and
Coordination Centre (NMECC), 232
National sovereignty, 92

NATO Shipping Center, 234
Natural resources, 93, 298–99
Naval forces, 92, 296n49
Naval intelligence, 126–28
Naval Oceanography Portal, 141n38
NDPVF (Niger Delta People's Volunteer
    Force), 20, 272
NDV (Niger Delta Vigilantes), 19, 20, 272
Nediyawan (Sea Tigers), 211
Net assessment, in maritime strategy
    development, 74–76
Netherlands, The, 21
New People's Army (Philippines),
    260n15
Niger Delta People's Volunteer Force
    (NDPVF), 20, 272
Niger Delta Vigilantes (NDV), 19, 20, 272
Nigeria: anti-violence responses of, 274;
    armed maritime crime in, 50, 266;
    corruption in, 53, 271; hijackings
    in, 52; insurance war-risk zone for,
    267; ISPS Code and, 114, 122n28; oil
    bunkering in, 267–69, 273; organized
    tribal militias in, 272, 273
Nincic, Donna, 243
Nirmalan, Maj. (Sea Tigers), 217, 218
Nishantha, Arulananthan (Illankot-
    tuwan), 216
NMECC (National Maritime Enforce-
    ment and Coordination Centre), 232
North America: CSI at ports in, 114;
    geography of and development in,
    298; Latin American cocaine exports
    to, 270; migration of manufacturing
    from, 107
North Asia, migration of manufacturing
    from, 107
North Korea, 212, 213, 216
Norway, 210

OBNI (Office of Naval Intelligence;
    US), 127
"Oceans Beyond Piracy," 52–53

Offensive strategy, 77
Office of Maritime Domain Awareness
    (US Navy), 125
Office of Naval Intelligence (ONI; US),
    127
Offshore oil platforms: attacks in Gulf
    of Guinea, 267; incident manage-
    ment for, 194; PSC protection of, 57;
    target analysis for, 41
Oil bunkering, 1, 2; corruption and, 271;
    in Gulf of Guinea, 267–69, 273
Oil spills: cost of, 91; *Deepwater Hori-
    zon*, 53, 195–97; environmental dan-
    ger of, 53; *Exxon Valdez*, 183, 187; ICS
    in response to, 187, 195–97; *Torrey
    Canyon*, 111
Oil supplies, through Malacca Strait, 225
One Earth Future Foundation, 52
Open registry. *See* Flags of convenience
    (FoC)
Operational management of maritime
    violence, 72, 79–81, 300
Operations: in ICS, 190–91; joint harbor
    operations centers, 110–11; port,
    21–22, 94–95
Outlaw sea, 1, 6n4
Out of the Mountains (Kilcullen), 244
Outreach, by maritime agencies, 99
Oversight, 99
Ownership of port facilities, 109, 110
Oyagha, Rear Admiral, 273

Palestinian militant groups, 283
Palestinian terrorists, 112
Panama, 51, 129
Panama Canal, 18, 65n21
Passenger ferries. *See* Ferries
Passenger ships, 15. *See also* Cruise lin-
    ers/ships
Passion, in institutional leadership,
    148–49
Pathmanathan, Selvarajah (Kannadi
    Pathmanathan, K.P.), 210

Pathmanathan, Selvarasa (Tharmalin-
gam Shanmugam Kumaran, Kuma-
ran Pathmanathan, K.P.), 210–11, 213
Pentagon, suicide strike on (2001), 13, 15
People's Liberation Force (PLF;
Nigeria), 272
Performance motivation, 154
Personnel. *See* Workforce of seagoing
personnel
Personnel movement, by terrorists,
20–23
Peru, 53
Phantom ship phenomenon, 51–52
Phaovisaid, Darin, 238
Philippines: Coast Watch System,
132, 258–59; corruption in, 53; dispute over Sabah, 247; Enhanced
Defense Cooperation Agreement
with United States, 258; ferry and
small craft attacks in, 229; human
smuggling and, 212; insurgent and
terrorist organizations in, 246–48;
kidnappings in, 249–50; Lahad Datu
incident, 251–53, 255–56; MDA of,
126; Muslims in, 245, 246; New People's Army in, 260n15; regional cooperative responses to piracy, 232; and
Sulu Sea violence, 245; *Super Ferry 14*
bombing, 17, 48n27; Zamboanga City
attack, 253–56
Pink, Daniel, 154
Piracy, 1, 2. *See also* Armed maritime
crime (AMC); attacks between 1980
and 1984, 128; combined with terror-
ist/insurgent goals, 250; convergence
of maritime terrorism and, 23–24;
criminal justice structures and, 271–
72; defining and reporting, 226, 228;
financial impact of, 52–53; in Gulf of
Guinea, 266; IMB definition of, 49,
50; IMB Piracy Reporting Centre,
131; Malacca Strait piracy case study,

224–39; phantom ship phenomenon,
51–52; preoccupation with, 243; and
PSC protection of ships, 59; root
causes of, 48n25; in Somalia, 289; in
Sulu Sea, 246; UNCLOS definition
of, 63n2; in Yemen, 287–89
Piracy Reporting Centre (IMB), 131
Pirates: capacity of, 86n12; objectives of, 24
Plans, in ICS, 191
Policy, maritime, 97
Political management of maritime vio-
lence, 72, 76, 78–79, 81, 83
Political stability, armed maritime
crime and, 53
Pong Su, 131
Population: in anti-violence strategy, 74;
world, 6n2
Port facility security assessment, 112
Port facility security plan, 112–13
Ports: assessing operations, 94–95; cargo
inspections at, 20; characteristics of,
109–10; darker side of, 104–5; immu-
nity to whole sale closure of, 19; as
transition zone, 94; vital role of, 104
Port security: assessing, 94–95; interconnectivity of, 4 (*see also* Global
port security); need for, 104–5;
September 11, 2001 attacks and, 105;
in Sierra Leone, 2; vetting of port
personnel, 21–22
Port shutdowns, to cause economic destabilization, 18
Poverty: in island/archipelago nations,
298; in Niger delta, 272, 279n32
Power plants: incident management for,
194; target analysis for, 41, 44
PPPs (private-public partnerships), 110
Prabhakaran, Velupillai, 204, 209,
210, 213
Pratheepan, Thavarasa (Sampras Thavaraja, Tambi Sampras), 218
Preventive governance initiatives, 101

Prioritization of defensive efforts, 30–32, 39–42. *See also* CARVES target analysis model

Private-public partnerships (PPPs), 110

Private security companies (PSCs), 57–62

Problem set, understanding, 300

Professionals, maritime, 99

Programs, maritime, 99

Protection of natural resources, assessing, 93

Provisional IRA, 22

PSCs (private security companies), 57–62

Public security, in target-analysis model, 36–37

Purpose, in institutional leadership, 142, 147–49

Radar, coastal, 135–36

Raheem (LTTE spokesperson), 205

Rajah Suliaman Movement, 17

Ransom payments, 54–57, 226, 229

Rasakumar (David), 206

Ras'ee, Ali Ahmed, 283–85, 288, 290

Raymond, Catherine Zara, 236

Raytheon, 132

Razak, Najib, 236

Recognizability, as target-assessment criterion, 34, 47n15

Recuperability, as target-assessment criterion, 33

Red-teaming, 46

Regional cooperation: in Gulf of Guinea, 85; in Malacca Strait piracy response, 232–37; ReCAAP, 233–34; in Sulu Sea area, 257–59

Regional Cooperation Agreement on Combating Piracy and Armed Robbery Against Ships in Asia (ReCAAP), 233–34

Regional intelligence fusion centers, 111

Reporting: of armed maritime crime, 266; of contacts of interest, 137

Resilience, as target-assessment criterion, 34. *See also* CARVES target analysis model

Resources: communication, investment in, 46; competing demands for, 54; management and allocation of, 178n29, 298–99; of Maritime Security Institutions, 301; natural resources, 93, 298–99

Restorative governance initiatives, 101

Revolutionary Armed Forces of Colombia (FARC), 271, 274, 280n39

Richardson, Michael, 18

Risk assessment: Automated Targeting System, 115; for maritime terrorism (*see* CARVES target analysis model); as prerequisite for good strategy, 82; for terrorism, 30–34; use of naval power and, 92

Risk management, in institutional leadership, 154–55

Risks, threats vs., 87n22

Riverine systems, lack of surveillance of, 11

Robbery, armed, 1, 2. *See also* Armed maritime crime (AMC); Theft; of ships at harbor, 50, 51; in territorial waters or on high seas, 51 (*see also* Armed robbery at sea)

ROE (rules of engagement): for PSCs, 60; for use of force in armed conflict, 291–92

Roll on, roll off *(ro-ros)*, 17

Rome Convention for the Suppression of Unlawful Acts Against the Safety of Maritime Navigation, 112

Ro-ros (roll on, roll off), 17

Routes of passenger vessels, 16–17, 27n28

Ruhani, Golala, 287

Rule of law, for Yemen, 287

Rules of engagement (ROE): for PSCs, 60; for use of force in armed conflict, 291–92

SA (situational assessment), 181
SADC (Southern African Development Community), 133
SAFE Framework of Standards to Secure and Facilitate Global Trade (SAFE Framework), 115–16
SAFE Port Act (Security and Accountability for Every Port Act of 2006), 114–16
Safety. See maritime safety
Sajahatra Bangsamoro Program, 251
Saleh, Ali Abdullah, 283, 287
São Tomé, 274
SAR. See Search and rescue
Saracen International, 59
Scanning technology, 119
Schedules of passenger vessels, 16–17
"Sea blindness," 4
Seafarer identity documents (SIDs), 117
Seagoing personnel. See Workforce of seagoing personnel
Sea-lanes of communication (SLOCs), 12, 18–19
Seaman Guard Ohio, 67n46
Sea Pigeons, 22
Search and rescue (SAR): domestic, 94; maritime, 93–94, 187; UN Search and Rescue Convention, 95
Search and Rescue (SAR) Convention (1979), 95
Sea robbery, 300. See also Armed robbery at sea
Sea Tigers of LTTE (case study), 203–22; arms procurement and, 213–14; capabilities of Sea Tigers, 206–8; destruction of fleet, 216–20; fighting power of LTTE, 208–10; human smuggling, 211–12; origins of Sea Tigers, 205–6; shipping network of

LTTE, 214–16; support for LTTE international network, 210–11
Security. See also Maritime security; Port security: balancing freedom and, 45; border, 4, 283–87; competing demands for resources, 54; human, 92; at passenger terminals, 16; public, in target-analysis model, 36–37; for sustainable development, 299; and taming of "outlaw sea," 1; in Yemen, 283–87, 289, 297n52
Security and Accountability for Every Port Act of 2006 (SAFE Port Act), 114–16
Seishin, MV, 219
Senegal, 270
Senpakavenan (Senpgaselvan, Semba), 219
September 11, 2001 attacks, 13, 15, 105, 129, 217
Sewel, MV, 17
Shapiro, Andrew, 59
Shinwa, MV, 216, 220
Shipping: disruption of international shipping system, 19; Gulf of Guinea attacks on, 272–73; international maritime transport system, 20–23; LTTE network for, 214–16; safety in, 91; in sea-lanes of communication, 12, 18–19; through Malacca Strait, 225
Ships as weapons, 243
Ship Security Alert System, 238
Shopping arcades, target analysis for, 41–42, 44–45
Shoshin, MT, 217–18
SIDs (seafarer identity documents), 117
Sierra Leone, 2, 270
Silappasan, Lt. Col. (Silambarasan, Ranjan), 217
Sinek, Simon, 142, 148
Singapore: claims to Strait of Malacca, 225; commercial terminal in, 22, 28n41; counterpiracy capability of, 230–31; human smuggling and, 212;

Information Fusion Centre, 132–33; LTTE weapons from, 212; Nigeria's agreement with, 274; personal freedom concerns in, 37; regional cooperative responses to piracy, 232–37

Singapore, Strait of, 18

Situational assessment (SA), 181

Sivarasan (Sea Tigers), 206

Skeleton crews, 54

SLOCs (sea-lanes of communication), 12, 18–19

Slovenia, 126

Smart boxes, 21

Smuggling, root causes of, 48n25. See also Maritime smuggling/trafficking

Sobithan (Sea Tigers), 219

Soft targets, 31

SOLAS (International Convention for the Safety of Life at Sea), 91, 111, 113–14, 136

Somalia: al-Shabaab in, 23; and AMC off Horn of Africa, 54; border patrol and, 284; counterpiracy drives in, 24; illegal emigration to Yemen from, 285; piracy in, 289; Puntland maritime force in, 59; UN embargo against arms trade to, 285–86

Somali-based syndicates, ransom payments to, 55–56

Somali Basin, 50, 52, 57

Soosai (Sea Tigers), 205, 209, 222n11

South Africa, 133

South Asia, armed maritime crime in territorial waters of, 49

South China Sea, 162–63

Southeast Asia: armed maritime crime in territorial waters of, 49; decrease in piracy in, 235; LTTE weapons from, 213; migration of manufacturing to, 107; phantom ship frauds in, 52; terrorist groups in, 229

Southern African Development Community (SADC), 133

South Korea, 17

Sri Krishna, 219

Sri Lanka: defeat of LTTE in, 203–4; IUU fishing in, 103n11; war against Sea Tigers of LTTE, 92, 203–22

Sri Lankan air force, 203, 218

Sri Lankan army, 204

Sri Lankan navy: current role of, 221–22; leadership in, 144; LTTE supply interdictions by, 203; in Sea Tigers defeat, 208, 214, 217–20

Staff. See Workforce of seagoing personnel

Stakeholders: external, institutional leadership and, 155–57; maritime agencies' coordination of, 99; in maritime security, 142–43

Standardized Emergency Management System (California), 186–87

Start with Why (Sinek), 142, 148

Steed, John, 23

Stephen (Lt. Col. Maniyan; Sea Tigers), 218

Strait of Bab el-Mandeb, 23, 65n21

Strait of Gibraltar, 18

Strait of Hormuz, 18, 65n21

Strait of Malacca: as choke point, 65n21; effect of closure of, 18; geography and importance of, 224–26; piracy in (see Malacca Strait piracy [case study]); regional approaches to piracy mitigation, 85; as terrorist target, 229

Strait of Singapore, 18

Strategy. See also Maritime strategy development: capacity and, 299, 300; comprehensive, 302; functions of, 71–72; government toolkit for, 72–74; horizontal dimension of, 33; political and operational levels of, 72; successful, prerequisites for, 82–84

SUA (Suppression of Unlawful Acts) Convention, 276

Suez Canal, 18, 65n21
Suicide attacks: AQIM, 1, 2; LTTE, 209, 210, 214; Sea Tigers, 208, 210; on September 11, 2001, 13, 15, 105, 129, 217; on USS *Cole*, 283
Sulu Sea region, 245–46
Sulu Sea violence (case study), 243–59; countering threats of, 256–59; groups' engagement in maritime violence, 249–50; Lahad Datu incident, 251–53, 255–56; lessons learned about, 255–56; Mumbai paradigm and, 250; Philippine insurgent and terrorist organizations, 246–48; region of Sulu Sea, 245–46; Zamboanga City attack, 253–56
Sunbird, MV, 213
Super Ferry 14 bombing, 17, 48n27, 250
Suppression of Unlawful Acts (SUA) Convention, 276
Surveillance platforms, 90
Sustainable development, 299
Sustainable wealth, 301–2
Symbolism, as target-assessment criterion, 35. *See also* CARVES target analysis model

Tactics, in target-analysis model, 37–39
Tamil New Tigers (TNT), 204
Tan, Tony, 237
Target-analysis model, 30–46; end product of, 42–45; and governments' risk assessment for terrorism, 30–34; prioritized list of targets from, 39–42; public security in, 36–37; tactics and tradecraft in, 37–39; thinking like a terrorist in, 33–35; value of debate in, 45; weighting factors in, 35–36
Targets. *See also* Maritime targets: soft and hard terrorist targets, 31–32; transportation systems as, 46n2
Tchuto, José Américo Bubo Na, 271

TCOs (transnational criminal organizations), 129–30
Technology: cybersecurity threats, 117–18; in global port security, 118–19; for MDA, 135–36; to offset cost of maritime governance, 90
Terminals, 104; commercial, 22, 28n41; infrastructure for, 104; LNG, 17–18, 34, 47n13; oil, 19, 20, 27n33; passenger, security at, 16
Territorial seas, institutional jurisdictions within, 3
Territorial waters: criminal maritime incidents in, 50; lack of surveillance of, 11; ransacking of vessels in, 51
Terrorism, 300; autonomous criminal conduct and, 177n26; conceptualization of, 244; criminal law provisions for, 174n9; insurgency vs., 6n3; international law on, 154; Lahad Datu incident, 251–53, 255–56; Malacca Strait as target for, 229; maritime (*see* Maritime terrorism); maritime intelligence and, 128; next major strike of, 11–12; offenses included in, 176n24, 178n27, 178n28; piracy blended with, 250; root causes of, 48n25; visible acts of violence and, 13; in Yemen, 290; Zamboanga City attack, 253–56
Terrorists: alliance of pirates and, 23–24; capacity of, 86n12; "comfort zones" of, 229; conservative nature of, 12–13; hijacking of ships by, 38; objectives of, 24, 35; planning cycle for, 38–39, 48n26; thinking like, 33–35; training and staging areas for, 38
Thailand: human smuggling and, 212; LTTE weapons from, 213; regional cooperative responses to piracy, 232
Theft: oil bunkering, 1, 2, 267–69; at sea (*see* Armed robbery at sea); from ships at harbor, 50, 51

Thermal sensing technology, 119

Thinking: globally, 301; like a terrorist, 33–35

Threats: changing environment of, 127–30; to coastal cities, 244–45; cybersecurity, 117–18; ecosystem of, 1, 2, 298; global response to, 105; government concerns about, 92; land-based dimensions of, 163; net assessment of, 74–76 (*see also* Risk assessment); risks vs., 87n22; transnational, 127–30

Titles, ICS, 188–89

TNT (Tamil New Tigers), 204

Togo, 274

Tongnova, MV, 214

Torrey Canyon oil spill, 111

Trade. *See* International foreign trade

Tradecraft, in target-analysis model, 37–39

Traditional maritime security, 92

Training, of MDA workforce, 137–38

Transnational criminal organizations (TCOs), 129–30

Transportation systems: international maritime transport system, 20–23; ports as nodes in, 94–95; as terrorist targets, 46n2

Trust: in broken window approach, 82; building, 87n23; in institutional leadership, 146, 150–51; interagency, 83

UN. *See* United Nations

UNCLOS. *See* United Nations Convention on the Law of the Sea

Ungoverned spaces, 88

UN High Commissioner for Refugees (UNHCR), 285

United Kingdom, 269

United Nations (UN). *See also* International Maritime Organization (IMO): Conference on the Law of the Sea, 139n7; embargo against arms trade to Somalia, 285–86; High Commissioner for Refugees report, 285; *International Trade Yearbook,* 120n2; Search and Rescue Convention, 95

United Nations Convention on the Law of the Sea (UNCLOS), 121n9; AOR and AOI under, 134; on armed maritime crime, 50; limitations of, 162–63; nations' obligations under, 127; origin of, 139n7; on partitioning of global maritime domain, 163; piracy defined by, 63n2; praise for, 162

United States. *See also individual laws, organizations, and treaties:* cargo inspections in, 20; CARVER target-analysis process in, 33–34; closing port security gaps in, 110; counterterrorism support to Philippines, 248; cybersecurity standards for ports, 118; and defeat of LTTE in Sri Lanka, 203; and domain awareness in Gulf of Guinea, 275; Exclusive Economic Zone of, 296–97n50; history of incident management in, 184–85; Latin American cocaine exports to, 274; limitations of MDA in, 125–26; LTTE weapons procurement efforts, 218; and Malacca Strait security, 235, 236; personal freedom concerns in, 37; port personnel vetting in, 21–22; and PSC protection of ships, 59; September 11, 2001 attacks, 13, 15, 105, 129; stakeholders in maritime security in, 143; and UNCLOS treaty, 139n7; War on Terror, 85n18

US Agency for International Development (USAID), 94

US Coast Guard, 296–97n50; closing port security gaps by, 110; cybersecurity standards and, 118; *Deepwater Horizon* oil spill, 195–97; ICS and, 187; Prohibition interdiction efforts of, 139n3; training missions to

US Coast Guard (*continued*)
    Malacca Strait nations, 235; vulnera-
    bility-analysis process of, 48n19
Use of force, 291–92
US Navy: Malacca Strait escorts by, 235;
    maritime domain awareness con-
    cept of, 243–44; Office of Maritime
    Domain Awareness, 125; Office of
    Naval Intelligence, 127; training mis-
    sions to Malacca Strait nations, 235
US Navy SEALs, 147, 150
US Office of Naval Intelligence (ONI), 127

Vasanthan (Captain Miller), 209
Vessel flag registry: cabotage laws,
    121n10; global port security and,
    107–8; under international law, 164;
    for phantom ships, 51; and ships car-
    rying weapons, 61; threat assessment
    and, 129; UNCLOS on, 121n9
Vessel trafficking services (VTS), 136
Vicious cycle, 85n2
Vinod, Captain, 220
Violence. *See also* Maritime violence: in
    Philippines, 246; visible acts of, 13
Virtuous cycle, 85n2
Vision, in institutional leadership, 149–50
Visual observation posts, 135–36
VTS (vessel trafficking services), 136
Vulnerability, as target-assessment crite-
    rion, 34, 35. *See also* CARVES target
    analysis model

War on Terror (US), 85n18
Waste dumping, 93
Ways, in maritime strategy develop-
    ment, 76–78
WCO (World Customs Organization), 115
Weapons: on PSC-protected ships, 61;
    on *Seaman Guard Ohio*, 67n46; in
    West Africa, 267
Weapons movement, by terrorists, 20–23
Weather prediction data, integrated, 136

White, Jonathan W., 128
"Wicked" problems, 299–300
Widodo, Jokowi, 303n8
Workforce of seagoing personnel: on
    ferries, 16; global port security and,
    116–17; in merchant shipping, 129;
    trend toward skeleton crews, 54
World Customs Organization (WCO),
    115, 116
World Factbook (CIA), 120–21n3
World Tamil Movement, 214
World Trade Center, 2001 attack on, 13, 15

Xe, 66n33
Xin Los Angeles, 129

Yemen: al-Qaeda in the Arabian Penin-
    sula in, 23; border security in, 283;
    drugs sold in, 295n27; illegal immi-
    gration in, 284, 285, 294n15; maritime
    security issues for, 282–83, 297n52;
    navy warships of, 292n3
Yemen Coast Guard (case study),
    282–92; and applying rule of law,
    287; arms smuggling, 285–86; border
    security, 287; Combined Maritime
    Forces and, 293n13; drug smuggling,
    287; illegal fishing, 289; illegal immi-
    gration, 284, 285; illegal smuggling,
    284–87; international cooperation
    on maritime security issues, 284,
    288–89; law enforcement culture
    and, 290–91; mission of, 283–84;
    operational capabilities of, 289–90;
    personnel structure in, 293n9; piracy
    reduction by, 287–89; terrorist at-
    tacks on, 290; trafficking of Somali
    migrants, 284–85

Zamboanga City (Mindanao) attack,
    253–56
Zinni, Anthony, 283
Zoning of maritime domain, 163